EUGÉNIE

THE EMPRESS AND HER EMPIRE

For Stella

EUGÉNIE
THE EMPRESS AND HER EMPIRE

DESMOND SEWARD

SUTTON PUBLISHING

First published in the United Kingdom in 2004 by
Sutton Publishing Limited · Phoenix Mill
Thrupp · Stroud · Gloucestershire · GL5 2BU

British Library Cataloguing in Publication Data
A catalogue record for this book is available from the British Library.

ISBN 0-7509-2979-0

Typeset in 11/14 pt Sabon
Typesetting and origination by
Sutton Publishing Limited.
Printed and bound in England by
J.H. Haynes & Co. Ltd, Sparkford.

Contents

Contents

Contents

Acknowledgements

When I was a small boy my grandmother would tell me what a wonderful time the Second Empire had been for France. Her mother and her aunts were educated in Paris during this period, at the convent of the Sacré Coeur where the Empress Eugénie had been a pupil, and when older they were presented to the empress at the Tuileries. They tried to copy her clothes, despite having seen a dogfight take place beneath a crinoline, even if their widowed mother was unable to afford Mr Worth's prices. One of the aunts married a soldier called Claude de Beausire-Seyssel, a trooper in the Cent Gardes (Napoleon III's bodyguard), who was very distantly related to the Bonapartes, and my grandmother would proudly relate how the emperor always addressed her Uncle Claude as '*mon cousin*' even when he was on duty. My great-grandmother collected sepia carte-de-visite photographs of the imperial family that I still possess, some of which have been used as illustrations for this book. Because of these faded family memories I like to feel that, however faint and tenuous, I have a personal interest in writing about the empress.

Among the many people who have helped me with advice or encouragement, or both, I would especially like to thank Jacques Perot, director of the château de Compiègne – and also of the Musée de l'Impératrice and of the Musée du Second Empire – who has welcomed me to the château on more than one occasion and who told me of the recently published memoirs of his forebear Léon Chevreau, a guest of Eugénie at Compiègne; Vincent Droguet, keeper of the château de Fontainebleau, who let me see Eugénie's remarkable study, currently being restored; Dom Cuthbert Brogan, prior of Farnborough Abbey – where Eugénie's presence can still almost be felt – who memorably showed me the imperial tombs, besides providing valuable information; Professor Aileen Ribeiro of the

Acknowledgements

Courtauld Institute who vetted the chapters on Eugénie's clothes and on the *couturier* Worth; Professor Andrew Cziechanowiecki who told me of the Polish attitude towards Eugénie; my cousin Chantal Hoppenot who obtained publications that were not easy to find outside France; André Dzerzinski who drew my attention to Eugénie's link with Lourdes; Susan Mountgarret who checked the proofs and compiled the index; my agent, Andrew Lownie; my very patient editor, Elizabeth Stone; Sara Ayad, who found most of the pictures; and Anna Somers Cocks who suggested that I write the book.

I owe a special debt to Dudley Heathcote for allowing me to reproduce a hitherto unpublished photograph of Eugénie in about 1905, which was given to him by his aunt, her lady-in-waiting Emilie d'Allonville (later Marquise Dusmet de Smours).

I am also grateful to Anne Lesage of the Agence Photographique of the Réunion des Musées Nationaux, and to the staffs of the British Library, the Cambridge University Library and the London Library.

Prologue: The Wedding of 1853

Paris, 30 January: the congregation is startled when, for a wedding march, the orchestra strikes up a swaggering tune from Meyerbeer's *Prophète* as the imperial couple enter Notre Dame. It is too theatrical, like much else in the vast, rather dirty cathedral – a sham Gothic porch over the main door, plaster statues of the first Napoleon against the columns, and blue imperial banners hanging everywhere. At the right of the two prie-dieux in front of the altar sits ex-King Jerome of Westphalia, a rouged old wreck with dyed hair, flanked by his sneering son and daughter; at the left sit a large group of Bonapartes and Murats, who until recently have been living in near poverty. They are the only royal personages, since the marriage has taken place in too much haste to invite guests from other countries. But there are six cardinals in scarlet, together with resplendent ambassadors, officers in brightly coloured uniforms and ministers in the new imperial court dress.

A small, thickset man in his late forties with short legs, a goatee beard and waxed moustaches, not particularly impressive even when glimpsed from a distance, the Emperor Napoleon III wears a lieutenant-general's uniform (dark blue tunic and red trousers) with the sash of the Légion d'honneur. The Golden Fleece at his neck is presumably worn in tribute to the Spanish lady, eighteen years younger than himself, whom he has married the day before, in a civil ceremony at the Tuileries.

The congregation at Notre Dame stares curiously at the dignified bride coming up the aisle on her husband's arm. Until yesterday Doña Eugenia de Montijo, Countess of Teba, she is in white velvet sewn with diamonds; her full, three-layered skirt is trimmed with priceless old English lace, her tight bodice is sewn with sapphires and orange blossom, and round her waist is Empress Marie-Louise's sapphire girdle – her three-quarter length sleeves reveal long, jewel-studded gloves. Her red hair has been arranged by the famous coiffeur Félix, curls flowing down the neck from the chignon to which her veil is fastened, and she wears the diamond and sapphire tiara that Empress Josephine had worn at her coronation in 1804. Yet the new empress's face is even whiter than usual. The ladies of her household are watching her with obvious anxiety.

The service is taken by the archbishop of Paris, Monseigneur Sibour, the choir singing Cherubini's Coronation Mass, with a *Sanctus* by Adolphe Adam – better known for his ballet music. When the pair leave Notre Dame there are shouts of '*Vive l'Empéreur!*', '*Vive l'Impératrice!*', and during the winter night that follows the sky over Paris will be lit up by fireworks.

Despite the crowds, the cheering is confined to a few areas around the cathedral and the Tuileries. The Parisians have come to watch out of curiosity, not from loyalty. Just how long can this new Second Empire last? Only recently established after a brutal *coup d'état*, it is opposed by royalists and republicans, distrusted by the Great Powers. The British ambassador, Lord Cowley, thinks that Napoleon III's régime will soon collapse, reporting that 'the impression becomes stronger every day, that all inside is rotten and that, with few exceptions, we are living in a society of adventurers'.

As for the beautiful new empress, well-informed French observers mutter that she is just an adventuress – what today we would call a gold-digger. If her father is supposed to have been some sort of Spanish grandee, her mother (about whose private life there are lurid rumours) is not even faintly aristocratic but the daughter of a bankrupt Scottish fruit and wine merchant in Malaga. The entire fashionable world knows that for years Eugénie and her mother have been trawling the capitals of Europe in search of a rich husband. The emperor's inner circle is horrified: his foreign minister is threatening to resign.

During the wedding Lady Cowley has sketched the new empress inside her prayer book. Kneeling at a prie-dieu, Eugénie's chin rests pensively on her hand. Has it dawned on her that by marrying a crowned dictator she will become the most powerful woman in the world?

The Second Empire belonged as much to her as it did to him. Until very recently this period was considered an aberration in French history, Lord Cowley's 'society of adventurers', dismissed by one historian as 'little more than a military parade flitting in front of a masked ball'. Nobody could forgive the emperor for his defeat by the Prussians in 1870, for France's humiliation and the loss of Alsace-Lorraine. But a new view has emerged, that the empire was in reality the French version of England's high Victorian age, a period of prosperity, of economic and social progress, and that Napoleon III was a man who was in advance of his time, an earlier de Gaulle, even an earlier Mitterrand.

Eugénie, too, deserves a reassessment. The last woman to reign over France (and the only one to reign over the Paris we know today), she personified the allure of the Second Empire that one glimpses in Winterhalter's portraits and the music of Jacques Offenbach. 'Eighteen years of self-indulgence, folly and wild gaiety, of love affairs and unbelievable elegance', a survivor recalled wistfully. 'For a short time, too short a time, it seemed as if we were glittering ghosts from the spendours of the eighteenth century.' In many ways the Second Empire was a final flicker of the *ancien régime*.

When she first became empress her role was that of '*la reine Crinoline*', presiding over the great balls at the Tuileries (the '*fêtes impériales*'), that were attended by thousands of guests, when her clothes and jewellery, her taste in furniture, began to be copied all over the world. But later she grew more concerned with influencing her husband's policies, then with making them. No woman had wielded such power in France since the sixteenth century. She gave style to the pressure for women's emancipation, which was increasing imperceptibly everywhere.

A natural feminist, she admired other women's achievements in a male world, trying to persuade the Académie Française to admit a female writer besides appointing the first female member of the Légion d'honneur. 'Nothing used to anger me more than to hear I had no political sense simply because I was a woman. I wanted to shout back, "So women have no political sense, do they? What about Queen Elizabeth? Maria Theresa? Catherine the Great?"'

As will be seen, she undoubtedly played a crucial role in shaping her husband's foreign policy.

Since most French writers of her time were republicans or royalists, and because of the Second Empire's overthrow at Sedan in 1870, the empress has been given a bad name by the majority of French historians as *'une femme néfaste'* – a baneful woman. They tend to agree with her long-standing enemy Thiers, that she 'began as a futile woman and ended as a fatal woman', while until the new feminist climate they damned her as a woman who dared to interfere in politics.

'She cannot really be said to have had a character at all, being too much of a woman to have one and, I would suggest, far too prone to the fluctuations of the feminine temperament', was the considered opinion of one of her best-known historians, Ferdinand Loliée, writing during the early twentieth century in *La vie d'une Impératrice*. 'She felt and she did not reason. She acted without realising where her actions would take her – and with her she took the emperor of the French.'

Loliée was biased against the empress before he even put pen to paper. Subtly hostile, always ready to admit that she possessed one or two 'feminine' good qualities, so as to give the impression of being unprejudiced, his insidiously negative approach and beautiful prose have had a far wider influence – and still have – than is generally appreciated, especially in France. In reality his attitude towards the empress derived from republicanism and the political smears that circulated immediately after the fall of the Second Empire.

This book is an attempt to refute 'authorities' such as Ferdinand Loliée. While I cannot claim to have unearthed any important new material – probably nothing significant remains to be found – I have tried to give a different portrait of Eugénie by taking her seriously and by being open-minded. I have concentrated on the historically important years of her life when she was empress and given less time to those of her exile.

For good or ill, she was the most powerful woman of the nineteenth century – even Queen Victoria, as a constitutional monarch, was forced to leave policy to her ministers. All too many Frenchmen resented the empress's influence because she was a woman, yet Bismarck called her 'the only man in Paris'.

ONE

How to Become an Empress

born may 28, 1826

GROWING UP

In <u>1826</u> Granada was a dusty, untidy place, the Alhambra so ruinous that tourists feared its crumbling red walls and owl-infested towers would vanish within a generation. Yet noblemen lived in the city, including, at 12 Calle de Gracia, a handsome count with red hair and a patch over one eye. If he tended to avoid society, his beautiful wife adored it and would have preferred to live in Madrid, but her husband had been sent to Granada under house arrest.

On <u>28 May</u> an earthquake shook the city. Taking refuge in the garden, the pregnant countess was stricken with labour pains and gave birth in a tent to her second child, another daughter, who was christened Maria Eugenia Ignacia Augusta. Long after, Eugenia said she was sure that being born during an earthquake had meant that great things lay in store for her.

Her father's name was Don Cipriano de Guzmán y Palafox y Portocarrero, Count of Teba, and he belonged to one of Spain's oldest families, the Guzmáns, claiming descent from the Visigoth kings who had reigned over the peninsula before the Moorish conquest. Cipriano's branch owned vast estates, but as a younger son he had inherited very little. Born in 1786, he served with the Spanish marines at Trafalgar where a British musket ball crippled his left arm. Welcoming the French invasion of 1808 and the Bourbons' replacement by King Joseph Bonaparte, he joined the French army, fought against the Spanish patriots and the British, became a colonel and lost an eye, leaving Spain with the French when Wellington drove them out. Loyal to Napoleon until the end, he was among the last defenders of Paris in 1814.

1

Understandably, when he went home to Spain Don Cipriano was distrusted by King Ferdinand VII. To make matters worse, he was a liberal, who told everyone that what the country needed was a constitution. Even so, in 1817 the king behaved with surprising kindness over his marriage, which, because Cipriano was a member of a great family, required royal approval.

The count's bride, whom he first met in Paris in 1813 when she had just left her finishing school, was not quite so blue-blooded. The story (recently repeated by a French biographer) that the family of her father, William Kirkpatrick (1764–1837), were Jacobites who had gone into exile with the Stuarts before being finally ruined by Prince Charlie's defeat, is a myth. A penniless Lowland Scot, the seventh of nineteen children, William emigrated to Malaga and joined the firm of a Belgian merchant, M. Grivégnée, who exported fruit and wine, specialising in fine grapes for the table. Turning Catholic and marrying Grivégnée's daughter, William became a comparatively rich man, sufficiently respected to be appointed United States consul by President Washington on the recommendation of an American business friend, Mr George Cabot of Massachusetts. Later, however, William seems to have gone bankrupt.

If the Jacobite story is untrue, William did at least belong to a distant branch of a family of Dumfriesshire gentry, Kirkpatrick of Closeburn, who had been Scottish feudal barons since 1232 – although a Scots laird was not the same thing as a Spanish baron. He produced a family tree drawn up by the Lord Lyon King of Arms that was accepted by the *reyes de armas*, the Spanish heralds. Ferdinand then gave his assent, writing graciously on Don Cipriano's petition, 'Let the noble Teba wed the daughter of Fingal.'

Born at Malaga in 1794, 'Doña Maria Manuela Kirkpatrick de Closeburn' was a tall, black-eyed, black-haired beauty, whom most people liked at first sight – not just handsome but strong and practical, intelligent and amusing. She shared Cipriano's admiration for Napoleon if not Cipriano's anticlerical views. Unlike her husband, however, she was full of boundless social ambition.

Predictably, Don Cipriano supported the Liberal revolt led by Colonel Riego that broke out at Cadiz in January 1820 and spread throughout Spain, setting up a chaotic constitutional government that was plagued by royalist risings. When it was crushed by a French army three years later, Cipriano was only saved from execution by his wife's pleas. These must have been amazingly eloquent since most of his friends were hanged, shot or garrotted, sometimes even quartered as well – their bodies hacked in four by the executioner. Fortunate merely to be imprisoned, Cipriano was released at the end of 1823 and permitted to live with his wife and child at Granada near his little estate, under police surveillance.

Soon after Eugenia's birth the restrictions of house arrest came close to ruining Cipriano. Worn out by vice – and probably syphilis – his elder brother Don Eugenio, Count of Montijo, had married a prostitute, installing her in the Montijo Palace at Madrid, the Casa Ariza in the Plazuela del Angel. The lady then announced she was pregnant. Since Eugenio was by now paralysed, this was clearly a plot to steal his fortune. It was vital for Cipriano or his wife to visit Madrid, but the police refused to allow them.

Hearing that King Ferdinand would be at a ball at Valladolid, Maria Manuela decided to attend, knowing that as the wife of a Spanish grandee she had the right to dance in the same quadrille as the king. Ferdinand asked for the good-looking countess to be presented and she made such an impression that he gave her leave to visit Madrid. Here she found what she had suspected: her sister-in-law had brought a baby boy into Casa Ariza, intending to pass him off as the Count of Montijo's son. Having thought Maria Manuela was imprisoned in Granada, when confronted by her the woman collapsed, admitting that she had never been pregnant and claiming she had merely wanted to adopt a child.

Liberal politics came into vogue in Spain, however, after Ferdinand's fourth marriage in 1829 to Maria Cristina of Naples. The king and his new queen hated the heir to the throne, his brother Don Carlos, and when Maria Cristina gave birth to a daughter, the king decided to abolish the Salic Law (introduced from France) that prevented women from succeeding to the throne. As Don Carlos was the white hope of the reactionaries (henceforward known as Carlists), the Liberals warmly supported its abolition and Ferdinand appointed Liberal ministers.

Cipriano was freed from arrest in 1830, moving to a larger house on Granada's Calle del Sordo and making frequent visits to his estate at Teba nearby. Eugenia and her sister Paca rode with him as soon as they could manage their ponies. They also visited Madrid, staying at Casa Ariza or at Casa de Miranda in the country outside, a much-loved house with beautiful gardens that had belonged to the Guzmán since the fifteenth century. Maria Manuela began to entertain at the Calle del Sordo. Among her guests was Washington Irving, living in the ruined Alhambra to write his book about the palace, who told stories to her daughters. Another was a young French writer whom Don Cipriano met on the stagecoach between Granada and Madrid, Prosper Mérimée, the future author of *Carmen*, who was fascinated by Spain. Long after, he reminded her of the 'beautiful tales' she had told him about Andalusia.

Meanwhile, Cipriano made his children wear the same linen dresses winter and summer, and would not buy them silk stockings for parties. Nor would he keep a carriage, making them go everywhere by pony. It did them no harm – a sketch shows two tough, sturdy little girls. Eugenia adored her father, who shared her colouring (white skin, pale face, red hair and blue eyes) and never forgot her rides with him to Teba. Cipriano talked a good deal to her, especially about his hero Napoleon. He may even have spoken of his pleasure at the news that Charles X of France had been overthrown and replaced by Louis-Philippe.

Ferdinand VII died in 1833, bequeathing Spain a two-year-old Isabella II and civil war. Don Carlos soon raised his standard, supported by every reactionary and true son of the Church – there were risings in the Basque country, Navarre, Catalonia and Valencia. Outside the cities the Carlists made alarming progress, the widowed queen proving a disastrous regent. Don Cipriano strongly supported Isabella's cause, but Maria Manuela had a sneaking sympathy for 'Carlos V' – because at first his troops appeared to be winning.

Cipriano's brother died the year after, on 16 July. In the Spanish way the house was draped in black with the coffin left open for a last farewell. On seeing her dead uncle's face, Eugenia tried to jump out of a window, but next day she saw something even more frightening. For some time a Carlist army had been marching on

Madrid, preceded by reports of massacre. Worse still, hundreds of men and women were dying from cholera, which killed within twenty-four hours – there were rumours that Franciscan friars, who were Carlist sympathisers, had poisoned the wells. On 17 July shouting was heard in the small square outside Casa Ariza and Eugenia opened one of the closed blinds to see what the noise was about. Screaming and struggling, a brown-robed friar was being dragged out of the church opposite, which had been set on fire – knives flashed, then they were kicking a dead body.

Don Cipriano became Count of Montijo, inheriting great estates. The prostitute countess was pensioned off, Maria Manuela adopting the baby, and the family were free to move into Casa Ariza. Yet Madrid was too unsafe. Eighty priests had been murdered during the riot in which Eugenia saw the friar knifed, while people were still dying from cholera. Cipriano decided that his wife should take the girls to Paris. He himself would stay behind.

It would not be an easy journey. The Saragossa road was blocked by Carlist guerillas while towns on the road up the coast would not admit travellers from Madrid for fear of cholera. But among Maria Manuela's friends was a famous bullfighter, Francisco Sevilla, who was due to fight at Barcelona. He refused to enter the ring there unless they let the Countess of Montijo pass through the city and helped her reach the frontier. The authorities gave in – postponing Francisco's *corrida* would mean a riot. She and her children set out on 18 July, without waiting for Don Eugenio's funeral, travelling in a slow, mule-drawn coach.

During the last two days Eugenia, only eight, had seen a dead man's face for the first time and another man murdered. She and her sister sensed their mother's anxiety, but with the bullfighter's help everything went off smoothly and they reached France on 29 July. She wrote to her father, 'None of us is dead, which is what really matters.' After a short stop at Perpignan, they went to Toulouse where they spent several nights, then on to Paris, riding in one of the unwieldy public diligences that trundled along the new, straight, Napoleonic roads, spending each night at an inn.

The Paris at which they arrived was that of Balzac, Alexandre Dumas and Victor Hugo, of Chopin and Berlioz, an untidy city of narrow, winding old streets with about a million inhabitants. Many of today's landmarks were there – the Place de la Concorde, the Madeleine, the Palais de Luxembourg, the Bourse, the rue de Rivoli, the column of melted cannon in the Place Vendôme. Already, buses ran regularly, crowded in the rush hour and stinking of cigar smoke inside, while the main streets were gaslit. As always, it was cheerful, with well-attended theatres and wonderful restaurants.

Yet the Orleanist monarchy, established four years earlier, was undeniably dull. So were the policies of its ministers such as M. Guizot, to whose clarion call, *'Enrichissez-vous!'*, fellow bourgeois were responding by creating the hellish world of *Les Misérables* for French workers while making their own fortunes. The régime's drabness also owed a good deal to King Louis-Philippe, who made a point of walking through Paris in a top hat and with an umbrella, pretending he belonged to the bourgeoisie. He forbade gentlemen to wear court dress or knee-breeches at the Tuileries while, *en bon bourgeois*, he carved a joint of meat when the royal family dined together. The only colourful note was the red of the troops' trousers and kepis.

Doña Maria Manuela sent her girls to the most fashionable school in Paris, the Convent of the Sacré Coeur in the rue de Varennes, whose pupils came mainly from the aristocratic Faubourg Saint-Germain. Mornings were spent in not too demanding lessons; afternoons in learning the manners of a lady and how to help the poor; evenings in prayer and reading the lives of the saints. It was a very limited education, but at least Eugenia was taught to write proper French while the nuns instilled in her a compassionate Catholicism that stayed with her for the rest of her life.

Don Cipriano joined them in the summer of 1835. If he had become a rich man, he was as austere as ever: once again, Eugenia and Paca could only wear linen dresses and cotton stockings, and were not allowed to carry umbrellas or go for carriage rides. He had plenty to tell them about Paris, no doubt showing them the site of the battery at Montmartre where in 1814 he had given the last order for cannon to fire in defence of the Emperor Napoleon. Perhaps, too, he told them how after Waterloo the emperor's troops had hidden him in their barracks from the Bourbon police.

He made the girls read the *Mémorial de Sainte-Hélène*. A brilliant piece of propaganda from the grave, this was a book that cast an extraordinary spell over their generation. 'I have given France and Europe new ideas that will never be forgotten', claimed Napoleon, boasting 'My enemies will find it hard to make me disappear.'

By the mid-1830s Napoleon's legend had become a cult. '*Toujours lui. Lui partout*', sang Victor Hugo. He dominated the memoirs of every great man and painters vied at producing Napoleonic battle scenes, while there were portraits, busts or prints of him in countless drawing-rooms. Hoping to attract a few rays of reflected glory for his own lacklustre régime, Louis-Philippe restored the emperor's statue to the top of the column in the Place Vendôme and ordered the completion of the Arc de Triomphe.

In November 1835 Cipriano, who was Senator for Badajoz, returned to Spain where the Liberals had split into two squabbling factions. The confiscation of Church lands was outraging Catholics and the Carlists were far from beaten. It would have been madness to bring his family home. Maria Manuela told a friend that if the Carlists won they would certainly shoot her husband.

Eighteen months later, she and her daughters crossed the Channel, landing in the England of *The Pickwick Papers*. She wanted them to learn English – they had had an English governess in Paris, Miss Cole – so they were sent to a boarding school in the recently built watering place of Clifton, a small, Regency town overlooking the River Avon near Bristol. Eugenia was miserable. The English girls called her 'Carrots' because of her red hair; and she tried to change the colour with a lead comb. She wrote to her father, however, that she would be his interpreter if he came to England. With a little Hindu friend, she decided to run away to India, the two eleven-year-olds sneaking down to the Bristol quayside and clambering on board a ship, but luckily a mistress saw them.

After only a few weeks Maria Manuela decided that a governess could teach them English and in August they returned to Paris, accompanied by a Miss Flowers. A timid young woman, she had difficulty controlling her charges – when she tried to make Eugenia rise at seven, her pupil would hold out five fingers from under the blankets, meaning another five minutes in bed, and when they had passed would hold out five more. The girls went back to the Sacré Coeur. On their father's instructions, they also attended a physical training school, run on Pestalozzi methods by a Spaniard, Colonel Amoros, who like Cipriano had fought for Napoleon. This was probably the first strenuous exercise that Eugénie had ever taken, apart from riding her ponies, and she enjoyed it.

Don Cipriano reappeared in Paris in autumn 1837. The war still dragged on in northern Spain, but the enemy's best general had died and they had failed to capture any of the major cities. Ostensibly for reasons of health, his visit may have been because he feared that his marriage was in danger. His wife had more or less stopped writing to him, and he knew she was entertaining lavishly. Although they lived together until his departure in January 1838, afterwards Maria Manuela sent him very few letters.

In a report of autumn 1838 Colonel Amoros tells Eugenia's parents that their daughter enjoys physical exercise, that her character is 'good, generous and firm' and her temperament 'sanguine and nervous'. This fits with what we know from other sources. She was very highly strung, almost hyperactive, never able to keep still or stop talking, even during meals, in an age when children were not supposed to speak unless spoken to, often having long conversations with herself, and obsessively fond of her father – one biographer comments that her letters to him sound like 'an impatient woman in love'. When only nine, she wrote, 'I'm so looking forward to your coming here that I think you're going to arrive every day, although it's three weeks since I asked you if you were coming soon.' In other letters she says, 'Dear Papa, I want to throw my arms around you'; 'Dear Papa, when are you coming, my heart is sighing for you?'

Sometimes she seems very grown up. 'It's just not possible to live in Paris any more as they're always trying to kill the king', she complains early in 1837. 'Yesterday the gas blew up, breaking lots of windows, and we were told it happened because people had set light to it. What was so funny was how all the soldiers came running with their guns, afraid that it was a revolution.' This is written by a girl not yet twelve, who in the same letter tells her father that she is looking forward to reading *Robinson Crusoe* and *The Swiss Family*

Robinson. She also mentions Napoleon, reminding Cipriano he has told her to read a book about Napoleon, and that what happened to him on St Helena made her cry.

Meanwhile, Doña Maria Manuela was meeting as many of the great as possible, including Legitimist diehards such as the Duc de Richelieu and Orleanist leaders like the Duc de Broglie, and also a young Bonaparte, Princesse Mathilde. Nor did she neglect literary lions, renewing her acquaintance with Prosper Mérimée, by now the author of several successful books and recently appointed Inspector General of Historic Monuments. A trim, birdlike man, very well dressed, with black hair starting to go white, a high forehead and a nose that enemies called 'snout-like', if not a grandee he had polished manners and a marvellous sense of humour. Lonely despite his constant party-going, he was grateful for her friendship, writing regularly to her for the rest of his life, while she valued someone so scholarly and amusing, who knew everyone worth knowing. It is unlikely that he slept with her, however – he told Stendhal, his closest male friend, that the countess was definitely not his mistress.

Mérimée played games with Maria Manuela's daughters, took them for walks – buying cream cakes – and even to shooting galleries where they learned to use pistols. He admired Eugenia's high spirits, calling her 'a lioness with a flowing mane' (*une lionne à tous crins*), referring to the red hair that still embarrassed her. He helped them with their homework – they were day girls at the Sacré Coeur, not boarders – and improved their rather Spanish French. It was his idea that they should make a first visit to the theatre and in September 1838 he and Maria Manuela took them to a production at the Comédie-Française of Corneille's *Horace*, in which Camille's role was played by the sixteen-year-old Rachel (who was to become one of the century's greatest classical actresses). He brought Rachel to some of Maria Manuela's receptions, where she thrilled everybody with recitations from Racine. Eugenia was dazzled, announcing that when she grew up, she too would be an actress.

'Mr Mérimée' also became a trusted ally of their governess, the dismal Flowers, calming her down after the girl's unending attempts to run away and roam the streets of Paris. On one occasion, inspired by the nuns' teaching on the need to be kind to outcasts, the two

9

children walked after a hearse because the sole mourners were its coachman and two mutes – 'not a wreath, not a single lily, not even a dog', recalled Eugenia. They followed it all the way to the Père Lachaise cemetery, where they attended the lonely funeral.

Among Mérimée's outings with the children was a walk to see the recently completed Arc de Triomphe at the end of the Champs Elysées, on which was inscribed a roll-call of the emperor's victories, while in 1836 he introduced their mother to a fanatical Bonapartist, a shy, burly man with a round face fringed with thick black whiskers. This was the novelist Henri Beyle, better remembered as 'Stendhal'. Painfully aware that he had not had the success he deserved, the novelist liked the handsome Spanish countess who talked about his books to him. He began to call on her every Thursday evening.

He told the girls about his hero the emperor, who on one glorious occasion had seized him by the lapel and actually spoken to him. Despite having nearly died on the retreat from Moscow – surviving on a lump of tallow – he thought Napoleon's return from Elba 'the most romantic and beautiful enterprise of modern times', and when it was dangerous to do so had dedicated a book to 'His Majesty Napoleon the Great, Emperor of the French, detained on the island of St Helena'. Convinced that Spanish blood flowed in his own veins, he felt he had found a worthy audience in these children from Spain.

'He came in the evening and sat us on his knee to tell us about Napoleon's campaigns', Eugenia remembered. 'We couldn't eat our dinner, we were so eager to hear. Every time the bell rang, we ran to the door. Finally we brought him in triumphantly, each one holding him by the hand, and sat him in his armchair next to the fire. We wouldn't even let him draw breath, reminding him of which of our Emperor's victories he had told us about last time, since we'd been thinking about it all week, waiting impatiently for the magician who knew how to bring Napoleon back to life.' Part of the magic came from his treating the girls as grown-ups. 'We wept, we groaned, we went crazy', recalled Eugenia. Sometimes their mother told the girls to stop bothering 'Monsieur Beyle' with their questions, but he encouraged them. Eugenia never forgot their evenings with Stendhal.

In 1840 she would write from Spain to tell him how pleased she was that the emperor's body was being brought back to France for reburial at the Invalides.

Another friend to whom Mérimée introduced Maria Manuela was his mistress's husband, Gabriel Delessert, the Prefect of Police. Delessert sent his daughter Cécile to Colonel Amoros's gymnasium where she became Eugenia's best friend. In November 1836 Mme Delessert took Cécile and the two Montijo girls to catch a glimpse of Louis-Napoleon Bonaparte, the emperor's nephew, when he was imprisoned in the Conciergerie after a farcical attempt to mount a *coup d'état* at Strasbourg. This was the first time that Eugenia saw her future husband, shortly to be deported to the United States. No doubt she was disappointed, as he did not look in the least like his uncle. Nevertheless, everything was conspiring to make Eugenia a dedicated Bonapartist. Her father's example was almost enough to do so, while Stendhal completed the process. In her words, 'He gave us his fanaticism.'

Late in 1839, Don Cipriano's doctor sent an urgent message from Madrid. He was dying, unlikely to last long. A coach journey across the Pyrenees in midwinter might give the girls pneumonia so, never worried about her own iron health, Maria left them with Miss Flowers and hurried back to Spain. She did not tell Paca or Eugenia how ill their father was – perhaps she did not even realise it herself. Travelling on the fastest coaches available, it took her ten days to reach Madrid and on arrival she found him beyond recovery. He died on 15 March.

Meanwhile, the girls thoroughly enjoyed their mother's absence. The normally gentle Paca became fiendish, tormenting the spineless Flowers so dreadfully that the latter appealed to 'Mr Mérimée' for help. He seems to have restored order, giving Paca a good scolding.

Mérimée guessed that Maria Manuela would stay in Spain. He wrote, 'I have been so fond of those children that I simply can't get used to the idea of not seeing them again for such a long time. They are leaving at a time in a woman's life when a few months can change them completely, and I know I'm going to lose them. If one parts from a friend like you, one is fairly sure of finding her again one day, just as she was, but instead of our two little friends,

I'm afraid that I shall meet two prim and haughty young ladies who have quite forgotten me.'

Stendhal, too, was depressed at the departure of the girls, whom he had not seen for several months as he was busy writing. Wondering how to give them a really exciting account of the battle of Waterloo, he had suddenly become inspired, producing his greatest novel, *La Chartreuse de Parme*. 'Monsieur Beyle has disappeared,' Eugenia had reported indignantly to Don Cipriano early in November. 'He's told the porter where he lives to say he's gone shooting if anyone asks for him.' He dedicated chapter three of *La Chartreuse* to them, in a cryptic footnote – the letters '*P y E*' – but never saw them again, dying before they returned to France.

As the weather had improved, Doña Maria Manuela wrote to Miss Flowers, telling her to bring her daughters to Madrid. She did not say that Don Cipriano had died. The three left Paris on 17 March. *En route*, snow blocked the road over the Pyrenees, so that they were held up for nearly a week on the frontier, at Oloron Sainte-Marie beneath the mountains. When they reached Madrid, the children were at last told that their father was dead. Paca collapsed in hysterics. Without a tear or a word, Eugenia went upstairs and shut herself in her room for two days.

SPAIN

The next few years transformed Doña Eugenia. If a Parisian childhood had given her a lasting command of French and a love of France, now she developed traits traditionally regarded as Spanish – a harsh pride and a rigid sense of honour, an elaborate courtesy, a boundless generosity and a deep religious faith, together with an incapacity for moderation. 'She became used to living inside a world she had created for herself', says Lucien Daudet, who knew her when she was an old lady. 'She steeled her soul, that Spanish soul, toughening it ruthlessly, ignoring human weakness and despising compromise, to such a degree that she became unyielding and unconquerable in her determination, blindly, unswervingly straightforward.'

Don Cipriano had left her mother very rich indeed, with an income equivalent to £20,000 a year in contemporary English money and those two fine houses at Madrid, Casa Ariza and Carabanchel. Extravagant and ambitious, no longer held in check by an austere husband, Doña Maria Manuela began to entertain lavishly, her receptions becoming a popular feature of Madrileño social life. Eager to obtain a high appointment at court, she ran after influential statesmen. Above all, she was determined her two pretty daughters should make marriages no less dazzling than her own.

The statesmen were shabby figures, Eugenia learning a good deal about an unsavoury form of politics. Although very young and definitely not a Carlist, in September 1839 she wrote to tell Stendhal of her contempt – 'It's not nice' – when after a bribe the Carlist General Maroto betrayed Don Carlos by ordering the troops under his command to surrender, ending for the moment what was to be a perpetual dynastic war. Next year the leading *Progresista* General Espartero (the man who had bribed Maroto) seized power, becoming Spain's first military dictator and banished the Regent, Isabella II's mother. In 1843 he was toppled in turn by another dictator, the *Moderado* General Ramón Nárvaez, who banned the press and gave the firing squad a new role in Spanish politics, shooting not just Carlist diehards but over 200 of Espartero's *Progresistas* without the tiresome formality of a trial.

Eugenia watched her mother flatter these petty tyrants, who had made themselves masters of Spain. Even a slight acquaintance left her with an intense dislike of corrupt, self-styled liberals, whether *progresistas* or *moderados*. Very different from her father, they concentrated on making fortunes out of confiscated Church lands or exploiting government contracts. Together with many other Spaniards, including even her mother in certain moods, Doña Eugenia yearned for a really capable ruler who would clear up the mess, a Spanish Napoleon.

Early in 1843 Eugenia danced with a young Frenchman who, like the Louis-Napoleon Bonaparte she had glimpsed at the Conciergerie in Paris, bore the emperor's name, but in contrast to Louis-Napoleon resembled their uncle in appearance. Later known as 'Plon-Plon', Prince Napoleon was the son of the emperor's youngest brother, ex-King Jerome of Westphalia, and had come to Spain hoping to marry Queen Isabella, although she was only twelve and matchmakers no longer took Bonapartes seriously. If unbalanced, with a cruel wit, he was also highly intelligent despite extreme opinions – he loathed Christianity and was a 1790s republican rather than a Bonapartist. There is a legend that he tried to seduce Eugenia and never forgave her for rejecting him, but the real cause of their lasting dislike for each other is more likely to have been the instinctive antipathy of natural opposites.

In 1843 Bonapartism was a sentiment, not a political programme, no more than nostalgic hero-worship of the emperor, whose uninspiring heir, the ex-King Joseph of Spain, did not die until 1844. The next heir, their brother, ex-King Louis of Holland, died the following year. Before Louis's death, despite two inept attempts at a *coup-d'état*, his son Louis-Napoleon could not properly call himself the Bonapartist pretender and had no followers other than a handful of adventurers. Plon-Plon was a figure of even less importance.

The ball where Eugenia met him was a fancy-dress ball at Casa Ariza for the carnival on the night of Shrove Tuesday. She went as a Highlander in tartan, her sister dressing in Polish costume '*à la Cracowienne*'. Doña Maria Manuela was the first Spanish hostess to give costume balls, those at Casa Ariza becoming so popular that Queen Isabella began to copy them. Maria Manuela gave three a year – for the carnival, for St Eugenia's day in November and for Paca's birthday in January.

This particular ball was part of the celebrations for Paca's forthcoming wedding to a distant cousin, the fifteenth Duke of Alba, holder of Spain's most ancient dukedom and the richest man in the realm. Only twenty, he was a shy, tongue-tied young man, perhaps because of his ugliness – portraits show a gnome-like face with a very long nose and a thick-lipped mouth hiding behind a heavy moustache and goatee beard. When at Madrid he lived in the magnificent Liria Palace, filled with superb old masters. The girls had first met him in Paris, Doña Maria Manuela having long ago marked Alba down. Surprisingly, in view of his ugliness, both fell in love with him. Their mother decided that Paca should have the glittering prize.

The duke had proposed in 1842, being immediately accepted, but for reasons unknown the wedding was postponed twice before it finally took place in February 1844. Among the reasons seems to have been Eugenia's distress at losing him, and which culminated in a suicide attempt – she drank milk in which she had dissolved the poisonous heads of phosphorous matches.

Eugenia sent the duke a farewell letter. 'People [her mother?] treat me like a donkey, punishing me in front of everyone, it's more than I can bear', she complained:

My blood boils and I don't know what to do. Clever people think nobody in the world is as happy as I am, but they're wrong. I'm unhappy because I make myself unhappy. I should have been born a century sooner, as these days all my dearest ideas seem ridiculous and I'm more frightened of being laughed at than dying. I love and hate violently, and I don't know which is better, my love or my hatred. I have an awful mixture of passions inside me, all wild; I fight them, but I always lose, and my life is going to end miserably, in a whirl of passions, virtues and follies.

. . . Perhaps you'll say I'm romantic and silly, but I know you're generous enough to forgive a poor girl who has lost all those she loved and who is being treated so cruelly by everyone, even by her mother and sister and, dare I say it, by the man she loved best, for whom she would have begged, whom she would even have allowed to dishonour her. Don't say I'm mad, please, but pity me; you don't realize what it is to be loved and rejected. But God will give me courage; he never denies it to those who need it, and he's going to give me the courage to end my life quietly, deep inside some gloomy cloister, so that no one will know I ever existed.

Some people are born happy; you're one of them, and God grant it always stays that way. My sister is a good person; she loves you, your marriage can't be delayed much longer, and then nothing will be missing from your happiness. If you have children, love them equally; remember they're all your children and never hurt their feelings by showing more affection for one than another. Follow my advice and be happy. This is what is wanted for you by your sister, Eugenia.

In a postscript she adds, 'Don't try to stop me, it's madness. I shall end my life far away from the world and its affections; nothing is ever impossible with God's help and I've made up my mind as my heart is broken.'

A little surprisingly, Eugenia not only became fonder than ever of Paca but, in spite of what she had insisted on seeing as Alba's heartless rejection, almost as devoted to her brother-in-law and their children. At seventeen, however, her wounds had time to heal, even if they left a few scars – especially on her relations with her mother.

She had plenty to distract her. Despite telling Alba that she should have been born a century earlier, she was a 'socialist' at sixteen, having read Fournier's *Le nouveau monde industriel*, with its proposals for abolishing all authority and establishing communes of men and women, the *'phalanstères'*. She spoke so often about this utopia during Maria Manuela's Sunday evening receptions that she became known as *'la jeune phalanstérienne'*. An instinctive feminist (if fully developed feminism was unimaginable at that date), what probably appealed to her most in Fournier's socialism was his view that marriage enslaved women and needed radical reform.

Eugenia was also a keen liberal, sympathising with the *progresistas* shot down daily in the streets of Madrid, hiding one in her mother's house when he was being hunted for his life after killing a political opponent. She quarrelled in public with Maria Manuela over her opinions, no doubt expressed a little too intensely, threatening to throw herself down a marble staircase.

'Even as a girl I had a taste for politics', Eugenia explained in old age:

It was a taste inherited from my mother, in whose house I became used to hearing statesmen, diplomats, generals and journalists expounding all day long. You can imagine how extreme politics were in the time of the Regent Queen Cristina, Nárvaez and Espartero. But I was bored by the squalid infighting of political parties, by all their murky little rivalries, petty intrigues and wretched manoeuvring. What did interest me were the really big questions, the ones where national prestige was involved and when a nation's reputation was at stake.

At one of her mother's receptions Nárvaez sneered that no woman had a right to political opinions because she would run away on seeing a bayonet – Doña Eugenia's response was to seize a knife and stab herself through the arm.

In the summer of 1845 she went with Doña Maria Manuela to take the cure at a small watering place in the Pyrenees, Eaux-Bonnes, where she met a woman who influenced her political ideas profoundly. This was the dashing Mme Eleonore Gordon, whom they heard singing at a musical evening given by some French friends. The beautiful daughter of a captain in the Imperial Guard and the widow of a British officer, still in her late twenties, Eleonore was a lady of very easy virtue indeed and an 'adventuress', not a suitable person for a well-brought-up young girl to know. But Doña Maria Manuela, never prudish, was intrigued when she learned that the lady had been tried for her part in Prince Louis-Napoleon's abortive coup at Strasbourg in 1836, and asked to meet her. Mme Gordon turned out to be fascinating and, after regretfully declining her offer to arrange for them to visit the prince in prison at Ham, Maria Manuela invited her to come and stay in Spain.

During Mme Gordon's visit to Madrid, she converted Eugenia to a Bonapartism of which she had hitherto been unaware. Presumably Eleonore repeated what she had told the court in 1836: 'The cause I openly defend to the best of my ability is so noble, so splendid and so holy that it has become my religion, a religion of which I shall always be a loyal and faithful disciple.' She is less likely to have repeated her admission to the court that Louis-Napoleon 'produces the same effect on me as a woman', or confided that she had slept with the prince and two of his key supporters.

Indoctrinated with the Napoleonic cult by her father and Stendhal, Eugenia now realised that the emperor might have an heir worthy of him, very unlike the horrible Plon-Plon, and that there was at least a chance of a Bonapartist restoration. She learned about the prince's programme from his book *Des idées napoléoniennes*, published in 1839, in which he argued that while his uncle had kept all the Revolution's best innovations, Bonapartism was in no way revolutionary but simply meant to make France a fairer and more efficient place, replacing aristocracy by meritocracy and parliamentarianism by 'disciplined' democracy – Frenchmen must learn to live together. For the moment, however, Louis-Philippe appeared to be firmly in control.

Significantly, she developed a passion for violets, which were the Bonapartist flowers, as opposed to the Bourbon lilies. From now on she wore them whenever they were in season, in her hair or pinned in a bunch at her waist. When spring drew to an end and they became hard to find, she employed a shepherd to bring them down from the glens of the Sierra Nevada.

A natural athlete, Colonel Amoros's former pupil kept herself fit by riding the biggest stallions obtainable (sometimes bareback), fencing daily, becoming a fine shot and hunting regularly. She swam like an otter and enjoyed sailing, particularly if the weather was stormy enough to be dangerous. Her favourite resort for swimming and boating was Biarritz on the Atlantic coast, just across the frontier into France – not a resort at all when she discovered it in 1847 but a lonely Basque fishing hamlet. She also drove a smart English phaeton pulled by mettlesome ponies, at such a terrifying pace that she had several bad smashes, both she and her passenger being thrown through the air into a roadside ditch. (Prosper Mérimée wrote to her deeply unamused mother that any normal young man would be only too glad to share a ditch with Eugenia.)

Some of Eugenia's more colourful behaviour made Madrid's dowagers raise their eyebrows. She was rumoured to smoke cigars, while she could be seen at the bullring or at ranches where the bulls were reared, wearing outrageous clothes – a bullfighter's hat and bolero jacket, with red leather boots and a dagger stuck in her belt – besides cracking a riding switch instead of fluttering a fan. More shocking still, she flirted with the strutting bullfighters idolised by the Madrid mob, whom the celebrity-obsessed Maria Manuela invited to the parties at Carabanchel. She was known to make long, solitary rides into the countryside, visiting gipsy encampments to have her fortune told. During the great Easter fair at Seville she and a girlfriend disguised themselves as gipsy dancers, setting up a booth where they gave a performance that completely deceived some English tourists, whom they then astonished by speaking English.

Madrid itself offered plenty of amusement and a vigorous social life, Maria Manuela taking care to see they were always there for the season. By the time she was eighteen Doña Eugenia de Montijo had become a celebrity whose name was seldom out of the gossip columns, at every court function or fashionable reception. She enjoyed going to the theatre, but being almost tone deaf except with gipsy music, never went to the opera. She liked dancing, however, especially at costume balls where she appeared as a Sicilian country girl, a Spanish jewess or a Spanish gipsy, and she also danced regularly at her sister Paca's balls in the Liria Palace. In addition, she acted in amateur theatricals staged in the little private theatres of the Liria and Carabanchel, in 1845 receiving an ovation for playing her part so professionally in *El Hombre del Mundo* – written by one of her mother's innumerable young protégés, Ventura de la Vega.

Stories of Doña Eugenia's beauty, of her tawny hair, exquisitely poised little head, violet eyes and white skin, spread throughout Spain. When she was staying at a house in the depths of the country a bandit broke in and hid under her bed just to see her. Realising someone was there, she bemused him by sitting silently on the bed and dangling her stockingless legs before his eyes while quietly sending a note through her maid to alert the staff. Rushing in, they hauled the man out, but as he was dragged off he begged to kiss her feet, saying he was proud that he and she were both Spaniards.

Although fascinated by Eugenia, the future novelist Juan Valera (who was two years older) gives an unattractive portrait of her at this time – spoilt, noisy, petulant, wilful and bad-tempered, 'obsessed by physical exercise and intoxicated by the adoration of handsome men'. He prophesied that one day some worshiping husband was going to be 'tormented by this celestial, aristocratic and almost unbelievably rich young being'. But Valera only knew Eugenia from a distance.

Very highly strung, sometimes her nerves brought her near to collapse, and her mother took her abroad to recuperate. On one such occasion, when they were staying in the château at Cognac, an Abbé Boudinet offered to tell Eugenia's fortune. 'I see a crown', he prophesied. 'A duchess's coronet or a princess's?', Maria Manuela enquired eagerly. 'No, no, it's certainly a crown', replied the palmist.

'An imperial crown.' Everyone burst out laughing – in the 1840s the only empires were those of Austria and Russia.

Eugenia had countless suitors, the most eligible being the Duke of Osuna, who once saved her from drowning. Even if he was not so rich as Alba, Maria Manuela would have been delighted with such a son-in-law, but although he was genuinely in love Eugenia refused him. Nor would she marry her cousin José de Xifre. There was a French suitor, Prince Albert de Broglie, from the French embassy, and even an English suitor, Ferdinand Huddleston of Sawston Hall, Cambridgeshire. When Huddleston asked Mme Gordon to intercede for him, she came back with the dismal news that the lady 'would rather be hanged from a gibbet than marry an Englishman'.

As a hostess, Doña Maria Manuela was more interested in leaders than politics, particularly General Ramón Nárvaez who was President of the Queen's Council. An Andalusian cavalry officer, created Duke of Valencia after seizing power, he was 'an ugly, fat little man with a vile expression', according to Lord Malmesbury, who saw him in London, swearing, threatening and bullying in a harsh, coarse voice. A dedicated ladykiller in dandified clothes, his yellow moustache and goatee beard contrasted weirdly with his greasy black hair. Despite calling himself a '*moderado*', he disliked Liberals as much as Carlists. On his deathbed, he claimed proudly that he was dying without enemies – they were all dead, shot by his firing squads.

But Nárvaez ran Spain and Maria Manuela made friends with him. Soon he became a frequent guest at Casa Ariza and Carabanchel, surrounded by fawning aides-de-camp and vicious bodyguards. He found her parties useful as they were not only enjoyable but attended by everybody who mattered in Madrid. Eugenia got to know him fairly well and once or twice they had heated arguments. He thought she was a joke, with her crackpot Fourierist ideas and did not realize that she was a Liberal. Privately she thought that 'Don Ramón' was a murderer. Ironically, he told Maria Manuela she was lucky to have such a daughter.

Another guest at Doña Maria Manuela's by now legendary balls was the young Isabella II, hell-bent on pleasure. For reasons of political expediency, she had been declared of age in 1843 when only thirteen and was growing up to be drunken and promiscuous, surrounded by greedy favourites. Nárvaez married Her Most Catholic Majesty off as soon as possible. ('You don't know these Spanish princesses,' said a courtier. 'They have a devil in their bodies and if you delay for a moment, the heir to the throne arrives before the husband.') Despite a certain feeble charm the Infante Don Francisco, her first cousin, was the worst possible husband, effete and rumoured to be 'effeminate', the period's code for homosexual. Isabella loathed him.

After drinking too much at an uproarious banquet at the Prado, the queen consented to the marriage, which took place in October 1846. Eugenia, a frequent guest at court, was one of the bridesmaids. It was a double wedding, Isabella's sister marrying the Duc de Montpensier, a younger son of Louis-Philippe. The French were convinced that Francisco could not beget children and that one day Spain would have an Orleanist sovereign, but somehow Francisco managed to give the Queen a son and three daughters – which did not stop her from going to bed with guardsmen, singers and bullfighters.

The year 1846 also saw Ramón Nárvaez lose power, briefly. On regaining it in October the following year, he appointed Maria Manuela '*Camerara Mayor del Palacio*' – mistress of the robes and first of the queen's ladies. The fruit merchant's daughter from Malaga had risen very high indeed. Ignoring the court's reputation as the most scandalous in Europe, she revelled in the social possibilities, persuading Isabella to make Paca a lady-in-waiting and come with 'King Francisco' to a ball she gave for her younger daughter. She also obtained the queen's permission for Eugenia to use Don Cipriano's titles, and from now on Eugenia was the Countess of Teba. But despite doing a difficult job rather well and although Queen Isabella grew devoted to her, Maria Manuela had to resign after less than two months, in mid-December 1847. An ally of Nárvaez wanted the post for a friend.

Meanwhile, the new Countess of Teba had at last taken a suitor seriously. If the handsome, amusing young Pedro, Marqués de Alcañices, was not in the same league as Alba, he could offer her a great fortune and eventually even a ducal coronet, while although an often frivolous man of pleasure, at the same time he had an impressive personality, commanding and intelligent. One day he would play an important role in Spanish politics. Since the correspondence was destroyed, the romance has to be reconstructed, most of what evidence survives coming from Ethel Smyth, who was told by one of Eugenia's nieces. The biographer Jasper Ridley thinks Alcañices has been mistaken for Alba, but Harold Kurtz accepts the story. It certainly agrees with what we know of Eugenia's temperament.

As Kurtz says, the most likely date is during 1848 – not in the summer as he suggests, but more probably in the early months of the year, the height of Madrid's social season. After acting with Eugenia in the Carabanchel theatre, 'Don Pepe' began flirting more and more seriously, finally declaring his passion in long letters. She responded, falling desperately in love, and with her uncompromising nature, must have made up her mind to marry him. Then she noticed that whenever she was staying at the Liria Palace he came daily. Suddenly she realised she had been the victim of a cruel stratagem. He was not in love with her at all – he had designs on her sister.

Again, Eugenia tried to poison herself, refusing an antidote. As she lay in the Liria Palace dangerously ill, Pepe came to her bedside, whispering, 'Where are my letters?' Crying, 'You are like Achilles's spear that healed the wounds it made', she swallowed the antidote. After two humiliating disappointments, Alba, followed by Alcañices, the poor girl can scarcely be blamed for distrusting men. It was time for mother and daughter to leave Spain.

THE HUSBAND HUNTER

Disappointment at having lost her great court appointment made Doña Maria Manuela more determined than ever to find a splendid match for Eugenia, and she was ready to search all Europe for the right husband. She cannot have foreseen how long it would take, however, while unwisely she ignored the fact that her daughter had no particular wish to marry, having already discovered some very good reasons for distrusting men.

For anyone quite so proud and fastidious as the young Countess of Teba, it was another humiliation to be made to seem a vulgar, gold-digging fortune hunter who was being hawked around by a matchmaking mama. As Don Cipriano's daughter, Doña Eugenia knew very well that she had no particular need of social position or money. She possessed a perfectly good title of her own – indeed she had several, including a duchy – while one day she was going to be an extremely rich heiress. She was not yet old enough to appreciate the cruel disadvantages of nineteenth-century spinsterhood.

As Eugenia said of Maria Manuela to an English friend many years later, when feeling old and charitable, 'She wanted to make everybody happy, but in her own way, not in theirs.' There were always potentially explosive tensions between mother and child, and especially at this time; it must have been very difficult for Eugenia to forgive Maria Manuela for deciding that Paca and not she should marry Alba. Even so, she admired her mother's courage and determination.

In theory, since the Countess of Montijo and the Countess of Teba belonged to that close-knit international ruling class which in those days stretched from London to St Petersburg and from Stockholm to Naples, and whose common language was French, the doors of great houses in every European capital should have been open to them. No doubt, too, they expected to meet kindred spirits – some of whom might even be potential husbands – at all the fashionable spas and watering places. Yet in practice it turned out to be not quite so easy.

Leaving Spain, they first of all went back to Paris. From here in March 1849 Doña Eugenia wrote to Paca, saying that she had gone with Maria Manuela to a party given by Princesse Mathilde Bonaparte, 'where I knew absolutely nobody. No one said a single word to me'. After the social triumphs of Madrid which she had always taken for granted, it was a new experience to be ignored by her own kind.

Eugenia adds:

I'm going to tell you something that will really make you laugh. The other day, when we were looking for an appartment we saw an enormous one in the Place Vendôme that appealed very much to Mamma, who said to me: "Don't you see how well this would suit us, as we would be able to give receptions here." You can imagine how I trembled. Mercifully we are now in a tiny appartment into which not more than ten people at most can fit, which helps to reassure me a little.

The story underlines the incompatibility between mother and daughter.

Paris had recently been shaken by a political earthquake whose tremors were felt by nearly every European government. In February 1848 the uninspiring monarchy of King Louis-Philippe had been unexpectedly swept away by the 'Revolution of Contempt', the king escaping from the Tuileries in a cab, with his whiskers shaved off and wearing dark glasses, to flee across the Channel under the name of 'Mr Smith, an English tourist'. As Prosper Mérimée had written to Doña Maria Manuela at the time:

> The Revolution was the work of 600 men, most of whom had no idea what they were doing or what they wanted. Now it has done its work. The little tradesmen who howled 'Long live reform' are saying today that it has ruined them. Government, opposition and National Guard each behaved with unbelievable stupidity. The only thing that we can do is try and keep some sort of authority and save whatever is left. While law and order have no doubt been restored and Paris is becoming her normal self again, you see very long faces everywhere. Bankruptcies are beginning to occur. There is immense uneasiness as people are living in fear of a future no one dares to predict.

The early months of the Second Republic had seen plenty of bloodshed. When the Paris mob rose in June, it was shot down mercilessly, 5,000 being killed and another 12,000 transported to Algeria. By the time Maria Manuela and Eugenia arrived, for the moment at least the new makeshift régime seemed to be in control but no one could say if it was going to last or whether the army would bring back the monarchy – many officers were staunch royalists.

Horrified by the reports of bloodshed and social upheaval that were coming out of the capital, throughout France the majority of the bourgeoisie and the peasantry hoped that the monarchy would return as soon as possible – many older people remembered the Terror very well, and also the financial chaos of the 1790s. What prevented any chance of a restoration, however, was the existence of two competing royalist parties, the Legitimists supporting the Comte de Chambord ('Henry V'), the grandson of Charles X, deposed in 1830, and the Orleanists supporting the Comte de Paris ('Philip VII'), Louis-Philippe's grandson.

Desperate for firm rule, in December 1848 France elected an ersatz monarch in the person of Prince Louis-Napoleon Bonaparte, who became the republic's Prince President and installed himself in the Elysée. Mme Gordon's sacred dream was beginning to look as though it might come true.

Only a few weeks after she arrived in Paris, Doña Maria Manuela secured an invitation to the Elysée for herself and her daughter, and in April 1849 they were presented by Prince Félix Bacciochi, the *chef-de-protocol*, to Louis-Napoleon. As someone who adored beautiful women, after chatting with Maria Manuela for a noticeably long time – normally he was a man of very few words – the Prince President then began to speak to her daughter. 'Monseigneur', Eugenia tactlessly informed him, 'we have often talked about you with a lady who is truly devoted to your cause.' 'What is her name?' 'Mme Gordon.' On hearing the name, Louis-Napoleon broke off the conversation hastily, and quickly moved on. Did the pretty young Spaniard with the red hair know that Eleonore Gordon had been his mistress? If so, why had she mentioned her to him? Was it some sort of invitation? Was she perhaps lascivious, like her queen in Madrid?

Some weeks later Maria Manuela and Eugenia received an invitation to dinner with the Prince President, not at the Elysée, but at the Palace of Saint-Cloud near Paris, where he was staying to escape from the midsummer heat, and also to take refuge from an alarming epidemic of cholera among the capital's poorer classes. Thinking that this was going to be a large, formal party, the two ladies put on their most stately dresses and best jewellery.

Instead of taking them to the Palace of Saint-Cloud, however, the carriage sent to fetch them drew up at a small house in the park, over a mile from the palace. Here they found not the great gathering they expected but only Louis-Napoleon and Prince Bacciochi. The dinner for four dragged on in painful embarrassment through a long, hot summer evening. As soon as they rose their host took Eugenia's arm, proposing a walk in the park, while Bacciochi took Maria Manuela's. Quickly, Eugenia told Louis-Napoleon that he must escort her mother, who then insisted that she was feeling tired and demanded that the carriage should take them home at once.

Eugenia and Maria Manuela realised that the invitation had been a stratagem inspired by lechery. They immediately left Paris, moving to Brussels, escorted by the lovelorn Duke of Osuna, and then spent a few weeks at the smart Belgian watering place of Spa. Eugenia was always 'taking the cure', so frequently that one cannot help wondering if she was suffering from psychological problems, not unlikely in a young woman who was so highly strung. Certainly, she had not enjoyed her months abroad, and neither had Doña Maria Manuela. In September Eugenia wrote to Paca of their sense of isolation, of being in exile. 'Instead of today [her mother's birthday] being one of rejoicing and feasting, it was really very sad, to be so far way from you all. . . . At lunch Mamma and I did nothing but cry.'

In November they returned thankfully to Madrid, to Doña Maria Manuela's accustomed round of dances and receptions, of visits to Queen Isabella at the Prado. The guests at a particularly successful fancy-dress ball held at Casa Ariza for the carnival of 1851 included over twenty august ladies of the highest rank, ranging from duchesses to countesses, together with all the Spanish cabinet ministers of the moment and most of the ambassadors to Madrid, but not Marshal Nárvaez, who had again fallen from power.

In April 1851 mother and daughter went abroad to London, in order to see the Great Exhibition. Here they ran into Nárvaez, accompanying him to a reception given by Lady Palmerston at her house in Carlton Gardens. A former foreign secretary, the Earl of Malmesbury recorded that at the reception he had seen 'the Spanish beauty, Mademoiselle Montijo . . . very handsome, auburn hair, beautiful skin and figure'. He was especially impressed by 'her lovely complexion'. During this visit to England Doña Eugenia and her mother also stayed with Ferdinand Huddleston, still besotted, at his country house in Cambridgeshire, Sawston Hall, where she enjoyed riding his horses over the flat dreary fields.

By July they were in Wiesbaden, yet another smart watering place, and which was also the capital of a tiny independent state, the duchy of Nassau, with its own miniature army of 5,000 men (one of those comical little German principalities of the sort that would one day be caricatured so uproariously by Offenbach in *La Grande Duchesse de Gerolstein*). From Wiesbaden they travelled to Paris, but were only there for a few weeks, during which time they did not bother to call on the Prince President.

By the end of November they were back in Spain for the winter, remaining in Madrid until May the following year, when they drove across the frontier up into the French Pyrenees to take the cure again, at Eaux-Bonnes. The husband hunting was not being very successful. Doña Maria Manuela must have despaired at her daughter losing the chance of marriage to a man – or, rather, a duke – such as Osuna. Yet an even greater catch was not beyond the bounds of possibility.

THE BIG FISH

Doña Maria Manuela watched what was happening in France with the keenest interest. When she and her daughter had met the Prince President in 1849 he had been elected for a mere three years and all the 'informed' political observers assured everyone that he would definitely not enjoy a second term. They underestimated him. For on 2 December 1851 he brought off a brilliant *coup d'état*, making himself president for a further ten years. Obviously it was only a matter of time before he would be proclaimed Emperor of the French. An hereditary emperor was clearly a much greater prize as a husband than a president who might easily be voted out of office. Admittedly, ever since 1789, the French had been addicted to revolutions – no régime had lasted for as long as twenty years – but that did not lessen the glamour of a throne.

Doña Maria Manuela always thought on the grand scale, and while she may not have known much history she knew from Donizetti's opera *Anna Bolena* how a strong-minded lady without royal blood had captured King Henry VIII by refusing to sleep with him. At that horrible little dinner party near Saint-Cloud three years earlier, Louis-Napoleon had shown unambiguously that he had fallen under the spell of her daughter's beauty, and as a natural matchmaker and social mountaineer, Maria Manuela began to see glittering possibilities.

Plenty of basic information about the Prince President was, of course, easily available. He had been born in 1808, the son of Louis Bonaparte, King of Holland and of Hortense de Beauharnais, the Empress Josephine's daughter by her first marriage. Brought up as an exile in Switzerland by Queen Hortense, he had launched two badly planned and under-supported coups against Louis-Philippe which had both ended in abject disaster. In restoring the Napoleonic Empire, however, he was revealing that he possessed considerable political ability.

Prosper Mérimée supplied intimate details of the all but emperor Louis-Napoleon, which were not easy to obtain. We do not know exactly what Mérimée said in his letters at this time, because Eugenia destroyed the important ones, but we can make a fairly accurate guess. He must have warned them frankly that the man was an almost pathological lecher, with a semi-official mistress living at Saint-Cloud – a rich English courtesan called Miss Howard, who had helped to finance his *coup d'état*. If Prince Bacciochi was his *chef-de-protocol* at the Elysée, he also acted as his procurer.

In common with most French intellectuals, not to mention most French politicians, Mérimée could not believe that this exotic new Bonapartist régime run by adventurers and opportunists was likely to last very long – whether in the form of a republic or an empire. In any case he thought the priapic Prince Louis-Napoleon would make Eugenia a bad husband and lead her a miserable life.

But his letters to Madrid failed to deter Doña Maria Manuela. Nor did they deter her daughter. From the very beginning the prospect of marrying the future emperor had attractions for Doña Eugenia, which may seem surprising in so fastidious a young woman. One would have thought there was a good deal about him which repelled her. Not only was he eighteen years older, but he was far from handsome, with a puny physique. A small, dumpy man, his legs were too short for his body, which gave him an odd, crab-like walk. His head was too big, with a huge hook nose and fishlike pale blue eyes, while his heavy, expressionless face was hidden by a goatee beard and a thick moustache whose long, waxed antennae he twirled constantly when nervous. He dressed badly, in sombre, clumsily cut clothes, and because he chain-smoked cigarettes his pockets were always full of tobacco ash. Slow, almost dull in manner, he spoke very little, only after careful thought and then with a sing-song, slightly German accent that was due to his Swiss upbringing.

On the other hand the Prince President possessed extraordinary charm, a charm on whose impact contemporaries remark again and again. Much of it came from the impression made by his calmness, gentleness and obvious kindliness – he was seldom known to lose his temper, and never with inferiors or servants – while he had beautiful manners. His lack of good looks was redeemed by an oddly fascinating expression, sphinx-like yet benign, and a remarkable smile which would suddenly light up his dark features. He seems to have been one of those rare human beings to whom, without knowing why, most people take an instinctive liking.

His lack of physical allure did not bother Eugenia since she was largely indifferent to male beauty. No one could have been uglier than her brother-in-law Alba, yet once she had loved Alba to distraction. (In middle age she once said, with obvious conviction, 'After the first night it no longer matters much whether a man is handsome or ugly, and at the end of the first week it's always the same thing.') Nor is she likely to have succumbed to an arcane sexual chemistry. What Eugenia found attractive, long before she set eyes on him, was *who* Louis-Napoleon Bonaparte was – the heir of his uncle and the Napoleonic legend incarnate. A convinced Bonapartist, she had always been ready to devote herself to the imperial cause. Despite that humiliating attempt to seduce her at Saint-Cloud, she had written to Felix Bacciochi, shortly before the coup of 1851, to offer the Prince President financial assistance should it fail. (The gesture shows how closely she and her mother were watching his progress.) She was convinced that the Bonapartist cause would triumph in the end.

29

There was another reason why this complex young woman should find him immensely interesting, even if she did not fully realise it until later. He and his legend embodied power, enormous power, and as a husband he could offer her influence on a vast scale, something which in those days was largely denied to her sex. Generally the very few women who possessed influence on such a scale did not use it – like the insanely irresponsible Queen Isabella of Spain. Even so, Eugenia undoubtedly believed that the marriage might give her at least some chance of making the world a better place. For although she had by now abandoned her Fourierism and her socialism, she remained an idealist.

Finally, one should not overlook the simplest of all reasons why the prospect of marrying the Prince President appealed to Eugenia. In May 1852 she had reached the ripe old age of twenty-six and was only too well aware that, according to the harsh conventions of her time, she was entering spinsterhood. This was a state of life that automatically condemned a woman to a condition of pity and contempt, since during the first half of the nineteenth century it was very difficult for any woman without a husband to find a proper, respected role in society, however rich she might be in her own right.

Both mother and daughter must have been fully aware that in pursuing the Prince President of France they risked losing touch with reality. Eugenia's chance of succeeding was one in a hundred. But Doña Maria Manuela – from whom the real initiative surely came – was never a woman to be daunted by the odds being heavily against her.

By midsummer 1852 everyone in France, even at such quiet little watering places as Eaux-Bonnes, was saying that when Prince Louis-Napoleon became their emperor he would immediately set about founding a dynasty. He needed to find a bride who would be able to bear him children as quickly as possible, since he was already forty-four. Presumably he would choose a foreign princess from one of Europe's great ruling families. In June the diarist Comte Henri de Viel Castel heard a well-founded rumour that the Prince President was going to marry Princess Carola of Vasa, a member of the former ruling house of Sweden who had the added advantage of possessing Beauharnais blood. Carola refused his proposal, however, marrying the king of Saxony instead. There were equally well-founded rumours that he was on the look-out for a German princess. Gossip of this sort was not exactly encouraging for Doña Eugenia's hopes.

At the same time Louis-Napoleon's long-standing mistress was pestering him to marry her. Everybody suspected, correctly, that he was still sleeping with Lizzie. Admittedly Viel Castel noted that at supper during a ball at the château of Saint-Cloud where his mistress was present, 'his love for Miss Howard did not stop him from stroking the thighs of the lovely Marquise de Belboeuf, who appeared to be neither surprised nor flattered'. Viel Castel also tells us that at the end of October Lizzie went to a state performance at the Paris Opera in honour of the Prince President. 'The more respectable element among the audience was horrified at seeing Miss Howard, the President's mistress, sitting in a prominent box and covered with diamonds, which gave a most unfortunate impression.'

Eugenia and her mother were back in Paris by early October, occupying the apartment at 12 Place Vendôme with the big rooms that Maria Manuela had so much admired on a previous occasion, as being particularly suitable for giving receptions. She intended to give as many as possible, since she needed to make all the useful contacts she could, in order to further her matchmaking. The faithful Ferdinand Huddleston had rented an equally splendid flat nearby and from its windows they watched the Prince President's triumphant return from a hugely successful tour of southern France, during which (in a widely quoted speech at Bordeaux) he had declared soothingly, 'The Empire means peace.'

Wearing full-dress uniform, Louis-Napoleon Bonaparte, Prince President of France, rode a mettlesome chestnut charger through the streets of Paris on his way to the Elysée, dramatically keeping several paces ahead of his glittering staff. Looking much better on horseback than he did on foot, he made a fine, soldierly impression, which was what the people expected from someone who was the great Napoleon's nephew – few of them can have realised that his experience of military life had been limited to a short spell with the Swiss army, as a humble captain in the Berne militia. There were big wooden arches over every street along the route, decorated with flags and bunting which bore the unequivocal words, '*Vive Louis*

Napoleon Empéreur!' while medals bearing the legend '*Napoleon III Empéreur*', were on sale at every street corner.

The normally cynical Parisian crowd cheered him wildly. Older citizens commented with astonishment that it looked extraordinarily like the '*Joyeuse Entrée*' of the old kings of France and Navarre when taking possession of their capital of Paris on succeeding to the throne – just as Charles X had done less than thirty years before – which was precisely what they were meant to think.

Doña Maria Manuela immediately set about obtaining invitations to the Prince President's official receptions at the Elysée and Saint-Cloud, and found no difficulty in doing so. Félix Bacciochi, the *chef-de-protocol* (recently promoted to chamberlain), whom they had met in 1849, was only too ready to oblige. No doubt he fancied he could still see possibilities in Doña Eugenia; he retrieved from his files her letter of November 1851, offering financial aid for the Bonaparte cause – which so far he had not bothered to show to Louis-Napoleon – and now gave it to him. When she and her mother attended the receptions, however, everything was very decorous, the Prince President behaving impeccably.

Louis-Napoleon had already revived the imperial hunt, installing a vast pack of hounds at Fontainebleau, where Eugenia was invited to a meet on 13 November. More than a firm seat and ability to take fences were required because there was so little jumping, the field being expected to show a command of dressage as well as skill at finding their way through the forest. Lent a big English thoroughbred, she impressed everyone by her horsemanship and was the first up with the hounds when they caught their stag. Next day, Louis-Napoleon sent her the horse as a present, the start of a whirlwind courtship. 'You can't imagine what people are saying about me since I was given that beastly horse', an embarrassed Eugenia told a friend at the Spanish embassy. Soon she would have good reason for feeling self-conscious. Everyone in Paris was beginning to watch her with fascination, especially if they saw her talking to the Prince President.

On 21 November a small ball was given at Saint-Cloud, to mark the first day of a long-awaited referendum in which every adult French citizen (women excepted) would be asked to approve the restoration of the Napoleonic Empire. The ball's guest list was largely restricted to the future emperor's leading supporters, many of whom looked more like adventurers than politicians. The Austrian ambassador, Baron Hübner, observed disdainfully that the list included 'a few Bonapartes together with a mob of obscure creatures who were equally inelegant'. He agreed with a haughty old French lady that the atmosphere was definitely 'a little too democratic', adding that 'this sort of thing and, still more, democratic manners, is certainly not to Louis-Napoleon's taste. But as a creation of universal suffrage, he can scarcely deny his own roots, and at such a time he would certainly be most unwise not to stress them. However, he's going to find it rather expensive.' The ambassador's assessment did not do justice to the shrewd Prince President, who knew the value of moving with the times.

Professionally sharp-eyed, the Austrian also noticed with interest that 'the young and beautiful Mlle de Montijo was being paid a great deal of attention by the President'. What Baron Hübner is unlikely to have known is that Doña Eugenia, as a committed Bonapartist of very long standing, was geninely delighted by the prospect of a Napoleonic restoration, which had been her dream since childhood. Needless to say, nothing could have endeared her more to Louis-Napoleon.

'Mlle de Montijo, a young Spanish blonde of the highest birth has been the object of the Prince's attentions ever since her stay at Fontainebleau', the Comte de Viel Castel carefully recorded in his diary for 25 November. He comments with considerable insight (especially remarkable since it was the first time that he had set eyes on Eugenia) that 'The young lady certainly has a most prepossessing manner and does not lack a keen sense of humour, but she is much too strong minded ever to be ruled by her heart or her emotions.'

The Second Empire was proclaimed on 2 December, followed by a *Te Deum* at Notre Dame. In every city throughout France cannon roared out salutes, church bells pealed, bands played Napoleonic marches and there was a public holiday – all without a single hostile demonstration. The Prince President had become Napoleon III, Emperor of the French, moving from the Elysée into his uncle's former Palace of the Tuileries, which was more suited to His

Imperial Majesty. The transformation cannot have displeased Doña Eugenia. But she was blissfully ignorant of the fact that on 13 December the French ambassador in London was going to solicit Queen Victoria's approval of the emperor's formal request for the hand of Her Serene Highness Princess Adelaide of Hohenlohe-Langenburg, still only seventeen, but possessing the invaluable asset of being the daughter of Victoria's half-sister.

'Mlle de Montijo is at all the receptions', M. de Viel Castel noted on 23 December. He added pruriently, 'she enjoys very noticeable favour, but I don't think that she has submitted to a conqueror's yoke' – meaning that so far she had not gone to bed with the Prince. 'Her mother, who was formerly known as the Comtesse de Teba, used to be very easy-going and about 1825 she had my brother Louis for a lover.'

When Viel Castel wrote this, Eugenia and her mother had already been staying at the château of Compiègne for several days, invited to spend Christmas with Napoleon III, and a hundred other guests. His unfortunate foreign minister, Edouard Drouyn de Lhuys, had been frantic with worry at the prospect of a *mésalliance* ever since the hunting party at Fontainebleau the previous month and the present of the horse, even if Louis-Napoleon had told him not to worry. But at Compiègne Drouyn de Lhuys could see there was every reason for worrying. What would happen to that sensible marriage with Queen Victoria's niece?

Another guest, Baron Hübner, was bowled over by Eugenia, despite believing her to be an advanced liberal and practically a revolutionary. In a lyrical dispatch the ambassador sent to Vienna a month later, he raves about 'the noble and regular beauty of her features, the brilliance of her complexion, the elegance of her slight and supple figure', writing of 'an expression of gentle melancholy the result of a strange and almost tragic adventure', of 'the wild oddness and energy of her spirit'. It is clear from his dispatch that he also enjoyed Doña Eugenia's conversation, 'which recoiled at nothing'. In addition, he credited her with 'a force of will and a physical courage which one rarely meets even among the women of the people'. Surprisingly, the man who wrote this paean of praise was a reactionary who loathed progressives.

Fascinated by the relationship between Eugenia and the emperor which, he claims, reminded him of a tale from *The Arabian Nights*, Hübner says there was a peculiarly nasty plot at Compiègne to persuade her to sleep with Louis-Napoleon. Despite having been Maria Manuela's guest at Casa Ariza, the Marquise de Contades (a very unsavoury lady and the mistress of the emperor's henchman, Colonel Fleury) was 'the soul of the cabal who wished to prevent the emperor marrying by giving him a new mistress. She said to Mlle de Montijo that, after all, remorse was better than regret, to which the Spaniard answered, "Neither remorse nor regret!"'

The emperor's aides-de-camp and the gentlemen of his household teased their unhappy master as much as they dared about his beautiful guest, placing bets on the date on which she was likely to give in and sending witty letters about the 'siege' to their friends. Their barely concealed amusement made him more frantic than ever. Horace de Viel Castel even has a story – probably unfounded but revealing about the atmosphere at Compiègne – that the emperor actually tried to break into her room.

During this nightmarish visit, originally planned to last for only a few days but which at the host's insistence dragged on for nearly a fortnight, Doña Eugenia had to put up with the sidelong glances and knowing smiles, the sniggers and whispers, of the rest of the party, aware that behind her back every sort of insinuation and calumny was circulating. The British ambassador, Lord Cowley, who was among the guests, went away completely convinced by opponents of the marriage that 'Mlle de Montijo' was just an adventuress. He reported, 'The Emperor's entourage is getting seriously alarmed at his admiration of a certain Spanish young lady, Mademoiselle Montijo by name. Her mother, an Englishwoman [sic] by birth, is, with the young lady, playing a bold game, and, I cannot doubt, hopes that her daughter may wear the Imperial Crown.' Later, Cowley added, 'The Emperor is going it finely with the young Montijo.' He also said that Drouyn de Lhuys was wondering how he could continue as foreign minister if Napoleon married her.

Eugenia needed considerable courage to remain at Compiègne until the party ended and to cope with an increasingly amorous emperor. Hübner tells us that when with Napoleon she was 'the image of virginal reserve', but as soon as he was out of sight, 'her highly excitable nature reasserted itself'. He also claims that when the emperor, by now 'the victim of a frenzy of passion', was galloping beside Eugenia through the forest of Compiègne and was under the illusion they were alone when in fact they were within earshot of the fascinated house party, he had begged her to go to bed with him. 'Mlle de Montijo pulled her horse up short, and looking the Emperor steadily in the eye, said "Yes, when I am Empress!"' That evening she did not come down to dinner and for the rest of the visit her manner was glacial when speaking to her host. From then on, says Hübner, Napoleon began to think seriously of marrying her. Clearly, something like the incident in the forest must have happened to make up his mind.

The Spanish envoy at Paris, the Marqués de Valdegamas, believed, however, that he had done so a month before the party at Compiègne. He reported to Madrid that in November, when Napoleon had been strolling with Eugenia through the park at Fontainebleau during a break from hunting, he discovered that both their watches had stopped at precisely the same moment. Now it so happened, according to the Spanish envoy's dispatch, that the emperor had only just received news from the Jardin des Plantes at Paris that a mysterious, exotic plant, which had never been known to flower since the year when his uncle had married his grandmother Josephine, had suddenly blossomed spectacularly. No less superstitious than his Corsican forebears, Napoleon immediately decided that the two phenomena must definitely be linked and, by some unfathomable process peculiar to himself, that this meant that Eugenia was predestined to share his throne.

There is yet another story, told by Doña Eugenia's great-nephew the seventeenth Duke of Alba. While admitting that the tale might not perhaps be accurate in every detail, the duke was nonetheless convinced that something like it must have happened at some point during Louis-Napoleon's courtship. According to Alba, Eugenia and her mother had been watching a military parade by the newly restored Imperial Guard in the Place du Carrousel from a window somewhere in the Tuileries when, after the parade, the emperor rode his horse beneath their window, shouting, 'How can I come up to you?' Eugenia shouted back, 'Only by way of the altar.'

What is certainly beyond dispute, even among historians, is that the Emperor Napoleon III had reached his decision about whom he ought to marry within three days of Doña Eugenia's departure from the château of Compiègne on 28 December 1852. When the Comte Walewski, the French ambassador in London, came to the Tuileries on New Year's Eve to discuss an irksome but surmountable difficulty that had arisen over the Hohenlohe-Langenburg marriage – the girl's devoutly Protestant parents seemed unwilling to give their permission – the Emperor shook his hand warmly and, ignoring whatever he was trying to say about Princess Adelaide, told him, 'My dear fellow, I've been captured.' He then explained his intention of marrying Mlle de Montijo. Horrified, Walewski played for time, begging him to wait for just a bit longer and to reconsider his decision. Next day, however, the Hohenlohe-Langenburg Princess formally declined Louis-Napoleon's proposal.

Yet there were still a number of extremely formidable obstacles for Doña Eugenia to overcome, together with some even more daunting enemies. At the worst, the emperor might manage to control his passion, listen to his advisers and say goodbye to her.

MARRYING A DREAM

Despite the emperor's frank admission to Comte Walewski on New Year's Eve, he had not yet proposed to Doña Eugenia, so that she was far from sure he would marry her, especially when there was so much opposition. She and her mother must have been in a state of agonising tension in the early days of 1853. After all, Napoleon III was the most eligible man in Europe.

Her enemies – enemies because the emperor was in love with her – could not believe he would make her his consort. At the New Year's ball at the Tuileries, when going in to supper Eugenia was shrilly rebuked by the minister of education's wife, Mme Fortoul, for daring to go in front of her, a breach of official precedence. She politely gave way at once, but was so upset that Napoleon noticed and came up to ask the reason. 'I have been insulted, Sire, and I refuse to be insulted again.' 'After tomorrow, no one will ever dare insult you', promised the emperor in a deliberately loud voice. But tomorrow came and went without a proposal.

The most vicious enemies were the 'royal Bonapartes' – ex-King Jerome, once puppet-monarch of Westphalia, and his children Plon-Plon and Mathilde. The new emperor's last surviving uncle, Jerome was opposed to his nephew marrying at all, as it might deprive his son Plon-Plon of his 'rights to the throne', even if he prophesied that Napoleon would marry 'the first skirt who turns his head and then won't sleep with him'. Plon-Plon, who had tried to seduce Eugenia during her visit to Paris in 1849, expressed the view that 'You go to bed with women like Mlle de Montijo, but you don't marry them.' Mathilde begged the emperor not to marry Eugenia. She could herself had been briefly engaged to him in 1839, but instead had made a short-lived marriage to a grotesque Russian prince. She told her cousin that Eugenia possessed neither '*coeur ni con*'.

Drouyn de Lhuys, the foreign minister, argued that he was throwing away a dynastic alliance to marry 'an adventuress', but Napoleon ignored his threat to resign. Comte Walewski, Napoleon I's son by Marie Walewska, was equally hostile. Comte de Persigny, minister of the interior, grumbled, 'We didn't make the Empire so that the Emperor could go and marry some flower-girl.'

The ablest members of the Imperial Council, Achille Fould and the Comte de Morny, were wise enough not to express an opinion. Fould was an exceptionally shrewd and well-balanced man, while Auguste de Morny, Napoleon's illegitimate half-brother, was the cleverest of all his advisers. It is most unlikely that he complained, 'If she can't be royal, why can't she be a French countess instead of a Spanish one?' He was an old friend of Doña Maria Manuela, whom he had known in Madrid.

Apparently the emperor assured Eugenia he would marry her, but that she would have to wait until he had brought his ministers to heel. Certainly mother and daughter seemed at ease on 9 January when Viel Castel dined with them at 'a very cheerful supper' given by Princesse Mathilde:

The Comte de Morny was among the party and so were the Comtesse de Teba and her daughter Mlle de Montijo. The emperor always spends a lot of time with this young woman, who is elegant, likeable, intelligent and amusing. For over an hour the two were absorbed in a private conversation that nobody dared to interrupt. The emperor had obviously enjoyed himself when he left the ball at two o'clock in the morning. Mlle de Montijo responds to his attentions with grace and decorum; her mother and she are hoping for a marriage, using the most skilful tactics. Everybody pays court to Mlle de Montijo, asks to be remembered to her, begs her to intervene with the emperor. Ministers succumb to her charm, she is seen at all the receptions, and has quite obviously become the rising star.

The 'most skilful tactics' owed a lot to Prosper Mérimée, whose advice they relied on, however much he disapproved of the marriage. It was rumoured that he drafted Eugenia's letters to Napoleon – he may well have written her letter of November 1851 in which she declared undying loyalty to the Bonapartist cause. They could not have been so cheerful at Princesse Mathilde's party if they had not felt reasonably confident. Yet the emperor was certainly taking a very long time to propose. It was impossible to know what he was really thinking – he was not called 'The Sphinx of the Tuileries' for nothing. Even now, he might still change his mind. An exasperated Mérimée advised them to tell everyone they were about to leave for Italy.

Many people at the highest level were still convinced that the marriage would never happen. At a ball at the Tuileries on 12 January when Maria Manuela and Eugenia sat on a bench reserved for ministers' wives, Mme Drouyn de Lhuys hissed in Eugenia's ear that 'foreign adventuresses have no right to sit there'. (No one heard Mme Drouyn's exact words.) Both stood up in confusion. But the emperor hurried over, inviting them to join the imperial family on the dais, leaving Mme Drouyn to be reduced to tears by the spiteful smiles of other ministerial wives. When he danced with Eugenia later in the evening, remembering Mérimée's advice, she told him that she was leaving for Italy. 'I am not going to stay here and be insulted.'

'One can say that the ball had the effect of announcing the marriage', recorded Hübner. Yet even two days later we find Hübner bothering to note down a rumour that it would take place, and when he saw Eugenia at a dinner party that evening she was looking pale and tense – still waiting for a formal proposal.

Only on 15 January did the minister of the imperial household, Achille Fould, call in person at Doña Maria Manuela's flat in the Place Vendôme to deliver a letter from the emperor:

> Madame la Comtesse, a long time has passed since I fell in love with your daughter, and ever since then I have wanted to make her my wife. So today I have come to ask you for her hand, because no one could make me more happy or is more worthy to wear a crown. I beg, however, that should you give your consent, then you will not allow this project to become widely known before we have completed all our arrangements.

Doña Eugenia's reaction to this unambiguous proposal from Louis-Napoleon, which she had supposedly been seeking all these months, is doubly revealing. It shows that she had been far from sure he was going to propose, while at the same time it confirms beyond any doubt that she had been in love with the Marqués de Alcañisez. For she at once wrote to Don Pepe, asking him what he thought she ought to do. The Second Empire, it has to be remembered, was after all a police state and when the censors intercepted the letter, after removing the wax seal so that it could be opened, they immediately forwarded the letter to the emperor who, however, ordered them to replace the seal and to let the letter reach its destination. In reply, Alcañisez coolly sent his congratulations – obviously he had never been in love with her.

Mérimée shrewdly obtained from the Spanish heralds a certificate of Doña Eugenia's impeccably noble birth on her father's side. His object was to make her background look as imposing as possible in the official announcement of her marriage. The French people would learn that their ruler was to marry the daughter of someone who had been not just an obscure Napoleonic officer on half-pay, but one of Spain's great feudal magnates: 'Don Cipriano Guzmán y

Palafox Fernandez de Cordoba, Layos y la Cerda, Viscount of la Calzada, of Palencia de la Valduerna; Count of Teba, of Banos, of Mora, of Santa Cruz de la Sierra, of Fuentiduena, of Ablitas, of San Esteban de Gormas and of Casarubios del Monte; Marquis of Moya, of Ardales, of Osera, of Barcarotta, of la Algaba, of la Baneza, of Villanueva del Fresno, of Valdunquillo, of Mirallo and of Valderrabano; and Duke of Peñaranda.' The certificate stressed that the late Don Cipriano had been three times a Grandee of Spain of the First Class, and the hereditary Grand Marshal of Castile. Irrelevant as this string of archaic titles might seem today, they meant a surprising amount in romantic, mid-nineteenth-century France, to the innumerable readers of Alexandre Dumas's novels, with their thirst for a chivalrous past. They inspired respect even among the Legitimist and Orleanist noblemen whom the emperor hoped to win over.

Meanwhile, a pornographic smear campaign was mounted against the bride to be, of the sort once launched at Marie-Antoinette. Cowley mentions rumours 'it would be impossible to put to paper'. Eugenia 'has played her game with him so well, that he can get her in no other way but marriage, and it is to gratify his passions that he marries her,' says the ambassador. 'People are already speculating on their divorce.'

The day before the civil wedding the Senate, Council of State and Assembly were summoned to the Tuileries, to hear a speech by Napoleon III, copies of which were distributed throughout France. He explained that as 'a parvenu' among monarchs – 'a glorious title when bestowed by the votes of a great nation' – he preferred to marry 'a woman whom I love and respect' rather than some unknown princess. His future wife, he told them, was of high birth, French by education and a devout Catholic. He promised she would bring back 'the virtues' of his grandmother, Empress Josephine. Many foreign ambassadors were alarmed, nervous of anything that might weaken this brittle new régime. Even if they distrusted the emperor, they recognised his achievement in taming the revolution of 1848, which had undermined almost every European government. Should he fall, it would break out again, spreading through the continent. 'News of the marriage has had a bad effect in

41

the *départements*', Hübner reported nervously to Vienna, despite his high opinion of Eugenia. 'However democratic people may be, they would have preferred a princess.'

On the day Napoleon made his speech, Cowley informed London that the emperor 'has been captured by an adventuress'. The few Bonapartists who approved of the marriage, 'wish to keep the Court in a degraded state because they profit by it' – implying that Eugenia could corrupt it further. The foreign secretary, Lord John Russell, wrote back, 'A marriage to a well-behaved young Frenchwoman would, I think, have been very politic, but to put this "intrigante" on the throne is a lowering of the Imperial dignity with a vengeance.' 'The emperor's foolish marriage has done him an infinity of harm in the country', Cowley claimed soon after. 'It was, of course, ill received at Paris, even by the emperor's friends, and it has set all the women against him. Clergy and army disapprove.' 'The emperor's selection of a private individual to share his throne has caused, in the female portion of society, a degree of jealousy it is really difficult to conceive', reported the *Illustrated London News*, 'and, alas for the gallantry of Frenchmen of the nineteenth century, they find nothing better to do than repeat the scandals originating in the *boudoirs* of the fairer part of creation.'

We know how Eugenia felt from a letter she wrote to Paca. 'Soon I shall be alone here, without any friends,' she said. 'Everyone's fate has a sad side: for example, I who used to be so obsessed with my liberty am in chains for the rest of my life: never by myself, never free, amid all that court etiquette, of which I'm going to be the principal victim.' She continued, 'Two things will save me, I hope, my faith in God and my desire to help the unlucky classes who are deprived of everything, even work. If the hand of Providence has given me such a high place, then it must be so that I can bring together the sufferers and those who could aid them.' She recalled how once, when they had been discussing politics long ago, their old maid Pepa had said, 'Women are born to knit stockings.' 'But I always knew I wasn't born for that and felt I had a proper role in life. I had a presentiment I might be of some use to my country; if I am half French now, I can't forget the land of my birth, where my poor father lies buried.'

She tried to explain her feelings about her future husband, 'a man of irresistible strength of will, yet without obstinacy, capable of the biggest and the smallest sacrifices; he'll go and look for a wild flower in a wood on a winter's night, crawling back to a fire to dry, just to please the whim of a woman he loves. Tomorrow he will risk his crown rather than not share it with me; he doesn't count the cost of what he does; he is always ready to hazard his future on the throw of a card, which is why he always wins.'

The civil marriage took place in the Tuileries on the evening of 29 January, Doña Eugenia wearing a dress of rose-coloured satin trimmed with lace, her gold and diamond tiara set off by a wreath of jasmine. She wrote to Paca that she was as pale as the jasmine, and felt she was acting in a play when people addressed her as 'Your Majesty'. For three-quarters of an hour they filed past her, cardinals, generals and ministers bowing, ladies curtseying – the Bonapartes barely concealing their fury. She did not tell Paca that she had been booed on her way to the Tuileries. Even so, she pleased the Parisians by declining the municipality's present of a diamond necklace worth 600,000 francs, asking for the money to be used to endow an orphanage for girls. Next day she is said to have pleased them again by curtseying to the crowd and smiling when she alighted from the coach on her arrival at Notre Dame for the wedding. According to the *Illustrated London News*, however, 'pale and trembling from deep emotion, she passed, bowing, with a mixture of timidity and dignity, to the assembled multitudes; yet all failed signally to waken any demonstration of heartfelt welcome or applause'.

While the church was packed with French dignitaries, embarrassingly there were no foreign royalties, partly because the emperor had changed the date from 10 February on account of so much opposition to the marriage. If she sensed the congregation's hostility, she showed no sign whatever of being cowed. In white velvet, ablaze with diamonds and enveloped in 'a sort of cloud or mist of transparent lace', she was both graceful and dignified according to a British spectator, Lady Augusta Bruce. The service was conducted by the archbishop of Paris, Monseigneur Sibour, who had tried to brighten up his soot-blackened cathedral. Hübner was unimpressed. 'Walls, pillars and vaulting were covered with garishly coloured pasteboard', he reported. 'There was a profusion of flowers and candles, plenty of flags, and very little taste.' He thought the march from Meyerbeer's *Prophète* most unsuitable. Worse still, 'not a single cheer greeted Napoleon and his future partner. One can only explain this indifference, not to say contempt, by supposing that the most egalitarian nation in the world feels humiliated by the ruler of France making a marriage that is less than royal.' If Hübner too admired Doña Eugenia's dignity, he also commented on her pallor. Next day he added, 'We now know that on the route taken by their Imperial Majesties' coaches, coming and going, the public remained cold. No cheers, no boos.'

Among the many Spanish spectators on the balconies of hotels along the route was a lady who had been at the civil ceremony and had noticed the priceless pearl necklace worn by Eugenia. She quoted an old Spanish proverb, 'The pearls women wear on their wedding day symbolise the tears that they are going to shed.' Some romantic historians see these words as only too prophetic of what Eugenia would suffer as empress of the French.

TWO

Imperial Splendour

When Eugénie (no longer Eugenia) married Napoleon III in 1853, he was the most powerful ruler in the world. No other country in western Europe possessed such a large population as France. If England was richer, her army was tiny, and in any case her ruler was a constitutional monarch. There were other absolute rulers, but their countries were not so prosperous or so centralised – the Austrian Empire was a ramshackle collection of peoples, the Russian barbarous and inefficient.

From the very beginning, Eugénie was determined to help her husband, a contribution that became more and more throughout the reign until she began to influence policy-making. To appreciate her increasingly important role in the Second Empire, one has to understand both the political system and the emperor himself.

In marrying Napoleon III, she had of course married Bonapartism incarnate. This was never easy to define as a political creed, even at the time, and historians are still unable to agree on precisely what it meant under Napoleon III. Most of them disapprove of it for being authoritarian and undemocratic and for eventually ending in disaster. Only in recent years has there been a fairer reassessment of the Second Empire. What makes it so baffling is that it gradually became liberal instead of absolutist.

Essentially Bonapartism was inspired by the dynamic personality and ideas of Napoleon I, who, as Thiers put it, was 'the man who made France feel the deepest emotions she ever experienced'. The Bonapartist programme was to combine strong and efficient government with the achievements of the French Revolution, reconciling monarchical and Catholic traditions with the new

45

egalitarian ideas. In addition, it promised to give France a glorious place in world history – past, present and to come. 'I once held, and still hold, a deep personal belief that for France the Empire is the only real democracy,' declared Baron Haussmann as late as 1890. 'Our country is the most single-minded in the world and has to have a single-minded government – it must be ruled by one man alone.'

The French Empire established by the first Napoleon Bonaparte in 1804 had been an absolutist, militarist state which recreated France after the chaos that had followed the Revolution, while at the same time conquering Europe. The constitution he granted in 1815, in a bid to gain popular support during the Hundred Days, was an aberration. In exile on his remote Atlantic island the brooding ex-emperor forged the myth contained in his political testament, the *Mémorial de Sainte Hélène*, which had captured the young Eugénie's imagination. 'I saved the Revolution as it lay dying,' he claimed. 'I have given France and Europe new ideas which will never be forgotten.' His wars had been a campaign of liberation and not of conquest, he insisted, waged only to create European unity.

As has been seen, Eugénie had derived from her father, Stendhal, Mérimée and the *Mémorial*, a belief in a 'tyrant of genius', who by applying the great emperor's ideas would bring prosperity and happiness. If never under the illusion that her husband was 'a tyrant of genius' or even a particularly strong character, she recognised that he was a highly intelligent, well-meaning and fundamentally honest man, with deeply held convictions. Above all, she believed that he offered the best, indeed the only chance of putting Napoleonic ideas into practice, which was why he fascinated her. In these early days she was impressed by his seemingly unfailing political judgement and by the magical way in which he would use his sphinx-like charm to win over the most stubborn opponents. She was certain that he could give France authority, glory and social reform.

The Orleanist constitutional monarchy of King Louis-Philippe had signally failed to give France any of these things. Elected by an electorate of less than a quarter of a million well-to-do male voters (out of a population of 30 million), its corrupt governments had been uninspiring, to put it mildly; the leaders had squabbled constantly with each other, while being at the same time undermined by the king's intrigues. Orleanist foreign policy had been chicken-hearted, determined to avoid at all costs the hazards of war with other European powers – when not conquering Algeria, the army's job was to hold down the working class. Although a period of economic and industrial expansion, the Orleanist years had been the sordid age of *Les Misérables*, and in the end the Orleanists had lost touch with the French people as a whole. If the revolution of 1848, the 'revolution of contempt' as Lamartine called it, was a confrontation between workers exploited beyond endurance and a ruthless bourgeoisie, most of France had become bored by a régime that possessed so little panache.

Despite being a reaction against Orleanism, the Bonapartism of 1853 was as far removed from the warlike empire of 1804 as from the 'constitutional' empire of the Hundred Days. 'The Empire means peace', Napoleon III insisted, even if he hoped to undo the European settlement of 1815. He claimed that his was a more democratic system than parliamentary government; only he could save the poverty-stricken majority of the people from the bourgeoisie, who would otherwise use a parliament to enslave them, while any really important decision would be referred to the nation in a referendum. This was what Bonapartism meant when Eugénie married him, and she became one of its most enthusiastic exponents.

The Second Empire coincided with an economic boom, and soon the French equated Bonapartism with prosperity. Napoleon hoped also to introduce social reform, since there was a genuinely socialist element in his thinking, and, encouraged by Eugénie, he did a great deal to help industrial workers. In the little country towns his *Préfets* installed pro-government mayors, who undermined the tyranny of the big landowners and built roads, making sure that the peasants voted the right way in referendums.

The elected Corps Législatif of 260 members, which replaced the National Assembly, met for only three months a year and could not initiate bills, although it was allowed to suggest amendments – its sole function was to approve laws and the budget. The Senate was nominated by the emperor. As for being a police state, Paris had no more policemen than London, and when Napoleon III needed to employ force he relied on the army, although he rarely used it. He was a very moderate despot.

The empress took care to make friends with her husband's ministers. She had no trouble with Achille Fould, the President of the Council of State and the emperor's chief minister, an amiable Jew who liked most people – and a financial wizard who ran the day- to-day government of France. The emperor's bastard half-brother, Auguste de Morny, Queen Hortense's son by the Comte de Flahaut (and Talleyrand's grandson) was even more important. Although a speculator and man of pleasure whose salon was generally full of financial sharks and 'actresses', he gave unfailingly sound advice to Napoleon, who made him first a count and then a duke. Princesse Mathilde disliked him, partly because he was a former Orleanist, sneering that if anything went wrong under Morny's arrangement, then 'Louis-Philippe would feel himself avenged'. Yet he ran the Corps Légistlatif brilliantly, preparing the way for a constitutional régime. Patronising if affectionate, at times he all but dominated his brother, who was a little frightened of him. Always sensitive about their relationship, the emperor was horrified to learn that Morny had hung a portrait of their mother in his drawing-room. Early in 1853 he sent Eugénie to ask him to remove it. 'The less you boast about your parentage, the more you'll be treated as a brother,' she advised him, and they remained friends for the rest of his life.

Drouyn de Lhuys thought that his days as foreign minister were numbered after his opposition to the empress's marriage and his wife's rudeness. When the engagement was announced, he called on her before resigning. 'Thank you for the advice you gave the emperor about marrying,' she told him. 'It was the advice I would have given him myself.' He withdrew his resignation. (Drouyn had an odd taste in practical jokes – when the British embassy advertised for a wet-nurse, he called in a bonnet and a dress padded out with cushions, completely taking in poor Lady Cowley, who was horrified when she realised that the '*nourrice*' was France's minister for foreign affairs.)

Eugénie did not get on so well with the Duc de Persigny. Another adventurer, a former bankrupt and an ex-cavalry sergeant with a bogus title, he had been created a duke after the coup. Viel Castel says he 'looked as much like a nobleman as chicory does coffee'. However, he had won Napoleon's gratitude by his support during the seemingly hopeless 1840s. Slightly unbalanced if frenziedly loyal, Persigny was trying to build up a hard-line Bonapartist party, which was the last thing wanted by the subtle emperor. 'From the day of my marriage I was honoured with his hatred, a venomous, slandering hatred,' Eugénie recalled. 'Sometimes he could not stop himself calling me "The Spanish Woman" or "The Foreigner". He wanted nobody between the emperor and him – the emperor and the Empire were his sole property. . . . Imagine a boiler perpetually blowing up.' A compliment she forgot to pay herself was that Persigny regarded her as his ultimate political rival.

For the time being the empress could help her husband best in creating a splendid new court. It was a vital aspect of the empire, a key element of Bonapartist 'glory'. Napoleon III could have found no better partner.

THE '*FETES IMPERIALES*'

Among Napoleon and Eugénie's humbler courtiers was their American dentist, Dr Thomas W. Evans from Philadelphia. Famous throughout Europe for his new, gold-foil fillings and a mercifully light touch on the pedal-drill, he was indispensable, since the emperor had unusually sensitive teeth. 'Less rigid in its etiquette than most European courts, and at the same time more splendid in its ceremonial forms', was Evans's considered opinion of the Tuileries. He was justified in thinking it 'the mirror of fashion for the whole world'.

There had been no court life since the 1830 revolution. Although Louis-Philippe had lived in the Tuileries, he had been busy being the 'Citizen King' – any sort of display would have damaged his image. But Napoleon III believed that the French preferred pomp and ceremony, which in any case were good for the Parisian luxury trade. Together, he and Eugénie recreated the court of the first Napoleon, surpassing even that of the tsar's in opulence. France was rich and could afford it, while nobody must be allowed to forget that she was a monarchy. Colonel Fleury, the emperor's aide-de-camp, was responsible for the court's initial organisation, improved by the emperor and empress throughout the reign.

As soon as the Second Empire was proclaimed, Napoleon moved into the Tuileries, on and off the residence of France's rulers since 1789. This was a very long, narrow building with an imposing if monotonous façade, at right angles to the rue de Rivoli and joining the wings of the Louvre, the latter already a museum. (Burned down in 1871, all that is left of the Tuileries today are the pavillions at each end and the gardens.) The other imperial palaces were at Saint-Cloud, just outside Paris, Compiègne and Fontainebleau. Built under the *ancien régime*, they had close links with Napoleon I, as the emperor remembered from his childhood.

The Maison de l'Empéreur, the imperial household, was revived, Napoleon appointing a Grand Almoner, a Grand Chamberlain, a Master of the Horse and a Grand Huntsman, with innumerable chamberlains. He brought back knee-breeches and court dress, which had not been seen since 1830, putting the household into gold-embroidered coats of scarlet, violet, green or pale blue. Even his doctors were clad in gold-laced blue uniforms with white breeches, including the 'Surgeon dentist to the Emperor', Dr Evans. Male guests at court were obliged to wear evening dress with black breeches and black or white silk stockings. But only footmen had to powder their hair and, if very different in style, the pomp was no more elaborate than at Buckingham Palace.

The Imperial Guard was revived to form a military household, thirty-seven squadrons of cavalry and thirty-three battalions of infantry, who paraded daily on the Place du Carrousel (the square enclosed by the Tuileries and Louvre), their massed bands playing stirring imperial marches: *Partant pour la Syrie, La Reine Hortense, Le Chant du Depart* or *Veillons au Salut de l'Empire*. Here, like his uncle before him, the emperor reviewed them on horseback, with white-headed old veterans of the Grande Armée at his side.

However, the troops most associated with the régime were the Cents Gardes and the Guides. The former, eventually 150 strong, were gigantic young cavalrymen recruited from the Imperial Guard. One of the sights of Second Empire Paris, armed with carbines they rode beside Napoleon's carriage in sky-blue tunics, steel breast-plates and plumed helmets, mounting guard at his palaces. Commanded by Colonel Fleury and modelled on those of the First

Empire, the Regiment of Guides were really hussars, in busbies, green tunics and dolmans, and red trousers, riding grey chargers.

As Dr Evans noted, despite its grandeur the atmosphere at the Tuileries was far less stuffy than at other European courts of the time. It reflected a wish to combine past and present, to mix *ancien régime* noblemen with new men still inspired by the Revolution. There was a place for everybody, for aristocrats of the bluest blood and for the self-made with brand new titles or no titles at all. (Napoleon III created only 52 titles, compared with Louis-Philippe's 98 and Napoleon I's 1,145.)

Some people laughed. Everybody knew that the Grand Marshal of the palace, Marshal Vaillant betrayed his peasant roots by a phobia for the sugar-beet worm, besides having a cousin who was a hatter in the rue de Rivoli. Horace de Viel Castel tells us that the father of the minister for the imperial household, Achille Fould, was bankrupt three times and that *his* father had been a servant, while as for the Grand Huntsman, 'Marshal Magnan's father was a porter who sometimes waited on his master's table with his son's assistance.' No doubt Viel Castel's sneers were echoed in royalist châteaux all over France, but they had little effect. Each of these men was good at his job – even if Vaillant, who pretended to tremble when in the emperor's presence, was often abominably rude to other courtiers.

As soon as she married, the 'adventuress' Eugénie had to fill the role of imperial hostess and did so with astonishing speed. She had no problems about asserting her authority, even if (as Viel Castel noted with relish) more than a few ambitious ladies who wanted to shine at court did not altogether enjoy having to address yesterday's equal as 'Your Majesty'. Although she had never even run a house before or entertained on her own account, Eugénie was not Doña Maria Manuela's daughter for nothing, and, as we have seen, she had had plenty of experience of court life and of court intrigues at Isabella II's Madrid.

Hübner saw the new empress at a ball at Saint-Cloud in July 1853, blazing with diamonds 'of fabulous value' that belonged to the French crown jewels. 'She looked weary and, if as beautiful as ever, I found her changed . . .'

She is no longer the young married woman, the new consort whose timidity added to her natural appeal; this is someone who knows that she is the mistress of the house, making it plain by the way in which she carries herself, by how she gives orders to her ladies, by a slightly disdainful air, a bit blasé but always watchful, with which she passes through the drawing-rooms, nothing escaping her eye.

It is only fair to explain that on this particular occasion Eugénie was not feeling well and was certainly not at her best. In contrast, Dr Evans, who knew and understood her far better than Baron Hübner, wrote of 'the lovely Empress . . . always with a pleasant word, or a sweet smile, or a bow of recognition for everyone'. Very highly strung, her good looks were easily affected by ill health or exhaustion, which may explain why the descriptions of her vary. Emile Ollivier, who saw her the same year, found 'something flat and dull in her face', but in those days he was a ferocious young republican who had not yet rallied to the empire.

Eugénie had her own household, many of whose members were paid enviably large salaries. The Grand Mistress was the coldly severe Princesse d'Essling, a tiny little woman with fragile good looks and a permanent, insincere smile. The person who did most of the work, however, was the first *dame d'honneur*, the far from fragile Duchesse de Bassano, a plump, handsome and somewhat haughty Belgian noblewoman who had married the emperor's amiable Grand Chamberlain. She had the demanding job of vetting each one of the countless ladies from every country in the world who were determined to be presented at court. There were six other *dames d'honneur* in the team, each one doing a week on duty, waiting in turn on the empress, although sometimes all seven were in attendance on her together.

Like Mme de Bassano, not all the *dames d'honneur* were French; for example the Spanish Marquèsa de Marisma, who had been a friend of Eugénie's since childhood and was known as 'the most amiable woman in Paris', and Baronne de Pierres, born Miss Thorne, an American. A shy and timid girl upset by the slightest thing, she was nevertheless a superb horsewoman who usually rode by the Empress's side when she hunted at Compiègne or Fontainebleau and whose transatlantic slang delighted her. In secret the baroness smoked a clay pipe, an odd habit for one of Winterhalter's beauties.

The ladies were immortalised by Franz Xaver Winterhalter, a German from Baden who looked a most unlikely artist with his stiff bearing, formal clothes and high black stock. When he painted Eugénie with them in 1855 he had already painted the courts of Louis-Philippe and Victoria, transforming the English queen and her consort into figures of Renaissance splendour. In this group portrait, which has been called the empress's 'Decameron', all the sitters are shown in full dress and bare shouldered, Eugénie wearing her favourite mauve. ('Not a man in it', commented her husband.) Winterhalter painted other portraits of the empress, although contemporaries say he never did justice to her beauty. Photographs, as well as paintings, also capture something of Eugénie and her entourage. Comte Olympe Aguado was the court photographer when what the English called 'sun-pictures' were still regarded as semi-miraculous. There were others, too, such as Edouard Delessert and Gustave Le Gray. Their faded sepia prints sometimes succeed in conveying faint, ghostly glimpses of Eugénie's world.

Some English visitors, accustomed to their own prim court, were shocked by the ladies' relaxed behaviour. 'I returned to Paris in the Royal carriage – a large omnibus', the earl of Malmesbury would write in 1862. 'Madame de Pierres, an American, née Thorne, and the Duchess de Morny, a Russian, just married, smoked all the way in the Empress's face, notwithstanding her plain hints against the proceedings. She is much too good-natured to her *entourage*, but enhances her singular beauty by the most natural gaiety.' (Eventually Eugénie forbade anyone save the emperor to smoke in her presence.)

In the earl's opinion, her ladies nearly all dressed in 'vile' taste. 'Their hair is dragged off their faces so tightly that they can hardly shut their eyes, and their scarlet accoutrements, jackets, cloaks, etc., as they happen to be very fair, make an *ensemble* indescribably unbecoming.' Yet most people thought they looked delightful – as did Eugène Boudin, when he painted them promenading with Eugénie along the beach at Trouville in 1864.

There were also the gentlemen of the empress's household, who wore her uniform of pale blue coat and white silk breeches. Among them was her principal chamberlain, Comte Charles de la Pagerie, an ugly little man, who was always grimacing nervously. Although still in his early forties, he was the Empress Josephine's nephew, seemingly his sole qualification for anything. Eugénie teased him unmercifully. When she told him to imitate the sun, he would twist his face into a ball and then scream, '*Voilà le soleil!*', while if ordered to imitate a turkey he would run round the room, gobbling at the top of his voice. He was much in demand for charades. She possessed a more effective chamberlain in the Comte de Cossé-Brissac, a nobleman of impeccable lineage and manners, who knew how to handle haughty members of the old aristocracy whenever they condescended – and many of them did – to visit the court of the Bonaparte usurper.

The background of the men and women who held court posts shows how central Napoleon I's inspiration remained. The Grand Chamberlain, the Duc de Bassano, was the son of the great emperor's war minister; the master of ceremonies, the Duc de Cambacères the son of his chancellor; and the *premier veneur*, the Prince de Moskova, was the son of Marshal Ney, while the chamberlain, Prince Bacciochi was the son of Napoleon's sister, Elisa. They formed the apex of the 'old' Napoleonic nobility (not yet fifty years old, sniffed Legitimists) and dominated Second Empire society.

Between New Year and Lent four astonishingly lavish balls were held at the Tuileries, culminating with a costume ball for the carnival on Shrove Tuesday, each attended by 5,000 guests. There were also the empress's '*Petits lundis*', her Monday evening receptions and dances in the palace's salon *bleu*, to which at least 500 people were always invited. Then there were the masked balls occasionally given by ministers at their ministries. In addition, there were balls for foreign royalties visiting Paris. All this was known collectively, with a hint of sarcasm, as the *fêtes impériales* – best translated as 'Imperial merry-making'. If there had been court balls under the restored Bourbons between 1814 and 1830, nothing quite like it had been seen since the eighteenth century.

White was *de rigueur* for ladies' dresses at the Tuileries, if only because it had been the custom at the first Napoleonic court, with gowns of tulle, velvet or gauze, trimmed with vast amounts of embroidery and lace; Eugénie sometimes appeared in a dress trimmed with ivy. Long trains, no shorter than three metres and no longer than four, hung from their bare shoulders, the empress wearing a red or purple velvet train on important occasions of state.

Guests at the Tuileries had to arrive in carriages, cabs being forbidden, so that on evenings when the balls were being held the entire length of the rue de Rivoli, from where they approached the palace, was jammed by a seemingly endless line of vehicles. Presumably their impatient occupants were supposed to be consoled by the fireworks which were bursting over the Seine. Having at last reached the Pavillon de l'Horloge in the centre of the Tuileries' interminable façade, they went up a broad staircase into the Galerie de la Paix, a huge Cent Garde with carbine and fixed bayonet standing motionless on each step. Dancing, which began at 9.30 p.m. precisely, took place in the Galerie de la Paix, where the imperial couple had their thrones, gilt chairs draped in red velvet that fell in folds to the floor. Flanking the thrones were red velvet chairs for members of the imperial family – old King Jerome and Princesse Mathilde being often in evidence, Prince Napoleon rarely. The emperor and empress invariably opened the dancing themselves, in a quadrille with the most illustrious guests. The music consisted mainly of waltzes by Waldteufel, Strauss or Olivier Métra, Waldteufel frequently conducting in person.

The memoirs of American guests are unusually vivid since, having no court life at home, they tended to be more observant than Europeans. Mrs Charles Moulton – Lillie Greenough, born and brought up in Cambridge, Massachusetts, and the wife of an American banker resident in Paris – has left us a cameo portrait of Eugénie holding court at the Tuileries. While skating one January day in the Bois de Boulogne, the emperor and empress (whom she had never met before) had suddenly come up and asked her to teach them to skate, since they could scarcely stay on their feet on the ice. An invitation to one of the big balls followed, so Lillie was vetted formally by the daunting Duchessse de Bassano, who found no difficulty in giving her approval.

At the Tuileries, Lillie admired 'the superb Cent Gardes, standing like statues', before she and her mother-in-law were taken by an usher to the grand master of ceremonies, who passed them on to a lesser master of ceremonies, who took them into the ballroom. 'Each lady showed to great advantage as, on account of their crinolines, they had to stand very far apart,' wrote Lillie. The ballroom, she noticed, was lit by wax candles instead of gas. After the *quadrille d'honneur*, 'Mme Moulton' (wearing her old wedding dress) was sent a message from the empress to come and talk to her. The note was brought by Prince Achille Murat, who took the young American up to the throne.

'I can't imagine a more beautiful apparition,' said Lillie. 'She wore a white tulle dress trimmed with red velvet bows and gold fringes; her crown of diamonds and pearls and her necklace were magnificent. On her breast shone the great diamond (the Regent) which belongs to the Crown.'

Learning that Mme Moulton could sing (she had been trained by Malibran's brother), Eugénie invited her to a Monday evening reception. ' "*Le petit lundi*" of the empress was not so *petit* as I had expected; there were at least four or five hundred people present', reported Lillie, who nervously sang them some American songs (including 'Swanee River'), and was warmly applauded by the emperor and the empress.

Lillie Moulton and Dr Evans, the dentist, show us what nonsense it is to suspect that Eugénie was anti-American, as one or two historians have suggested. Evans has been accused of sycophancy yet he wrote long after the empress had lost her throne. 'Everyone likes him, and every door as well as every jaw is open to him', said Lillie. 'At the Tuileries they look on him not only as a good dentist, but as a good friend.' If a bit fulsome, Evans was clearly no fool. He tells us that during the Second Empire, 'It used often to be said that "Paris is the heaven of Americans".'

Certainly there were always plenty of them to be seen at the Tuileries and in 1869 General John A. Dix, United States envoy to France, told the American colony, 'We are invited to participate most liberally – far more liberally than at any other court in Europe – in the hospitalities of the Palace.' Eugénie, who spoke English, obviously enjoyed American company. Evans wrote that General Ulysses S. Grant was fascinated by her 'never failing kindness to Americans'. No less obviously, the liking was reciprocated. General Dix recalled how he loved to watch the empress at receptions, 'moving about with a gracefulness all of her own'.

Formal dinners at the Tuileries were served by a footman behind each chair and eaten off silver-gilt, with dessert plates of old Sèvres: Eugénie barely noticed what she ate. Very occasionally there was unseemly behaviour. One day she heard loud laughter. A napkin having fallen off a lady's lap, the Marquis de Gallifet had dived beneath the table to retrieve it, but had failed to re-emerge. 'He's been on the Mexican campaign and thinks he's still under canvas', Napoleon told the angry Eugénie. She experimented with dinners that separated the sexes, men and women sitting at different tables, but no one enjoyed them, apart from a handful of natural feminists like the empress herself.

There was of course a private side to Eugénie's life at the Tuileries. Every day at noon Baron de Pierres, the American's husband and equerry in charge of the stables, came to see if she needed a carriage, and when she went for a drive he rode at its side. The Grand Mistress, the principal lady-in-waiting, the private secretary, the librarian and the reader also came to this midday audience. The private secretary organised her engagements, the librarian brought a selection of books, since the empress spent a good deal of time reading in her boudoir, and the job of the 'reader' was not to read but to go through her correspondence and answer letters. At about one o'clock a carriage was sent to bring the two ladies-in-waiting on duty to the palace from their apartments; their role was essentially decorative and if there were no public engagements or if Eugénie did not go for a drive, after lunch the carriage would take them home for the afternoon. However, the Grand Mistress, the ladies and one or two of the household gentlemen always dined with the empress.

The shrewish Mme Pollet was a key member of the team. Supposedly the daughter of a Carlist general, 'Pepa', who had been with Eugénie since she was a girl, she was a cross between maid and 'companion', running the empress's wardrobe, keeping her accounts (paying dressmakers' bills, sending donations to charity) and looking after her jewels. Still young, she suffered from phobias, convinced that she was dying and that assassins lurked behind the curtains. Bad-tempered, she was always being rude to the ladies-in-waiting or upsetting the servants, much to Eugénie's irritation. But although she occasionally screamed at Pepa, she could not do without her.

The empress had a tiny circle of close friends whom she received before dinner at about six o'clock, notably Cécile Delessert and her mother, with another old acquaintance, Mme de Nadaillac. The circle included Princesse Mathilde, who pretended she had grown fond of her despite waging a relentless campaign of character assassination, the emperor's niece, Anna Murat, who married the Duc de Mouchy – just the sort of marriage between the old and new aristocracies that Eugénie liked to see – and, later, Princess Clothilde, the unfortunate young Savoyard who married Plon-Plon. Paca's children came when they were in Paris. Few others were ever admitted to the empress's private apartments.

Gaiety was not confined to the Tuileries. In 1859, for example, there were masked balls at the office of the minister of state in the Louvre (M. Fould), at the ministry of foreign affairs in the newly opened Quai d'Orsay (Comte Walewski) and at the chamber of the Corps Législatif in the Palais Bourbon (Comte de Morny). Normally austere rooms were draped in silk and full of exotic flowers while sweet champagne – the Second Empire liked it sweet – was served inexhaustibly to the guests, who wore fancy dress or dominoes with masks. Accompanied by the empress, Napoleon came to all three balls, under the impression that his mask disguised him, but everyone recognised his slow, sidling walk and the way he twirled his moustache.

Splendour and elegance made Paris once again the capital of Europe. Under Napoleon III France regained the ascendancy she had lost at Waterloo. Not only foreigners were dazzled. Many Frenchmen, and Frenchwomen, mourned for the old, pre-1789 monarchy that octogenarians could still remember. Just as the First Empire had to some extent satisfied their nostalgia, so did the Second, and a shrewd awareness of this lay behind all the spectacular balls and glittering parades. Although Legitimists in the Faubourg Saint-Germain tried to pretend that only *nouveaux riches* or painted whores visited the Tuileries, they were impressed despite themselves. Built on what seemed to be rock-solid prosperity, the Second Empire looked more and more like the heir of the *ancien régime*, and an increasing number of royalists, even of republicans, began to go to court.

Much of this success was due to the empress, but few observers realised the effort that it had cost her, guessed at the melancholy and pessimism beneath the smile of the woman who presided over the *fêtes impériales*. 'I am the chief slave in my realm, isolated in the midst of everybody, without a single friend,' she complained to her sister as early as spring 1853. 'Often I am so tired when I arrive at a city that the very thought of a ball or a dinner makes me want to cry,' she wrote to Paca while on progress seven years later, lamenting that sovereigns have to flatter people unceasingly – 'all young girls must be pretty, all artists must be talented'.

SAINT-CLOUD AND FONTAINEBLEAU

The imperial couple spent half the year away from Paris. After becoming empress, Eugénie never felt entirely at ease in the capital, while in any case the Tuileries was too hot and uncomfortable during the summer months. Even in winter they stayed at the château de Saint-Cloud, only forty minutes' drive away but in open country. Elegantly rebuilt by Louis XIV, who gave it superb gardens, with lakes and avenues, the palace had been a favourite residence of both Marie-Antoinette and Napoleon I. The imperial couple played at country life here, receiving as few visitors as possible, strolling in the park or through the fields. The emperor stocked the park with fallow deer imported from England. 'In the mornings. I often saw the empress driving in a pretty little dog-cart, after being installed in it by Gamble, the English groom who ran the stables', Filon, who became the Prince Imperial's tutor during the late sixties, recalls in his memoirs. In the afternoon she and her court would go for a drive in chars-à-bancs through the woods, to the model farm or to Malmaison. 'Gentle, peaceful days alternated with the pomp of levees and receptions, but Saint-Cloud was not far enough away from Paris to stop politics intruding into the sovereigns' lives', Filon remembers:

Paris was always present in our eyes and minds and the great, frowning capital seemed like a silent enemy. Twice a week we saw a long procession of ministerial carriages drive slowly up the avenue and we knew as if by instinct that every carriage was bringing fresh problems . . . . in consequence, the empress's life at Saint-Cloud was two entirely different worlds. She shared the simple pleasures with those around her – her very real worries could only be guessed from the odd word that she let slip from time to time.

Early in May, earlier if possible although it was a difficult place to heat, they went to Fontainebleau, loveliest and most romantic of all the French palaces. Despite the tragic memories that it evoked – Napoleon I had abdicated here in 1814 – Napoleon and Eugénie enjoyed the hilly, wooded country and, above all, the stag hunting. The imperial staghounds were kennelled at Fontainebleau, except in the autumn. 'Traditional French hunting is unique, quite different from English hunting', explains Princesse Metternich. 'Everything is conducted according to ancient custom and you need to see harbourers using their lime-hounds to find a stag and watch those wonderful whips blowing their horns at full gallop to appreciate its skill and grace.' Even the ungainly Achille Fould, ignoring a good deal of laughter, climbed onto a horse – nearly losing his life when an infuriated stag charged him.

Under the nominal direction of General Fleury as Master of the Horse, Eugénie's stable usually contained about twenty animals, mainly English thoroughbreds bought for her by Baron de Pierres. Thanks to her Spanish upbringing, she had no difficulty in riding the most temperamental and hard-mouthed horse.

On hunting mornings, the empress put on a green riding habit with crimson facings and a gold-laced, three-cornered green hat. Gentlemen wore crimson-faced green coats, buckskin breeches, jackboots and tricornes, and carried swords. After a late breakfast she drove with her guests to a meet in the forest at noon, where horses were waiting, fast carriages being provided for those who did not ride. The pack moved off with feudal pomp through rows of liveried footmen, hunt servants blowing fanfares. Early in the morning a *limier* (harbourer) would find a runnable stag so that hunting began without delay, the field guided by signals from the great brass horns telling them along which woodland ride to gallop. For the rest of her life Eugénie wistfully recalled the horn music ringing through the forest:

'*J'aime le son du Cor, le soir, au fond des bois.*'

She liked to see the stag at bay, fighting the hounds, even if normally she was kind to animals. The emperor killed it personally, dismounting and using a gun instead of a sword amid the whoops of the *hallali*. Often he got too close and once he nearly lost his life when the enraged stag charged him; he escaped by throwing himself flat on the ground. Watching, Eugénie was almost as shaken, but it did not stop them hunting.

The empress returned to an English tea with the guests, followed by a hip-bath – her dressing-room floor covered in hot towels, maids bringing huge jugs of hot water – before presiding over a hunter's dinner. Afterwards, everyone went to the windows overlooking the Oval Courtyard to watch the *courée*, a re-enactment of the hunt. As flaming torches of tarred wood lit the courtyard below, the horns sounded and hounds rushed into the circle. Standing over the skin which held the entrails, the huntsman waved its antlered head at them, the snarling pack being beaten back twice until allowed to fight for its reward to the music of horns.

A sleepy little town, Fontainebleau welcomed the court's visits. Since their visits were fairly brief, invitations to the palace were comparatively few and largely restricted to their inner circle.

Napoleon reviewed the garrison and decorated the officers while Eugénie inspected the local orphanage, attending its sports day and handing out sweets. On one occasion local workmen sang a chorus in the Jardin Anglais, 'The Imperial Hunt', and were given champagne by the emperor, who drank their health. Young people would dance country dances in a forest glade to entertain the empress.

The hounds met only twice a week so there were other amusements. These included sailing on the lake in front of the palace, in boats like tiny gondolas with sails, that were always capsizing – Eugénie was particularly proud of a real gondola rowed by a genuine Venetian gondolier. Roller-skating took place indoors, with footmen strategically positioned to stop crinolined ladies from crashing into the walls. There were plays in the minute theatre and surprise visits to the colony of painters who lived in the forest.

Octave Feuillet, the novelist and playwright who was the imperial librarian, describes a firework display organised by Eugénie:

All the town had been invited while people came from Paris. The courtyards, flowerbeds, terraces and paths round the lake were invaded by a huge crowd as soon as their majesties and their guests had crossed the Fountain court to stand in the English garden. Leaning over the fence between the garden and the courtyard, the empress chatted gaily with the delighted spectators, singling out a poor, ragged little urchin who was quite overwhelmed . . .

Suddenly the sky was lit by red, blue and silver light, by showers of gold, and (in Eugénie's words) the château looked 'like a picture by Gustave Doré'. The evening ended when

a legion of ghosts on horseback carrying torches came trotting down the avenue de Maintenon into the palace. It was the empress's Régiment of Dragoons beating the retreat with flambeaux . . . they rode in a circle, hunting horns and cavalry bugles sounding alternately. It was strange, superb. In the setting of the old Palace, the horses, torches and helmets mingled as if in a tournament, seemed like some magnificent fête from Valois times.

More than once, Eugénie took her guests to see the animal painter Rosa Bonheur, a flamboyant lesbian. The court always dined in the great Galerie François I and when about to enter the room one evening, the empress and Napoleon heard shouting outside the palace. What seemed to be a fat man in a velvet suit was waving an invitation and demanding to be let in. When it turned out to be Rosa, both burst into uncontrollable laughter. Nevertheless, as will be seen, Eugénie had genuine admiration for her.

The empress descended without warning on another fine artist in the vicinity who painted animals, Gabriel Descamps. A third local artist taken up by the court was a M. Jadin, who was invited to hunt regularly. Inspired by Oudry's tapestries, *The Royal Hunts of Louis XV*, Jadin produced a series of paintings of the imperial hounds which were tactfully applauded until the end of the Second Empire.

Among foreign royalties who came to stay at Fontainebleau was Maximilian II of Bavaria (father of mad King Ludwig) in 1857, the emperor driving him through the forest in a dog-cart to a picnic in the wild gorge at Apremont. The year after, the town cheered Queen Sofia of Holland, the Crown Prince of Württemberg and the Duke of Nassau's brother – all of them close friends of the imperial family. In May 1861 Napoleon received an embassy from the Shah at Fontainebleau. For the first time Eugénie was present at a reception of envoys, she and her ladies appearing in their richest clothes and jewels. The Persians were so impressed that the emperor asked her to sit next to him when receiving an embassy here from the king of Siam in June the same year. The scene was immortalised in a vast canvas by Jean-Léon Gérôme, who shows the silken-robed Siamese crawling on their hands and knees along a red carpet towards Napoleon and Eugénie. The court had been warned not to laugh. Far from laughing, it was horrified at seeing human beings grovel like animals. Balancing a huge gold cup filled with gifts on his head, the leader crawled with such obvious pain that, rising from his throne, the emperor walked down to the man and gently raised him to his feet. 'We might have fewer courtiers in France if they had to do that sort of thing', he joked afterwards. 'Perhaps that's why the King of Siam likes it.'

Despite its beauty, Octave Feuillet had reservations about Fontainebleau. It was, he felt, a little too haunted, 'a bit too sad and solemn'. (Nor, as a hypochondriac, did he care for being dragged by the empress through the mud on long, cross-country walks with the rest of the court, generally in the pouring rain, to see the picturesque 'rocks'.) Yet Napoleon and Eugénie liked it the best of all their homes and during the later 1860s, when their régime was becoming unpopular, they planned to spend more time here than at Saint-Cloud – from whose terraces they could see an increasingly hostile Paris. New heating was installed, while the empress designed a new study for herself. However, they were overtaken by events.

Eugénie

HOUSE PARTIES AT COMPIEGNE

From 1856 until almost the end of the reign, the enormous autumn house parties that took place at the great château of Compiègne, north-east of Paris, formed an essential part of Second Empire court life. Very unlike the parties at Fontainebleau, even if there was plenty of hunting, they were not only much bigger – because there was far more room in the château (a hundred people at a time could be invited although generally the number was about seventy) – but there was always an unexpected guest list.

From Capetian times until the Revolution, the kings of France had hunted here in a forest that stretched for miles. During the mid-eighteenth century the ancient château had been rebuilt for Louis XV by Ange-Jacques Gabriel, at that time France's most gifted architect, as a palace seen from the front and a country house seen from behind – a brilliant mixing of formal and informal. Since it was one of the four châteaux where French monarchs held their councils of state, the royal bedroom adjoined the council chamber. Compiègne had been where Napoleon I was happiest with Marie-Louise and became one of the palaces in which he preferred to meet his subjects. His nephew and niece were no less fond of it.

It was the carefully chosen guest lists that made the Compiègne house parties so memorable. Napoleon III and Eugénie followed a precedent set to some extent by their uncle, of meeting on social terms as wide a selection of Frenchmen and their wives as possible. Lasting for a week, the parties averaged about three every year, from the end of October to the middle of December, the ultimate compliment being an invitation to more than one. There was a serious party for statesmen and important officials, a smart party for leaders of fashion, and a deliberately mixed party for diplomats, soldiers, musicians, writers and artists. William I, the new king of Prussia, was entertained here in 1861, but without the usual mixed party. However, this was a rare exception.

Compiègne was ninety minutes from Paris by rail, an imperial express leaving what is now the Gare du Nord at 2.30 p.m., its salon carriages equipped with armchairs and newspapers. The château contained over 1,300 rooms, so that on arrival everybody

64

was given a bedroom and a sitting room. They were asked to be in the Grand Salle des Fêtes by 7.00 p.m., ladies dressed for dinner but not in the white gowns worn at the Tuileries, gentlemen in informal court dress: ordinary tailcoats with knee-breeches. Here they would be ceremoniously welcomed by Napoleon and Eugénie, who from then on behaved as host and hostess rather than sovereigns.

In November 1857 the British foreign secretary, the Earl of Clarendon, asked Lord Cowley to give him some idea of what life was like at Compiègne house parties. 'It is difficult to describe . . .', the ambassador replied, with a distinct lack of enthusiasm:

> The empress instead of letting people alone, torments herself and them by thinking it necessary to furnish constant amusements for them – such amusements generally suited to some people and not to others, but the emperor and empress are both so natural and unaffected, and there is so little ceremony and etiquette that the life is not disagreeable for a short time. . . . Breakfast is at eleven, then there is either hunting or shooting, or some expedition. Dinner about eight o'clock, which never lasts more than an hour. In the evening there is dancing to a hand organ (a dreadful trial to one's auricular nerves) or charades or cards. . . . The hand organ is employed because the emperor fancies that regular musicians would tell tales – so a wretched chamberlain has to grind all evening.

A Whig nobleman, Cowley did not enjoy mixing with intellectuals who were not gentlemen. The 'hand organ' was a primitive Debain mechanical piano which could only play a few tunes, hence his anguish. But often Waldteufel, who had an apartment in the town, played dance music on a proper piano.

A few years later, Lillie Moulton was invited and she gives a more enthusiastic account. At the station, 'I think the whole twelve thousand inhabitants of Compiègne were gathered there to stare at us.' About sixty guests were taken to the château in ten green chars-à-bancs, each drawn by four horses, the luggage going separately. Her own included eight day costumes ('counting my travelling suit'), her green riding habit for hunting, seven ball dresses and five tea gowns. Accommodation for herself and her husband consisted of two bedrooms, two servants' rooms, an ante-chamber and a large salon whose walls, curtains and furniture were covered in pink and mauve brocade. She much preferred the modern chaise longue and armchairs in white and green in her bedroom to the stiff First Empire furniture in the salon.

Despite being used to the Tuileries, and although the party was supposed to be comparatively informal, at first Mrs Moulton found herself a little daunted by the grandeur of Compiègne. The Cent Gardes were very much in evidence, fifty footmen with powdered hair in red and white liveries served dinner, a military band in the courtyard outside the dining-room playing throughout the meal. Eugénie was wearing a superb diamond tiara and a collar of huge pearls. After dinner, however, the atmosphere grew more relaxed, everyone going into the ballroom where they waltzed to music provided by Waldteufel – 'the French Strauss' – in person or by the famous mechanical piano which, whatever Lord Cowley might say, Lillie considered an altogether delightful instrument.

Occasionally there was singing in the evening, and during her visit Lillie sang to the court, among her American songs being 'Nelly Bly' and 'Swanee River' at Napoleon's special request – he also asked for 'Massa's in de Cold, Cold Ground', which he remembered from his visit to America, but she did not know the words. Sadly, Prince Murat's suggestion that the entire court dance a Virginia reel ended in disaster – 'the emperor refused to be swung', complains young Mrs Moulton.

Other evening amusements during the '*séries*', as Compiègne house parties were called, included Japanese billiards, while full use was made of the château's pretty little theatre. Sometimes actors were brought from Paris or the guests mounted a play themselves – after one appearance on the boards, despite frenzied clapping, Eugénie was shrewd enough to realise that she had no gift for acting and did not try again. More often the theatre was used for charades, for whose organisation the architect Viollet-le-Duc had a special talent. In one of them Lillie Moulton impersonated 'a mechanical doll sent from America'. There was also a rather dull-sounding parlour game of dictations full of grammatical pitfalls. Evenings at Compiègne always ended with tea in the empress's salon.

The salon, Eugénie's private drawing-room, had an ante-chamber furnished with Italian Renaissance cabinets, inlaid tables and vitrines. The salon itself was very large, filled with tables on which bibelots were strewn, screens made of eighteenth-century engravings and low, modern armchairs. Its walls were hung with magnificent old tapestries and cases of fans, while there was a painted ceiling in what seems to have been rococo style. Books, obviously in the process of being read, were lying about everywhere.

What Lillie Moulton particularly liked about the empress was her lack of self-consciousness. 'None of the many portraits painted of her, not even Winterhalter's, do her the least justice; no brush can paint and no words can describe her charm', said Lillie. When the poor girl crept into the château's dining-room late for lunch, a frightful breach of court etiquette, especially when she had been invited to sit next to Napoleon, Eugénie immediately restored Lillie's self-confidence with an understanding smile down the table.

The imperial hunt was kennelled at Compiègne during the autumn months when the '*séries*' were being held. The hounds always met at noon, at the Puits du Roy ('The King's Well') in the middle of the forest, a spot which was the focal point of eight long and very wide woodland rides. If the hunt went according to plan, a stag was run down and killed in time for everyone to return to the château for tea. The empress presided over the tea, which was served in the Salon de Musique, Napoleon slumped amiably by the fire in his favourite, plum-coloured armchair. After dinner, standing on the balconies, the party watched the torchlit ceremony of the *curée*, which at Compiègne was held in the Cour d'Honneur; Eugénie, who felt the night cold keenly, was muffled in furs.

Every morning at nine a valet brought tea, coffee or chocolate according to choice to the guest rooms, together with a card listing the programme for the day. Lillie gives an example:

Dejeuner à onze heures
Chasse à tir à deux heures.
Comédie Française à neuf heures.

Excellent guns, ammunition and loaders were provided for any guest of either sex who wanted to join the shooting party, which was served by unusually helpful gamekeepers and an obliging horde of beaters. But although she knew how to, Eugénie never shot birds, merely watching the guns.

Generally there was shooting on the first day, 'promenades' in the forest (regardless of the weather) on the second, hunting on the third, and rabbit and rook shooting in the park on the fourth. Simpler outdoor amusements were always available, however. 'Do you wish to walk?', said Lillie. 'You can tramp up and down the one-thousand-metre-long trellis walk, sheltered from wind and rain. Do you wish to drive? There are carriages of all descriptions, chars-à-bancs, landaus, pony-carriages, and even a donkey cart, at your service. Do you care to ride? There are one hundred and fifty horses eating their heads off in the imperial stables waiting for you. Whatever you do, you are expected to be in your rooms before four o'clock, which is the time the empress will send for you, if she invites you to tea.'

Mrs Moulton witnessed an unsuccessful attempt to introduce croquet to Compiègne, Napoleon having recently ordered a croquet set from Paris. According to Lillie, 'The emperor, bored to death, slowly disappeared and the empress suddenly discovered that her feet were cold and went away, and couples flirtatiously inclined began wandering off.'

The party was invited to attend the local army manoeuvres, a faintly ridiculous mock battle during which enormous quantities of blank ammunition were fired, and which always ended in a triumphant victory for French troops. Eugénie and the ladies wore their green hunt uniform for the occasion. 'The empress looked radiantly beautiful, her well-fitting riding-habit showing her fine figure to the greatest advantage', Lillie tells us.

On another afternoon there was an expedition to see the great fourteenth-century château of Pierrefonds on the edge of the forest of Compiègne, the guests, wrapped in furs and rugs because of the cold, travelling in the green, four-horse chars-à-bancs which each held eight passengers. They were accompanied by Viollet-le-Duc, 'the pet architect of the emperor', who was restoring the château.

(As at Carcassonne, Viollet-le-Duc's so-called 'restoration' was in fact a wildly inaccurate reconstruction.) Lillie found it interesting, but very cold and tiring, even though she enjoyed the beautiful drive through the woods.

Not everybody was quite as enthralled as Mrs Moulton by the *séries*. 'The Compiègne gathering is an odd one', Viel Castel had sneered enviously in October 1856. 'The court has come up with a thoroughly unsuitable guest list. Literature is represented by the Comte Alfred de Vigny . . . who paints his face and licks his lips to make them pinker, looking just like an old woman dressed up as a man contrary to police regulations. He doesn't write any more, for fear of making a mess of it.' Even so, Vigny (who remembered the courts of Louis XVIII and Charles X, having been an officer in their household troops) was delighted to be invited – 'puffed up' (*gonflé*) is Viel Castel's description.

What was surprising about this particular *série* was that it included so many *ancien régime* names, because all the old aristocracy were supposed to be irreconcilable Legitimists and boycott the imperial court – the Prince de Beauvau-Craon, the Prince de Bauffremont, the Comte de Caumont la Force, the Marquis de Caulaincourt, the Comte Frédéric de Lagrange. A less unexpected guest was Baron de Rothschild, an old and valued friend of Eugénie from before her marriage, 'who will perhaps divert the company with some financial calculations', sniffed Viel Castel. 'Auber and Meyerbeer will talk music with Verdi, Horace Vernet and Isabey will exchange puns. The Marquess of Hertford is no doubt very clever and amusing, but you have to fill in the background with ministers, generals and officials and if, after all that, you don't admit the company is most elegant and select, then you're hard to please.' But Comte Horace de Viel Castel's sarcasm came from knowing that he was too insignificant to have any chance of being invited himself.

In contrast, Mrs Moulton was fascinated by the company she met at Compiègne a decade later. One night she sat next to the poet Théophile Gautier, who entranced her, telling her about his educated cats, and who then sent her a poem. She made friends with the Marquis de Gallifet, who was the most dashing cavalry colonel in the entire French army. (A future hero of the 1870 war and scourge of the Communards, in his old age he would be immortalised by Proust.) The marquis told her how he had been shot in the stomach and left for dead in Mexico, but had crawled to safety 'holding my entrails in my képi'. She was taken into one lunch by Baron Haussmann, the great rebuilder of Paris. At the final lunch Gustave Doré passed round the table an album of caricatures he had drawn during the week, with a 'sketch of Her Majesty driving a chariot like the "Aurora" in the Rospigliosi gallery'.

No doubt after one of the *séries*, Prosper Mérimée wrote, 'I feel half dead. Fate never intended me to be a courtier', although he added loyally, 'You can't imagine a more amiable hostess.' But Mérimée was a professional intellectual, nervous about his image and deeply embarrassed at having been made a senator at Eugénie's request.

On the last morning the pleasure of Lillie and her husband was a little marred by the major-domo bringing them a bill for a huge tip – 600 francs. The whole party grumbled about the tips on the train back to Paris, despite learning that Compiègne cost 10,000 francs a day to run, with 900 people to feed. Eventually a guest complained in the newspapers and the emperor, who had no idea of what had been happening, angrily banned all tipping. But next year Lillie eagerly accepted another invitation to Compiègne.

BIARRITZ AND THE VILLA EUGENIE

The pressures on Eugénie grew throughout the reign. Years afterwards, she was to confide in a close friend, 'If only you knew what we had to endure!' It was not just the claustrophobic, demanding life in the great palaces, always on show and in the public eye, hemmed in by stifling pomp and etiquette, that was such a strain on her, but the ever-increasing worries – about her husband's compulsive infidelities, about a dangerous international situation that deteriorated steadily and about the régime's sheer insecurity at home, more than just a few times expressed in determined attempts at assassination by bomb, revolver or dagger. (After one particularly narrow escape she commented, 'It's our business to be shot at.') Often her life as a sovereign at the Tuileries, even at Compiègne, must have seemed barely tolerable to a woman who was so highly strung and who in any case was by nature a free spirit, fiercely independent, and who loathed any form of constraint on her personal liberty. She needed a special refuge where she could relax and be herself.

Fortunately, Eugénie had already found it at Biarritz, that obscure, south-western fishing village on the shore of the Bay of Biscay, just north of the Spanish frontier, which she had first discovered in 1847. She loved its pleasant weather, so much gentler than the weather in northern France even if often interrupted by storms; but she took a perverse pleasure in storms. When she returned to Biarritz a few months after her marriage, there were still only a few hundred people in the village, all of them Basque-speaking fishermen and their families, while the only building larger than the little church and the local lighthouse was a ruined castle, the château d'Atalaye. The landscape was 'wildly picturesque', with a magic coastline of little bays, caves and grottoes, together with the Pyrenean mountains for a background. But the couple also explored inland, driving through the Landes. One of the expeditions was to visit new mineral springs near Grenade, where a tiny spa (which still exists) was subsequently established, with the name 'Eugénie-les-Bains'.

In 1854 Napoleon III built the empress a large, rambling and luxurious house to the north of Biarritz, as an annual haven. He christened it, 'The Villa Eugénie', although it was really a palace and much bigger than a mere villa. The Villa Eugénie was not without splendour, seven Gobelin tapestries of Don Quixote being priceless. Surrounded by iron railings, the house was protected by Cent Gardes and a detachment of the Imperial Guard in barrack-like lodges at the gates. There were few guests (Mrs Moulton never received an invitation), only one or two statesmen or foreign royalties. Each year, Eugénie spent several weeks at the villa, nearly always with her husband, and frequently with her mother and sister as well. Not only did she walk or drive along the beach as much as possible, watching the waves endlessly, but every morning in her voluminous bathing dress she swam in the sea – preferably when a storm was approaching – swimming very far out from land, from a small boat and escorted by three or four reliable fishermen, to ensure that she would be well beyond the range of any prying telescope. She also liked to sail up and down the Bay of Biscay with Napoleon in their luxurious yacht, although seldom for more than a day, or up the River Irun or along the Spanish coast. (Yachting was a taste which she preserved into her old age.) In addition, she enjoyed driving herself along the shore or through the pretty countryside around Biarritz in a fast dog-cart, with only a single lady-in-waiting for company.

Sometimes, accompanied by Napoleon and a small group of friends, the empress would ride into the mountains for a picnic in some Pyrenean glen or to drink from the mountain springs of mineral water at Cambo. A favourite expedition was to ride up to a peak such as La Grande Rhune, 3,000 feet high, from the top of which they could look down into Spain. Then, leading their horses by the bridle, the party would clamber down the mountain on foot to where carriages were waiting to take them back to the Villa Eugénie. Driving home through the dusk, escorted by outriders carrying flaming torches, they would stop and dine at an isolated tavern, remote but renowned locally for its good country food and wine.

Occasionally, Eugénie would take the emperor to Bayonne a little further up the coast, whenever bullfights were taking place in the town. It was a sport for which she retained a Spaniard's ineradicable passion and which she tried, unsuccessfully, to popularise in France. (Once she arranged a bizarre, not to say grotesque, boar and cow fight at the Trianon, personally goading the cows with a lance; when the cows, unusually savage animals imported from Spain, turned and charged her, she calmly avoided them, although her terrified ladies ran away screaming.) Needless to say, there was a certain amount of criticism from the not very effective 'animal rights' lobby of the day, while republicans attempted to portray her in pornographic pamphlets as a bloodthirsty pervert who took sexual pleasure in such horrible spectacles. On the whole, however, as is so often the case with people who enjoy hunting – or even bullfighting – she was genuinely fond of most animals, especially horses.

A barely credible yet solidly documented adventure, resembling some wild tale from one of Alexandre Dumas's novels, took place during the Biarritz holiday of 1858. After the empress had met and made friends with 'Monsieur Michel', a handsome French Basque who was the most successful smuggler in the entire Pyrenees – and the most powerful since he controlled all the main smuggling routes between France and Spain – he boldly invited the emperor and herself to dine with him at the lair high up in the mountains where he hid his contraband. Although Michel was not much better than a brigand, they knew they would be perfectly safe in his hands because all the French Basques were fanatical Bonapartists, and they accepted. Accompanied by a small, carefully picked escort, the imperial party was guided by smugglers along secret, hair-raisingly precipitous paths up to a huge cave, below a mountain peak just across the Spanish border. Tables and chairs were waiting in the cave, which was lit by torches. Throughout a splendid meal the night outside was illuminated by fireworks, while the smugglers sang and danced, serenading the guests with guitar music. Their host enthusiastically joined in the dancing himself as soon as the meal was over. 'The empress simply could not stop herself', says an admiring eyewitness, a doctor who had come with the imperial party. 'Throwing off her hat and cloak, she started to dance a particularly graceful fandango. She was completely unaffected and altogether enchanting, the look on her face being one of pure delight. We all of us felt that the empress had come back to the land of her birth and that, for a moment, she had regained the freedom of her early days.'

'The freedom of her early days' is a highly significant phrase. Those precious six weeks spent each year at Biarritz, after midsummer, were certainly the closest that Eugénie came to recovering it, and to releasing at least some of her frustration. Here the etiquette of the Tuileries, even of Compiègne, was relaxed to the barest minimum and there was a good deal of boisterous horseplay. On more than one occasion, the same courtier-doctor tells us that the empress and her ladies chased the emperor and his gentlemen through the villa, flicking them with twisted napkins and making them jump over tables and chairs.

When Prince and Princesse Metternich first came here in September 1859, Pauline Metternich was astonished to find the empress sitting quietly at a big round table playing patience, her ladies reading or sewing as they sat with her. It reminded Pauline of life in a country house rather than in a palace. She noticed, however, that when the emperor came in, Eugénie rose to her feet – as she always did so, 'even when one was alone with her in her study or her private drawing-room'. Nevertheless, she called her husband 'Louis', never 'Napoleon'.

Pauline Metternich went on a mountaineering expedition with Eugénie, who wore a broad-brimmed Spanish hat. Tough as she was, Pauline found it hard going, but when they halted for a picnic, the empress of the French danced a vigorous and lengthy fandango. Everyone else was exhausted by the ascent. A tearful Mme de la Bedoyère begged to be left to die, and had to be carried down by relays of mountaineers, Eugénie grumbling, 'My ladies are always ill, by land or by sea.'

The household dreaded her love of the sea, as Pauline makes clear in '*Une promenade en mer*'. One afternoon in September 1859 the empress insisted on everyone accompanying her despite a high wind. Blown across the Bay of Biscay like the Flying Dutchman, all save Eugénie were seasick, the ladies, led by Clothilde de la Bedoyère, sobbing and screaming. The boat was almost sent to the bottom by huge waves when trying to re-enter Biarritz. By now it was 2.00 a.m. and Napoleon was waiting on the jetty. 'We haven't had much luck with our little voyage', the empress told him nervously. 'This is the last time you go on one of these escapades,' he replied, the only time Pauline ever saw him in a bad temper.

But nothing would stop her. In October 1867 Mr Whitehurst, the *Daily Telegraph* correspondent, watched Eugénie's little steamer 'staggering too and fro, and occasionally shipping a sea'. When a gale blew up the captain tried to land his passengers at Saint-Jean-de-Luz, but the boat hit a rock. 'In a few minutes the empress was sitting in water up to her waist, and the prince was almost out of his depth.' Keeping their heads, they were rescued in the nick of time, but the panic-stricken pilot jumped overboard, hit his head and was drowned.

'Twenty years ago no Frenchman would have believed that this little Basque village could have become the seat of an imperial Court', wrote Whitehurst, noting that the site of the Villa Eugénie had been bought for £12. Now the smart world spent holidays at

'Eugénieville', buses bringing day-trippers from Bayonne or San Sebastian. There were hotels and a casino. Eugénie continued to mountaineer and picnic – as well as to sail – yet the first thing Felix Whitehurst saw on arriving was 'a compact crowd . . . following the emperor and empress, who were strolling up the high street'.

AN INSECURE REGIME

One of the Second Empire's greatest historians is the royalist, Pierre de la Gorce, even if wrong in believing that it was doomed from the start. His description of France in the days immediately after Eugénie's marriage cannot be bettered:

> This is the state of the country in spring 1853. Too many festivities, as tiring as hard work; important reforms on the way to fruition; a remarkable growth of public wealth; a future sure enough to allow for long-term planning; a frivolous but well-meaning society; no liberty but not so as to miss it very much; extremist politicians powerless or cowed; fine minds alienated or ignored, but no general awareness of so much lost talent; an all-powerful government, sufficiently moderate to limit itself and not be tyrannical.

The new, Bonapartist France seemed a rich, contented land. The economic misery of the 1840s had vanished, together with the spectre of a return to the upheavals of sixty years before. 'Nobody can deny that the Emperor is a most extraordinary man, and that he has raised France to a position in Europe which she had long since ceased to occupy', Lord Cowley would comment in 1856.

Yet, in Pierre de la Gorce's words, 'there were seeds of decline and misjudgement, although so deeply buried that no-one could possibly foresee they would ever ripen'. Beneath the surface Legitimists and Orleanists were resentful, and republicans simmering – everyone recalled how the last two régimes had been toppled by revolution. And the Bonapartists lacked able leaders, Alexis de Tocqueville sneering that the Second Empire was 'a paradise for the envious and mediocre'. The biggest danger, however, lay in Napoleon III's foreign policy. He wanted to show the world that France was *the* power in Europe by helping Italy and Poland win their freedom.

England had headed every European coalition against France, so Napoleon was eager to secure her goodwill. His opportunity came in July 1853 when Tsar Nicholas I occupied the Danubian principalities (Romania) and assembled a fleet at Sevastopol in the Crimea, obviously planning to seize Constantinople ('that object of eternal Muscovite desire' as one of Napoleon's ministers put it). England was outraged. Here was the emperor's chance of an Anglo-French alliance. In any case, war against Russia would please all those who pitied the Poles and who hated Russian tyranny, while saving the Holy Places in Palestine from Russian domination would please Catholics. Hostilities became inevitable in November when the Russians blew the Turkish navy out of the sea, although France and England did not declare war until February 1854.

So far Eugénie had had little influence on foreign affairs, but we know that Napoleon showed her ambassadors' dispatches, explaining his policy. From the first he used her to sound out foreign envoys and argue his point of view, as is clear from Hübner's reports, and sometimes Cowley's. She was opposed to the war – a defeat might bring down the Second Empire – even if she disliked the idea of the Holy Places being ruled by Russian Orthodox, referring to what she called 'the antagonism between the Greek cross and the Latin cross'.

During the summer of 1854, 70,000 troops assembled at Boulogne (from where, half a century ago, the great Napoleon had hoped to invade England), marching, counter-marching, firing volley upon volley of blanks, in manoeuvres before the emperor and on one occasion the Prince Consort, who crossed over from England. Napoleon personally inspected the French expeditionary force, 25,000 strong, accompanied by the empress who, riding in front of the forest of red képis, wore instead of a bonnet a broad-brimmed Spanish hat with a white plume. Roars of '*Vive l'Impératrice!*' showed that the army knew a beautiful woman when it saw one. They knew, too, how she had given a humble infantryman a lift in her carriage when he was cut off from his unit.

In September the French landed in the Crimea, to be joined by 25,000 British troops. They had a fine commander in Marshal Saint-Arnaud. Within days, the allied army had driven back the Russians at the Alma and were able to invest Sevastopol, but Saint-Arnaud died of a heart attack. The siege dragged on, the allies barely surviving the Russian winter which had destroyed the Grande Armée in 1812, in disease-ridden dugouts.

In its early stages the war earned the Second Empire some badly needed popularity. Displacing countless families during the rebuilding of Paris, together with a bad harvest and soaring food prices had caused widespread unrest by the end of 1853, but now Napoleon was cheered to the echo. Republicans applauded a war against tyranny, while *L'Univers*, the main Catholic newspaper (most Catholics were Legitimists) welcomed a 'crusade' against the Orthodox. The empress helped to exploit this popularity, suggesting that, besides being given a hero's funeral, Saint-Arnaud should have a street and a bridge named after him.

But Sevastopol refused to surrender, false rumours of its capture causing bitter disappointment. By early 1855 the emperor was unpopular again, Lord Cowley noting that a professor had been hissed for praising him during a lecture, that the empress was rumoured to be buying property with stolen public money. He also reported that Napoleon was desperate to 'get out of the scrape in which we are in the Crimea'.

The Legitimists now hoped for a defeat in the Crimea that would bring Napoleon III crashing down. His best organised and most dangerous enemies, they had never accepted the Revolution of 1789 and were united in believing that France was embodied by the exiled Comte de Chambord. They ran secret royalist clubs all over the country, even infiltrating freemasons' lodges, besides owning over fifty newspapers that were fuelled by press releases from a centralised news agency. Although Chambord was one of those Bourbons who had learned nothing and forgotten nothing, so many army officers supported him that his party never ceased to be a threat.

Far less dangerous, the Orleanists supported the rival pretender, the Comte de Paris. Liberals who accepted the Revolution and wanted an English-style parliamentary democracy, they had an eloquent if treacherous spokesman in Adolphe Thiers and a few genuine idealists such as the Comte de Montalembert. Their opponents accused them of being cynical trimmers, unpatriotic Anglophiles who were planning to rob the poor.

Throughout the reign republicanism grew among intellectuals and the urban working class under some extremely capable leaders – Ledru-Rollin, Jules Favre, Jules Ferry and, in the final years, Gambetta. The noisiest republican was Victor Hugo (well described by the late Professor Richard Cobb as 'France's national bore'), ex-Legitimist, ex-Orleanist and ex-Bonapartist, who ranted from his refuge in the Channel Islands. He denounced the emperor in *Napoleon le petit* as a bloodstained tyrant who had massacred the Parisians during his coup, 'cheered on from the money-market by Fould the Jew, from the Church by Montalembert the Catholic; cherished by women eager to become whores, by men hoping to be made *prefets.*'

The emperor tried hard to win over as many Legitimists as possible, presenting Bonapartism as an alternative to royalism. He joked that the empress was really a Legitimist – had she married a Frenchman from the old nobility, she might easily have become a passionate supporter of 'Henri V'. As a good Catholic, she managed to persuade at least some of her co-religionists to vote for her husband.

Politicians rather than idealists, a fair number of Orleanists came over to Napoleon. He also succeeded in converting several leading republicans, men such as Victor Duruy, whom he appointed inspector of schools and later minister for education. Another convert from republicanism was Emile Ollivier, once a savage critic of the régime, who ended up as its first minister.

Since Eugénie did not have a son until 1856, strictly speaking the emperor's heir was the aged ex-King Jerome, a deplorable old rake who by now was on his last legs. An unmitigated disaster as ruler of Westphalia during the First Empire, his one moment of glory had been at Waterloo where he advised his brother to die on the battlefield, offering to die with him. Between Waterloo and the Second Empire he had lived off women. Created a marshal of France, President of the Senate and Governor of the Invalides,

Jerome was given a huge pension and the Palais Royal, the former home of the Orleans family, with twenty-four drawing-rooms.

The obvious heir, however, was Jerome's son Prince Napoleon – Plon-Plon. Born in 1822, physically he was the image of his glorious uncle but like him in no other way. Intelligent, often charming, the friend of Georges Sand and Flaubert, he was crippled by a lack of realism and an insane temper. He had developed a curious republican Bonapartism of his own, hoping to succeed his cousin as First Consul like the Bonaparte of 1799, not as emperor, but his radical policies and extreme anticlericalism would have torn the Bonapartist party in half. 'If ever he comes to the throne, which God forbid, then France will have a bad time of it', observed Viel Castel in July 1854.

Hübner called Plon-Plon 'the scourge of the Imperial family' and he certainly had a very odd relationship with his cousin. Anna Bicknell, a governess at the Tuileries, tells us, 'He was jealous of the emperor's pre-eminent position, as of something stolen from himself; but, though in a state of chronic rebellion, he never hesitated to accept all the worldly advantages which the title of "cousin" could obtain for him.' She adds that 'his temper was violent and brutal; his tastes were cynically gross, his language coarse beyond what could be imagined. . . .' More than a few contemporaries confirm her description. 'He hated the emperor', Eugénie said of Plon-Plon. 'He never forgave him for embodying the Napoleonic legend and restoring the Empire.' He loathed the empress too, because, according to his secretary, he lusted after her and knew he could never get her. Returning his hatred, and probably sensing the reason for it, she invariably treated him with a cold, maddening politeness.

Yet Napoleon forgave Plon-Plon again and again, because he had declined an offer by a group of Bonapartists to make him leader in 1848. Anna Bicknell said he 'felt a sort of indulgent affection for Prince Napoleon'.

Although Plon-Plon had never seen a shot fired in anger (and had even run away from his military academy as a boy), when the Crimean War broke out he demanded to be made commander-in-chief of the allied forces. The emperor declined, but let him accompany the reserves as a general. As soon as he landed, he wrote telling his father to have a steamer waiting. 'Should the emperor be assassinated, it would be essential for me to return as quickly as possible.' The emperor was furious when he heard. The prince speedily earned a reputation for cowardice, his name 'Plon-Plon' being changed by the troops to 'Craint-Plomb' (frightened of bullets). 'The miserable creature may be a prince but he certainly isn't a Frenchman', commented Viel Castel.

The ablest Bonaparte was King Jerome's daughter, Princesse Mathilde, charming, insincere and tough, who lived unhappily with her Dutch lover, 'Handsome Emilien', the self-styled Comte de Nieuwerkerker, ignoring his chronic infidelity. A failed sculptor (despite a fine portrait medallion of Eugénie), Nieuwerkerker was made director of the Louvre and superintendent of museums, becoming an important figure in artistic circles. Mathilde's salon, in the rue de Berry or at her château of Saint-Gratien near Enghien, was genuinely distinguished, including Rossini, Flaubert, Sainte-Beuve, Pasteur and the Goncourts among its regular guests, impressing even Mérimée. Because of her literary friendships she has been portrayed far too sympathetically. 'You can't imagine how beautiful she was in the early days of the Empire', Eugénie is supposed (by Paléologue) to have said of her. 'She had the profile of a medallion, eyes that really sparkled and shoulders that looked like sculptured marble.' But photographs of the 1860s show a heavy-jowled, thickset little woman, resembling Plon-Plon in skirts. Mathilde was jealous of Eugénie for taking the position that might have been hers. Despite some fierce arguments she concealed her hatred, while tirelessly slandering and abusing the empress behind her back. Some of her more venomous remarks were recorded with relish by the Goncourt brothers, who were royalists.

There were dozens of imperial relations living in France, each one paid a handsome civil list pension: Bonapartes, Murats, Bacciochis and Primolis. A few were respectable, such as Cardinal Bonaparte, the philologist Prince Lucien Bonaparte (an expert on Basque) or the blue-stocking Comtesse Primoli. Most were worthless, however. After numerous scandals the bullying, duelling and womanising Prince Pierre Bonaparte, popularly known as the 'Corsican Wild

Boar' was commissioned as a colonel in the Foreign Legion to keep him out of the country, yet somehow he managed to get himself spectacularly cashiered despite his name, and returned to Paris where he married a prostitute.

Several others were almost as embarrassing as Pierre, especially the grandchildren of Caroline Murat and Elisa Bacciochi. Ten Murats were receiving pensions, having rushed back from North America where they had established themselves during the lean years, the biggest nuisance among them being the head of the family, Prince Lucien Murat. More than one diplomatic row was caused by his publicly insisting that he was rightful king of Naples and, untruthfully, that the imperial government supported him – when crippled by gout, the grotesquely fat Lucien had himself carried in a chair to the Folies-Bergère every night. Count Camerata, Elisa's grandson, lost a fortune gambling on the stock exchange and asked Jerome to help him – the avaricious old king refused, so Camerata shot himself.

Relations like these did serious harm to Napoleon III's image, and emphasised that the Second Empire depended on his survival. There was an attempt on his life practically every year, although the royalist pretenders had forbidden their supporters to kill him, while few republicans cared to risk ending under the guillotine. The would-be assassins were nearly always Italian 'patriots', enraged by his sending troops to defend the Papal States. Hübner saw him in 1855 just after Pianori had shot at him when he was riding down the Champs Elysées. 'They need a knife if they're going to hit their mark', laughed the emperor, but Eugénie was sobbing hysterically.

By February 1855 Napoleon was in despair over the Crimea. Plon-Plon was spreading rumours that Sevastopol was impregnable and that the Anglo-French expedition had failed, while Morny and Fould were urging him to make peace. He was also growing nervous about Austria's attitude. By March he was seriously thinking of taking command in the Crimea, hoping to win some sort of victory and then ship his army back to France to deal with any crisis that might threaten – he would rely on a naval blockade to bring Sevastopol to its knees.

Eugénie was horrified. What if he should be defeated in the Crimea? She was delighted when, to dissuade him, the British government invited the emperor and empress to visit England in April as guests of Queen Victoria.

THE VISIT TO ENGLAND

The Victorians remembered Napoleon I rather as we do Hitler and regarded France as a land of frog-eating maniacs. They were astonished to learn that 'Boney's' nephew was coming to England, Prince Albert commenting privately that George III's ghost must be turning in its grave. (The dear old king had been in the habit of asking the boys at Eton, 'I hope you hate the French?') France was no less astounded by the prospect of her emperor being welcomed by her ancient enemies. If the prime minister, Lord Palmerston, deserved credit for so imaginative an invitation, so did Napoleon III for accepting it.

Queen Victoria was less than enthusiastic. One of her aunts, the late Queen Louise of Belgium, had been a daughter of Louis-Philippe, a king whom Victoria had always respected. 'The emperor's reception here ought to be a boon to him and not a boon to us', she wrote tartly to her foreign minister.

The emperor and empress set sail from Calais on 16 April 1855 on board the *Pélican*, a fast mail-steamer, accompanied by the *Pétrel* which carried Eugénie's hairdresser M. Félix together with her wardrobe and jewel boxes. Thick fog descended during the crossing, and Eugénie was sick. Met at Dover by Prince Albert, who accompanied them for the rest of the journey, they went on by royal train to London, where they alighted at a long-forgotten station (Bricklayers' Arms, in the Old Kent Road) and then, in an open carriage with an escort from the Household Cavalry, drove across London to Paddington, to board another royal train for Windsor. The empress's tact in wearing a tartan dress was much appreciated, as was the friendly way she waved back; the cheering crowds grew so out of hand that the party was held up for two hours.

Queen Victoria and her children greeted them at Windsor Castle. She may have been a dumpy little woman, but her dignity was overwhelming. The exhausted Eugénie was then horrified to learn that the *Pétrel* had been delayed – not only was Félix unavailable, but she would have to go down to dinner without her jewels. She borrowed a plain blue silk dress from one of her ladies, who did their best with her hair, a bunch of forget-me-nots replacing the jewels. Such simplicity charmed her hosts, however, and the queen began to refer to 'the dear sweet Empress' in her diary. Noticing how nervous she was, Victoria explained to Napoleon that Eugénie did not find her position easy, 'from not having been brought up to it'.

Next morning the emperor was made a Knight of the Garter in St George's Chapel. 'At last I am a gentleman,' he joked. An accomplished flatterer, he soon captivated the very human Victoria, with his quiet manner and good humour – 'his voice is low and soft', she observed. He told her, 'I feel bound to Your Majesty for ever', adding that no one could spend a few days with herself and Albert without succumbing to the charm of 'the happiest of families'. In the fascinated queen's view, he possessed 'indomitable courage, unflinching firmness of purpose, self-reliance, perseverance, and great secrecy; to this should be added great reliance on what he calls his *Star*.' Her analysis was not far from the truth.

In the evening there was a state banquet, and then a ball in the Waterloo Gallery – tactfully renamed for the evening. Victoria danced happily with 'the nephew of our great enemy, the emperor, now my most firm ally . . . '. She grew enchanted by the empress, 'so gentle, graceful and kind, and so modest and retiring'. She had already endeared herself by playing with the royal children and 'talked away to me with Spanish liveliness.' Victoria noted that Albert liked and admired Eugénie in a way he did very few women.

Next day the royal family took their guests to London, where they stayed at Buckingham Palace. Driving through wildly cheering crowds, the emperor and empress lunched at the Guildhall with the Lord Mayor, and went to the opera in the evening, the imperial anthem 'Partant pour la Syrie', being played with real enthusiasm on both occasions. Everybody raved about Eugénie except for Benjamin Disraeli, who disliked both her looks ('Chinese eyes') and her manner ('too natural for a sovereign'). Victoria and Albert saw them off at the station when they left for France on 21 April. The fourteen-year-old Princess Royal, who had become devoted to the empress, wept when they said goodbye; the queen herself had moist

Eugénie

eyes. After the carriage door had been shut, Napoleon reopened it and jumped out in tears, flinging his arms around Victoria and kissing her on both cheeks.

The French were delighted by the visit's success. 'The emperor and empress returned from London today', Hübner noted sourly. 'People say they are intoxicated by the tremendous welcome they received from John Bull.' Napoleon was convinced the Anglo-French alliance would continue and that he had overthrown the anti-French peace settlement of 1815.

Pianori's attempt at assassination in May brought home to the emperor that the Second Empire depended entirely on his survival and he abandoned any thought of visiting the Crimea. It meant leaving Plon-Plon in charge and the Prince was unreliable. The war dragged on.

VICTORIA AND ALBERT IN PARIS

On 18 August – the feast day of St Helena, Comte Horace de Viel Castel observed – Queen Victoria and Prince Albert sailed into Boulogne, with the Prince of Wales and the Princess Royal. They were met by the emperor who rode with them to the station where they boarded a train for Paris. Arriving when it was nearly dark at the Gare de Strasbourg (now Gare de l'Est), the royal party drove in six carriages (the sovereigns with the Princess Royal in the first, the fourteen-year-old Prince of Wales with Plon-Plon in the second), along the boulevards and the Champs Elysée, across the Bois de Boulogne, to the lovely château of Saint-Cloud in the countryside. Troops lined the entire route. A crowd 800,000 strong, some standing on the rooftops, cheered them in the dusk, waving banners with greetings in English. The empress was waiting for them at Saint-Cloud, where their rooms were hung with Gobelins tapestries and Lyons silks, furnished with the finest Louis XV or Louis XVI cabinets, with Flemish or Venetian old masters.

The Goncourt brothers relate maliciously how, anxious to outshine Windsor Castle and Buckingham Palace, Eugénie had borrowed some of the items from the Louvre, and had done the same thing at the Tuileries. Since the queen had listed the pictures she hoped to see at the Louvre, she was astonished to find them in her hostess's palaces. But such details could not spoil the visit. 'Nothing, no description, can give you any idea of what Paris has looked like for the past week', Viel Castel wrote afterwards. 'Streets and boulevards were a forest of banners with triumphal arches everywhere, all bearing the arms or monograms of the British and French sovereigns.'

'I am DELIGHTED, ENCHANTED, AMUSED and INTERESTED', Victoria wrote in her diary. 'The Emperor has done wonders for Paris.' With Albert, she inspected and admired an international exhibition that displayed exhibits from every European and American country – even from Russia despite the war, Russian businessmen having been given safe conducts. There were glittering balls at the Tuileries and the Hôtel de Ville, and a visit to the Conciergerie where the emperor had been imprisoned. There was an evening when by torchlight during a thunderstorm the royal family saw Napoleon I's tomb at the Invalides. The queen told her son to kneel down, although privately she thought the shrine looked like a swimming bath. When she and Albert went to the Opéra, at their departure the audience sang 'God save the Queen', gave three cheers and then sang 'God save the Queen' again.

Napoleon drove the Prince of Wales through Paris in a dog-cart, pointing out the sights. 'I wish I were your son', sighed the future Edward VII, remembering his stern existence at home. It was the start of his lifelong love of France.

The climax was a ball in the Galerie des Glaces at Versailles, the 'Hall of Mirrors', which had not seen such splendour since 1789 – understandably, as Eugénie had chosen an eighteenth-century print for its inspiration, '*Une fête sous Louis Quinze*'. She was waiting to welcome Victoria, looking, in her guest's opinion, 'like a fairy-queen or nymph'. The empress stood at the top of the great marble staircase, which was covered with a purple carpet, its balustrades almost concealed by masses of orchids, ferns and mosses, and lined by Cent Gardes. Her white dress was thickly sewn with diamonds and bunches of green grass, while there were more diamonds at her waist and in her hair.

At ten o'clock sharp the gardens were suddenly lit by rockets and Chinese candles, then 'a million fireworks' painted Windsor Castle in the night sky, after which Napoleon and Victoria, Albert and Eugénie, opened the ball. There was little dancing, people preferring to admire the magnificent decorations in the palace and the park. However, the emperor insisted on waltzing with the Princess Royal. Even Viel Castel agreed that the evening had been 'beyond all praise'.

The nine days went by, more and more amiably, the emperor and Prince Albert even singing duets in German. 'His German is perfect', commented the queen approvingly. Throughout, Napoleon was, as the foreign secretary Lord Clarendon put it, 'making love' to Victoria. He took her for a long walk in the park at Saint-Cloud, during which they discussed European politics with the utmost frankness and he paid her some highly agreeable compliments. 'Isn't it odd, Lord Clarendon', she confided later, 'the emperor remembers every dress he has seen me in.' She was in ecstasies over his tact, his dignity, his modesty. 'I know very few people in whom I feel so ready to confide or to speak to so frankly. I felt, I can't quite explain it, so safe with him.'

The friendship between Eugénie and the queen grew still stronger. She confessed to Victoria that she was pregnant and that, despite two previous miscarriages, she expected to bear a child. The queen was full of sympathy and useful advice. As the end of the visit approached, both the Prince of Wales and the Princess Royal, who had begun to worship the empress, begged her to ask their mother to let them stay for a few days longer in Paris.

The emperor took the royal family out to their yacht in his barge when they left from Boulogne on 27 August. Victoria's visit had been no less of a dazzling success than his own to England. 'Throughout her stay the celebrations have been superb,' Viel Castel admitted – despite observing, when Plon-Plon received the Order of the Bath, 'the Queen would have done better to give him a cake of Windsor soap'.

Moreover, the visit made the French forget, if only for a little while, the war in the Crimea. Early in September, however, their troops finally stormed the Malakhov, the key fort to Sevastopol, which surrendered – and then it was only a matter of time before Russia gave in. When the Imperial Guard returned and Napoleon rode at their head, the Parisians threw flowers beneath his horse's feet, and the subsequent peace conference in Paris made it seem that France was once again the leading power in Europe. Yet both Victoria's visit and victory in the Crimea would turn out to be surprisingly hollow triumphs.

The emperor, said General Fleury, was deeply impressed by the queen's 'knowledge of the politics of all Europe and by the obviously very active part she took in the British government's foreign policy'. Poor Napoleon did not realise that however many state papers she read, and however much she liked 'my nearest and dearest ally', she had little influence. Now that Russia had been kept out of the Mediterranean, England lost interest in a French alliance that could easily mean being dragged into another war.

All that survived was the friendship between Eugénie and Victoria. When the imperial couple spent four days at Osborne in August 1857, Victoria told Lord Clarendon that she would have liked them to stay much longer, as she felt 'none of the *gêne* of royalty in the society of friends like them'. Ironically, only a few years before, the queen's advisers had been telling her that the empress was a 'Spanish adventuress', yet during the state visits the two women had found a surprising amount in common. They would meet again only occasionally and very briefly until 1870. However, they remained genuinely devoted friends for the rest of their long lives.

THREE

'Queen Crinoline'

A SON AND HEIR

During the early years Eugénie did not find much time for politics, so busy being a hostess and trying to bear a child, with entertaining and setting the fashion. Parisians called her '*La Reine Crinoline*'.

She knew that the régime's survival depended on her having a son. Plon-Plon was a most unsatisfactory heir, while a daughter could not inherit the throne. Her attitude to sexual matters did not make life easy for her. 'Physical love, what a filthy business '*quelle saleté*', she complained to Cecile Delessert, after her honeymoon. 'Why do men think of nothing else?'

Once, only half-joking, the empress said men were 'just animals, bears walking on their hind-legs and opening their mouths to frighten poor little women. They don't bite, however. They simply rattle their chains. Then they dance. Then they give in. Then they pay the bills.' Often she regarded them as semi-human. Yet she developed an eye for a good-looking one, horrifying Archduke Maximilian by saying she had seen 'a delicious sailor' when out driving. 'If I wasn't a believer, I would have taken only too many lovers,' she told Émile Ollivier in 1867. 'Love is the only good thing there is.' Ollivier comments in his journal, 'She's never had affairs, only flirtations . . . I've seen her at a ball, letting herself be kissed by a man.'

On the other hand she admired beauty in women and to some extent chose her ladies for their good looks, sometimes having their portraits painted. Once she gave a dinner party for the emperor at which the guests were the twenty most beautiful women in Paris. Too much should not be read into this, however – the sapphist Ethel Smyth, who knew her well in old age, tells us 'she had no sensuality in her nature'.

A pre-Freudian biographer, Roger Sencourt, argues eloquently that Eugénie belonged to a specific type, and that 'women (or men) who have this Platonic enjoyment of the beauty of their own sex, if they marry, marry those who gratify their ambitions and not their senses . . . . It explains both her disgust with, and her long loyalty to the first man she had loved.' In Sencourt's view it explains, too, her combination of excitability and hot temper with kind-heartedness and generosity.

After two miscarriages, which had made her thoroughly miserable, when Eugénie found herself pregnant again in June 1855, she only saved the child by going to Eaux-Bonnes. 'If I had left it longer, I would not have been able to have children at all', she confided to Paca. She went into labour at about midnight on 14 March. Close members of the imperial family were asked to witness the birth. Plon-Plon took his revenge. 'The Prince stood in the doorway wearing his eye-glass, coolly examining the unfortunate woman who, having thrown almost everything off in her convulsions, was practically naked,' Princess Bacciochi recalled. 'The Prince said, "How can you call a woman pretty with legs like that."'

After twenty-two hours, Eugénie gave birth early on the morning of 16 March. She almost died. Barely articulate, the emperor suddenly cried, 'Save the empress!' and the doctor used forceps to extract her child. Later, the doctor said he had never seen such suffering. It was a boy. Overjoyed, Napoleon rushed out of the room in tears and embraced the first five people he saw, then pulled himself together, muttering, 'I can't kiss you all!' As dawn broke, cannon at the Invalides fired a 101-gun salute. On the same day, the emperor amnestied all political prisoners. No longer heir, Plon-Plon refused to attend the private christening, but Mathilde smoothly congratulated the empress on saving the dynasty. Two days later, when market women from Les Halles brought flowers to the Tuileries, Napoleon let them see the baby. Then the diplomatic corps solemnly filed past the cradle, Hübner noting that he had blue eyes and was wearing the red sash of the Légion d'honneur. Cardinal Patrizzi arrived from Rome bringing the Golden Rose – twenty-three gold roses in a gold vase – the highest honour the papacy could give to a woman.

89

LonLou born March *Eugénie* 16, 1856

No SEX ever again

There was more rejoicing when peace was signed with Russia on 30 March, marked by a splendid military parade. 'Returning to the Louvre at about one in the morning, I met processions of workers in the streets and on the boulevards, carrying torches and cheering the emperor and peace', records Viel Castel. 'Who would have recognised the France of 1848?' Yet there were shadows. Dr Fergusson, one of Queen Victoria's physicians, had examined Napoleon and found signs of premature ageing. As for Eugénie, she was unable to walk or even stand until the end of May – doctors warned that another child would kill her and that she must never sleep with her husband again.

The Prince Imperial's formal christening by Cardinal Patrizzi took place at Notre Dame on 14 June. The child was named Napoleon Eugène Louis Jean Joseph, Pope Pius IX being the boy's godfather. (His parents called him 'Lou-Lou' when he was very small, then 'Louis'.) Hübner said he had never seen a more beautiful service, but Lord Cowley thought it more theatrical than religious, adding that the crowds showed little enthusiasm. Even so, Thomas Couture's painting of the occasion was one of the most successful official pictures to emerge from the Second Empire.

The child was given a formidable nanny, Miss Shaw, chosen because she was English, while the abbé Deguerry, curé of the Madeleine – afterwards murdered by the Communards – gave him religious instruction. He was made a grenadier of the Imperial Guard when only eight months old and issued with a soldier's red pay book. A photograph taken when he was five shows him proudly wearing a grenadier's bearskin. His first proper tutor was M. Monnier.

For a time M. Lévy of the College de Vanves came to the Tuileries every day, bringing a group of his boys so that the prince could study with them. At the end of each week Lévy announced the class's marks, always beginning, 'First, His Imperial Highness the Prince Imperial' – then taking another boy aside, he would whisper 'You were first, the prince came fifteenth.' All this changed in 1867 when General Frossard (a former *polytechnicien*) became his 'governor' and the empress appointed Augustin Filon as his tutor, on the recommendation of Victor Duruy. He was assisted by Ernest

Lavisse who taught the boy history. Augustin Filon, as loyal as he was gifted, turned out to be an excellent choice.

Eugénie wanted her son brought up with the icy dignity of a Spanish duke, approving highly of Carpeaux's patrician statue of him with his dog Nero, which was exhibited in 1865. When she was away, however, 'Lou-Lou' played games like hide-and-seek with other small boys all over the Tuileries, making what his father called 'a hellish noise'. Yet if she rebuked the emperor for not stopping him, he would answer, 'Why spoil his happiest years?' Father and son enjoyed playing together with the model railway in the park at Saint-Cloud. The child picked up slang from his friends; when his mother told him off, he replied 'You speak French quite well for a foreigner, Mamma, but you don't really understand our language.'

Everybody liked the little boy, even the crusty Mérimée. So too, despite herself, did Princesse Mathilde, who joyfully quoted him – '*Maman* has already said some silly things [*bêtises*] today.' – and gave him one of the new bicycles as a birthday present.

There were more implications for Eugénie than simply bearing an heir, however; she had made real the Bonapartes' claim to be a dynasty as well as saviours of the Revolution, the 'fourth dynasty', who ruled in succession to Capetians, Valois and Bourbons. Napoleon III ordered a tomb at Saint-Denis, so that he would lie among the old kings, and spoke of his son as *L'Enfant de France* – the term for a royal child during the *ancien régime*. Above all, under the imperial constitution, Eugénie would now become regent when her husband was away on campaign or should he die before 'Lou-Lou' came of age.

THE MOTHER AND THE GRANDMOTHER

Throughout changes in her life that inevitably resulted from marrying a ruling sovereign, Eugénie remained devoted to her mother and sister. Nobody could ever take their place as the confidantes of this deeply reserved woman. If for obvious reasons it was quite unthinkable that Doña Maria Manuela should stay in Paris, Paca was another matter, although there was plenty to keep her in Spain. Since she could not see them, Eugénie wrote often, long and revealing letters still preserved in the Alba family archives.

Her mother had had to leave Paris six weeks after Eugénie's wedding, with the utmost reluctance. 'I have two incurable faults, which will soon be found out,' she had admitted before the marriage, 'I am a foreigner and I am a mother-in-law.' She might have added a third, that she was known all over Europe as a compulsive intriguer – her old friend Lord Clarendon warned her bluntly that she would find it difficult to stay in her son-in-law's capital. Even so, she obviously hoped to remain at her daughter's side. However, the emperor soon insisted that she must leave. He paid her off handsomely (if so indelicate an expression may be used) through three secret bank accounts, so that she went back to Spain even richer than before. Despite joking bravely about her enforced departure, she was resentful and once or twice in her letters to Mérimée refers slightingly to Napoleon as 'Don Louis' or 'Don Isidore'.

Maria Manuela found an impeccable excuse for returning to France with Paca in the late autumn of 1855, however, which was to be present at her grandchild's birth. She stayed in the Albas' great house in Paris (long since demolished), just off the Champs Elysée and near today's rue Lincoln. This was the former Hotel de Lauriston, which Eugénie had purchased for them from the Lauriston family and then refurbished luxuriously at her own expense. Republicans grumbled sourly that the empress was plundering the nation's coffers for the sake of her relations.

After this Maria Manuela came back fairly regularly, although only for comparatively short visits. Brief as they were, she was seen as something of a joke by the Parisians, on account of her rather too splendid carriages, her stately, self-conscious promenades down the Champs Elysées accompanied by her maid and footman, and her excessively lavish parties in the 'Hôtel Alba' – which were invariably full of handsome male guests, even if they always included the indispensable Prosper Mérimée.

All the same, Maria Manuela was sufficiently nervous of her son-in-law to ration her visits to the Tuileries. Taking her cue from the Albas, she declined any special treatment, refusing to sit on red velvet chairs near the imperial couple, unlike Plon-Plon and Mathilde.

Occasionally she was invited to stay at Biarritz, and sometimes Fontainebleau or – more rarely – to the *séries* at Compiègne.

However, Doña Maria Manuela found life at home in Spain far from disagreeable. Her position as mother of both the empress of the French and the Duchess of Alba made her one of the indisputable leaders of Madrid society, and her receptions at Casa Ariza and Carabanchel were attended with more enthusiasm than ever. Queen Isabella appointed her honorary Camera Mayor, which gave her considerable influence at court without any of the irksome duties of a mistress of the robes. Hers had been the sort of beauty that lasts, so that well into her seventies, tall, dignified and exquisitely dressed, she remained a splendid-looking woman.

Eventually, however, she lost the sight of her flashing dark eyes. 'When my mother realised she was going blind, she made almost unbelievable efforts to conceal it, not just from strangers but even from herself', Eugénie told Filon. 'She would insist on finding her own way, besides telling others where they should go, so that she was always knocking over furniture, hurting herself against the walls she could not see and trying to walk through closed doors. It was simply impossible for her to acknowledge that she was beaten by a physical weakness.'

In many ways Paca had been altogether different from her mother and sister, in both looks and temperament, although despite harsher features she possessed a certain family resemblance to Eugénie. A thin brunette, she had always seemed frail and did not share their iron health. Everybody had liked her for her friendliness and sense of humour. Her son Jacobo – 'James' – and her daughters Maria and Louise (the future duchesses of Tamames and Medinacoeli) spent a good deal of time in Paris, where they were constantly at the Tuileries with their aunt.

Mme Carette had never seen Paca, who died before her appointment as a lady-in-waiting, but she had met many people who knew her. She describes her as 'an adorable woman . . . for the empress such a sister really was the unfailingly affectionate comrade, the ultimate confidante and faithful heart which every human being needs during the trials of life.' Gushingly expressed as this may be, it appears to have been the truth.

Paca had been unable to come to Paris as often as she would have liked because of her husband Jacobo's demanding position in Spain and his enormous estates, in whose management he took a very serious interest. Although he had once broken her heart, by now Jacobo was Eugénie's trusted friend, and he remained one as a widower. At her request, he lent her the letters between his ancestor, the great third Duke of Alba, and King Philip II – until her death she continued to be fascinated by Spanish history.

Despite everything that had happened, the bond between mother and daughter stayed as strong as ever, particularly after the loss of Paca – even if sometimes Eugénie still laughed at Doña Maria Manuela. Although she would never admit it, what made the bond so strong was that, as empress, she never really felt at ease with more than one or two Frenchwomen, however fond she may have been of her ladies.

A good deal of her remained Spanish, however much she tried to hide it. In April 1860 Cowley wrote to Lord John Russell that Eugénie had asked him if the British ambassador at Madrid could help 'friends and relations' who were in trouble after a Carlist plot. She would not do so herself, clearly anxious not to remind her French subjects of these friends and relations in Spain.

EUGENIE AS DECORATOR

In the Duc de Morny's *La corde sensible ou les Dadas favoris*, a revue performed at Compiègne in 1862, one of the characters gives advice on how to flatter the empress. 'It's no use telling her she's beautiful, amusing or good', he explains. 'What you must do is say is that no decorator can rival her at choosing furniture, picking materials and creating a drawing room.' It was one of her passions. Rejecting the fashionable 'Henri II renaissance' in favour of rococo, she evolved her own special style.

Her decoration at the Tuileries went up in flames in 1871, but you can still catch glimpses of it in paintings and memoirs. She had had a daunting task, since after being constantly adapted for centuries the palace was a rabbit warren, with endless, windowless corridors lit even in daylight by smoking oil lamps that made them unbearably hot and stuffy. There was no running water, everyone washing from jugs. By 1860, however, comfortable new apartments had been completed. Eugénie's were on the first floor.

The first of her drawing-rooms was the *salon vert*, whose walls had leafy green friezes on a green background, with green parrots and woodpeckers over the doors, dominated by a vast mirror reflecting the gardens. The waiting-room, the *salon rose*, was hung in rose silk, its ceiling painted by Chaplin with a *Triumph of Flora*, Flora being a portrait of the empress. Guests were received in the *salon bleu* where scallop-shaped blue pelmets matched the chairs' blue needlework and small blinds of dark blue gauze could be drawn over the windows to soften the light. Plaster medallions on the walls held portraits of her ladies. The three rooms were lit by wax candles in rock-crystal chandeliers, and filled with clocks, bronzes and vases of old Sèvres or lapis-lazuli, while the furniture was mostly from the eighteenth century, much of it marquetried, with gilt armchairs.

A painting of Eugénie's private salon by Giuseppe Castiglione shows a drawing-room and study joined by a curtained arch, with long windows looking out onto the Tuileries gardens. The high walls are covered in green silk, the draped curtains and furniture in red velvet, and the mahogany wainscot, window-frames and doors are picked out in gilt. In the drawing-room, on the eighteenth-century porphyry fireplace stands an ornate oromolu clock of the same period, topped by Cupid and Psyche in white marble, which is flanked by two Chinese bronze lamps. On the walls hang small landscapes and portraits of the emperor, Paca, Anna Murat and the dauphin. The furniture includes a buttoned sofa, a Chinese screen of crystal and a Louis XVI cabinet on which there is a bust of Marie-Antoinette, while the carpet is a red Savonnerie. Through the arch, flanked by two tall red vases on gilt stands, what may have been Marie-Antoinette's writing table can be glimpsed in the study.

There are masses of flowers in the big vases and an immense jardinière. Eugénie was fond of orchids from China, India or Mexico, forced in the Tuileries' hot-houses, but she loved simple flowers too – roses, carnations, geraniums – while she had a passion for ivy. 'Her writing table was fenced off by a crystal screen over which graceful climbing plants hung in green festoons, making her look as if she was in some tropical forest', Augustin Filon tells us.

Her son played in her study, her husband coming to smoke his eternal cigarettes. Nobody else was allowed to smoke here, however, since she had developed a loathing for tobacco and could generally smell it at 25 metres. She seldom visited him in his own stiflingly overheated rooms on the floor above, partly because they stank of nicotine – whenever she wanted to see the emperor of the French, she would bang a gong at the foot of his staircase.

Eugénie always sat in a low armchair with the light behind her, near the door and next to the fireplace, resting her feet on a stool, a green silk screen protecting her complexion from the heat. At her left, by the fire, was an ebonised worktable of several tiers strewn with papers that served as her desk – although generally she wrote letters on her knees, very fast, in a large, neat hand – while at her right was a revolving bookcase.

Loliée claims that she never read books, but left them lying around to give the impression of wide reading. In reality, she read voraciously, keeping a commonplace book that ran into many leather-bound volumes kept in a special bookcase. Filon, who unlike Loliée, had actually visited her study, tells us the entries that occurred most frequently in the volumes were taken from Bossuet, Châteaubriand, Lamartine, de Maistre, Victor Cousin and Donoso Cortés. Besides reading, she had what almost amounted to a mania for filing documents in cabinets which stood in the study – in those days filing meant tying letters in bundles with coloured tape and then docketing them with handwritten slips.

The empress's bedroom was dominated by an uncomfortable-looking state bed on a raised platform and by a commode on which stood the Golden Rose – Pepa always made the sign of the cross when passing it on her way to the dressing-room. There was an oratory next door, where she heard Mass on weekdays.

The best place to see Eugénie's '*Louis XVI-Impératrice*' style is at Compiègne, where some of her interiors have been brilliantly re-created. The Third Republic had tried to banish all trace of the Second Empire, dispersing its furniture, even its carpets, to ministries or embassies. Since the 1950s, however, some of the empress's furniture has been reassembled here, while the fabrics which she used have been reproduced from samples still possessed by the Mobilier National (formerly Mobilier Impérial), the state furnishers.

Her style was a blend of the *ancien régime* with comfort. Nostalgia for the days before 1789 was already widespread, and inspired by her heroine Marie-Antoinette she pioneered a revival of interest in eighteenth-century furniture – acquiring as much of the queen's as she could, made by such ébénistes as Weisweiler, Riesner, Oeben and Carlin, besides commissioning copies. With this, she mixed cosily upholstered nineteenth-century sofas and *confortables* (easy-chairs) together with little gilt or ebonised Italian chairs from Chiavari, all carefully arranged to encourage conversation.

The Salon de Musique gives a particularly good idea of the style. Its panelling is hung with an eighteenth-century Gobelins tapestry and a nineteenth century one from Beauvais, while the ornaments include plenty of Sèvres and Chinese porcelain. Two magnificent red lacquer cabinets (incorporating Chinese panels of about 1775) are set off by Marie-Antoinette's armchairs from Saint-Cloud in red silk, supplemented by a buttoned *canapé* (sofa) and *confortables*, likewise in red silk.

Eugénie remodelled the Salon de Réception, once Louis XVI's bedchamber, adding extra pier-glasses as well as more elaborate plasterwork and gilding. What look like Louis XV tables and chairs are copies by Selme from 1859, while the floral upholstery and yellow damask curtains were supplied by Beauvais. The 'conversational' chairs are in a yellow damask that matches the curtains.

Her only totally new room is the Galerie Natoire, built in 1858 as a covered way to the palace theatre. An architectural pastiche in the Louis XVI manner, it is hung with six paintings by Natoire (from the 1740s) of Don Quixote's adventures, which began as designs for a set of tapestries.

One comes very close to Eugénie in these imaginatively restored rooms at Compiègne. All that is missing is the astonishing profusion of heavy-scented flowers, both hothouse and native, that filled them winter and summer alike.

The style can also be seen at Fontainebleau, whose tiny theatre, rebuilt and enlarged in 1857, echoes Marie-Antoinette's theatre at

Versailles. Eugénie covered it entirely in a pale gold silk known as 'bouton d'or'. What is even more striking is how she displayed her collection of oriental art. Starting with a wedding gift from the emperor (two Chinese vases of beaten gold), this eventually included the French army's loot from the Summer Palace at Peking, together with the presents from Siam and Japanese porcelain bought from Morny's executors. Eugénie came to Fontainebleau early in April 1863 in order to inspect progress on building her *Salon Chinois*, after discussing furnishings at the Garde-Meuble at Paris, returning in July to supervise the collection's installation.

The Chinese Salon is approached through an ante-chamber that contains the larger Siamese presents, such as the pagoda. Looking onto the lake, the Salon's walls are covered with carved panels of Chinese design while three great ironwood cabinets display the smaller pieces of ivory, jade and goldwork. Huge candelabra and a gigantic incense burner, great Chinese vases and two mighty Dogs of Fo contrast with Cordier's statue of an Arab woman, a Sèvres jardinière and portraits of Louis XV and his queen. (Winterhalter's painting of the empress among her ladies hung here too, but is now at Compiègne.) Six sofas in striped green silk make it habitable – there is a mechanical piano in case the court should wish to dance. A smaller room, opening off the Salon, displays the bulk of the collection – jade, rock crystal and porcelain, ivories, bronzes and cloisonné enamels. 'Anyone except Eugénie might so easily have turned the room into a kind of museum', comments Filon, who had known it well. 'But she created what you might call a corner of the abode of "The Son of Heaven".'

Entered through an ante-chamber hung with Chinese papers in lacquered frames, her study here (still being restored), was no less oriental, with lacquered panels and Chinese cabinets, lit by a Chinese lantern. Leather armchairs gave the room a masculine appearance, very unlike her study at the Tuileries.

At Fontainebleau Eugénie showed herself even more imaginative than King George IV had been at Brighton. Few contemporary decorators knew how to make such inspired use of the plunder that was flooding in from the East. The restoration of the Salon Chinois in 2000 was a revelation.

AN EMPRESS DRESSES

No one had set the fashion in France since the empress Josephine. Marie-Louise had been too young to make much impression, while Louis-Philippe's queen Marie-Amélie and his daughter-in-law, the Duchesse d'Orléans, were frumps. Eugénie succeeded brilliantly, her clothes being copied throughout Europe and across the Atlantic, even in the sultan of Turkey's harem.

Initially, she was not very interested in smart clothes, but was forced to dress up for her countless official engagements. Ideally, she preferred to wear a plain dress of wool or faille (cheap silk) which was what most women wore every day; driving through Paris, often she merely put a smart cloak over her dress. She once said she had never spent more than 1,500 francs on a gown. When Princess Metternich first met her, she was wearing a black skirt and a red flannel shirt with a black leather belt. Instead of lounging in a dressing-gown, for years she did without one, dressing as soon as she rose, until finally Mme Carette bought her a ready-made red flannel wrapper for 84 francs at one of the new department stores near the Louvre.

Eugénie's first triumph was to popularise the crinoline. Invented in 1856, the 'cage-crinoline' was a bell-shaped petticoat stiffened with hoops of steel wire that replaced the petticoats previously used to create width. 'Crinolinomania' conquered France, Britain and the United States within months. According to *Punch*, 'Dr Punch has ample grounds for the belief that the persons first affected were the ladies attached to the Imperial court; and that the symptoms of the mania were primarily betrayed by the young and lovely empress.' In a letter of 1856 Ernest Barthez (the Prince Imperial's doctor) said that if the emperor teased Eugénie about her 'cage', she told him she didn't know how she had ever managed to do without one – the doctor thought she liked it because she could dispense with layers of petticoats and use her legs.

A boon in hot weather, the crinoline gave ladies a certain stateliness while enabling them to walk with a gliding motion that had definite sexual allure. (Significantly, the last women to discard the cage after it went out of fashion were expensive prostitutes.)

Despite its drawbacks – entering a carriage or even just sitting down needed great skill, so that travelling was a nightmare – the cage crinoline remained indispensable for over a decade.

One can gain an idea of how completely women's clothes differed from today's by imagining how Eugénie began her morning at the Tuileries during the 1850s. She entered her dressing-room to wash, 'a vast room' according to Mme Carette. Besides tall pier-glasses on the walls that reflected each other and a cheval glass, its main features were a washstand with jug and basin (a hip-bath underneath) and a dressing-table draped in lace over a blue silk cloth. On the table stood Queen Hortense's silver-gilt dressing-case, flanked by scent bottles and by pots that contained rice powder for her white complexion, kohl for a line beneath lower her eyelashes and rouge for the lobes of her ears. As she washed, four dummies descended on a lift through a trapdoor in the ceiling from the wardrobes overhead, in response to orders screamed by Pepa down a speaking-tube. The dummies were dressed in the four outfits the empress would wear that day – the system gave rise to rumours that she was dressed in a single movement, by a machine like a candle-snuffer.

First, Eugénie stepped into her 'pantaloons', long drawers that opened down the middle and fastened with a drawstring, to enable the wearer to use a chamberpot without undressing. Then she slipped into a silk under-petticoat, before her maids – supervised by bad-tempered little Pepa – laced up a corset of woven horsehair stiffened with whalebone to hold her breasts in a tight, narrow-waisted bodice. Next the maids put on silk stockings and pointed boots of glacé kid, varnished leather or embroidered satin, tying garters above the knee and buttoning the boots' cloth sides with a special hook – her feet were no bigger than a child's. A ballooning petticoat went on, reinforced with horsehair and hoops of split cane. (Although known as a 'crinoline', this was not the 'cage'.) Finally, with the aid of pulleys the maids lowered on her cage, another silk petticoat and dress itself, from the tall stand onto which they had been moved from a dummy.

She wore day dresses of wool or poplin, of silk, velvet or plush, in every colour of the rainbow, plain or patterned. Among them was the new English mauve called 'Perkins's Purple' (since it suited her violet eyes), made with a recently invented aniline dye, and 'Magenta', named after the French victory, which was another new aniline dye. She was fond of pastel shades such as dove grey, cream or buttercup yellow, because they had been favourites of Marie-Antoinette. Cashmere or Paisley shawls took the place of coats, while long, buttoned gloves of soft leather or silk, kept in flat boxes and extended with stretchers, reached halfway up her arms.

Demure, face-framing bonnets had held sway for sixty years, tied under the chin by a bow and with a frill behind, but she liked a broad-brimmed straw hat when relaxing in the summer. She always wore her own new hairstyle '*à l'Impératrice*', with her hair pulled back (over round pads) from a central parting so as to reveal her ears, instead of combing it down flat on either side of her face or letting it hang in ringlets.

Unless she was at Biarritz, the empress changed her clothes several times a day, and never wore a formal gown more than once. Every six months she gave the discarded dresses to her ladies, who sold them for a high price – often to Americans since there was a good market in New York where they were hired out – and at least one imperial gown appeared on the stage of a Paris theatre.

During the 1850s her dressmakers were Mmes Vignon and Palmyre, Mme Félicie made her shawls and cloaks, and Mme Lebel or Mme Virot supplied her bonnets. Her riding habits came from Henry Creed, her husband's English tailor who had a branch in Paris. In 1860 she began to order her morning dresses from the newly established Mme Laferrière.

Today Second Empire clothes may seem excessively elaborate. Mme Carette tells us that even simple dresses were hard to wear, requiring an upright bearing which had to be taught in childhood, by such instruments of torture as backboards. Yet the men of the time loved them. 'There is an acme of dressing, just as there is of genius', sighed the philosopher-historian Hippolyte Taine in 1867. 'A perfect toilette is worthy of a poem. Taste and judgement are needed in placing and contrasting each ribbon or silk rose on soft, silvery satin, on palest mauve, against the softness of sweet colours made sweeter still by layers of lace, tulle flounces and billowing frill

. . . It is all the poetry left to us, and how women are aware of it!' (Admittedly Taine had developed some very odd theories – he believed that Englishwomen possessed exceptionally large feet, evolved to cope with the marshy, rain-sodden soil of *'perfide Angleterre'*.)

The French crown jewels, unseen since 1830 because Louis-Philippe would not let his consort wear them for fear display might harm his bourgeois image, consisted of gems bought by Napoleon I and the restored Bourbons, together with those of the Orleans family. Among the few from before 1789 were some magnificent pear-shaped diamond earrings, which were doubly precious to Eugénie because they had belonged to Marie-Antoinette. She often wore the great Regent diamond, an Orleans heirloom, on her breast. The largest of the crown diamonds was yellow, 'as big as a nut' and set in smaller white diamonds in a comb-like ornament, but she stopped wearing this after learning its history. Swallowed by one of the mob during the sacking of the Tuileries in 1848, it had perforated his intestines and was recovered in the subsequent autopsy. 'It's a daring little rascal who has plumbed the very lowest depths of society', joked the emperor.

Eugénie had many diamonds reset. Impressed by the work of such jewellers as Oscar Massin and Lemonnier, she preferred a naturalist style – currant-leaves, flowers or ears of corn – for her tiaras, sprays and shoulder knots, her crescents and aigrets. In 1855 she brought a reliquary cross from Bapst, in 1867 a spray of lilac blossom from Massin. Her favourite piece, however, was a clover-leaf in emeralds set with diamond dew – Napoleon's first gift to her. At the Tuileries ball for the Carnival of 1863, when she went as a Venetian *dogaressa*, Mrs Moulton says that she was 'literally *cuirassée* in diamonds and glittered like a sun-goddess. Her skirt of black velvet over a robe of scarlet satin was caught up by clusters of diamond brooches.'

Sometimes Eugénie wore a huge dog-collar of pearls, for which she had a passion, in particular for the rare black pearls from Mexico. Until then, black pearls had not been much prized, but when her interest became widely known their price soon overtook that paid for the finest white ones.

102

She liked to give presents of jewellery; Lillie Moulton, for example, received a bracelet of large rubies and diamonds set in three heavy gold coils, with Eugénie's name and the date engraved inside. During her visit to England in 1855 she gave the young Princess Royal, in Queen Victoria's words, her own 'beautiful watch of rubies and diamonds and a beautiful little chain, seal and watch-key . . . Vicky was in ecstasies.'

MR WORTH AND FASHION

When, in the 1860s, the dashing Princess Metternich danced at one of the great Tuileries balls wearing a startlingly beautiful dress of white tulle sequined with silver, an entirely new material that was sewn with fresh daisies, Eugénie asked her who had made it. 'An Englishman, madame, a rising star,' answered Pauline. 'What is his name, pray?' 'Worth, madame.' 'Such a star should have some satelites,' said the empress. 'Tell him to come and see me at ten o'clock tomorrow morning.'

When the 'man-milliner' (a term coined by Charles Dickens) arrived at the Tuileries, as a test Eugénie asked him to make a ballgown, and to choose the material and style. He returned the same day with a dress of beige brocade. She sniffed, saying, 'I hate brocade – it looks like curtain material.' The emperor came in and Worth told him that wearing brocades would please the silk-weavers of Lyons, notorious republicans. Napoleon and Eugénie took the point. Soon Worth became dressmaker to the empress, and by the end of the year his dresses were being ordered in London and New York.

Eugénie had reason to patronise Worth and ignore his being a man – until now male couturiers had been unknown. He measured and cut his patterns with such skill that a dress needed only one fitting instead of half a dozen. Employing teams of seamstresses (who toiled twelve hours a day, six days a week), later supplemented by the new sewing machines, he delivered a garment to the Tuileries the morning after Eugénie had ordered it, faster in an emergency – once he made her a dress in under four hours. His materials – tulles and muslins woven with fine silver or gold wire, failles, chiffons and taffetas, satins, velvets and brocades, laces and embroideries – all save the lace specially manufactured for him at Lyons – were exquisite, his design and workmanship superb. He always ensured that no one else anticipated what the empress would wear. She ordered hundreds of outfits from him, because he knew what would suit her.

The magic of these marvellous dresses, enhanced by the *frou-frou* of silk petticoats and the gleam of wonderful jewellery, is almost impossible to imagine today. ('We heard the rustle of silk and satin, the soft jangle of swinging bracelets and chains', Filon recalls, remembering a door opening on a certain evening at Compiègne. 'It was the empress.') Only Winterhalter can give us a faint inkling, as he does in his portraits, especially in those of the Duchesse de Morny, Princess Rimsky-Korsakov and Princess Metternich, transformed into a beauty.

Worth was more than a gifted dress designer. In a few years he changed the way in which women of even modest means dressed throughout the world. In 1863 at Eugénie's request he designed a 'walking crinoline' with skirts 10 centimetres shorter than usual so that she could go for country walks without getting muddy. She made her ladies wear the skirts first, to prepare public opinion, then wore them herself. Five years later he summoned up the courage to make a dress without a crinoline, which Pauline Metternich promptly introduced at court. Basically, a narrow skirt of very thick satin with no hoops or stiffened petticoat and falling straight to the ground, this caused a sensation as wide skirts had been in vogue since the 1820s. It was immediately copied by Eugénie, condemning her once beloved 'cage' to extinction. He revived the alluring bustle, which had not been seen since the seventeenth century and among his other innovations were jackets (with or without sleeves), and shirts with skirts.

However, Worth was not entirely responsible for ending the bonnet's long tyranny. Eugénie had worn broad-brimmed 'Vandyke' hats with plumes before she was even aware of his existence – Viel Castel recorded that in July 1857 she and her ladies rode through Paris in them. But he introduced other types of hat that finally killed off the bonnet. In 1860 he persuaded Princess Metternich to wear a little pillbox toque he had designed, and soon the empress could be seen in one, and then even in a bowler (derby) hat. The ubiquitous shawl was replaced by a scarf or a mantilla, a fashion pioneered by Pauline, who appeared without a shawl at the Longchamps race meeting.

The empress's patronage made Worth's clothes not merely popular but essential for every rich lady who wanted to be fashionable. In consequence the Maison Worth in the rue de la Paix was besieged daily by the smartest women in Paris, especially on days before the balls at the Tuileries. While each lady sat with her maid in one of its luxurious fitting rooms, waiting for the great man to give a dress his finishing touches or to suggest yet another, she was regaled with a lavish helping of foie-gras and a glass or two of Sauternes.

'The men believe in the Bourse and the women believe in Worth', observed Felix Whitehurst. 'I confess that, opposed as I am to the "unbridled extravagance of women", I look on with supreme pleasure at a luxury which, while reminding me of the decadence of Rome, now indicates only the wealth of France.' The 'master of the robes', as some courtiers called him sardonically, became indispensable. Eugénie showed her appreciation by inviting his wife to all the Tuileries balls while Princess Metternich asked her to all the receptions at the Austrian embassy – both made a point of talking ostentatiously to Mme Worth, so that no one dared to snub her.

Worth's prices soared, and, understandably, his name was loathed by husbands or fathers who had to foot the bills. Some people saw the funny side, however. 'I am informed that the last thing in dress is a "puff-petticoat", which sticks out like a bunch, and causes the female form divine to look rather like the Gnathod or Dodo', Whitehurst reported irreverently in the *Daily Telegraph* in March 1868 after the bustle had made its appearance. 'It is said to have routed sleep from the couch of oft-recorded Worth, who laboured night and day at its invention. When this truly great man is composing, he reclines on a sofa, and one of the young ladies of the establishment plays "Verdi" to him; he composes chiefly in the evening and says that the rays of the setting sun gild his conceptions.'

It has to be admitted that success turned Mr Worth's head. He liked to pose as one of history's more memorable artists, wearing floppy cravats and enormous velvet berets that scarcely suited his walrus moustache and bottle nose. Taine heard that the dressmaker was comparing himself to Delacroix and Ingres, even to the first Emperor Napoleon. Yet never for one moment did he forget that he owed his success and his millions to Eugénie's patronage. As long as he lived, he sent her Bonapartist violets every year on her birthday and when the Second Empire fell he continued to insist that she was still his empress, stubbornly displaying the imperial warrant over the main entrance to the Maison Worth and ignoring the risk of having his windows broken. When he died in 1895 Eugénie sent a telegram to his widow – 'In my prosperity and in my sorrow, he was always my most devoted friend.'

Republicans and even royalists claimed, wrongly, that Eugénie's expenditure on clothes during her reign rivalled Marie-Antoinette's, that she was a symbol of unbridled luxury, ignoring the prestige she gave to French fashion. Yet any fair-minded observer realised that she could not afford to dress cheaply – had she done so, the opposition would have been the first to criticise. 'The empress's taste for luxury was wildly exaggerated', writes Mme Carette indignantly. 'Luxury is an attribute of monarchs – beautiful and intelligent women are supposed to dress well.' And what other imperial or royal lady of 1860 would have dared to be the first to patronise a 'man-milliner'?

WITCHCRAFT

Bertrand Russell once observed that spiritualism was the suburban form of witchcraft, but it was considered neither suburban nor witchcraft during the Second Empire. Even the great Dominican Lacordaire, the most brilliant preacher of the day and a member of the Académie Française, thought there might be something in it. In 1854 Princesse Mathilde and Pietri, the Prefect of Police, both tried table-turning. Napoleon and Eugénie experimented soon after, without much enthusiasm.

Three years later, an unusually gifted medium named David Dunglas Hume arrived in Paris, a young Scot who had discovered his powers while living in the United States. Twenty-two, haggard and skeletal, with nice manners, he not only communicated with the dead but foretold the future. Converted to Catholicism by a celebrated Jesuit, Fr Ravignan, he confessed that he was tormented by spirits but promised to give them up. They returned, however – at least, he said they did – and he began to talk to them.

On 13 March 1857 Horace de Viel Castel wrote, 'All Paris is talking about the American sorcerer.' Hume had been taken up by Prince and Princesse de Beauvau-Craon, holding seances at their house where, when he went into trances, claps of thunder sounded, bells pealed, tables and chairs danced round the room, pianos and accordions played, while handkerchiefs came out of the guests' pockets and tied themselves in knots.

Fascinated, Eugénie invited Mr Hume to hold seances at the Tuileries, the first taking place in a seldom-used room. A heavy armchair suddenly lumbered across the room towards him and then the chair on which he was sitting rose slowly into the air – he also floated out of the window. Later the spirits of Napoleon I and Queen Hortense spoke to him, together with those of Pascal, Rousseau and St Louis. So, too, did Don Cipriano, who held the empress's hand – 'It's my father's hand!' she cried. The emperor grasped it too, exclaiming, 'My God, it's cold!' The Duc de Mortemart actually saw the spectral fingers.

Not everybody was convinced, however. Comte Walewski, minister for foreign affairs, warned that Hume was known to use conjuring tricks, was wanted by the police in several countries and was believed to be a Prussian agent. The Tuileries indignantly refused to credit these allegations, especially after scientists called in to investigate could find no explanation.

Throughout her life Eugénie was inclined to believe in messages from the world beyond. She took fortune-tellers very seriously indeed, and leafed through the Bible to find texts hinting at the future. It was a sign of her growing influence over Napoleon that, for a moment, he too was taken in by the 'American sorcerer'.

'Have you ever heard of a certain charlatan by name Hume, half English and half American, who pretends to raise spirits, etc.?', Cowley asked Lord Clarendon. 'He has been here for the last month and has complete hold over the emperor and empress who both believe in his spiritual powers.' The ambassador added that after the emperor had asked Hume to raise the spirits of Napoleon I and Louis-Philippe, he was told they were both in the room with him. '"Wait a little", said Hume, "and Your Majesty will feel their presence." Soon afterwards H.M. experienced a violent kick on an unmentionable part of his sacred person.'

'But, seriously speaking', Cowley continues, 'it is impossible to conceive that such a man should be so easily gulled, and as he receives this Hume at all times and *alone*, the Police are seriously alarmed.'

Eventually, Hume went too far, foretelling that the Prince Imperial would never become emperor. Eugénie immediately insisted on Napoleon calling the police. On 28 March Viel Castel noted with relish that the sorcerer, 'who summoned up the dead in the presence of the emperor and empress' had been sent to the Mazas prison 'as a thief and sodomite', and would be expelled from France to avoid a highly embarrassing trial.

Dr Barthez suspected that privately Eugénie continued to think he was genuine enough but had lost his powers. In 1862 Lord Malmesbury and the emperor discussed 'Home [*sic*] and spiritualism, which I saw he half believed in; and as he had been speaking of the many doubtful pictures in the Louvre, I suggested that it was desirable that Mr Home should call up Titian's spirit and ask him whether he really painted the portrait of Francis I.' Malmesbury adds that Napoleon III 'looked displeased'.

It is only fair to remember that others besides Eugénie believed in Hume. Among them was the exiled Victor Hugo, whom the sorcerer visited in the Channel Islands and obligingly put in touch with Molière.

HUSBAND TROUBLE

Not even Eugénie's admirers could deny that she was excitable. Prince Metternich (Hübner's successor as Austrian ambassador) refers to her *'fougue caractéristique'*, her natural fieriness. Sometimes she was alarmingly impatient and irritable, controlling with difficulty an anger which verged on hysteria. Most of it was caused by Napoleon's infidelity.

In many ways he was an ideal husband. Gentle and considerate, rarely losing his temper and never shouting, he shared his triumphs, was supportive and had a good sense of humour. In addition, he was obviously very proud of his wife. He possessed one fault, a weakness for pretty girls. Princesse Mathilde told Viel Castel (or a mutual friend) how in 1857 at a ball at the Tuileries she saw the emperor looking worried and asked him why.

'I have a bad headache,' he answered. 'And I'm being chased by three women.'

'What!', gasped Mathilde. 'How did you get yourself into such a mess? Three women! It's madness.'

'Do you see that one, over there,' replied Napoleon, 'that blonde on the ground floor? I'm trying to disentangle myself from her.' This was Mme de la Bedoyère, one of Eugénie's ladies-in-waiting.

'Next, I have a lady on the first floor, who is certainly very beautiful, but has no personality. She's insipid – she bores me.' This was the Piedmontese Mme de Castiglione.

'Then there's the blonde on the second floor who's marked me down and is hunting me.' This was Mme Walewska, the foreign minister's wife.

'But the empress?' asked Mathilde.

'Ah, yes, the empress.' He explained. 'I was faithful to her during the first six months of our marriage, but I need my little distractions, even if I always go back to her with pleasure.'

Virginie de Castiglione was the first rival of whom Eugénie was aware. The affair began just before the Prince Imperial's birth. A magnificent creature who dressed outrageously in transparent muslins, she had an oval face, sultry dark green eyes and luxuriant black hair, while according to Viel Castel her nymph-like waist did not need corsets and 'her bust bids defiance to the rest of her sex'. Lord Hertford paid a million francs for a night with her, which was so vigorous that she was prostrate for three days.

In July 1856 at a *fete champêtre* near Saint-Cloud – 'a regular orgy', reported Cowley, 'the men dancing with their hats on' – the emperor took Mme de Castiglione rowing in a small boat, then disappeared into the woods with her. Eugénie was so angry that although weak from child-bearing she tried to dance, but fell over. Virginie and her husband were invited to Compiègne. Previously on the edge of bankruptcy, a smiling Count Castiglione commented,

'I'm a model spouse who sees nothing and hears nothing.' But his wife caused a sensation by storming out of the Palace theatre, Napoleon running after her and leaving the empress alone in their box. In February 1857 her costume as 'Queen of Hearts' at a ball at the Quai d'Orsai thrilled the men and horrified their wives, a see-through shift of gold muslin with golden hearts outlining her splendid bosom. 'The heart is a little low tonight', observed Eugénie.

Gossip said Virginie had been ordered by her husband's cousin Count Cavour (the Piedmontese prime minister) to seduce the emperor and win him over to the cause of Italian unity. But Cavour knew she was too stupid for such a task, even if she bragged later that united Italy was her creation. Her job was simply to report anything she heard in bed.

Her boasting alerted her lover's enemies to the fact that he visited her house in the avenue Marceau by night. It nearly cost him his life. When he was leaving at three in the morning in April 1857 men armed with knives (Italians, hired by exiled republicans) ambushed his carriage, seizing the horses' heads. The coachman managed to beat them off with his whip, galloping back to the Tuileries. Napoleon had already been growing tired of the brainless Virginie, whose sole charm lay in her sensuality, and soon after he ordered her to leave France. She bore him a son whom he entrusted to his dentist. Evans brought the boy up to be a dentist, too, under the name of Dr Hugenschmidt.

In January 1858 Viel Castel wrote, 'Almost none of the younger ladies at court fails to set her cap at the emperor and, since he isn't too discreet, people quickly know whom he fancies.' Napoleon waited for them to chase him, choosing the one he wanted. 'I don't believe in attack', he would say. 'I defend myself and sometimes I give in.' He gave in rather a lot.

'The emperor's ladies are all open-mouthed at having found a very pretty Pole in high favour at Plombières', Cowley wrote on 15 July 1857. The first to capture him after Virginie's dismissal, this was Comtesse Walewska – the 'blonde on the second floor' whom the emperor had mentioned to Mathilde.

The Comtesse's vain, venal husband was Napoleon I's son by his Polish mistress Walewska, and he looked a bit like his father, which was where the resemblance ended. A former ambassador to London – Queen Victoria could not stand him – he had recently replaced Drouyn de Lhuys as foreign secretary, although Napoleon did not think too highly of his abilities. 'I tell him to do something and he does it in a disobliging or an extravagant manner', he grumbled to Lord Cowley. In contrast, his elegant wife Marie-Anne (a Florentine, not a Pole) was intelligent and very good company. 'With the exception of Mme Walewski, the ladies who surround the empress are decidedly vulgar', thought Lord Malmesbury, Bismarck said she was the only amusing woman in France besides Eugénie, and even Morny respected her. A natural diplomat, while Mme Drouyn was insulting Eugénie during Napoleon's courtship, Marie-Anne was whispering in her ear, 'I congratulate you on the destiny that awaits you.'

'Comtesse W . . . is definitely the new favourite', Viel Castel noted in September. 'W . . . struts in the shadow of his wife's new *dignity*.' 'The way in which she threw herself at the emperor was the theme of everybody's conversation', Cowley informed Clarendon after a week at Compiègne in November. 'She had neither eyes nor ears for anyone else.' In the imperial train on the way down to the *série* Princesse Mathilde had seen 'her very dear cousin' mounted on Marie-Anne's knees as if riding a horse, kissing her mouth and pushing his hand down her bosom. Walewski pretended to be unaware of the affair, after receiving a valuable country estate in the Landes.

'Mme W. . . hides her good fortune as little as possible, to convince as many people as she can of her power over the emperor', Viel Castel observed. 'A short time ago she went to the empress and with superb effrontery told her, "I am forced to beg Your Majesty not to invite me any longer to your private *soirées* since people are accusing me of being the emperor's mistress and I don't want such a calumny to harm Your Majesty's opinion of me. I hope you will keep me at a distance until these vile rumours die down." Deeply moved, the empress kissed her and their friendship has grown even closer.'

Although Marie-Anne saw off Clothilde de la Bedoyère, the other blonde whom Napoleon mentioned to Mathilde, by March 1859 she was making a scene at a ball because he had flirted with a 'Mme G . . .'. By January 1860 it was rumoured that a 'Mme C . . .' was enjoying the imperial favour and that her husband, a naval lieutenant, had been promoted to captain for no apparent reason. This was the month when Walewski ceased to be foreign minister. Yet in November that year Cowley assured Lord John Russell, 'Madame is more powerful and more in favour than ever.' However, she finally lost her hold during the next few months.

'W. . . . is very shaken', Viel Castel cackled diabolically in November 1861. 'His wife's credit is at an end, and she is to be found among the ranks of reformed sultanas.' The diarist then relates gleefully how when Marie-Anne had admired one of Viollet-le-Duc's gargoyles at Pierrefonds, saying 'What an expensive drain-pipe', Marshal Vaillant had answered, 'Less expensive than yours, Madame.' Someone present reproached him for being 'too lively'. 'You just don't understand', replied the coarse old minister for the household, 'drainage like that costs us four million francs a year'. Her reign was definitely over.

For a while there was no *maîtresse-en-titre*, Napoleon sleeping with any good-looking and easy woman who happened to catch his fancy, as he had done even during Marie-Anne's ascendancy. When some unusually pretty young ladies were presented at court, Eugénie muttered grimly, 'I'd like to know which one of them hasn't slept with the emperor.' A staircase led discreetly from the imperial study to a bedroom above. If he was brought a girl whom he found unattractive, he would say, 'I am summoned by my papers', and she would be shown out.

Napoleon III's papers did not always summon him, however. According to the Goncourt brothers, when a girl met with his approval she was taken to a room to undress before being led naked into another where her sovereign, also naked, was waiting, the chamberlain on duty telling her, 'You may kiss His Majesty on any part of his person except for his face.' But Mme de Taisey-Châtenoy says that the emperor generally wore a mauve silk nightshirt in which he looked undistinguished, and that, personally, she had found his performance in bed equally lacking in distinction.

Unable to share a bed with her husband because another pregnancy might easily kill her, in desperation the empress attempted to make herself more interesting. One method she tried was photography. She posed as a smiling odalisque in a harem, wearing Turkish trousers and reclining seductively on silk cushions, and also as a pensive bride in white with her veil thrown back. Perhaps in private she dressed like this once or twice for the emperor, but obviously it made no difference. Ordinary studio photographs taken during the early 1860s, show her with a tense, melancholy expression.

Even when Eugénie did not know who her rival was, she lived in a state of constant suspicion. The strain took its toll. The last straw was the death of her beloved sister Paca at Paris in 1860, after a long illness – an undiagnosed disease of the spine. Paca died on 16 September, but the emperor, who had been informed, did not tell Eugénie until a week later, so as not to spoil their cruise to Algeria on the imperial yacht. She found it hard to forgive him.

Almost without warning, the empress suddenly left for England on 14 November, under the name of the 'Comtesse de Pierrefonds', with only two ladies-in-waiting, two gentlemen and ten servants – the personal maids and valets, and the footmen who were needed to look after a mountain of trunks and hatboxes. 'The Empress of the French arrived in London, and drove with her suite to Claridge's Hotel in hack cabs', an astounded Lord Malmesbury noted on 16 November. 'The following morning she went shopping on foot, and to the Crystal Palace in the afternoon.' Afterwards he added that she had been cheered wherever she went and 'was evidently delighted'.

From London the imperial party then made a long, exhausting journey up to Scotland in a jolting, unheated steam train, sitting all the way in an ordinary first-class carriage swathed in cloaks and rugs against the cold, equipped with foot warmers and picnic baskets. Part of the reason for going north was to consult Dr Simpson at Edinburgh, the world expert on diseases of the sort that had killed Paca, since although not a hypochondriac Eugénie was a firm believer in what would now be termed 'preventative medicine'. After he had confirmed that she was basically in good health, she climbed up Arthur's Seat, turning back halfway up because of the cold. Then she went to her friend the Duchess of Hamilton at Hamilton Palace near Glasgow.

In December she returned to London, staying at Claridge's. She spent two days at Windsor with Victoria and Albert, who found her thin and sickly looking. 'She gave me a melancholy impression as if some deep grief and anxiety weighed upon her', wrote the kindly perceptive queen, who liked her as much as ever. Clearly there was some other motive besides grief at Paca's death for her absence from France, almost certainly a severe rift with her husband, but there is no firm evidence.

Napoleon was waiting at Boulogne to welcome her home and there was some sort of reconciliation between them – for the moment. 'Great is the despair in the harem of the Tuileries', Cowley could nonetheless write in April 1862. 'The Empress would not appear at a ball for the Queen of Holland on Monday night, and was reported very sulky.' Whoever the woman was, it does not appear to have been a particularly important affair. A new 'distraction' that emerged in 1863, however, was much more serious than for some time. This was Marguerite Bellanger, whom an early twentieth-century biographer* calls 'a new and vulgar amour', and whom Viel Castel does not even deign to mention. A big, statuesque peasant, twenty-five years old, with yellow hair and a pink complexion, she came from a little village in the Loire Valley near Saumur and her real name was Julie Leboeuf, a name that suited her coarse good looks. In Paris she had become a walk-on actress and what we might perhaps describe today as a part-time call-girl.

Probably brought to the Tuileries during the summer of that year by one of Napoleon's procurers, Marguerite made a deep impression, which was due to more than physical qualities. She was, quite simply, great fun, cheerful and good-natured, the archetypal whore with a heart of gold, and had acquired a remarkable collection of 'friends' – politicians, courtiers, soldiers and actors – for whom she gave little parties. Once again, Napoleon was infatuated, installing her at a small house in Paris at Passy and an even smaller one at Montretour, just outside the park at Saint-Cloud. In February 1864 she gave birth to a son.

At times the 'friendship' proved too strenuous for Napoleon, worn out by years of sexual excess. Returning late one August night from Montretour, he collapsed, although he quickly recovered. The

*Roger Sencourt, *Life of the Empress Eugénie*, London, 1931.

empress was horrified – this new mistress was killing him. If he died now, the Prince Imperial could never inherit the Second Empire, since it would fall apart at once.

What took place the following morning has been described by a recent biographer* as a scene straight out of *La Dame aux Camélias*. Accompanied by Napoleon's private secretary (and procurer), old Mocquard, the empress of the French called on Marguerite at Montretour. 'Mademoiselle, you'll kill the emperor', she informed her. 'If you love him, you must go away tomorrow. It has to stop and I order you to leave. I shall pay you but you must leave, now.' Astonishingly, Marguerite stood her ground. 'Your husband comes here because he's bored and tired – if you don't want him to come, then make him stay at home by being nice and kind, good-humoured, gentle.'

Eugénie went back to Saint-Cloud and gave the emperor an ultimatum, but he refused to abandon Marguerite. Unable to eat or sleep, the empress fled to Schwalbach, a watering-place near Hesse. Nothing had changed when she returned in October, Cowley reporting that the atmosphere at Compiègne had been 'most painful'. 'The emperor and empress are hardly on speaking terms. . . . She taxes him with his present liaison to his face – calling the lady the scum of the earth.' She told the Walewskis that she had always known of his infidelities. 'I've tried everything, even to make him jealous', she confided, rather pathetically. 'It made no difference, but now that he's lowered himself to this *crapule* [scum] I can't take any more.'

'Spanish blood and Spanish jealousy have often begotten imprudences, but I have never heard of such an imprudence as the visit of Eugénie to Marguerite', thought Lord Cowley. 'It was certain to end in miserable failure as the damsel would feel sure of better provision from the husband than the wife and at the same time be able to give him a *preuve éclatante* of her disinterested love.' Yet he felt sorry for the empress. 'The fact is that she had worried herself to death over the emperor's liaison with Mlle Bellanger', he wrote later. 'This worry had fallen upon her nerves and produced loss of appetite, nausea, etc. . . .'

*Jean des Cars, *Eugénie: la dernière impératrice*, Paris, 2000.

Mercifully, Napoleon suddenly grew tired of Marguerite, and by the summer of the next year he had pensioned her off – handsomely. A courtier commented that by now he was so terrified of Eugénie's scenes that 'he would set all Europe on fire to avoid them'.

In August 1865, when the emperor and empress were at Neuchâtel, the horses of the carriage in which her ladies-in-waiting were sitting bolted after an engine driver sounded his steam-whistle. Hurled out, Princess Anna Murat and Mlle Bouvet (Mme Carette) were badly hurt. Napoleon and Eugénie organised their removal to hospital, and the empress spent the night with them. The experience seems to have done much to bring the pair together again.

Even so . . . 'The Emperor is setting up a new flirtation with a Countess Merci d'Argenteau', wrote Cowley in April 1867. 'She is young, pretty, and being deserted very much by her husband, has taken to poetry and painting. It is supposed that she will not surrender but will try to prevent the Imperial mind from its perverted ways.' He added, 'I shall look out for squalls on the other side of the ménage.' However, the Imperial manhood was by then a thing of the past.

One lasting effect of the 'distractions' and the scenes which resulted, an effect never admitted by either, was to strengthen Eugénie's increasing domination over her husband.

FOUR

Zenith

On 14 January 1858 the programme at the Paris Opéra, then in the rue Lepelletier, included among other items the ballet from Auber's *Gustave III*. Although this ended with an assassination, Napoleon and Eugénie, who liked the composer, decided to attend. At 8.00 p.m., three-quarters of an hour before the performance, Colonel Pieri, a well-known Italian republican, was arrested outside, armed with a pistol, a knife and a grenade. No one bothered to tell the emperor but the equerry on duty had sent a troop of twenty-four lancers as escort, unaware that he preferred to be without one.

As they arrived at 8.30, three grenades packed with bullets were thrown at their carriage, exploding in succession under the wheels. The first grenade put out the street lighting, plunging the street into pitch darkness, and smashed both the opera house and carriage windows, a glass splinter cutting the emperor's lip, another splinter grazing the empress's eyelid. The carriage doors were forced open, the 'most horrible faces she ever saw' peering in; but they were policemen's faces.

Getting out in the dark onto the broken glass, among the screaming men and horses, Eugénie's white dress became spotted with blood. (Someone in the crowd seized the chance to kiss her bare shoulders.) 'Stop worrying about us,' she said. 'This is our job. Help the wounded.' Napoleon wanted to help the injured himself. 'Don't be silly,' she muttered, pushing him into the opera house, where they received an ovation. His face was twitching, but Eugénie's was totally composed. They were cheered all the way back to the Tuileries.

'The poor little boy, of whom the emperor speaks so feelingly', commented Lord Cowley, 'would of course have no chance. By the

117

way, talking of him, I am told that when everybody had left the Tuileries on the night of the *attentat*, the emperor and empress went to the poor child's room where their firmness forsook them both and they burst into tears, the emperor crying most bitterly.' On reaching the palace, they immediately went to the Prince Imperial's bedroom – had they been killed, what would have happened to him?

Seventeen of the lancers were wounded, one fatally, the final casualty list (including spectators) being ten dead and one hundred and forty wounded. The attackers had meant to knife Napoleon and Eugénie amid the chaos, but were thwarted by the police's quick reaction. Tracked down and arrested, they proved to be three more Italians, led by Felice Orsini, whose aim was to turn France into a revolutionary republic that would unite Italy under a similar régime. Orsini and Pieri were sentenced to death.

Orsini behaved so impressively during his trial that the empress tried, unsuccessfully, to save him from the guillotine, knowing he would be less of a threat in prison than as a martyr. She was no less realistic when it was learned that the plotters had been living in England and had had their bombs made in Birmingham, and she refused to join in the furious outcry in Paris that jeopardised Anglo-French relations. Nor did she lose her head when a jury in London acquitted a Frenchman called Bernard, the brains behind the conspiracy. Britain declined to take further action, even if Palmerston was apologetic. She wrote privately to Lord Cowley, saying that it was not 'the daily fear of seeing my husband and son struck down in my arms' which upset her so much as that Bernard's acquittal gave the impression 'these men have your moral support'.

In February Napoleon announced that in the event of his death the empress would be Regent. 'A beautiful woman, a baby in her arms, saving France with the aid of an heroic army, conjures up so moving a picture for Frenchmen that the emperor's elimination by bomb at any moment has become an almost negligible factor', laughed the cynical Hübner.

During the plotters' trial their counsel had read out a letter from Orsini to Napoleon III. 'Remember, if Italy is not free, then European peace and your Majesty's own peace of mind are no more than empty dreams.' Ironically, the emperor agreed – he coveted the role of champion of 'oppressed nations'. Only Austria, the still mighty central European power that dominated Germany, had a stake in a disunited Italy, occupying Lombardy-Venetia and keeping garrisons in the 'duchies' (Tuscany, Parma and Modena) and part of the Papal States. In March 1858, three weeks after Orsini had been guillotined, Eugénie hinted to the Piedmontese ambassador what was in her husband's mind. Casually, she told him that the Italian peninsula ought to be three kingdoms – north, central and southern. 'The emperor is warming up for Italy again', Cowley warned during the same month. 'Orsini's letter and the dread of Italian stilettos would some day drag him into action if he knew how to begin.'

Allying with Piedmont was how to begin. There was no doubt that its king, Victor-Emmanuel II, was a joke. 'I've discovered something wonderful', he had told a lady during a state visit to France in 1855. 'Parisiennes don't wear drawers – heaven has opened before my eyes.' Clarendon told Cowley that when he read out his dispatch at 10 Downing Street, 'the roars of laughter in the Cabinet might have been heard at Westminster Bridge'. But behind Victor-Emmanuel was a ruthless minister, Count Cavour.

Napoleon and Cavour met secretly at Plombières in July 1858. Here they agreed that after driving Austria north of the Alps, Piedmont would take Lombardy-Venetia, while the duchies and most of the Papal States would form a new 'Kingdom of Central Italy' with Plon-Plon as king. The pope would keep Rome, however, and the king of Naples would be left in peace. France's reward was to be French-speaking Savoy and Nice – although *'Nizza la Dolce'* was the birthplace of Garibaldi.

The Franco-Piedmontese alliance was cemented by a marriage in January 1859 between Plon-Plon and Victor-Emmanuel's sixteen-year-old daughter, Princess Clothilde. Few people liked seeing the frail, plain girl sacrificed to such a man. However, Clothilde – very soon a member of Eugénie's inner circle – was tougher than she looked, a fiercely devout Catholic obsessed with the next world, who treated courtiers with chilling haughtiness.

The emperor then began to see the disadvantages of an Italian war. Cavour had already made Piedmont the most anticlerical state in Europe, dissolving its monasteries, and France's Catholics were going to be increasingly angered by the alliance, as well as outraged at the seizure of papal territory. The Austrian army, which had routed the Piedmontese army ten years earlier, knew every inch of the ground – it could defend the wide Lombard rivers or fall back into the fortresses of the Venetian 'Quadrilateral'.

Although at first Eugénie had welcomed the prospect of liberating Italians from Austrian rule, when the war's implications sank in, she started to oppose it. She realised that instead of three or four client states it might create a strong, united Italian kingdom capable of allying with France's enemies, besides threatening the papacy.

Napoleon hoped for a congress of the great European powers that could find a peaceful solution, but in April 1859 Austria sent an ultimatum to Turin and before the end of the month France and Austria were at war. When the emperor rode through Paris at the head of the Cent Gardes to take the train to the front he was cheered, even by workers from the Faubourg Saint-Antoine. Republicans were delighted, Catholics suspicious. After a tearful farewell, he left Eugénie to govern France as Regent. Without any experience of warfare, he was taking a huge gamble by personally commanding his army in the field. The empress was so worried that as soon as he had left, she drove to five churches in succession to pray for him.

Her prayers were answered, since the Austrians were commanded by the spectacularly inept Count Gyulai. The campaign was over in two months, the French defeating their opponents in two fiercely fought battles, Magenta and Solferino – losses on both sides at Solferino amounted to 6,000 killed and 30,000 wounded or missing. When the casualty reports reached Paris Eugénie was horrified. After driving the Austrians out of Lombardy, however, the French did not fancy attacking the great Quadrilateral which barred their way in Venetia. They also knew that Prussia was mobilising and might enter the war on Austria's side at any moment. In July Napoleon made peace with Emperor Franz-Joseph at Villafranca. Piedmont received Lombardy, Savoy and Nice going to France, but Austria kept Venetia. Soon, just as Eugénie feared, Piedmont – now the 'Kingdom of Italy' – had occupied central Italy including most of the Papal States, and within little more than a year the entire peninsula.

Napoleon led his victorious troops through a cheering Paris, showered with flowers, but although he did not realise it he had won a pyrrhic victory. Far from being grateful, the new 'Italy' blamed him for leaving Venice in Austrian hands while the great powers were angry with him for starting a war that might have engulfed Europe. 'May God destroy the wicked French' was Prince Albert's prayer. The emperor's dream of a lasting Anglo-French alliance vanished in smoke.

Even so, for the moment Napoleon III appeared to be stronger than ever. This was the zenith of the Second Empire.

EUGENIE AS EMPRESS-REGENT

Eugénie's first regency lasted from Napoleon's departure for the front on 10 May 1859 until his return on 17 July. She then possessed absolute power, chairing the Council of Ministers once a week – Mérimée mentions a meeting that went on for five hours – besides receiving copies of all reports on internal and external affairs. There was no trouble from Plon-Plon, who had been sent to Italy in command of an army corps occupying Tuscany. She enjoyed her duties so much that she said she was afraid of being bored when they came to an end.

'Since the absence of the Emperor the Councils of Ministers at the Tuileries have not been less frequent than when his Majesty was at Paris', reported the clearly astonished correspondent of the *Illustrated London News* on 11 June. 'Each of these Ministerial meetings, which are held in the Salle des Conseils, is presided over by the Empress Regent, who displays the same grace and intelligence in her new position that she has hitherto shown in all those to which her high station has called her.' The paper published a full-page engraving that showed the extraordinary spectacle of a mid-nineteenth-century woman ruler surrounded by her ministers. 'All documents hitherto signed by the emperor now bear the sign-manual of the empress Eugénie', it added. 'The numerous State occupations of the empress Regent since the departure of her august husband for the seat of war in Italy have not prevented her from pursuing her favourite charitable projects. In a recent visit to the Orphan Asylum, in the Faubourg Saint-Antoine, the whole of the industrial population turned out to give her Majesty a hearty welcome.'

After addressing the Senate and the Corps Législatif at the end of May – receiving an ovation – she spent most of the time at Saint-Cloud, however, only driving into the capital for the meetings of the council or for 'poor peopling'. She wrote to Paca in Madrid that 'Paris is absolutely quiet and the mood of France has seldom been more reassuring.' There was tremendous interest in the war, with an insatiable demand for newspapers and maps, and rumours of victories aroused wild enthusiasm. Yet she remained very uneasy, worried that Austria might at any moment find formidable allies.

It was a letter from Eugénie that alerted the emperor to danger from the Germanic Confederation (the kingdoms, duchies and free cities comprising Germany, whose senior member was Austria) and, above all, to danger from Prussia. 'The Germans regard the river Mincio [the Venetian frontier] as crucial for their country's security', she explained. 'That frontier has now been crossed and German public opinion is anxious that something should be done to help Austria.'

Describing how Prussia was exploiting Austria's difficulties in order to strengthen her own position within the Confederation, she said that Berlin had already demanded the mobilisation of all Federal troops and was insisting they must be placed under Prussian command, despite protests from Vienna. Whatever happened, if the French advanced any further beyond the Mincio a Prussian attack from the Rhineland was certainly on the cards. 'Feeling is running very high in Germany', she warned. 'The old 1813 mentality has re-emerged and no amount of assurances of peaceful intent on your part is going to satisfy Prussia.' Her assessment was confirmed by reports in the British press that the Confederation would soon assemble 350,000 troops and that Prussia was starting to look like an armed camp.

She also quoted Lord Palmerston – who had recently become prime minister again – as enquiring, 'Does France really want to establish another Prussia on her south-eastern frontier?' She commented, 'Very well put, in my opinion', and in the same letter she asked her husband bluntly, 'Will you be able to put a stop to this unity movement?'

Eugénie made the most of any good news from the front. As soon as she received a cable from Napoleon announcing his victory at Magenta, the massed cannon of the Invalides fired salutes while copies of the telegram were distributed to be read out in the Paris streets – 'A great victory: 5,000 prisoners, 15,000 of the enemy killed or wounded.' That evening she and Princess Clothilde drove in an open carriage along the boulevards, and were cheered rapturously the whole way. 'The entire Saint-Germain quarter was illuminated by bonfires and fireworks', wrote the patriotic Viel Castel. She had a *Te Deum* sung by the archbishop of Paris at Notre Dame, and asked for one to be sung in every parish church in France. When the captured Austrian colours arrived from Solferino, Eugénie had another *Te Deum* sung at Notre Dame on 3 July, attending it with the three-year-old Prince Imperial. On the way from the Tuileries to the cathedral, their carriage was completely filled with flowers thrown by the crowds.

She kept a watchful eye on the French press, giving a personal warning – delivered one morning by an official from the Ministry of the Interior – to the republican journal *Le Siècle*. Its violently anticlerical editor, who had welcomed the news of risings in the Papal States, received a stern reminder that the Second Empire had every intention of protecting the papacy. As he knew, three such warnings to a paper meant compulsory closure.

The prefects of all departments sent weekly political reports to Paris, which Eugénie read carefully, together with the reports from the police. Apparently, only the most fanatical Legitimists disapproved of the war while the republicans were delighted by it. What shocked her, however, was learning for the first time the sheer intensity of republican hatred for her husband's régime. Royalists might be won over to an alternative form of monarchy, but clearly republicans would never accept Napoleon III, who during his coup on 2 December 1853, after arresting their leaders in their beds, had ordered his troops to shoot them down in the streets and had then transported thousands to the penal settlements in Algeria or Guyana. 'You wear the memory of 2 December as if it were a shirt of Nessus' (the poisoned shirt which nearly killed Hercules), she told the emperor later. 'Yes, I think of it every day', was his reply.

While in favour of wooing individual republicans, the empress now became convinced that it would be dangerous – probably suicidal – for Napoleon to try to liberalise the Second Empire, as he was already planning. In her view he was seen as having shed too much blood.

Ferdinand Loliée, at his most insidious, attributes Eugénie's interest in politics to vanity. 'To be a decorative sovereign, unfaded by the passing years, still gave her pleasure whenever she looked in the mirror, but it did not flatter her self-importance quite enough', he sneered. 'She had to show the world that she had more serious gifts, those of a politician. . . . How could she hold back so much that was in her – character, imagination, pride at being able to make her fancies take wing?' He adds, 'people were going to experience them and, more than once, regret them'.

In reality, the catalyst had been reports from the prefects and the police revealing to Eugénie the extent of republican hostility, convincing her that the emperor's plans for a new constitution were flawed. Only by involving herself in politics could she hope to modify them and save the Second Empire for her son. If liberalisation was inevitable, it must wait until the reign of Napoleon IV.

THE SECOND EMPIRE MEANS PROSPERITY

'The Napoleonic idea is not an idea of war, but a social, industrial, commercial and humanitarian idea', Napoleon III had argued passionately, even before he achieved power, and he meant every word. He succeeded in ruling France for twenty-one years, longer than has any other man in the country's modern history.

Hostile historians have sometimes called his régime a 'carnival empire', implying that it was based on nothing more substantial than the *cancan*. No doubt it may often have seemed frivolous, but behind the parades and the masked balls there was solid economic muscle, industrial and financial. 'Bonapartism, in its most simple interpretation, meant prosperity', is Theodore Zeldin's definition.

Napoleon's entire reign was a time of full employment with steadily rising wages, in contrast to the lack of work during the miserable 1840s. This transformation was of course largely due to the gathering pace of the industrial revolution that was sweeping the western world, but it owed a good deal to the contribution made by the emperor. He was obsessed with a healthy economy. The World Exhibition at Paris in 1855 was one of his ideas, a gigantic trade fair where France's booming new industries could display their products.

He encouraged a programme of railway building that accelerated France's industrialisation – from 1,800 in 1848, by 1870 the rail network had increased to 17,000 kilometres of track. Manufacturing and mining were assisted by generous government concessions (even if some of them went to commercially minded courtiers). Communications were revolutionised, so that by the end of the reign there were 1,500 telegraph stations compared to seventeen in 1852. New-style banks, persuading ordinary people to invest their savings, helped to provide the money to finance this rapid progress.

Since the railways opened up formerly inaccessible markets, agriculture also benefited. At the same time chambers of agriculture were founded to introduce better farming methods, which were even taught in village schools. These were accompanied by schemes for land clearance, afforestation and drainage, the emperor being personally responsible for draining wide areas of Champagne, the Sologne and Gascony. Local taxes that had previously hampered the movement and the sale of crops were abolished. New roads were built throughout the country.

Carried by new steam trains – and steam ships – France's exports rose by 400 per cent. Napoleon, an enthusiastic apostle of free trade, had smoothed the way by signing treaties with most of the countries of western Europe, including England, which either abolished or lowered customs duties. Some romantics suggest with a certain exaggeration that in doing so he anticipated the European Community.

Looking back, Eugénie could claim that her husband had, as she put it, 'given France long years of prosperity'. If not directly involved, she discussed commercial and financial problems with him, aware of the close relationship between secure employment and support for the Second Empire. She also performed a decorative but valuable role in opening trade fairs and factories.

In August 1860 the empress visited Lyons, a socialist city with a record of violence and even of armed insurrection, whose main industry was silk manufacture. From the police reports she had read during her regency she knew that its silk-workers remained hostile. Carrying out a lengthy tour of the city's major silk factories needed real courage; using all her charm she received a surprisingly friendly welcome, however, and was cheered for her skill at operating a shuttle-loom. Besides contributing to charities, she began to wear regularly the heavy Lyonnais brocades, until then unfashionable, in a determined effective bid to popularise them.

From genuine compassion as well as politics, Eugénie always encouraged Napoleon III in his unending efforts to improve conditions for the working classes. He fostered plans for mutual-aid societies and day nurseries, for legal and medical assistance, for old age pensions and accident insurance, founded orphanages and free nursing homes, and demolished slums, rehousing their occupants in 'industrial dwellings' that were bleak but healthy. He abolished the infamous *livret* without which a man could not be lawfully employed (a certificate signed by his previous employer stating that he did not owe him money). In 1864 he withdrew the ban on workers' associations and legalised the right to strike – nor did he reinstate it despite the ensuing wave of industrial action.

At the empress's suggestion, Napoleon, who genuinely believed in the 'dignity of labour', set up a species of *Invalides* for workers injured in the factories, rather than soldiers wounded in battle, just outside Paris. He insisted on a cheerful atmosphere and every man having his own room. The Asile de Vincennes had 430 bedrooms, treating at least 10,000 patients a year. Shocked at so many of the poor being discharged from hospitals before they had fully recovered and still unable to work, it was Eugénie's idea that there were proper facilities for convalescence and aftercare. At the same time, she saw that a similar hospital for women workers was established at Vesinet.

By the end of the reign the number of free hospitals in France had grown from 9,332 in 1852 to 13,278, of lying-in hospitals from 44 to 1,860 and of infant schools from 1,735 to 3,633. This increase owed much to imperial initiative, and often to imperial funding as well. The empress played a key role in providing a network of free dispensaries, public baths and communal cooking stoves.

'The work-people believe that the rich are their enemies and that the emperor is their friend, and that he would join them in an attempt to get their fair share, that is, an equal share of the property of the country', Mme de Tocqueville (the historian's widow) told an English economist in 1861, adding, 'I am not sure that they are mistaken.' Yet despite his efforts, until long after the Second Empire, working conditions continued to be dictated by supply and demand, the conditions of the brutalised men and women who are portrayed in Zola's novels – toiling for twelve hours a day, numbing their misery in drink or promiscuity.

The emperor and empress met with complete indifference from employers. During the American Civil War, when textile workers were laid off at Lyons because of the cotton shortage, Eugénie offered to set up a government fund to make good losses incurred by factory owners who kept them on, even if there was no work. Her proposal was rejected by the owners, because it meant state intervention. All she could do was to give the charities at Lyons money to buy and equip a château as a convalescent home for workers. Nonetheless, Napoleon and Eugénie did more to help the working classes than any previous rulers of France.

A NEW PARIS

Although their Palace of the Tuileries may have vanished, if Napoleon III and Eugénie returned today they would find no difficulty in recognising their capital. Until 1853, despite its elegant mansions and imposing public buildings, Paris remained a medieval city. According to an English guidebook of 1864, it had been 'a dense mass of old, lofty houses, only accessible by narrow and crooked streets, impervious to light and air'. As Balzac and Victor Hugo made clear, it was certainly very picturesque, especially the Gothic alleys of the Ile de la Cité or around the Châtelet, but at the same time dangerous and horribly unhealthy. The streets were a paradise for muggers, while filthy open drains ran down the middle of each thoroughfare. There was no proper water supply, everyone drinking from dubious wells: thousands died in the cholera epidemics of the 1830s.

While Louis-Philippe completed the Arc de Triomphe and the Madeleine, repaired some of the public buildings, widened a few streets and improved the paving, the Louvre remained unrestored, the Place de la Carrousel was obscured by shoddy houses and shops, and the Place de la Concorde and the Champs Elysées were still muddy, unpaved ground.

The emperor's chosen instrument for rebuilding Paris was a career civil servant, Georges Eugène Haussmann. An arrogant, overbearing man, most people disliked him. 'He is very tall, bulky, and has an authoritative way of walking ahead and dragging his partner after him, which makes one feel as if one was a small tug being swept on by a man-of-war', wrote Lillie Moulton after being taken into dinner by him at Compiègne. He behaved like this with opponents, ruthlessly forcing through demolition and reconstruction. But behind Haussmann stood Napoleon, who inspired the major projects. It was his idea to provide easy access between the new railway stations and the centre of Paris – for the sake of both business and pleasure – to clear away the warrens that hid the city's great monuments and, not least, to install modern drainage. 'It was the emperor who planned it all', said Haussmann, with a certain exaggeration. 'I have merely been his collaborator.' It was Napoleon who insisted that Les Halles should be made of iron.

When Haussmann was appointed prefect of the Seine, six months after Eugénie's wedding, he was summoned to an audience at Saint-Cloud where the emperor gave him his first, staggering briefing. It was a map marked with coloured lines, red, blue, green and yellow. They traced the new Parisian boulevards that Napoleon was determined to build – wide, well paved, tree-lined and gas-lit avenues that would replace the cobbled alleys.

First, Haussmann completed the rue de Rivoli, then he constructed the avenue Napoleon III (now avenue de l'Opéra), linking it with the Place de l'Opéra. Then came the '*grands boulevards*', radiating out from great squares, flanked by peripheral boulevards. Not content with boulevards, the emperor redesigned the whole of central Paris, and Hippolyte Taine did not exaggerate when he wrote that town planning on this scale had not been seen in France since Roman times. Among the tall, white buildings that went up were the huge markets of Les Halles, the Polytechnique, the Ecole des Beaux Arts and such government offices as the Ministry of Foreign Affairs on the Quai d'Orsai. The Louvre was completed, the Bibliothèque Nationale rebuilt and a new opera house begun. Two vast parks were laid out at each end of the city, the Bois de Boulogne and the Bois de Vincennes. Paris also acquired its first department store, the Bon Marché, which opened in 1853.

Within months of Haussmann taking office 50,000 buildings had been demolished, a process that went on almost until the end of the Second Empire. Slums vanished, the stench of former times disappearing with the oozing walls and the cesspits. Unavoidably, hundreds of thousands of Parisians were displaced. Up to now it had been normal for working men and clerks to live in the garrets or basements of bourgeois houses, but the rents in Haussmann's new mansions and apartments were so high that they were forced to move into the slums on the far side of the city. Tradesmen were ruined by losing their shops, and had to compete for any sort of work with labour coming in from the provinces on the railways – the population doubled before the reign was over. The emperor tried to help by providing special housing at low rents and free medical treatment, but on much too small a scale. Nothing earned him more hatred than rebuilding Paris, not even the coup of 1851.

Not only the poor were upset. Many mourned the loss of medieval Paris, the insensitive destruction of the old streets. Others were angered by the lack of compensation and by the enormous price of the new housing. Some very unpleasant rumours began to circulate about Haussmann's finances.

Even so, France soon realised that her capital had been transformed into one of the glories of Europe. Napoleon III had succeeded brilliantly in creating his dream city. By the 1860s he and Eugénie could drive through a gleaming Paris that had become, as they planned, 'the capital of capitals'.

PRINCESS METTERNICH: A NEW FRIENDSHIP

After the Prince Imperial's birth the court became more austere, but this changed in 1859 with the arrival in Paris of Pauline Metternich. Two years younger than the empress, she was the wife of the Austrian ambassador, a small, slight woman with wavy chestnut hair, simian features and a sallow complexion. If far from beautiful, she had a lively, amusing face lit by huge, dark eyes, shoulders that were admired by Winterhalter and a pretty bosom. (Asked why she had had her bust sculpted by Carpeaux, she replied 'I may be ugly, but I've got nice details.') What made her so attractive was an extraordinary dynamism, inherited from her half-insane Hungarian father Count Sandor. She was also totally Parisian in her attitude, despite her lack of French blood.

Pauline's husband, who was also her uncle, was the great chancellor's son. Only thirty, a handsome, amiable grand seigneur without his father's genius, a lover of music who was on friendly terms with Verdi and Wagner, he had been given the job of restoring good relations between France and Austria after the Italian war. His success owed a good deal to his wife.

The princess, whom Mérimée thought looked 'half great lady and half tart', soon became known as 'the prettiest *belle laide* in Paris' and acquired the odd nickname of 'Cocomacaque' ('Cocoa Monkey'). Her dress sense made her a leader of fashion, while her eccentricity amused most people, if not perhaps everybody. Known to turn cartwheels in her crinoline, she founded a smokers' club where she and her friends could enjoy cigars. She also played the piano, singing some extremely vulgar Parisian songs.

Long after first seeing Eugénie at Biarritz in September 1859 one recalled that impression: the empress was wearing her red shirt and the black skirt looped up for walking in the country that showed her ankles. (Old dowagers grumbled that she dressed 'like the dancers at the Opéra'.) Pauline was struck by her beauty and an easy charm that made you feel you had known her for years. She was also impressed by Napoleon III's pleasant manners and lack of self-consciousness.

'Madame la princesse de M. . . who affects the mannerisms and tone of the inferior type of prostitute, has become a great favourite of the empress, who now invites her to all her parties', sniffed

Horace de Viel Castel. 'She drinks, she smokes, she swears, she's ugly enough to frighten you, and she tells dirty stories.' Whatever the count may have said, in Mme Carette's opinion Pauline was 'a great lady to her finger-tips'.

One may perhaps wonder what endeared someone like this to a woman who disapproved quite so strongly of Offenbach. Yet Pauline Metternich had a good deal in common with Eugénie, coming from an aristocratic background instead of the steps of a throne, while as a girl she too had liked hard exercise and been a superb horsewoman and reckless driver. For all her oddity, she was highly intelligent and very amusing. Above all, she knew how to make the empress enjoy herself.

Despite Austria having only recently been an enemy, the Metternichs behaved with such tact that the Austrian embassy, then in the rue de Grenelle, became the smartest house in Paris, with endless dinners, receptions and balls. 'The Princess Metternich receives after midnight every evening', said Lillie Moulton. 'To sit up till twelve o'clock to go to her is very tiresome, though when you are once there you do not regret having gone. It is something to see her smoking her enormous cigars.'

Lillie went to a ball in the rue de Grenelle, among the other guests being Napoleon and Eugénie. Johann Strauss had been brought from Vienna for the evening and for the first time Paris danced to the 'Blue Danube'. 'We had thought Waldteufel perfect; but when you heard Strauss you said to yourself you had never heard a waltz before', Lillie tells us. She was also impressed by the princess's 'wonderful taste' as a decorator, admiring a new ballroom hung with lilac and pink satin.

Besides enjoying Strauss, Pauline Metternich was a pioneer Wagnerian and persuaded the emperor to invite the composer to give a performance of *Tannhäuser* at the Opéra. When it was hissed and booed, she stood up amid the tumult, cheering and beating the edge of her box with her fan till it broke – only making matters worse. Afterwards, she insisted fiercely, 'I did what I could to save Wagner's honour.'

'The court is disporting itself at Compiègne', Viel Castel recorded in December 1863. 'The young fry are playing charades and that restless little monster Princess de M. . . . is dancing in ballets.' She was particularly good at directing the plays staged during the *séries*, although she sometimes fell out with the cast. When Persigny's wife, who had very beautiful blonde hair, was playing a lady's maid, she refused to let her wear it loose. 'Do be kind and remember that her mother was a little crazy.' begged Eugénie, who loathed quarrels. 'My father was crazy too and I'm not going to give in,' said Pauline.

This performance was a *tableau vivant* rather than a play, a re-creation of Watteau's *Dejeuner Champêtre* – nostalgia for the days before 1789 – but often Compiègne productions were more up to date, and so was Pauline. In 1865 she made a memorable appearance in a review called *Les Commentaires de César*, in compliment to the emperor's book on Julius Caesar. As leading lady, she sang a song as a *vivandière* from the Zouaves, and another as a Paris cab-driver – smoking a pipe, speaking impeccable *argot* and swearing horribly. There was a repeat performance for charity at the Théâtre des Variétés in Paris two years later and, perhaps because it took place during a cab strike, she was cheered to the echo. Mme Carette tells us, she sang 'with more style and spirit than I ever heard in any theatre'.

The princess genuinely admired Eugénie, writing afterwards of 'her grace, her kindness, her ravishing beauty . . .'. She shared her interests in decoration and in clothes. At the same time, she persuaded her to be a little more adventurous and once or twice they seem to have travelled together on the top of Paris buses, unrecognisable in veils. There were rumours they did so disguised as men, and even of a successful hoax that they were going to attend a reception wearing tights – several thousand people gathered outside the building, only to be disappointed.

The empress grew so fond of Pauline that she commissioned Ernest Hébert to paint a sketch of her for the private salon at the Tuileries. She also kept a photograph of the princess in her bedroom.

FIVE

A Serious Empress

1865 – REGENT AGAIN

'The public judge by externals and thought I was only interested in smart parties and fashion, dresses and jewellery', Eugénie recalled. 'I was blamed for being frivolous. . . . If only they could have seen my notebooks.' Nevertheless, when Napoleon left for a tour of Algeria on 29 April 1865 he again appointed her Regent. As in 1859 she was given complete power. During this second regency we catch glimpses of what would now be called her feminism.

Once again it was not only Frenchmen who were taken aback by the very idea of somebody of her sex running the country. Cowley reported that 'The Queen of Holland tells me . . . the poor foolish woman can't conceal her joy at being *Régente*'. After the regency was over, he commented patronisingly:

> it has raised her in the opinion of those who had to deal with her, all admitting (even those who do not like her) that she showed remarkable tact and good sense in dealing with the business which she had to superintend. She always yielded her own opinions to those of the majority of her Council and was always to be found on the side of moderation and conciliation. She rather liked the display of power, and doing '*Madame la Regente*', but that is pardonable in a woman.

Yet she played a much more positive role than appears from Cowley's reports.

Eugénie showed that she could work with people who held different opinions from her own, notably with Victor Duruy. The son of a Gobelins tapestry weaver, with Michelet and Guizot he was one of nineteenth-century France's great popular historians as well as a distinguished academic. He was also a natural republican and an anticlerical. 'Let us improve the intellectual aristocracy of a people who want no other sort of aristocracy,' he once declared. However, he helped Napoleon with his life of Julius Caesar and was made Minister for Education in 1863.

Eugénie saw Duruy's ideas as a chance for Bonapartism to identify itself with educational reform, which she regarded as vital for France. As soon as she became regent, she asked him to explain his programme to her, supporting his bill for more primary education by lay teachers when it came before the Council. He wrote to thank her for her decisive intervention after it became law in May. Her support astonished not only Duruy but Catholics, who regarded education as the priests' business.

She continued to support Duruy after her regency was over. What particularly caught her imagination was his programme of further education for girls. Most Frenchmen, and not merely Catholic traditionalists, thought female education a waste of money – the Socialist Proudhon estimated women's intellectual and moral powers as at best one-third those of men – while only villages with over 800 inhabitants had a primary school for girls. When in 1867 Duruy proposed that fifty *lycées* should be founded for girls between sixteen and eighteen, he caused outrage, especially as they would have to be taught by men. Yet, as he said, he was merely proposing that girls should receive the same education as their brothers. The clergy, including even the liberal Bishop Dupanloup, claimed he was contradicting God's law and promoting social revolution by 'new and unheard of innovations . . . which would bring down what was left of the social order'. (Heaven knows what Viel Castel would have said, but by then the great chronicler had died.)

With the empress's support, Duruy succeeded in establishing his *lycées*. Even so, the Sorbonne refused to allow women to attend its lectures for another quarter of a century – although they had to tolerate the presence of Paca's daughters, sent by their aunt.

However, Eugénie's interest in women's education dated from before meeting Victor Duruy. When in 1862 a young schoolmistress, Julie-Victoire Daubié (author of *La Femme pauvre au XIXe siècle, par une femme pauvre*), tried to obtain a *baccalauréat* and the minister for public instruction refused because of her sex, Eugénie sent a message to the Council of Ministers to overrule him.

As regent she was able to do much more for women. Eager to widen their job opportunities, in the face of bitter opposition she forced the French postal service to employ women. Her most remarkable innovation, however, was to make a woman a member of the Légion d'honneur. Despite trying and failing to establish a new order for women that would be its female equivalent, she remained determined that female achievements should be acknowledged.

The painter Rosa Bonheur had been well known since the Salon of 1853, when her picture of a horse fair had won two gold medals. A lesbian who lived in the forest of Fontainebleau with a friend (and a lion, a yak and a gazelle), she cropped her head so that, as Mérimée observed, even if she wore a skirt it was hard to tell her sex. When she submitted a canvas to the Salon of 1855 the police warned the committee that the artist was a woman who dressed as a man. Rosa records in her pleasant, unpretentious memoirs how one spring morning in 1864 the empress called on her at her little château of By in the woods without warning, so that she barely had time to put on a dress. They discussed at considerable length her latest paintings and then the equality of men and women, Rosa being a passionate advocate of equality between the sexes. When they said goodbye, the artist kissed Eugénie's hand, and was embraced in return.

There had been talk of making Rosa a member of the Légion d'honneur, but the authorities had refused because she was a woman, compromising by giving the Légion to her brother, an embarrassingly mediocre painter. The empress was outraged, and in June 1865 it was announced amid general astonishment that 'Mlle Bonheur' had been appointed a member of the Légion. After signing the decree the regent went to By, pinning the cross on Rosa's lapel, kissing her and telling her how proud she was that it had at last been given to a woman.

Rosa was a friend of George Sand, one of her pictures inspiring Sand's famous pastoral novel, *La Mare au diable*. Another 'rebel against convention', Sand too had often dressed as a man, but was not really a feminist. Despite her republicanism and anticlericalism, the empress tried unsuccessfully to coax the Académie Française into admitting her as its first woman member – earning precious little gratitude from the novelist, who after sending fawning letters to the Tuileries caricatured her as the Spanish adventuress Mlle d'Ortosa in *Malgrétout*, set on marrying 'an emperor or a king'. Eugénie always ignored gossip about Sand's private life although Mérimée could have enlightened her. 'She is coldly debauched, out of curiosity and not by temperament', he told Viel Castel, who lists a dozen of her lovers (including Mérimée himself and Marie d'Agoult, a former rival). But the empress was no more concerned with Sand's private life than with Rosa's – she simply wished to honour the achievements of two great women. Another artist whom she encouraged was the young sculptor Adèle d'Affry, who used a man's name (Marcello) when exhibiting, to disarm prejudice.

Eugénie was equally keen on opening up the professions. When Miss Elizabeth Garrett found it impossible to study to become a doctor in England, she went to Paris where the empress persuaded the University of Paris to let her qualify. Aided by Victor Duruy – no longer minister for education but still a highly influential senator – Eugénie even founded an Ecole libre pour l'instruction médical des femmes (an institute for the medical education of women), to be staffed entirely by women professors. The idea had come to her on learning that doctors in Algeria were never allowed to visit harems. Authorised on 8 July 1870, it should have opened its doors the following October, but was overtaken by events.

During her regency the empress wooed opposition deputies in the Corps Législatif, inviting them to dine at Saint-Cloud and discuss questions they were raising in the Chamber. She was carrying on the work of her late brother-in-law Morny, who as president had been trying to turn them into a 'loyal opposition' on the English model, ready for France's transformation into a constitutional monarchy – even if she fervently hoped that it was not going to happen while she and her husband were still on the throne. Morny, who had died in March (from an overdose of aphrodisiac pills, it was unkindly rumoured), was the one statesman who might have ensured the Second Empire's long-term survival. 'He had it in him, if he had been honest, to have become a very great man', was Lord Cowley's verdict. 'People may say what they please, but Morny is a great loss to the emperor and the latter is much cut up.' The regent was only too ready to give permission for a statue of Morny to be erected at Deauville.

The republican 'irreconcilable' Emile Ollivier was among those whom Eugénie wooed when regent, warmly supporting his projects for penal reform. Hearing that La Roquette prison in Paris had a bad name, she paid an unexpected visit and was shocked to discover 500 children in solitary confinement, locked in cells day and night. She adopted Ollivier's solution with enthusiasm – camps from where the children could work on farms and go to school – siding with him against the 'experts'. When the emperor returned, she persuaded him to set up a commission with herself and Ollivier as members, to put the scheme into practice. She also spent an entire day in the Saint-Lazare penitentiary for women, talking to the prisoners, listening to their grievances to see if there was any better way of dealing with female crime.

In *L'Empire Libéral* Ollivier records his impressions of her as regent. 'I was struck by her ability to understand and discuss everything, by an intelligence that always saw the point, by sparkling conversation enlivened by an amusing wit and by sometimes passionate eloquence.' Sadly, Ollivier and Eugénie would later become bitter enemies.

The empress showed surprising restraint with Plon-Plon. When he made a speech in Corsica attacking the pope as the source of all reaction, she ignored demands by ministers for a public rebuke, merely ordering that his speech be censored and that he should be told to keep quiet. The emperor was so angry, however, that he sent a telegram from Algiers, ordering his cousin to resign at once as vice-president of the Council.

Her handling of the press was impeccable. She protested immediately at serious criticism of government policy, but did so as mildly as possible, without too strict an interpretation of the censorship laws. 'The empress-Regent is visible every day, looking very well, and apparently not much disturbed by the cares of office', noted the obviously somewhat surprised correspondent of the *Daily*

Telegraph on 7 May, although he realised she must be very busy, as he told his readers. 'She has daily "audiences", and almost daily Councils, besides the ordinary routine of State business – no slight business in itself.' President Lincoln had just been assassinated, and among 'diplomatists who have sought an audience is his Excellency Mr Bigelow [the United States minister to Paris.] The empress expressed to him her "profound emotion" on learning of the recent events in Washington, and added that she had written a private letter to Mrs Lincoln expressive of her deep sympathy.'

Napoleon returned from North Africa on 8 June, in time to accompany Eugénie to the Grand Prix de Longchamps three days later, the most important fixture in the French racing calendar and always the great social event of the summer.

Eugénie's second regency had come to an end after only six weeks, yet it shows how much she enjoyed power. 'The ministers never once quarrelled among themselves and I have kept them so well under control that I almost regret surrendering the reins', she observed complacently to Prince Metternich, who reported the conversation to Vienna. 'I shall tell the emperor I am handing over a firm and united government.' Mérimée had the distinct impression that from now on she intended to be an empress in the fullest sense of the word. Next year she began attending all important meetings of the Imperial Council as a matter of course, and presided in the absence of her husband.

EUGENIE AND THE POPE

Every Sunday at twelve o'clock the imperial family and their household heard High Mass in the Tuileries chapel, Napoleon III genuflecting and crossing himself. His faith may have been lukewarm, but he never forgot that most Frenchmen were Catholics. In 1849, when still Prince President, he had sent the French army to Rome, to put an end to Garibaldi's Roman republic and restore Pope Pius IX.

'I am Catholic to the roots of my being', Eugénie told Paléologue, but she was in no way a bigot, as her enemies alleged. 'Never in my time did the Tuileries see that ceaseless coming and going of cassocks that used to be seen under Charles X's reign', she insisted. 'In my day there was no clericalism at the Tuileries.'

The Legitimists claimed that their pretender, the Comte de Chambord, was the only man who could embody Catholic France. They accused Bonapartists of being anticlerical, not altogether without justice. Both Plon-Plon and Persigny were bitter enemies of Catholicism, the former becoming Grand Master of the French freemasons. (Garibaldi was Master of the masons in Italy.) The empress's obvious piety was therefore of considerable value to Napoleon.

There were two sorts of French Catholic. Ultramontanes wanted a declaration of papal infallibility and a return to the 'purer' belief of the Middle Ages, in order to fight modern materialism. The Comte de Montalembert declared 'We are the sons of the Crusaders and will never surrender to the sons of Voltaire', while the journalist Louis Veuillot thought it was a tragedy that Luther had not been burned. Their leaders, Montalembert, Veuillot and the Dominican preacher Lacordaire, welcomed Pius IX's *Syllabus of Errors* which condemned practically everything in nineteenth-century thought.

In contrast, the Gallicans wanted more independence from Rome, did not wish for a declaration of infallibility and tried to live with the intellectual climate of the day. Liberal Catholics like this were often Orleanists, yet Mgr Darboy, archbishop of Paris, and Mgr Dupanloup, bishop of Orleans, cooperated happily enough with the Second Empire. (Darboy was the empire's Grand Almoner, 'our principal chaplain' as Eugénie called him.) They tried desperately to reinterpret the *Syllabus of Errors* in a less obscurantist sense.

'I was something of a Gallican', the empress remembered. 'At least, I was certainly not shocked by Gallicanism.' She favoured the ideas of Darboy whom, as she constantly reminded people after his murder by the Communards in 1871, 'Pius IX never deigned to make a Cardinal'. She ignored the *Syllabus of Errors* and supported the freethinker Victor Duruy's educational reforms, disregarding papal fulminations about his 'impious designs'. It was on Duruy's advice that instead of accepting the standard abbé recommended by bishops, she appointed Filon as the Prince Imperial's tutor. She was shocked when Franz-Joseph signed a concordat giving the Church control of Austrian education and told Hubner that the concordat belonged to the Middle Ages.

Possibly her attitude owed something to Spanish Jansenism, inherited from her father, which was not so much the pre-destinarian creed of Port Royal as a conviction that the Church was badly in need of reform. (Don Cipriano's mother, the countess of Montijo, had been a Spanish Jansenist, harried and humiliated because of her views.) Like the Gallicans, Jansenists wanted a national Church, with most of the pope's powers transferred to the country's bishops.

Yet Eugénie believed it was vital to preserve the Papal States if the pope was to perform his mission as God's instrument on earth without interference. Only a French garrison saved what was left of them, the area around Rome, from being occupied by Victor-Emmanuel's troops. Withdrawing it would outrage every French Catholic and might even cause a Legitimist uprising.

At the same time Napoleon needed Italy as an ally and had to conciliate French anticlericals. Anticipating today's Vatican State, he suggested that the pope should stay in Rome but cease to rule, a plan which Eugénie rejected as impractical. She made such ferocious scenes that Lord John Russell joked that there would be a divorce citing the pope as co-respondent. When in May 1862 the Italian ambassador Cavaliere Nigra asked her to persuade the emperor to remove his troops, she shouted that Victor-Emmanuel was a bandit who had stolen the kingdom of Naples and that if Garibaldi took over Italy and 'strung him up', France would not lift a finger to save him. Reporting in June that for the moment Napoleon had abandoned all idea of withdrawing them, Metternich commented, 'I regard it as a triumph for the empress.' 'The emperor will seize upon any excuse or pretext to remain in Rome', wrote Lord Cowley in October, 'because he dreads the family discord and the effect upon public opinion.'

In January 1865 Eugénie told Cowley of her plan for all 'Christian princesses' to join in replacing the buildings over the Holy Sepulchre in Jerusalem by two churches side by side – one for Catholics, the other for Orthodox – with a central building between for other denominations. The Foreign Office quickly warned him,

'The Queen won't have the Holy Sepulchre at any price.' Nor would the pope. When Eugénie's friend Count von der Goltz made discreet enquiries through the Nuncio in Paris, he was told that Pius IX would never approve such a plan because the Holy Sepulchre rightly belonged to the Catholic Church alone. The tsar would have been equally hostile. If impractical, the plan shows that, ecumenically, Eugénie was years before her time.

Nothing weakened Eugénie's commitment to the temporal power. 'I am afraid the empress is [hell] bent on going to Rome', Lord Cowley reported from Compiègne in December 1866, commenting he could not see what she hoped to achieve. Yet it is easy enough to guess. Despite her opposition, Napoleon had by now withdrawn the French garrison, and she wanted to reassure French Catholics that, even so, he remained determined to preserve the Papal States. She abandoned the idea on realising that it would infuriate King Victor-Emmanuel's government.

Eugénie had no favourite priests, although for a time the Abbé Bauer preached so eloquently that he held a near monopoly of the Tuileries' pulpit. A rich Hungarian and a convert from Judaism, small, gaunt and hollow-eyed, he had been recommended by the Rothschilds. But success went to his head and he irritated the empress by wearing dandified cassocks with purple buttons like a monsignor which, according to rumour, were made for him by Worth. (After the fall of the empire he was caught sleeping with one of his penitents, defrocked and took up a new career on the stage.)

'An artless young Gascon maiden has had visions of a lady in white hard by a fountain – a sort of White Lady of Avenel tale', reported *The Times* sardonically at the end of August 1858. 'The fountain is only said to have spouted forth since the White Lady sprouted out from among the bushes at the entrance of the cavern. The young girl sees the vision and falls into ecstasies, while surrounding crowds can discern nothing.' The paper added that Louis Veuillot of *L'Univers* had written five columns on whether 'the Virgin Mary has once more descended upon earth, and, like Moses, has caused water to flow where none was seen before.' It commented that the visions would be credited by nobody 'superior to a profoundly ignorant peasant who is not a fit inmate for Charenton' – the madhouse. The Gascon maiden was Bernadette Soubirous and the cavern was at Lourdes, a small Pyrenean town not far from where Eugénie liked to climb. Soon the water was credited with healing powers and the Lourdais began to pray there, so the local authorities, anticlericals who shared the view of *The Times*, obtained an order to fence the grotto off from public access.

When the imperial couple arrived at Biarritz (to see a *corrida* at Bayonne in Eugénie's honour, with Spanish bulls) the archbishop of Auch asked Napoleon to withdraw the ban. The Prince Imperial's governess Mme Bruat and then the master of the empress's household visited Lourdes, and when the emperor sent Achille Fould – ironically, a staunch Jew – to withdraw the order, people suspected that Eugénie had intervened. If there is no firm evidence, it certainly looks as if the ban's lifting owed something to her prompting.*

The empress described herself to Filon as 'pious but not a fanatic'. Even so, she heard Mass on weekdays as well as on Sundays, spent long hours in prayer and helped the poor. Her most prized possession was the Charlemagne Talisman, a pearl and sapphire pendant holding a relic of the True Cross, that had been sent to Charlemagne by Haroun al-Rashid. Napoleon I gave it to Josephine and Eugénie found it among her wedding presents. She kept it by her bed when giving birth to the Prince Imperial – beyond question she believed in miracles.

At the same time she believed passionately in freedom of conscience. 'It is more against *unbelief* that we should fight rather than differences in belief', she told her mother. Horrified that the Spanish government should contemplate legislation against non-Catholics, she recalled how Louis XIV had expelled the

---

* Admittedly she never visited Lourdes, which was within easy reach of Biarritz. Nor is there any proof for Franz Werfel's claims in *The Song of Bernadette* (New York, 1942) that she had sent Mme Bruat for water from the grotto to heal the Prince Imperial and bullied the emperor into rescinding the order.

Huguenots from France. 'The Revocation of the Edict of Nantes was a terrible mistake. Are we going to repeat it in the middle of the nineteenth century? I hope not, precisely because I am a Catholic to the very depths of my soul.' She gave generously to Jewish charities after consulting the Grand Rabbi of France, and, if Ethel Smyth can be credited, while in England was almost shocked when Anglicans converted to Catholicism – although this may have been wishful thinking on Dame Ethel's part. Even so, she was convinced that most people could find salvation in the creed into which they had been born. 'There is but one justice before God', she told Dr Evans. 'And it belongs to all men alike, rich or poor, black or white, Catholic or Protestant, Jew or Gentile'. However, under no circumstances would she tolerate divorce.

Her occasional criticism of both pope and priests stemmed from being a genuinely liberal Catholic. Had she been born a century later, she would have approved of the modernisation of the Church set in motion by the Second Vatican Council. In later years her faith became so unostentatious that Ethel thought it a mere matter of form, before realising that, on the contrary, it was an 'inward need and a source of consolation and strength'.

Very Spanish, her creed was a bleak one. She expected suffering instead of joy, accepting whatever God might send, reserving her hope only for the life to come. It is likely that she rather than her son composed a prayer found on his body after his death:

Do not take away the obstacles in my path but give me strength to overcome them, do not disarm my enemies but help me conquer myself. . . . If retribution must fall, then let it fall on me. . . . Only in putting the past behind me can I find happiness. . . . Make me feel certain that those I love who are dead are watching what I do.'

The prayer contains a characteristic phrase of hers – 'how sad is the thought that makes us say, "Time effaces all."'

Her reputation for bigotry, stemmed from the smears circulated by anticlericals, who were angry at her support for the pope's temporal power. In reality, no one could have been a more tolerant Christian.

'POOR PEOPLING'

'All this frivolity did not prevent the new sovereigns from cherishing the very highest ideals', admits the austere Pierre de la Gorce. 'One of the Second Empire's oddest features was the way in which it combined charity of the most imaginative sort with dissipation, serious thought with utterly trivial pursuits. Amid the demands of her constant entertaining, the empress never forgot the social duties that went with her rank . . . she always showed a real desire to help the poor and suffering.'

Visiting the poor – 'poor peopling', as the Victorian English sometimes called it – was a normal enough activity for nineteenth-century ladies. What made Eugénie's visiting different was that she spent so much money on it. Napoleon allowed her 1,200,000 francs a year, òf which 100,000 went on her wardrobe, the rest on presents, pensions for retired servants and, above all, charity. 'I am frequently laughed at for wasting time in trying to make myself popular with the working classes', the emperor complained more than once. 'I don't think that it's a waste of either time or effort – and I'm sure Queen Victoria would agree with me.' Eugénie was not just attempting to please her husband but putting into practice her own extremely practical form of Christianity.

The poverty that existed in mid-nineteenth-century Paris was as marked as anything in Dickensian London. The capital described by Privat d'Anglemont in *Paris Inconnu* (1861) could be nightmarish, a city of alcoholism, disease and starvation, of brutal exploitation. Women in particular received pitiful wages. A tiny minority, such as the expert sewing girls who made the empress's dresses ('never costing more than 1,500 francs'), might perhaps earn as much as ten francs a day, but those working in most dressmakers' sweatshops were lucky if they got two and a half. A toiling laundress was only paid two. The wages of their menfolk were often not much more, and there was no provision for unemployment, illness or old age.

Acutely aware of this grinding hardship and misery, Eugénie was anxious that her son should learn what poverty really meant. 'He probably thinks the poor are people who don't own carriages', she told his tutor when the boy was eleven. 'It is essential that he understands and realises what it is, for him to listen to what these wretched folk have to say. No doubt a good deal of it is lies, but most of it is true. He must see for himself their ghastly homes, without any air or food, where happiness is an impossibility. He isn't fit to reign until he's done it.'

Whenever Eugénie was in Paris, a nondescript dark blue landau, without any coat of arms or other form of identification and driven by a coachman in a plain livery, might be seen leaving a side door of the Tuileries at least a once a week, usually in the mornings. Sometimes the landau went out more than once a week, especially in the winter during cold spells. It had small, curtained windows in order that no one could see from the street that inside was the empress, accompanied by a single lady-in-waiting, both of them so muffled in cloaks and veils that they were quite unrecognisable. The landau was setting off to visit a hospital, an orphanage, a school for poor children, a shelter for the destitute, a home for foundlings or just some family starving in an attic.

Eugénie kept an entire staff at the Tuileries whose job it was to let her know of any cases of hardship or of welfare institutions that urgently needed financial help or to inform her of requests for assistance from charities, even from individual men and women in distress. It was the indispensable Pepa's job to keep the accounts and make a note of donations.

The empress's first large-scale charity was paid for with the 600,000 francs that the municipality of Paris had offered her as a wedding present. Instead of spending the money on a diamond necklace as they suggested, she used it to found and endow an orphanage for girls in the Faubourg Saint-Antoine, a notoriously poverty-stricken district, where 300 poor girls were given a sensible education that would enable them to earn a decent living. As its patron, she visited it regularly until the very end of the Second Empire. In addition, she contributed large sums, generally anonymously and always with a minimum of fuss or ostentation, for homes and relief agencies all over France. Among these were convalescent homes for children at Falaise and Epernay, a convalescent home and lying-in hospital at Lyons, a hospital for scrofulous children at Berck-sur-Mer, and a relief scheme for old sailors at Dieppe. In and around Paris, besides her orphanage she helped to found a hospital for terminally ill young girls, a hospital for sick boys and a scheme to provide foster-parents, as well as convalescent homes for adults.

Her personal visiting never flagged. Shortly after Augustin Filon took up his post as tutor in 1867 he saw 'an old lady' in spectacles, with a large hat and a heavy veil, alighting from a carriage in the courtyard of the Tuileries. Raising her veil and removing her glasses, she laughed at him. It was the empress, returning from 'poor peopling'.

Even Ferdinand Loliée, Eugénie's most subtly disparaging biographer, could not fault her behaviour during the cholera scares of the 1860s. In September 1865, when she was at Biarritz in bed with a bad bout of 'flu, news arrived that the dreaded cholera (the nineteenth-century equivalent of the plague) had broken out in Paris and that people were dying every day. Parisians were fleeing from their city in terror. Napoleon rushed back, the empress following as soon as she could. Ordering her lady-in-waiting to stay in the landau, she visited the Beaujon, Lariboisière and Saint-Antoine hospitals, personally shaking each of the patients by the hand and telling them they were going to get better. Smallpox had broken out too, so in addition she insisted on visiting the smallpox ward at Saint-Antoine hospital, although this time she did not shake hands. Her visits reassured patients and staff, and did a good deal to halt the panic that was sweeping through the capital.

Next summer cholera broke out at Amiens, where public health was not so well organised as in the capital. The news reached Paris on 4 July, just when France was learning that Prussia had defeated Austria at Königgrätz the previous day. Ignoring the political crisis, Eugénie immediately took a train north and drove straight to the Hôtel Dieu, the city's main hospital. When Marshal Vaillant, who was escorting her, warned the empress to be careful, she replied, 'Marshal, this is how we women behave when we're under fire.' She toured every ward in the Hôtel Dieu, stopping at each bed and shaking every hand. Then she issued detailed instructions for sanitary precautions to be enforced throughout Amiens, supplied all hospitals with funds for extra food and medicine, gave money to people whom illness prevented from working, and arranged for the adoption of two small children orphaned by the epidemic. The bishop was alarmed at her disregard for her own safety. 'Do take special care of your health, Monseigneur', she told him drily on leaving. The municipality of Amiens described her courage as 'heroic'.

Eugénie's charity was invariably practical. During a tour of Brittany in 1855 a young lady, the daughter of a naval officer and grand-daughter of an admiral, was presented to her. Good looking and intelligent, she made a pleasant impression. When the empress heard, six years later, that Mlle Bouvet's father had died and that she and her mother were living in poverty, she wrote inviting the girl to become a lady-in-waiting and then gave her the post of reader. The future Mme Carette – she made a good marriage – always remained devoted to Eugénie, as may be seen from her memoirs.

INTELLECTUALS AT COMPIEGNE

Most intellectuals disliked the Second Empire for its absolutism and for the censorship, however mild. As this was a great era of French literature, the imperial couple were slandered with a venom that still stings, noisily by the republican Victor Hugo, slyly by the Goncourt brothers, who were Orleanists. In any case Napoleon III and Eugénie did not have very much in common with professional writers. No doubt, they had a few literary supporters – Mérimée, Vigny, Gautier, Sainte-Beuve, Sardou and Feuillet – while Taine admitted, 'The emperor understood his age better than anyone.' But that was all.

Throughout, the 'immortals' of the Académie Française, mainly Orleanists, were hostile, led by the Orleanist elder statesman Guizot. Any candidate of whom the Tuileries was known to approve, like Théophile Gautier, would find himself unelected. Despite declaring that he would never occupy his *'fauteuil'*, in 1860 the Dominican Lacordaire was elected to fill Alexis de Tocqueville's place because he had opposed the coup and had later attacked Napoleon in his sermons. But by the time of his investiture he had come out in favour of the war in Italy and Eugénie attended the ceremony at the Coupole. If she did so from curiosity, she was nonetheless keen to win the support of writers, composers and artists.

'I go to Monday receptions at the Tuileries', wrote Hector Berlioz in 1857 while he was composing *Les Troiens*:

The last time that I and Marie went, the empress had me presented to her, and we discussed my opera in detail; she asked what each act was about. Her 'gracious' Majesty (and she is) has read a lot of Virgil and I was amazed by her precise references to the *Aeneid*. My God, she's beautiful, just the sort of Dido I want. But perhaps not, as her wonderful looks might wreck the opera – the audience would howl down any Aeneas who even thought of leaving her.

Clearly Eugénie had taken a lot of trouble being nice to the prickly M. Berlioz, who was not one of nature's Bonapartists.

With the limited education of women of her time, Eugénie was ill equipped to cope with intellectuals, some of whom were extremely vain. Her only solution was inviting them to Compiègne. No women writers or artists were asked, except for the sculptor Marcello, although she came as a great lady under her real name, the Duchess of Castiglione-Colonna. One or two declined, such as the composer Meyerbeer and the painter Ingres. Others found difficulty wearing the obligatory skin-tight silk knee-breeches; the contortions of the novelist Jules Sandeau embarrassed even Mérimée. Such visitors generally slept on the second floor, the Galérie de l'Orangerie. In November 1864 Eugène Fromentin, the painter and writer (notably of an autobiographical novel, *Dominique*) informed his wife – writers' wives were not invited – that he was between Corvisart, the emperor's doctor, and Meissonnier the painter. The younger Dumas, author of *La Dame aux Camélias*, was next door and Gustave Flaubert further down the gallery. Émile Augier, the playwright, was on another floor. 'Is he warmer?' asks Fromentin. 'That's all we worry about. I have a lobby, a bed-sitting room, two dressing-rooms, a room for my servant, a whole forest of logs on my fire – and Siberia two steps away from my fireplace.'

Not so prickly as many writers, Octave Feuillet became something of a favourite with the imperial couple after his *Roman d'un pauvre jeune homme* was performed in the Palace theatre in 1858 – his plots always had happy endings. He was appointed imperial librarian and invited to stay no less than six times. He described one of his visits to Compiègne to his wife Valérie: 'I am very pleased at being placed directly over the park. . . . I look down long avenues hidden in the morning by a jewelled, shining frost, with marble gods and goddesses, trellises and flowerbeds and, in the distance, the tall forest towards Pierrefonds. I have only small rooms but they're very pretty.' Feuillet enjoyed writing charades and was even more amused by a tableau not of his devising, the 'Temptation of St Anthony', who was played by M. de Nieuwerkerker with Mmes de Morny and Girardin as female devils, while he found it hard not to laugh when, led by the aged Duke of Atholl, four Scots chieftains 'with naked legs' danced a Highland reel for the empress, 'a species of bizarre jig' (*une espèce de gigue bizarre*). He watched Gounod singing his own songs in a low voice, accompanying himself on the piano and 'rolling his eyes in a frightful way'. Eugénie, listening with her son on her knee, was moved to tears and had to leave the room. The composer was clearly enchanted at making such an impression.

Other musicians invited besides Gounod included Auber, Ambroise Thomas and Verdi, while among the artists were Delacroix, the younger Isabey, Horace Vernet and the sculptor Carpeaux.

The emperor showed more interest in science, which to him meant 'progress'. During a visit in 1865, Pasteur explained his current work on wine, giving a lecture for the *série*, Eugénie carrying his microscope and test tubes. He recalled happily that, for a moment, she 'gave the impression of being transformed into a laboratory assistant'.

'The bourgeois of Rouen would be even more astonished than they already are, if they knew what a success I've had at Compiègne', wrote Flaubert. 'I'm not exaggerating. Simply, instead of being bored, I've thoroughly enjoyed myself.' But the dressing and the strict timetable were trying. He had had reason before to be grateful to the empress. When prosecuted in 1857 for his 'immoral' novel, *Madame Bovary*, she had interceded with the judges. Similarly, when Baudelaire (never asked to Compiègne) was fined

300 francs he did not possess, on publishing *Les Fleurs du Mal*, he wrote to Eugénie, who had the fine reduced to 50 francs. Neither Flaubert nor Baudelaire nor, save for Vigny, any of the writer guests who was not already a Bonapartist, was completely won over to the Second Empire, but undoubtedly they all became less hostile. Inviting them was the *séries'* most positive feature.

'At Compiègne, the empress needed the utmost skill to perform her challenging and enormously varied obligations as hostess', Filon recalls:

> The guest list had first to be decided on and the *séries* organised so as to consist of fairly equal numbers of patricians, international figures, diplomats, artists, men of learning, pretty women and members of the Académie Française. These different elements had to be neatly balanced to harmonise; feuds and quarrels were taken into account when achieving variety and contrast while at the same time avoiding hurt feelings or misunderstandings. To do this required a knowledge of each guest's personality and background. . . . Many of them could testify to her triumphant success.

No other nineteenth-century court used hospitality with such imagination.

JACQUES OFFENBACH

Just as Mozart conjures up the *ancien régime*, so Offenbach's wild yet slightly melancholy gaiety conjures up the Second Empire. Napoleon and Eugénie attended the first run of several Offenbach operettas, and from the 1850s until the end his music was heard at every court reception.

The emperor ordered a command performance, *Les Deux Aveugles*, at the Tuileries to entertain the statesmen attending the Congress of Paris, and Eugénie encored the bolero. However, the empress soon began to disapprove of Offenbach's operettas, even if she quite enjoyed the music. What she disliked were the 'immoral' plots, full of sly jokes about the régime. Her husband laughed at them uproariously, but they offended her Catholic puritanism and

Spanish dignity. In 1855 Offenbach met a comic genius, a young civil servant called Ludovic Halévy who, with Henri Meilhac, supplied him with hilarious scripts.

If Eugénie had no objection to *Les Dragées du Baptême*, celebrating the birth of the Prince Imperial (Halévy did not write the words), she was horrified by *Orphée aux Enfers*, which came out at the Bouffes-Parisiens in October 1858. The philandering, bacchanalian life led by the gods on Mount Olympus – 'tired of nectar, ambrosia and virtue' – was clearly a skit on the Second Empire court, while the lustful Jupiter wore a beard and waxed moustaches just like the emperor. Nor can she have been amused by Pluto, disguised as a fly, seducing Eurydice. Far from being displeased, Napoleon sent the composer a bronze figure inscribed, '*L'Empéreur à Jacques Offenbach*', saying that he would never forget how much he had enjoyed *Orphée aux Enfers*. He approved his application for French citizenship, later making him a member of the Légion d'honneur.

Offenbach's next triumph was not until 1864, with *La Belle Hélène*. Nothing could have shocked Eugénie more. All about sex, its climax was a seduction scene, while for lewd minds the dream duet sung by Paris and Helen, '*C'est le ciel qui m'envoie*', verged on pornography. Helen was played by Hortense Schneider, a well-known courtesan as well as a diva. (She had had a son by the late Duc de Gramont-Caderousse, who once made an aquarium by filling a piano with champagne.) When she sang, 'Tell me, Venus, why do you enjoy making my virtue come cascading down?', young men in the boxes would yell, 'Cascade, Hortense, cascade!' 'An immense bacchanal, Venus turning the hellish hurdy-gurdy', grumbled Agamemnon, 'Pleasure and sensuality reign supreme' – everyone knew he meant the imperial court. The ludicrous march of the Greek kings echoed the march by Meyerbeer that had been played at Eugénie's wedding.

The empress failed to see that when the Greeks sang, 'It can't go on much longer, you know, it can't go on much longer', meaning the Second Empire, they did so to tease, not from disloyalty. Offenbach and his scriptwriters were not being satirical but merely laughing at the government to add to the fun, which Napoleon III understood very well.

The composer's combination of levity and immorality disgusted her. He always attended the Bouffes-Parisiens escorted by a troop of pretty actresses and rumour said that he slept with them. Ironically, Offenbach was in love with the empress, worshipping her from afar. On the one occasion he met her, presented after a performance at the Bouffes-Parisiens, he lost his nerve and could only babble that he had been born at Cologne, not at Bonn like Beethoven. No one could have been a more loyal subject.

In 1866 *La Vie Parisienne* poked less fun at the régime than usual, apart from describing Paris as 'the modern Babylon', and had a less 'immoral' libretto – if one ignored the heroine being a high-class tart or the extra-marital romps of the Swedish baron and his baroness. Had the empress seen it, she would have been outraged by a spectacular revival of *Orphée aux Enfers* in January 1867 in which the most famous *grande horizontale* in Paris, Cora Pearl (born Emma Crutch) appeared in pink tights as Cupid. She could not act, mouthing a few lines, but the men loved her legs, while her cockney accent brought the house down – '*Je souis Kioupiddon*'. Everybody in the audience knew that Cora was Plon-Plon's current mistress and that he had taken an apartment for her next to the theatre.

La Grande Duchesse de Gerolstein came out at the Théâtre des Variétés in April 1867 in time for the Exposition Universelle, the Second Empire's zenith, and was a dazzling success. 'Gerolstein' is a mythical German principality ruled by a lovely, capricious Grand Duchess (Hortense Schneider) who adores soldiers. She falls for a simple fusilier whom she immediately promotes to commander-in-chief, only to demote him when he rejects her advances.

Next year *La Périchole* tried to flatter the empress. It contained a beautiful song with the words 'He'll grow up tall because he's a Spaniard', alluding to the Prince Imperial's Spanish mother – but it was sung by Hortense. If the plot was based on a play by Eugénie's friend Mérimée, its plot about a viceroy who falls in love with a street singer and makes her a marquise reminded rather too many people of their emperor's private life, as did the '*cachot de maris recalcitrants*' (a prison for uncontrollable husbands).

When Offenbach's promotion to a senior grade in the Légion d'honneur was suggested during Eugénie's regency in 1870, she refused, making the thin excuse that he had been born a German. Her disapproval is understandable, however: he genuinely shocked the nineteenth century. In 1876, when he arrived in the United States for a concert tour, *The New York Times* commented that *La Belle Hélène* was 'simply the sexual instinct expressed in melody. . . . Priapism is put on a level with music.'

The irony is that the operettas of Jacques Offenbach recapture better than anything else the charm and allure of Eugénie's empire.

SIX

Clouds

THE MEXICAN ADVENTURE

Augustin Filon, the Prince Imperial's tutor and a man who understood the empress better than most people, said in his memoirs that she took all her political ideas from Napoleon III, 'in whose political judgment she possessed unquestioning confidence'. The emperor, he added, had unbounded respect for Eugénie's political intuition, consulting her again and again, although Filon commented that in his own view this high opinion was not quite borne out by events. Yet whatever Filon may have thought, her politics did not always mirror those of her husband, who often teased her for her Legitimist or at any rate conservative sympathies. And it was partly because of these very un-Bonapartist sympathies that Eugénie encouraged him to make one of the Second Empire's biggest mistakes.

She had been shocked by the fate of Italian sovereigns – banishment and confiscation of their property. For Austria this added insult to injury since the Grand Duke of Tuscany and the Duke of Modena were Habsburgs while the King of Naples was Franz-Joseph's brother-in-law. Something must be done to mollify the Austrian Emperor.

Eugénie always insisted that it was her idea to create a Mexican Empire and that she first suggested it to Napoleon in September 1861 when a young Spanish diplomat, José Manuel Hidalgo (a friend since childhood) was staying at the Villa Eugénie. For some time Hidalgo had been begging her to persuade her husband to send an army and save the Mexican upper classes from the godless revolution that was confiscating their estates. In fact Napoleon had already made up his mind to give Mexico a monarchy – pathologically secretive, he concealed it from Eugénie.

'But note: there was never a political move over which the Emperor had so long and so deeply brooded – for many years', the British prime minister, Benjamin Disraeli, remembered. 'In 1857 he mentioned to me his wish and willingness to assist in establishing a European dynasty in Mexico. . . . He looked upon its establishment as of high European importance.' Disraeli then explained why. 'It was his custom to say that there were two powers who hated old Europe: Russia and the U.S. of America.' And we know that Napoleon was far from along in holding such an opinion. 'Shall America become Europe's protector and master?', a French writer asked angrily in 1862.

Naïvely, the emperor believed that a Mexican empire might help to block the rise of the forthcoming transatlantic superstate. He also suffered from the delusion that the Mexican leader Benito Juarez and his 'radicals' were a tiny minority. In addition, he hoped that cotton could be grown in Mexico on a large-enough scale to make up for Confederate cotton declining imports which were destroying the French textile industry.

Eugénie told Napoleon and Hidalgo that Archduke Maximilian would make an excellent emperor. Franz-Joseph's younger brother and a former governor of Lombardy-Venetia, Maximilian was not yet thirty, handsome and dignified. The Italians had liked him, even if he was a bit pompous. On first meeting Eugénie in 1856, he had found her court 'completely lacking in tone' and was horrified by her shaking hands with her ladies. There was even a rumour that he was not a Habsburg but a Bonaparte, his real father having been the emperor's cousin 'Napoleon II'. Maximilian might have had reservations, but Eugénie was convinced that the gift of a throne could make an ally of Franz-Joseph. Napoleon agreed, hoping it would persuade him to cede Venetia to Italy.

Morny welcomed the idea, for personal reasons. Among the loans on which President Juarez had recently defaulted were Swiss bonds worth 15,000,000 pesos, in which Morny had a 30 per cent interest: unless there was military intervention, the president of the Corps Législatif was going to lose a great deal of money. Neither Napoleon nor Eugénie knew about the 'Jecker' bonds, so called after the bank which issued them.

Early in 1862 France, England and Spain sent a joint expeditionary force. At first Palmerston was enthusiastic about 'the monarchy scheme', which would 'stop the North Americans, whether of the Federal or the Confederate States in their projected absorption of Mexico', but then London and Madrid changed their minds, pulling out their troops. The French commander, Admiral Jurien de La Gravière, advised Napoleon to do the same. His advice was ignored, leaving a French army of under 3,000 men marching on Mexico City, to be humiliatingly routed en route by Juarez's guerillas. Declaring that in no circumstances would he negotiate with Juarez, the emperor sent out 30,000 more troops, who occupied the Mexican capital in June 1863, news that was cheered in Paris, although most people could see no need for the war. Napoleon had one sound reason, however – Mexican cotton, even if there was not enough of it.

In July an assembly of 'notables' in Mexico City offered the crown to Maximilian, General Bazaine arranging a plebiscite which approved the offer. Yet, understandably, the archduke was still very reluctant to commit himself. The situation was complicated by the Civil War that made French intervention possible. While the emperor refused to recognise the Confederacy, he tried to keep on good terms with both sides. In 1862 the Confederate government had offered him 22,000 tons of raw cotton, but it would have had to go through the Federal blockade on French ships and Napoleon declined, unwilling to risk war with the Union.

One must not forget that most European observers expected the South to win, as it very nearly did at Gettysburg. If this happened, then both the Union and the Confederacy would disintegrate, and none of the successor states would be strong enough to give Juarez sufficient help to overcome French intervention in Mexico, in which case Maximilian would have a reasonable chance of surviving. During the early 1860s the 'United States' were scarcely a good advertisement for republicanism, while there was what appeared to be a sound precedent for a monarchy in the New World – few American régimes seemed more solidly established than the prosperous Brazil of Emperor Pedro II, a member of the Portuguese royal family.

The concept of a Catholic monarchy in the New World had captured Eugénie's imagination – 'a dictorship that should bring liberty'. In February 1862, through Metternich and the Austrian ambassador in Brussels, she persuaded the Belgian king (Maximilian's father-in-law) to ask Queen Victoria to tell her cabinet that she had no objection to the scheme. In 1863 Eugénie visited Madrid to win over Isabella II, who was unhappy at the prospect of a Habsburg reigning over a country that had once belonged to Spain.

In March 1864 the archduke and his wife Charlotte (soon to be Carlotta) came to Paris where they were warmly welcomed. Maximilian, his jutting Habsburg lip hidden by weeping blonde side-whiskers even longer than his brother's, was impressive and Carlotta made an excellent consort, tall, stately and handsome, with large, expressive brown eyes. Eugénie and Napoleon had met the archduke before, but now they found his ideas more interesting – like them, he genuinely wished to make the world a better place.

After nearly refusing the crown, and reducing Eugénie to tears of frustration, Maximilian finally accepted. He arrived at Vera Cruz in May, having spent the voyage compiling a manual of court etiquette. Given a spectacular welcome, his régime was quickly recognised by almost every European country. However, Washington and Richmond refused to acknowledge him, while attempts to float a loan in Paris or London failed disastrously. He soon found that he ruled only by the grace of French bayonets, most Mexicans staying loyal to Juarez, who was an Indian like themselves. Intent on recovering their estates, the conservatives sneered at his good intentions and liberal ministers, and at a constitution that safeguarded the rights of manual workers.

As soon as the Civil War ended, the Union sent guns and volunteers to Juarez, and North American cotton began reaching France. Bazaine's men suffered such heavy casualties that in October 1865 he issued an order not to take prisoners. The situation continued to deteriorate. Early in 1866 Napoleon accepted that the adventure had failed, although the last French troops would not withdraw until 1867. Maximilian asked Bazaine to train a Mexican army but the marshal advised him to leave with the French.

Having bombarded Napoleon and Eugénie with letters, in August 1866 Empress Carlotta suddenly appeared in Paris. Eugénie called on her at her hotel, explaining that the emperor was too ill to see her (he was in agony, from a stone in his bladder). Carlotta made such a scene, however, that she gave way, asking her to come to Saint-Cloud the next day. When Carlotta arrived, the Mexican eagle was flying over the château and she was greeted by the little Prince Imperial wearing a Mexican order.

Napoleon told her gently that he could no longer go on helping Maximilian. France had already lost too many men. 'You've condemned us to death', cried Carlotta. He continued patiently that the Senate and Corps Législatif opposed any further involvement in Mexico, but she demanded that he mount a coup to make them change their minds.

Carlotta forced her way into Saint-Cloud four times more. On the last occasion the emperor said that her husband should abdicate – he would be found another throne in the Balkans and all Europe would admire him for 'sparing blood and tears'. She screamed, 'blood and tears, they're going to flow again and again because of you, in rivers of blood, all on your head'. When Eugénie offered her a glass of water, she threw it at her, howling, 'Murderers, I won't drink your poison.'

The Empress Carlotta then left for Rome, writing to Maximilian that Napoleon was really the devil in disguise. At Rome she told the pope that her ladies were trying to kill her and must be arrested. She had gone completely insane. Taken home to Belgium, she lived on, hopelessly mad, until 1927. The Emperor himself stayed in Mexico, refusing to abdicate or to leave the country, which, for the time being, was protected by French troops.

If Eugénie's judgment failed her over Mexico, her husband was equally at fault. She was certainly telling the truth when she said that her concept of a Mexican empire had been largely inspired by a wish to bring benefits to a backward country. 'We were misled,' she claimed with reason, 'We were told that the Mexican people would welcome the proclamation of a monarchy . . . several times – for example, after our troops entered Mexico city, after Bazaine's victories in the northern provinces or after Maximilian's warm reception at his capital – we had some cause to think that the expedition would be a success.'

Even so, as will be seen, sometimes she was shrewder than her husband.

REDRAWING THE MAP OF EUROPE

During the 1860s European politics were bewilderingly complex, but an account of them cannot be omitted if one is to understand Eugénie. As she herself insisted, what really interested her were foreign affairs, and we know that from the very earliest days of her marriage, Napoleon III had been in the habit of discussing policy with her – although he did not always tell her everything that was in his mind. Gradually she became obsessed with international relations in Europe, far more than with the problems of Mexico. At the same time, when her husband's health began to deteriorate he grew much readier to listen to her views and take her advice. Even if she was wrong about the Mexican empire, generally her instincts were excellent. No other woman of the nineteenth century possessed influence of this sort, on such a scale.

After the Crimean War was over, the emperor had tried, at first with reasonable success, to build closer relations with Russia, while attempting to keep on as good terms as he could with England. The new Russian emperor, Alexander II (the future liberator of the serfs), who was certainly a more imaginative and flexible man than his father Nicholas I had been, welcomed Napoleon's overtures. During the Italian war of 1859 he alerted France to the danger of Prussian intervention, sending his personal aide-de-camp, Prince Schuvalov, to Paris to warn the emperor, and to some extent Prussia was deterred from attacking across the Rhine by nervousness about Russian intentions.

As has been seen, however, Eugénie's dislike of the upheavals caused by the 1859 war, and her deepening friendship with the Metternichs, made her more and more inclined to see Austria and not Russia as France's natural ally. This was by no means a new approach – it had always been the policy of King Louis-Philippe's government and, during the Second Empire's early years, of the foreign minister, Drouyn de Lhuys. Moreover, a fair number of very influential Austrians saw Russia as their greatest enemy.

What finally destroyed any likelihood of a lasting understanding between France and Russia was the sudden re-emergence of the insoluble Polish question. The Kingdom of Poland had disappeared during the infamous 'partitions' of the last quarter of the eighteenth century, Russia taking the bulk of the country, Austria the south-west and Prussia the north-west, a tripartite occupation that was renewed by the 1815 settlement. A rising by the Poles against the Russians in 1831 had failed, despite arousing sympathy throughout Europe.

From the very beginning, Napoleon III had wanted to help the Poles. They had fought heroically for his uncle, who, if the 1812 campaign had ended differently, would almost certainly have restored their ancient kingdom. He had cursed the craven Louis-Philippe for not even protesting, let alone intervening, during the crushing of the 1831 rising.

By January 1863 when 'one fine morning the bombshell of the Polish insurrection burst about our heads', as Eugénie put it, the emperor's sympathy had grown still deeper, in common with most western Europeans. Not only did liberals feel pity for an enslaved nation but Catholics were angry at the oppression of their co-religionists; in Montalembert's words, 'Since the murder of Poland all Europe has been in a state of mortal sin.' Graphic reports of savage reprisals by the Russians caused widespread revulsion. The unequal struggle lasted for over a year, tens of thousands of Polish patriots being herded off in chains to Siberia.

In 1914 the empress discussed the insurrection with the diplomat Maurice Paléologue. All too often in *Entretiens de l'Impératrice Eugénie,** Paléologue put his own opinions and even his own words into Eugénie's mouth, sometimes altering what she had said to him (especially when it was about Kaiser Wilhelm II). Yet his account of

* Christophe Pincemaille (2000) dismisses the Entretiens as '*un faux grossier*' (a clumsy sham) and Kurtz (1964) calls it 'one of the poisoned wells'. This is excessive. A good deal in it is obviously genuine and of real value, even if one has always to be on guard against Paléologue's emendations and flights of fancy. Undoubtedly he had had many discussions with Eugénie.

her recollections of what happened in 1863 is convincing. Her mind retained all its clarity.

'You cannot imagine the magnificent impression made by this people suddenly rising in defence of their religion and their nationhood', she recalled. 'Nothing so heroic had been seen since the Spaniards' revolt against the French occupation . . . every church was a living centre of patriotism.' She was thrilled by the way compassion for Poland united the French. 'From republicans to Legitimists, from free-thinkers to clericals, from Jules Favre to Mgr Dupanloup, from the Faubourg Saint-Germain to the Faubourg Saint-Antoine, there arose the same cry of admiration for the Poles and of disgust with Russia.' For the first time she found herself in complete agreement with Plon-Plon – 'My ferocious enemy, Prince Napoleon'.

France, England and Austria sent notes to St Petersburg, advising Russia to give the Poles a constitution. The emperor assured a Polish leader in Paris, Prince Adam Czartoryski, that he intended to send them guns and then an army – he was prepared to go to war if he could find allies.

A fortnight after the rising broke out, Bismarck (Prussia's new minister-president) sent General von Alvensleben to sign an agreement with Russia allowing her troops to pursue 'rebels' over the Prussian border but declined a proposal by the tsar that Prussia and Russia should immediately declare war on France and Austria. Eugénie said that Bismarck's motive was 'separating France and Russia', yet relations between them had already collapsed. When Napoleon complained to Berlin about its own ill treatment of the Poles the British wrongly suspected he was planning to attack Prussia and seize the Rhineland frontier – the emperor had no wish to fight both Prussia and Russia.

Prince Metternich reported a conversation he had with Eugénie at the Tuileries on 21 February 1863. Producing a map of Europe, she said she would like to fly over it with him so that they could get a bird's eye view. ('What a flight, and what a bird', he joked in his dispatch.) She wanted to redraw the map, she told Metternich. She wished to see Poland restored under the king of Saxony, Russia being compensated at Turkey's expense. Prussia would get Saxony and

Hanover – surely something could be found in America for the Hanoverian king? Austria would cede Galicia to Poland and Venetia to Italy in return for Silesia, part of Germany south of the Main and Bosnia-Herzegovina. Italy would give up the Papal States and Naples. Constantinople would go to Greece. The empress admitted, without any embarrassment, that the scheme meant war with Prussia.

Historians have laughed at 'this extraordinary incident'. (William Smith comments, 'While thrones fell, dynasties were transplanted and fundamental problems were resolved by the feminine touch.') But Eugénie was flying a kite, her basic message being that France wanted an Austrian alliance. Metternich took it seriously enough to go to Vienna, to spend days discussing the plan with emperor Franz-Joseph and the foreign Minister Rechberg. They realised that it had Napoleon's support, but were too nervous to commit themselves. Meanwhile, Eugénie offered a practical diplomatic objective. Writing on 1 March, Lord Cowley said it was 'A Poland all but independent under a Grand Duke', in return for Russia being given a reasonably free hand in Turkey.

The emperor went on trying to save the Poles until the end of 1863, warmly encouraged by Eugénie, who was determined that France should do her best to rescue them. Sadly, apart from some mild diplomatic muttering, England and Austria refused to do anything concrete once they had sent their notes to St Petersburg. Sweden, on the other hand, even suggested a Franco-Swedish war against Russia – but the Swedes' motive was not so much to help the Poles as to regain Finland for Sweden. At home, Fould and Morny (always pro-Russian) were against military action in any form, insisting that diplomacy was the only way to find a solution.

In November 1863 Napoleon proposed that a European congress should meet urgently, to discuss rearranging the frontiers of the 1815 settlement together with the Polish problem. England and Austria immediately declined, the latter disturbed by Eugénie's blueprint for the future. In December, without much hope, the emperor repeated his proposal for a congress, to be attended instead by Russia, Prussia and Italy, to redraw the map of Europe on the lines suggested by Eugénie to Metternich. None of the powers involved would accept the invitation. Their refusal meant that all

Empress Eugénie in 1853, in robes of state. Franz Xaver Winterhalter's official portrait. (*Museo Napoleonico, Rome*)

Napoleon III in 1857, by Winterhalter. This is a flattering portrait of an ugly little man, who despite his appearance possessed considerable charm. (*Musée national du château, Compiègne: AKG London/Erich Lessing*)

Eugénie and Napoleon in 1853, examining plans for completion of the Louvre, by Ange Tissier (*Musée du château*

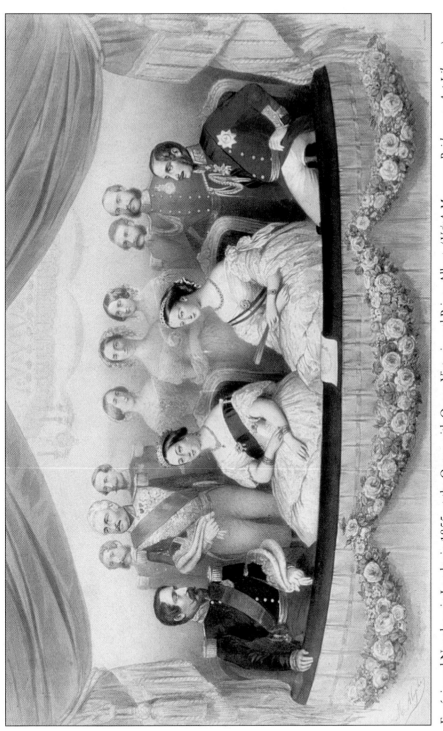

Eugénie and Napoleon in Londonin 1855, at the Opera with Queen Victoria and Prince Albert. (*V&A Museum: Bridgeman Art Library*)

Eugénie and Grand Prince Ferdinand of Tuscany in the uniform of the imperial hunt, at Compiègne in October 1856. Photograph by Comte Aguado. (*Chateau de Compiègne: RMN/Frank Raux*)

Eugénie, Napoleon and 'Lou-Lou', the Prince Imperial, in 1859. Doctors warned that trying to bear a second child would kill the empress. Photograph by Disdéri. (*Author's collection*)

The Prince Imperial in 1861, as a haughty Grenadier of the Imperial Guard. The prince's name was already on the regiment's muster-roll. Photograph by Disdéri. (*Author's collection*)

The astonishing spectacle of *a woman* presiding over a nineteenth-century cabinet meeting: the Empress Regent with her ministers in June 1859. (*Illustrated London News*)

Eugénie and Napoleon as a happy married couple in 1862. In reality the emperor was a wildly unfaithful husband and Eugénie a wife tormented by jealousy. Photograph by Disdéri. (*Archiv für Kunst und Geschichte, Berlin: AKG London*)

Eugénie's private *salon* at the Tuileries, by Castiglione. Her favourite room, hung in Indian silk, was always full of flowers.
(*Liria Palace, Madrid: Institut Amatller d'Art Hispànic-Arxiu Mas*)

Prince and Princess Metternich. Pauline (the 'Cocoa Monkey') was Eugénie's closest, if ultimately faithless, friend. She is wearing a dress designed by Mr Worth. Photograph by Disdéri. (*Archiv für Kunst und Geschichte, Berlin: AKG London*)

Above left: Otto von Bismarck (*Gothaischer genealogischer Hofkalender, 1870*)
Above right: King William of Prussia (*Gothaischer genealogischer Hofkalender, 1871*)

Eugénie's escape in 1870, restaged by actors for the former court photographer Comte Aguado. Two, not five, men had been present. (*Author's collection*)

The imperial family in exile at Chislehurst, December 1872. This is the last known photograph of Napoleon III, who was planning another *coup d'état*. (*Private collection: AKG London*)

Right: 'Napoleon IV' at twenty-one, in British uniform, from a photograph of 1877. He is wearing the mess kit of the Royal Artillery. (*Author's collection*)

Below: The death of the Prince Imperial in 1879 by Jamin. On the front of his body were found seventeen assegai wounds. (*Château de Compiègne: RMN – Jean Hutin*)

Eugénie's court in exile about 1905 at Villa Cyrnos, from an unpublished photograph, with Augustin Filon on the extreme left, and Franceschini Pietri next to him. (*Collection of Dudley Heathcote*)

his efforts to save the Poles had been in vain; without obtaining anything for them other than a worthless Russian promise to be 'merciful', he had merely succeeded in infuriating the tsar.

At the beginning of 1864 Napoleon failed to take advantage of the crisis over Schleswig-Holstein, until then ruled by the late king of Denmark, which had offered a chance of reforging the French *entente* with England. Even Lord Palmerston considered going to war when Austria and Prussia attacked Denmark in the spring – for one thing, it was the home of the recently married Princess of Wales – but, with his ingrained paranoia, he did not have enough confidence in the emperor. As it was, another, shrewder British statesman, Lord Clarendon, observed that merely by denouncing Bismarck as a deliberate disturber of the peace, who was using the war for Prussia to 'lord it over Germany', Napoleon would be regarded by all Europe as a public benefactor and get every German democrat on his side – without involving France in the conflict. Yet, prejudiced in favour of his Bernadotte cousins, the Emperor hoped that a weakened Denmark might be absorbed into a single Scandinavian state ruled from Stockholm.

Even after the Austrians and Prussians had overwhelmed the Danish army, 'liberating' Schleswig-Holstein, Napoleon misread the situation and became alarmed at the prospect of a continuing Austro–Prussian alliance. Eugénie realised, however, that Schleswig-Holstein would soon end up as part of Prussia. Making the best of a bad job, she commented that it was preferable to creating another under-sized German state.

Meanwhile, she was evolving an imaginative and not entirely impractical scheme for rebuilding the church of the Holy Sepulchre at Jerusalem. She hoped that a joint endeavour of this sort would result in a spirit of ecumenism and international cooperation, bringing lasting peace to a divided Europe. In essence, her project involved building two great churches side by side, one Roman Catholic and the other Orthodox, with a central nave which would be available to all the other Christian communions. The scheme was finally abandoned when in March 1865 Pius IX let it be known that only Catholics had the right to rebuild the church of the Holy Sepulchre – although the pope added graciously that he would make no objection should the empress wish to pay for restoring the church's dome.

Eugénie's growing determination to share in the shaping of French foreign policy was hampered by Napoleon III's habitual, bewildering inscrutability. Even to his wife he was always the 'Sphinx of the Tuileries', a man who was pathologically obsessed with secrecy. 'The emperor is not exactly communicative', Viel Castel had noted a few years earlier:

> He remains for whole days, so to speak, without opening his mouth and totally absorbed in his inmost thoughts. Calm and impenetrable, even with the people who are most in his confidence, his soul seems as adamantine as his face. Impressed by no one, no one is allowed to share in what he is thinking. He is like some meticulous craftsman, who has plenty of the highest quality tools, but no assistants. You cannot even hope to judge him by what he does, since its real significance is often missed by the keenest observers.

Nevertheless, Eugénie could often guess what was in the emperor's mind. At first he had told her no more than a little, so that – as he intended – she could repeat it to the foreign ambassadors, which was an extremely useful means of sounding them out or spreading rumours. Gradually, however, she developed opinions of her own, which were more traditionalist than the emperor's. This first became apparent over Rome, then over Mexico, then over Poland and finally over Austria. As Napoleon's health worsened, inevitably the empress's influence grew, while her ideas became clearer and firmer.

Eugénie had certainly begun to assert her own opinions, and very strongly, as early as 1861. Viel Castel, who obtained most of his information about her from Princesse Mathilde or from those in the princess's circle, recorded in June that year how she was already attempting to influence imperial policy over Poland. She had secretly contributed an anonymous article to a highly influential newspaper, the *Constitutionel*, in which she had attacked Russia and praised the Polish extremists. 'She would like us to support the rebel movement in that country as much as possible, whatever the cost', explains the diarist, who was writing at least eighteen months before the Polish insurrection of 1863. He adds, 'She is no less pronounced in her views about the confiscated Italian states.'

At breakfast in the Tuileries with the emperor one morning in May 1861, according to the diarist (or, more probably, to Princesse Mathilde, who was present), Eugénie spoke about nothing except international affairs, criticising French foreign policy so savagely that eventually the normally phlegmatic Napoleon rose to his feet, saying, 'Really, Eugénie, you seem to forget two things – first, that you are French and, second, that you are married to a Bonaparte.'

'I have great difficulty in making any sense of this woman's character at all, nor am I able to discover just what it is that she wants', the diary continues. 'Her love for the emperor is to a very large extent conditioned by ambition, her maternal instincts appear to be extremely unsatisfactory, and the way she behaves is more than likely to alienate the French people.' This is not the voice of Comte Horace de Viel Castel but of his informant, Princesse Mathilde Bonaparte, pursuing her unforgiving vendetta against Eugénie. She also supplied the Goncourt brothers with the same sort of vicious gossip. Mathilde's venomously bitter voice can be heard in the rest of the entry about Eugénie. 'She carefully makes friends with all the ladies whom the emperor *distinguishes* with his attention, approves of their relations with her husband, and by exploiting their influence tries to wield still greater power over him.' Yet, however prejudiced and unreliable Viel Castel or Princesse Mathilde may have been, there is no ground for disbelieving their claim that as early as 1861 Eugénie had been trying to dominate her husband and to put into practice a foreign policy that was sometimes very much her own.

OTTO VON BISMARCK

On 27 August 1864 a dying Horace de Viel Castel wrote his last journal entry. As a malicious connoisseur of scandal, what he said has always to be treated with caution, especially on 'the foul arena of politics', yet often he was shrewd. He tells us that, distrusted by Russia, Prussia and Austria, above all by England, France is totally isolated. 'She has let Denmark be defeated in the recent war, having been 'tricked by Mons. de Bismarck.' He ends, 'We are hastening towards our decline. Everything that was young about the emperor has grown old and what was not yet decayed even four years ago is now entirely so.' Although we can now see that Viel Castel's forebodings were justified, few would have agreed with him in the summer of 1864. Among the exceptions was Eugénie.

On 4 October 1865 the Prussian minister-president arrived at Biarritz. Despite being well over fifty, bald and walrus-moustached, he was a magnificent-looking man, built on the lines of a Wagnerian hero, who spoke excellent French in a deep, musical voice and had a keen sense of humour. Women liked him. The empress herself admired him, even if she recognised an enemy when she saw one. He was going to destroy Bonapartist France and his name was Count von Bismarck-Schoenhausen.

Napoleon and Eugénie had met Bismarck before. He had been presented to them as a member of the Prussian delegation to the Congress of Paris, while in 1862 he had spent several months in France as his country's ambassador. This time the gigantic Prussian charmed everyone at the Villa Eugénie, even Mérimée enjoying his conversation. He flirted with one of the ladies, the beautiful Comtesse de la Bedoyère, who took such a fancy to him that (according to Dr Barthez) Mérimée painted Bismarck's face on a piece of cardboard and put it on her pillow – going up to her bedroom after dinner, she rushed out, screaming, 'My God, there's a man in my bed'.

Otto von Bismarck treated the empress not just politely but with genuine respect. When he was ambassador he had described her as 'the only man in Paris', a surprising tribute from someone who did not usually accept women as equals. For all his charm, Eugénie knew that this was the most dangerous man in Europe. Having seen how ruthlessly he had behaved towards the Poles, she watched with alarm his outmanoeuvring of Austria.

The reason Bismarck had come to Biarritz was to find out what the emperor would do in the event of war between Prussia and Austria, the two men spending several days in secret discussion. He suspected that Napoleon hoped to avoid being caught up in hostilities and wanted the two German powers to fight themselves to a standstill, after which he could annex some territory. But the minister-president had to make sure. In strict confidence he explained that he meant to drive Austria out of northern Germany and, in addition, force her to surrender Venetia to Italy – Prussia was going to ally with the Italians. And he promised to give France either Belgium or Luxembourg.

Bismarck had guessed right. With his best troops away in Mexico, Napoleon had no wish to join in the fighting and was not going to commit himself, as he had done so disastrously to Cavour at Plombières in 1858. Unlike Cavour, however, Bismarck asked him to do nothing, while it would certainly be most gratifying if Venetia were to be given to Italy.

The minister-president went back to Berlin in a very good mood, merely saying that he had met 'two remarkable women', by whom he meant Eugénie and the lovely, but hare-brained, Comtesse de la Bedoyère.

An unadventurous foreign policy suited the emperor very well, partly because his health was starting to crack. Exhausted by a sexual appetite verging on satyriasis, he was also debilitated by chain-smoking – not cigars, unusually for the period, but cigarettes. Ominously, he was beginning to suffer from mysterious pains in the bladder.

The empress did not share her husband's optimism and dreaded the prospect of a victorious Prussia. Realising that the Second Empire's one hope of survival lay in an Austrian alliance, she begged Metternich to persuade Franz-Joseph to surrender Venetia. It would have a magic effect on French opinion. Convinced that in the end she would bring Napoleon round to her way of thinking, she assured Metternich that Austria could go to war knowing that France would quickly join in on her side – 'Yes, yes, the emperor is committed to neutrality, but only until the first shot has been fired.' She told him this again and again throughout March, April and May 1866, when on paper Austria was still Prussia's ally.

By now Eugénie was terrified of Bismarck. A baffling mixture of Lutheran piety and cynicism, a Prussian nobleman rather than a German nationalist, he was determined to serve his king by extending Prussian rule over all the states of Protestant north Germany, and eventually over those of the Catholic south as well.

To do so, he had to end Austrian domination of the Germanic Confederation, which meant war. If Prussia won, then France would be menaced by a power far more dangerous than Austria. Eugénie understood this at once, unlike the tired, self-deluding emperor.

When Austria ended her treaty with Prussia on 12 June, Metternich signed a secret pact with France the same day, by which Austria agreed to surrender Venetia and France promised to restrain Italy. But although war was imminent, Napoleon refused to abandon his neutrality.

Hostilities broke out on 18 June, Austria supported by the tiny armies of Saxony, Hanover, Hesse-Cassel and Nassau. Remembering the Italian campaign, everyone in France, including Eugénie, admired Austrian troops with their excellent artillery and were not surprised when they routed the Italians at Custozza a week later. The French were quite sure they would defeat the Prussians just as easily, contemptuous of its reservists and *landwehr*. Yet General Bourbaki, who had recently visited Berlin, warned them, 'Be as rude as you like about this army of lawyers and occulists but it will march into Vienna whenever it wants.'

While the emperor waited for a suitable moment to intervene, Eugénie tried to help the Austrians, giving Metternich the names of French firms that held large stores of lint and bandages. Above all she urged the necessity of sprinkling hospital beds with carbolic acid, 'which numerous experiments here have proved to be a preventative against typhus and fevers'.

On 3 July, brilliantly coordinated by Helmuth von Moltke, the Prussians smashed the Austrians at Sadowa (Königgrätz) in Bohemia, inflicting ghastly casualties. That evening the Austrian foreign minister, Count von Rechberg, telegraphed Metternich in Paris – 'only French armed intervention stands in the way of Prussia gaining exclusive domination over Germany'. Bismarck thought so too. Later he admitted he had never understood why the French did not cross the Rhine while the Prussians were still held up in Bohemia. Even 15,000 men would have been enough. 'The mere sight of your red trousers in the Duchy of Baden and the Palatinate would have raised all south Germany against Prussia. . . . I am not even sure that we could have defended Berlin.'

'The consternation here at the successes of Prussia continues to be very great', reported Cowley that night. 'I speak of high quarters.' Clearly he had been surprised by Napoleon's neutrality. 'The emperor is getting alarmed at his Frankenstein, and is turning his mind a little too late to the problem of how Austria is to be saved.'

On 10 July a Prussian envoy, Prince Reuss, received a veiled warning from Eugénie, who told him that the prospect of Prussian hegemony over Germany was making Napoleon very uneasy. 'With such a nation for a neighbour, we should run the risk of finding you one day in front of Paris before we had ever suspected it. . . . I shall go to bed French and wake up Prussian.' She told him that Prussia owed a lot to French neutrality and must not exploit her victory too much. France, she lied, 'desired nothing but peace'.

In reality Eugénie had been doing her best to make the emperor declare war. The fullest account of a crucial meeting of the Council at Saint-Cloud on 5 July is that which she gave to Paléologue in January 1905. When Drouyn de Lhuys, once again foreign minister, had insisted the only possible option was war, Eugénie broke in to ask Marshal Randon, minister for war, if the army was ready to invade across the Rhine. Without hesitation he replied that 80,000 troops could be concentrated immediately – 250,000 more within three weeks. At this, she demanded that the army should march at once. 'I felt that the fate of France and our dynasty's future were at stake', she recalled bitterly. She was supported by Drouyn and Randon.

Napoleon then asked other ministers for their opinion. Underlining the obvious, the Marquis de la Valette, minister for the interior, argued that opposing Prussia meant allying with Austria and therefore abandoning Italy. He was quite certain, he added inanely, that France could obtain any territory she wanted 'through friendly negotiations with Berlin'. His views were shared by Rouher, minister of state, and Baroche, minister of justice.

'When the Prussian armies are no longer kept busy in Bohemia and are able to turn and give us their undivided attention, Bismarck will merely laugh at our claims', Eugenie responded angrily. 'Prussia had no scruples about stopping you after Solferino', she reminded Napoleon. 'Why worry about doing the same to her after Königgrätz?

We gave way in 1859 because we could not find the 50,000 troops needed to bar the road to Paris, but today the road to Berlin lies open.' Again, both Drouyn and Randon warmly supported her.

The Council took three decisions. First, the Senate and Corps Législatif should be summoned urgently to vote the money needed for general mobilisation. Second, 50,000 troops should be concentrated on the Rhine immediately. Third, a stern note should be sent to Berlin, warning that France would not tolerate territorial alterations to which she had not given her consent. These decisions were to be announced next day in the *Moniteur* (the official gazette).

Although Randon was over-optimistic, the French could certainly have massed 50,000 troops on the Rhine very quickly, which would have brought the South German States into the war on Austria's side. Their sovereigns had no wish to be gobbled up by Prussia, even if a small and vociferous group in each little country wanted unification. While Württemberg had only 22,000 troops and Baden a mere 16,000, the Bavarian army was genuinely formidable with 190,000. The western areas of Prussia (Westphalia and the Rhineland) could have been invaded with ease, causing panic in Berlin. Moreover, the Austrians were regrouping, waiting for reinforcements from the Italian front.

War was the one way to stop Prussia overrunning all Germany. If she did, then it was merely a question of time before she attacked the Second Empire. A few days after Königgrätz, Victor Duruy warned the emperor that in order to consolidate her gains Prussia would 'humiliate France, just as she has humiliated Austria'. Rouher, France's nearest thing to a prime minister, did not agree, however. A subtle Auvergnat, in the words of Professor William Smith, he 'knew how to play on that weakness for intellectual speculation which so often hampered the Imperial will'. During the night after the Council he showed Napoleon reports chosen by La Valette and Baroche to give the false impression that war with Prussia would be very unpopular with the French.

The following morning the announcements did not appear in the *Moniteur*. At the next Council on 10 July Eugénie, Drouyn and Randon tried frantically to revive intervention, but failed. In a despairing letter Eugénie told Metternich, 'They are exaggerating today's danger to make us forget tomorrow's.' She ended, 'If only you could give those Prussians a really good thrashing.'

Her opponents in the Council dismissed what she wanted as 'a policy of adventure', but very soon Napoleon admitted to her that he had made a mistake. 'By then it was too late to retrieve it, since the chance had been lost', she remembered. 'At the time he seemed so utterly crushed that I trembled for our future.' On 23 July she told Metternich, 'He can no longer walk, no longer sleep, scarcely eat.' She had advised him to abdicate in favour of the Prince Imperial with herself as regent. Yet she never stopped trying to make Napoleon declare war, telling Metternich on 25 July that she was certain he would do so, when he visited the camp at Chalons in the autumn. (The French army was eager to cross the Rhine.) For the moment he was at Vichy, seeing no one except her ally Drouyn whom she had sent there. Meanwhile she was working on other ministers. Metternich was amazed at her determination. Eventually Napoleon agreed to move as soon as the Prussians advanced on Vienna, but on 26 July – the day Metternich wrote his dispatch – Prussia and Austria began negotiations for peace.

'The empress told Goltz that she looked upon the present state of things as *le commencement de la fin de la dynastie*', Cowley reported early in August, quoting the Prussian ambassador. 'This is exaggeration. What with Mexico, what with Italy, what with his late mediation, the emperor has no doubt fallen in prestige, but as yet there are no signs of public discontent.' A few days later, however, Cowley was saying that Napoleon would have to get some sort of compensation from Prussia to calm public opinion. But Eugénie was worried about more than prestige, telling Goltz on 20 August that Prussia's army was 'twice as strong as the French and asserting in jest that France had to guard against a Prussian invasion for the conquest of Alsace-Lorraine'.

Drouyn resigned in despair. His successor as foreign minister was the Marquis de Moustier. Lord Cowley had a low opinion of the marquis, writing, 'He hates business, it seems, and prefers the society of ballet-dancers to all others . . . he has made every place he has been in too hot to hold him.' This was at a time when Napoleon needed clear-headed advisers.

On 23 August Prussia and Austria signed the Peace of Prague, Prussia annexing Hanover, Hesse-Cassel, Nassau, Schleswig-Holstein and the free city of Frankfurt (whose mayor hanged himself). A North German Confederation was formed with the Prussian king as president, the South German States agreeing to a programme of military and economic cooperation. Emperor Franz-Joseph was so weakened within his own lands that he was forced to grant the Magyars autonomy, creating the Austro-Hungarian dual monarchy.

Regaining their equilibrium, Napoleon and Eugénie tried hard to give the impression that nonetheless all was well with the Second Empire. When Felix Whitehurst went to a ball at the Tuileries in January 1867, he found a scene of the utmost tranquillity. 'Good music pervaded the atmosphere, and when, to the "Belle Hélène", some twenty couples waltzed before the emperor and empress in the splendid Throne-room, the effect was very striking', he told readers of the *Daily Telegraph*. 'The emperor, who had been skating all day, looked very well; the empress, who was very simply dressed in white trimmed with white roses and ivy, reminded one of the empress of twelve years ago.'

Behind the scenes, however, the couple were desperately worried. France, indisputably Europe's greatest military power for the last seventy years, was now being challenged by what until recently had been only a minor power. As Cowley predicted, a 'policy of compensation' ensued after the Peace of Prague, Count Benedetti, the French ambassador at Berlin, informing Bismarck that his emperor would offer no opposition to Prussia taking over South Germany so long as France was given Belgium or Luxembourg. (Unwisely, he submitted the offer in writing.)

Realising Belgium was beyond his reach, Napoleon hoped to obtain Luxembourg, whose capital was then the strongest fortress in Europe. Its Grand Duke, King William III of Holland, was ready enough to sell it since it did not go through the female line and he had no sons. If the Luxembourgeois could not stay independent, they preferred union with France to absorption by Prussia, which had seemed more than likely after Königgrätz. In negotiations that he took care to keep secret from his Council – and, above all, from the staunchly pro-Austrian Eugénie – Napoleon offered Prussia an alliance against Austria in return.

Bismarck brusquely rejected the offer. He also revealed the emperor's designs on the Grand Duchy to the German press, which was outraged, furiously trumpeting that 'Luxembourg is a German country.' In Berlin and Paris there was serious talk of war. 'Nothing could be more agreeable to us than a war, which in any case cannot be avoided', purred General von Moltke. 'France fears that Alsace-Lorraine will be wrenched from her' was how Count von der Goltz in Paris explained the French attitude – devoted to Eugénie, he genuinely wanted peace. (Napoleon then confused the ambassador by confiding that France and Prussia 'were like two friends in a café who feel they ought to have a fight but who cannot think why.') Prince Metternich informed Vienna that the empress was complaining 'they were very much annoyed with Prussia', and adding that large-scale military preparations were in hand which should be completed by the end of the year.

The situation grew increasingly tense throughout the early months of 1867 – for a few nerve-racking days in the spring many well-informed observers in both Berlin and Paris thought that war was inevitable. 'All Friday things were in a terrible way, and the declaration of war against Prussia by France was in the mouth of everybody', an obviously very alarmed Mr Whitehurst, normally an optimist, told his *Daily Telegraph* readers in England on Sunday 21 April. 'The Bourse has been in a panic, the tone of society uneasy and the general feeling feverish.'

The crisis had passed by the end of the month. France was not ready to fight and Bismarck did not want to have a war – not just yet. A settlement was reached, Luxembourg ceased to be a member of the German Confederation while the Prussian garrison that had occupied its capital since 1815 was withdrawn, after dismantling the fortifications. However, the Grand Duchy became a neutral state instead of being handed over to Napoleon, who failed to get his 'compensation'.

During the exceptionally tortuous and distrustful negotiations over Luxembourg the French foreign minister, Moustier, made the remarkable statement that 'M. de Bismarck does not always act in bad faith.' Even so, the French had been completely outwitted, and it was another bitter humiliation for their emperor. Putting matters in perspective, with only too much justification Adolphe Thiers had reminded a sombre Corps Législatif in March 1867 that Prussia's victory at Königgrätz had been the worst disaster to befall France since the Allied invasion of 1814.

It was also a further triumph for the Prussian minister-president, giving Eugénie still more reason to fear him. Yet, despite everything – including what was to come – she could never bring herself to dislike the man. Forty years later, asked who were among 'the most *fascinating* personalities' she had ever met, she mentioned Bismarck first. 'When it was worth his while,' she said with a peculiar smile, 'no one could be a more adroit courtier.' The questioner suddenly realised that instead of boring the empress, as had so many other men, by telling her how beautiful she was, he had complimented her on her flair for politics.

EUGENIE AS MARIE-ANTOINETTE

In 1854, Winterhalter painted the empress in a garden at Versailles, in an eighteenth-century dress of pale gold taffeta and with powdered hair. Only the year before Hübner had watched the ninety-year-old Isabey picking up her fan – if Isabey, who had painted Marie-Antoinette, saw Eugénie dressed like this, he may well have thought that he was seeing a ghost. Princesse Mathilde told the Goncourt brothers it was ridiculous for the empress to compare herself with the queen, yet the two women had much in common. Disliked as foreigners, criticised for their clothes, jewels and parties, both were on insecure thrones and had a vulnerable child.

When Napoleon III asked Eugénie to marry him, he warned of the dangers and reminded her of Marie-Antoinette's fate, which frightened even Doña Maria Manuela. During her honeymoon the empress visited the Petit Trianon where the queen had played at being a milkmaid, and later installed a copy of the dairy in a small country house near Saint-Cloud. In future years she would warmly encourage the Petit Trianon's restoration, visiting it regularly – as if hoping to commune with the spirit of her predecessor. Sometimes the great antiquary Count Nieuwerkerker expounded learnedly on how the little palace must have looked in Marie-Antoinette's day, the empress listening with rapt attention.

As early as 9 May 1853, when Eugénie was pregnant for the first time, she wrote to Paca, 'I am thinking with terror of the poor dauphin Louis XVII, of Charles I, of Mary Stuart and of Marie-Antoinette. What is going to be my poor child's destiny? I would a thousand times rather that my son had a less glittering but safer crown.' In her far from infrequent moods of depression, Eugénie began increasingly to fear that her husband would be overthrown like Louis XVI, and that she too would die a terrifying death. Above all, she worried about the Prince Imperial. Would he end as horribly as the little Dauphin had in the Temple, sixty-three years before?

Viel Castel had noticed the empress's obvious emotion when shortly after her marriage she went to the Conciergerie to see the cell where Marie-Antoinette had been imprisoned during her trial, and from where she was taken to be guillotined. She also visited the National Archives to read the letter written by the queen on the night before her execution. One night she returned unexpectedly to the Archives, asking the keeper to show her the queen's last letter again, while she chose Maundy Thursday 1860 (when she was probably fasting) to revisit the cell at the Conciergerie.

Baron Hübner thought that her obsession bordered on the morbid. Staying at Saint-Cloud in April 1855 he was shown the imperial couple's private apartments, and observed, 'The empress's almost superstitious cult for Queen Marie-Antoinette may be seen in her own rooms (these were the rooms that had once been occupied by Marie-Antoinette):

In the bedroom that she shares with the emperor, only one picture hangs on the walls. It is an old print that depicts Louis XVI's unlucky consort. Clearly, 'Doña Eugenia' is convinced that she is going to die on the scaffold. She has said to me more than once, and when I smiled she went red. She mentioned, as absolute proof that a tragic fate awaited her, how when preparing her trousseau for her marriage she had been offered a lace veil that the queen had worn. It was really most tempting, but Mlle de Montijo simply did not have enough money to buy it. She was therefore overwhelmed – both elated and depressed – when opening her wedding presents she found sitting on top of them the same veil, the very same, that had once belonged to Marie-Antoinette.

In October the following year (only a few months after the demoralising ordeal when she had so painfully given birth to the Prince Imperial), the empress and Hübner had another conversation while he was staying at Compiègne, during which they discussed the queen and her execution. 'I would much rather be assassinated in the streets', Eugénie confided in the ambassador. 'I have lost all my *sang-froid*. Since my lying-in, I have had a deeply disturbed imagination.' Hübner comments condescendingly, 'Poor woman. It is no bed of roses being on a throne, even an imitation one.' Obviously an element of terror contributed to Eugénie's not infrequent bursts of ill-temper.

Understandably, the birth of the Prince Imperial made the empress think still more of Queen Marie-Antoinette and the dauphin. In London *The Times* reflected that since Louis XIV no French monarch had been succeeded by his son although almost none of them had been childless, gloomily prophesying, 'The Napoleon born last Sunday morning may be crowned the last of his line; or may add one more to the Pretenders of France.' During the weeks that followed the Orsini plot Cowley reported that 'The poor empress is tormented to death by anonymous letters telling her that the little Prince is to be carried off and the poor child is now never let out of sight of the house.'

Eugénie bought everything she could find that had belonged to the martyred queen, or might have belonged, as if it were a sacred relic. Horace de Viel Castel presented her with a ring worn by Louis XVI, together with Gravelot's sketch for the invitation to the ball for Marie-Antoinette's wedding (but, sadly, they did not earn him an invitation to Compiègne). Eventually her collection included furniture, jewellery, paintings, tapestries, bronzes, porcelain and letters – and books whose bindings bore Marie-Antoinette's coat of arms, particularly prayer-books. Among the most prized items were the queen's ivory and ebony mandolin, her jewel casket decorated in Sèvres and some exquisite chairs by J.B.B. Demay with the monogram 'M.A.'. In addition, a bust, a portrait or a print was prominently displayed in the empress's apartments at each of the imperial palaces.

In 1861 the British foreign secretary Lord Clarendon compared her vendetta with Plon-Plon to the feud between the queen and Philippe Egalité. After his embarrassing refusal to fight a duel with the Duc d'Aumale – one of the Orleanists pretender's uncles – she had expressed her contempt for Plon-Plon during a dinner at the Tuileries. 'He will never forgive the empress any more than Egalité did Marie-Antoinette, who was always abusing his *lâcheté*, and this chimes in curiously with her belief that she is in all things like Marie-Antoinette and that the same fate is reserved for her.'

Rumours of her cult circulated widely, revealing how frightened she was of a revolution and delighting the régime's opponents, republican or royalist. At the costume ball for the carnival of 1866, on 8 February, she received the guests in a dress of crimson velvet trimmed with sable and a matching toque with red and white plumes – modelled on what the queen had worn in one of Mme Vigée-Lebrun's portraits. A masked man sidled up through the crowd, to hiss in her ear, 'Some day you're going to die just like her, and your son is going to die in the Temple just like the dauphin.'

'Until 1860, so far as I can make out, most people thought that the empress's time was entirely taken up with dress and frippery', said Augustin Filon, the Prince Imperial's tutor. 'It was when Italian unity had begun to be very much the question of the day and when this unity, already half-achieved, had started to threaten the pope's temporal power, that whispers began to circulate about the empress's political influence.' This alteration in her public image was not unlike that undergone by Marie-Antoinette seventy years before. As early as 1862 Viel Castel noticed how the resemblance to the queen was being used to damage the empress's reputation during M. Thouvenel's sudden replacement as foreign minister by the pro-Austrian Drouyn de Lhuys. Eugénie was blamed by Thouvenel's enraged friends. 'I was told this morning that Marie-Antoinette perished because of her Austrian name, and that the *Spaniard had better take care of herself*', recorded the diarist. 'For some days now the unhappy empress has been considered capable of almost any crime – she is even said to be hoping for her husband's death so that she can become Regent.'

Just as the queen had been accused of plotting against the Revolution, so the empress was blamed for all the Second Empire's more unpopular policies at home as well as abroad. Filon heard that she was supposed to have her own political party, but never saw any trace of one during his three years at court. What is beyond dispute is that the hostility towards Eugénie noted by Viel Castel was growing stronger every day. There were rumours that she was responsible for the emperor's failing health, even for France's loss of standing as a world power after Prussia's victory at Königgrätz. However half-baked, such rumours may have been, they did her no good.

'It really is quite extraordinary how much our empress resembles poor Marie-Antoinette', wrote the loyal if not uncritical Filon, two years later when Eugénie's unpopularity had soared to alarming heights. This was after he had read the memoirs of Mme Campan, the queen's woman of the bedchamber during the Revolution. Filon noticed in Eugénie the same love of domesticity as the queen's, while he thought that he could see certain resemblances in their temperaments – the same mixture of haughtiness and affection, the same vivacity interrupted by moods of melancholy and bitterness. Yet Filon was shrewd enough to recognise at the same time the more sterling qualities that marked the two women – the same morality and decency, together with an honest, unaffected desire not only to please but to serve the French people.

By the end of the 1860s the Second Empire was losing impetus and obviously nearing a crisis. Eugénie's comparison of herself with Marie-Antoinette, which had begun in 1853 as little more than an affectation, partly romantic and partly superstitious, now seemed only too convincing. It looked as if she had good reason to fear that she might share the queen's fate.

THE WORLD TRADE EXHIBITION

'For everyone who grew to manhood towards the end of the Empire, the year of 1867 must stay firmly among recollections that can never be forgotten', wrote Pierre de La Gorce, born in 1846. 'A picture lingers on of a vast, cosmopolitan party given by France for the entire world.' He tells us, however, that those who saw it 'remember two feelings, a feeling of dazzling brilliance and a feeling of fear. . . . Never have people enjoyed themselves more frenziedly or more uneasily.' If it was the year of *La Grande Duchesse de Gerolstein*, it was also the year when Prussia consolidated the gains won at Königgrätz, and when the Mexican adventure ended in tragedy.

Augustin Filon, who took up his appointment as the Prince Imperial's tutor in the year of the Exposition Universelle, in September, was surprised by Eugénie's simple manner and way of speaking – noticeably more natural than that of her ladies. Her looks were beginning to go, her face already lined and her complexion a little faded, but her only make-up was a line of kohl under her eyelids. Filon was struck by her advanced views on education and the approval with which she spoke of Victor Duruy. 'What she said impressed me deeply, completely changing my idea of her as some haughty beauty reigning theatrically like a fairy queen in splendour', he wrote. 'Here was a woman with both brains and heart, who filled me with passionate loyalty.'

One of the best descriptions of the World Trade Exhibition in Paris is that of La Gorce. He tells us that the centre was the park known as the Champ de Mars, in which stood the Palais de l'Exposition, the principal showroom, ringed by galleries that displayed the latest marvels of industry and art, together with Egyptian temples, Greek porticos, Chinese pagodas, English and Dutch cottages, Tyrolean huts, Swedish log cabins and Turkish kiosks. (Among England's exhibits were a Bible stall and an Anglican church.) If some of the buildings were shoddy, the overall impression was one of astonishing colour and variety. There were restaurants, photographers' studios, dance halls, boutiques and casinos, police turning a blind eye to 'waitresses' in exciting versions of Bavarian, Dutch or Spanish folkdress.

The capital's streets had never been more frequented. The carnival went on and on, lasting for six months. In La Gorce's words, 'Paris became the abode of princes and meeting place of kings.' They included the Russian and Austrian emperors and the Turkish sultan, the kings of Prussia, Sweden, Portugal, Holland, Belgium and Greece, the shah of Persia and the khedive of Egypt. Among the heirs to thrones were the prince of Wales, the crown princes of Prussia and Italy and the hereditary prince of Sweden.

Clearly, Lillie Moulton had no reservations when she called the exhibition 'magnificent', and spent 100 francs on a season ticket which contained her photograph and her signature. She reported that the main building on the Champ de Mars was circular, a segment of the circle being devoted to the exhibits of each country. Outside were cafés that served the food of every nation represented. 'We go almost every day, and it is always a delight', wrote Lillie enthusiastically. 'The villa of the Bey of Tunis, a Buddhist temple, a Viennese bakery, where people flock to taste the delicious rolls hot from the oven, and where Hungarian bands of highly coloured handsome zitherists play from morning till night, and a hundred other attractions, make the Exposition a complete success. You pass from one lovely thing to the other. The gardens are laid through avenues of trees and shrubs where fountains play.'

On 17 May the Cowleys gave a ball for 2,000 guests at the British embassy in the rue du Faubourg Saint-Honoré. Albert Edward, Prince of Wales, was there with his brother the Duke of Edinburgh and many other royalties. 'Waldteufel played his wonderful music', wrote Whitehurst, 'and if any lady or gentleman thinks that Paris society does not like American drinks, that lady or gentleman is very much deceived.' The emperor and Eugénie came, Whitehurst reporting 'there was the prettiest picture – a Winterhalter it should have been – which I have ever seen in a ballroom. At the end, before a glass, and in a bower of flowers, sat the empress surrounded by her ladies-in-waiting and some of the best specimens of London and Paris beauties.' The Princess of Wales, the lovely Alexandra, had been left in England – still in his twenties, the future Edward VII meant to enjoy the Parisian fleshpots to the full.

The most august of the visiting sovereigns, Alexander II, emperor of Russia, arrived in Paris on 1 June, handsome, stately and coldly polite, exuding a Byzantine aura of divine right. He and his two tall sons, the Tsarevitch Alexander and Grand Duke Vladimir, were installed at the Elysée. The king of Prussia, William I, who came with Queen Augusta and Crown Prince Frederick William four days later, was not so daunting, a fine old soldier, who had unusually pleasant and kindly manners. Despite remarking with a certain lack of tact that Paris was looking even more beautiful than when he had seen it during the allied occupation of 1814, the septuagenarian monarch charmed his hosts, particularly Eugénie.

The even more amiable and much younger King Charles XV of Sweden was unaffectedly made welcome in Second Empire Paris, as a ruler belonging to a dynasty no less parvenu than the Bonapartes. In any case, he was also a kinsman, related to them through both the Bernardottes and the Beauharnais. His brother and heir, Prince Oscar, was equally welcome, flitting up and down the Seine on a private *bateau-mouche* and singing duets with Mrs Moulton. (The emperor was godfather to Oscar's little son.)

Count von Bismarck had decided to escort his king, much to Napoleon's irritation. Apparently quite indifferent to the stares of the fascinated French, the Prussian chancellor cut a striking figure in the dazzling white uniform and black thigh-boots of a major of Cuirassiers, the scabbard of his sabre clanking noisily along the pavement. He looked even more colossal when he wore his eagle-topped steel helmet. As a piece of subtle mockery that had been inspired by Princess Metternich, the fashionable colour this year for the ladies' new straight dresses was brown often set off by coral jewellery, a brown called '*la couleur Bismarck*'. (During the Königgrätz campaign, the brown-coated Austrian artillerymen had inflicted substantial casualties on the Prussian army.)

The real world broke in suddenly and unpleasantly upon the autocrat of all the Russias when he paid a formal visit to the Palais de Justice, where there were yells of '*Vive la Pologne!*' and '*À la porte!*' ('Get out!') from several of the younger advocates, who had not forgotten how the Russians were behaving in Poland.

La Grande Duchesse de Gerolstein had been running since mid-April, attracting enormous audiences who laughed and applauded rapturously, and afterwards sang its cheerful, catchy tunes in the streets of Paris. Its fame had spread to every European capital. An imperial gala performance was arranged for the visiting sovereigns.

In the imperial box, next to Napoleon and Eugénie, the Russian emperor and the king of Prussia sat side by side with Don Francisco de Assisi, king consort of Spain, King Louis and Queen Maria Pia of Portugal, Queen Sophia of Holland, the ex-King Ludwig I of Bavaria and his melancholy grandson Ludwig II, and the khedive, Ismail of Egypt. Behind them, but not seated, were the Tsarevich Alexander of Russia and his brother Grand Duke Vladimir, with Crown Prince Frederick of Prussia, Crown Prince Albert of Saxony and Crown Prince Umberto of Italy.

At the far end of the box, which was arranged as a drawing-room, stood a group of ambassadors, ministers and generals with their ladies – among them were Prince and Princess Metternich, Count von Bismarck in his white uniform, the aged Russian chancellor Prince Gortchakov, the Prussian ambassador Count von der Goltz, and those two faithful old warhorses Marshal Canrobert and General Fleury.

The empress, wearing rose-coloured silk with her shoulders bare, her throat adorned by a superb collar of pearls, seemed to glow with all the brilliance of her heyday. She had certainly come a long way from 1853, when not a single foreign royalty had attended her wedding.

Bismarck was seen to bellow with laughter, again and again, at the way in which the operetta mocked the tiny armies of the minor German states, so much so that it seemed almost as if he were laughing at some private joke. 'That's it! That's exactly it!' he said afterwards when, accompanied by General von Moltke, he paid a perfectly respectable, if for him unusually frivolous, visit to the leading lady, Mme Hortense Schneider. 'We are going to get rid of the Gerolsteins and very soon none of them will be left. I am grateful to you Parisian artistes for showing the world just how ridiculous they were.'

Unfortunately, and no doubt just as Bismarck hoped, most of the audience left the Théâtre des Variétés totally convinced that all German troops were no less laughable and ineffectual than those of General Boum-Boum and the Grand Duchy of Gerolstein.

If the empress found the libretto of *La Grande Duchesse* marginally less distressing than usual, one can only hope that she did not hear about the excessively patriotic behaviour of the operetta's leading lady, whose hospitable welcome for foreign royalty earned her the cruel name of '*les passages des princes*' and convulsed Paris with laughter. Hortense slept with a good few princes, including it seems the Prince of Wales. One of her numerous discarded lovers equipped himself with the flag of every nation and took the house opposite, hoisting and floodlighting the appropriate flag during each royal visit.

On the evening before the performance of *La Grande Duchesse* Eugénie invited her royal guests to a fête at Versailles, of such splendour that those who were there believed it could not possibly have been rivalled in any preceding age, not even in the days of Louis XIV. There were elaborate water pageants in the park that surrounded the great palace, which was illuminated by torches and flares, pageants accompanied by music from concealed orchestras of violins, together with a fleet of gondolas for the guests on the Grand Canal, then an epicurean supper for 600 in the Hall of Mirrors, and finally a brilliant firework display that reached its climax when 100,000 rockets lit up the night sky over Versailles.

In the small hours Princess Metternich encountered her friend the empress, creator of the feast, wandering happily by herself through the park, a white, gold-embroidered burnous thrown over her shoulders – 'admiring murmurs following in her wake like a trail of lighted gunpowder'. Yet, typically, the Princess reminds us, Eugénie was simply not interested in polite compliments about her appearance or her clothes – what she really wanted was to be congratulated on giving a good party. 'What do you think of my fête?' she asked Pauline, who replied sincerely enough, 'Worthy of Your Majesty.'

The 'révue de Longchamps' was always the climax of the French military calendar, a mixture of parade, picnic and national celebration, when the Parisians flocked out to Longchamps race-course to applaud the red-trousered army that was France's glory. This year the review was even more spectacular than usual, 60,000 men taking part in an attempt to impress the visiting sovereigns and their staffs – in particular the Prussians.

On 6 June 1867 tens of thousands of spectators cheered when Eugénie's carriage arrived at the saluting base, the empress smiling and bowing. She was followed by Napoleon III and his fellow monarchs on horseback, together with a host of crown princes and lesser potentates. Quick-stepping to the raucous military music of France, the infantry marched past. Then, to the staccato, braying fanfares of their mounted trumpeters came the cavalry in tunics and dolmans of dark blue, light blue or green. Among them were the empress's own personal regiments – her cuirassiers, carbineers, lancers and dragoons.

'When squadron on squadron charged with drawn swords upon their sovereigns and their escorts, and halted but a few paces from them with the cry of "*Vive l'Empereur!*" the thrill was magical', said Roger Sencourt, who, writing in the 1920s, could well have spoken to survivors who had watched the legendary review. 'At that moment there swept through the people and the army a conviction that French power was irresistible.'

Unlike the handful of keen-eyed Prussian officers and their king, very few among the spectators appear to have realised that, despite all the magnificent uniforms, the army's artillery was out of date. Even those rare French experts who did notice remarked proudly that these guns were the cannon that had triumphantly smashed the way into the fort at the Malakhoff in the Crimea, and had won the victories of Magenta and Solferino in 1859.

While the cavalcade of visiting sovereigns and princes was riding back from Longchamps, led by Napoleon III, a twenty-year-old Polish refugee called Beregowski fired a single pistol shot at the Russian emperor, but missed, the bullet passing through a horse's nostril and covering the tsarevitch with the animal's blood, and wounding a lady in the crowd. The young man was seized by the police before he could shoot again. 'Sire, we have been under fire together, which means that now we are brothers-in-arms,' said Napoleon smoothly. 'Our lives are in the hands of Providence,' replied the angry tsar in tones of ice. He had not forgotten how his host had encouraged the Poles to hope for independence.

On 10 June, the day before Alexander was due to leave France, when he was about to join a shooting party at Fontainebleau, the police discovered that there was a Polish conspiracy to ambush and kill him in the woods. In order to avoid further embarrassment by revealing yet another plot on his life, Eugénie engaged the tsar in conversation, dragging it out until it was too late for him to reach the party.

The only major European sovereigns not to visit the Exposition Universelle were Queen Victoria, by now the reclusive 'Widow of Windsor', and Queen Isabella of Spain who was about to lose her throne. Even the sultan of Turkey came. Deliberately, the pleasure-loving, ineffectual Abdul Aziz arrived late, after the tsar had gone, blazing with diamonds when he attended the exhibition's prize-giving on 1 July.

Just as Napoleon and Eugénie were about to leave the Tuileries for the prize-giving, they were told that Emperor Maximilian had been executed by a Juarist firing squad on 19 June. The news underlined France's humiliation by Prussia and made Franz-Joseph still less inclined to ally with a man who was ultimately responsible for the death of his brother – noisily derided as 'The Archdupe' by the French opposition.

'The glitter of the Exposition Universelle hid our country's discontent at home and its danger abroad', said La Gorce. 'But for how long? Napoleon III can seldom have felt more isolated than when he rode at the head of his cavalcade of kings. Everything was going wrong.'

'L'ESPAGNOLE' – THE SPANISH WOMAN

The Second Empire had lost its way. Napoleon III was failing spectacularly to win the 'glory abroad' that was a vital part of Bonapartism – Russia had crushed Poland, Prussia had become a menacing rival and now Mexico had shot his protégé Emperor Maximilian. France felt humiliated. Throughout history the French have always looked for a scapegoat and, already inclined to dislike Eugénie as a foreigner, they had no need to look further than the 'Spanish Woman'.

She was too intelligent to be unaware of their hostility, while she knew very well that she had stayed Spanish in temperament and outlook – when she spoke, her intonation if not her accent remained Spanish and she retained a deep Spanish bark of a laugh. Meeting the empress in her mid-seventies, Lucien Daudet realised at once that he was talking to a Spaniard.

On the morning after Napoleon had been informed of the Emperor Maximilian's death he summoned the chief of the Empire's secret police, Hyrvoix, to the Tuileries. How, he asked him, were Parisians reacting to the news?

'If you really want to know, Sire, it is not just Parisians but the whole nation who are thoroughly indignant and upset by the way this unlucky war has ended', answered the policeman. 'Everywhere you'll find that everybody is saying the same thing. They say it's the fault of . . .'

The emperor broke in quickly, 'Whose fault?'

'Just as they used to say in Louis XVI's time, "It's the Austrian's fault", now under Napoleon III they're saying, "It's the Spaniard's fault".'

No sooner had he spoken than Eugénie burst into the room – looking like 'one of the furies' in a white wrapper, her hair loose over her shoulders, her face red with anger, her eyes blazing, recalled the wretched Hyrvoix.

'Repeat what you've just said,' she demanded.

'All right, Madame, since it's my job to report the facts, but I hope Your Majesty will forgive me,' said the unfortunate policeman. 'I was telling the emperor that today's Parisians talk of the "Spanish Woman" just as, seventy or eighty years ago, they used to talk of the "Austrian Woman".'

'The Spanish woman, the Spanish woman!' shouted the by now infuriated empress. 'I've become French, but, if I need to, then I'll show my enemies that I know how to be Spanish.' Then she rushed out of the room, slamming the door.

'I am a ruined man,' exclaimed the terrified Hyrvoix.

'Oh no, you only did your duty.' Napoleon assured him.

Within a week, however, poor Hyrvoix found himself transferred from Paris to a post in a remote area of eastern France, in the Jura. Yet the policeman had merely been quoting from his agents' reports, which were accurate enough. More and more of the French were blaming 'the Spaniard' for anything that went wrong, just as they had Marie-Antoinette.

The story of Eugénie and Hyrvoix comes from *An Englishman in Paris* by Albert Vandam, a journalist who had developed an intense dislike of the empress, and should be treated with caution. Yet the incident is in character and undoubtedly reflects popular feeling in Paris at the time. Writing in 1905 the historian Jean Guétary had heard a similar story from 'a high functionary at the Tuileries'. 'Answer me frankly, Monsieur Hyrvoix', Eugénie asked the policeman. 'Am I popular?' Hesitating for a moment, Hyrvoix replied. 'Yes, Madame. . . . especially in the provinces.' Guétary says she never forgave him.

If that alarming burst of ferocity in response to Hyrvoix's unpalatable warning may give one the illusion that Eugénie was a virago, she left a more pleasing impression on most people who encountered her. Sixty-five years afterwards, the English historian Sir Charles Oman, who had watched her at a ceremony in the Tuileries gardens during the summer of 1868, remembered (in *Things I Have Seen*) 'a splendid figure, straight as a dart, and to my young eyes the most beautiful thing I had ever seen'. (She was wearing 'a zebra-striped black and white silk dress with very full skirts, and a black and white bonnet'.) He recalled how Napoleon III made a dismal contrast. 'On a bench overlooking the scene sat a very tired old gentleman, rather hunched together, and looking decidedly ill. I do not think I should have recognised him but for his spiky moustache. He was anything but terrifying in a tall hat and a rather loosely fitting frock coat.'

Significantly, Oman informed us that the empress 'was a commanding figure and dominated the whole group on the terrace while the emperor, huddled in his seat, was a very minor show'. The 'old gentleman' had only just reached his sixtieth birthday, but clearly to Oman he appeared to be almost senile. Although he sometimes revived for brief periods, and if the agonising attacks of pain resulting from the stone in his bladder were intermittent, he was very tired indeed. He had lost his once insatiable sexual appetite – there were to be no more 'little distractions'.

Unlike the unfortunate Hyrvoix, Augustin Filon was a member of the imperial household and knew the empress at close quarters. He became so devoted to her that eventually he would follow her into exile. His assessment of her marriage in the 1860s is probably fairly near the truth, if sometimes a little fanciful. 'I think she lived in a kind of fairy tale, fascinated by her extraordinary destiny,' he says:

Nearly twenty years separated the couple, and such a gulf is not easily bridged even by women who seem designed by nature to love men older than themselves. I don't believe that the empress was a woman of this sort. Her feelings for the emperor had never been passionate, although they were much stronger than mere friendship and had grown steadily deeper until the day when she discovered his infidelities.

Yet, despite his betrayal, like many women she continued to respond to certain aspects of Napoleon's personality, such as his kindness, gaiety and sense of fun, his oddly gentle voice and manner – all so surprising in an autocrat. Once he had caught her imagination as Bonapartism incarnate, and she never ceased to reverence him as emperor, never calling him 'Louis' or '*tu*' in public. Ultimately she saw him as 'a great, honest man who wanted to do good, even if often he pursued his aims crookedly'. In Filon's view, Eugénie found her role in supporting and encouraging her husband.

As for the emperor's attitude towards Eugénie, instead of the beautiful, alluring woman whom he had first 'loved for her moods of impatience, her nervousness and her foibles', he now loved her character and high standards. 'He regarded her as his second conscience,' claims Filon. Undoubtedly he consulted her more and more. She was his only confidante, although he still preferred to keep a good deal secret about his real aims.

In November 1868 the emperor contributed (under the name of A. Grenier) a curious article on Eugénie, written as if he were her father rather than her husband, to a new journal, the *Dix-Decembre*. 'Women's welfare is one of her main interests,' he wrote. 'She wants to improve conditions for them and has obtained recognition for Rosa Bonheur in the form of a decoration. . . No economic or financial question is beyond her grasp, and it is pleasing to hear her discuss these recondite problems with experts', he continued patronisingly. 'If her way of expressing herself is occasionally faulty, it is invariably colourful and lively, and she is remarkably precise in talking of business matters.'

One can dismiss Maxime Ducamp's claims that Eugénie 'had her camarilla, her court, her partisans', since he was a journalist notorious for his venom, but Filon, who unlike Ducamp knew the world of the Tuileries, has to be taken seriously. Nevertheless, when he suggests that the emperor pretended that Eugénie led a reactionary court party so that he could blame her for policies which the liberals disliked, one must reject the idea as nonsense: Napoleon did not want to harm his image by making his wife still more unpopular.

On the other hand, Eugénie undoubtedly opposed her husband on certain issues. Filon argues that 'the thought of setting herself up in opposition to the emperor, from whom she had taken all her political ideas and whose judgement she trusted absolutely, would never have occurred to her,' yet we know that she often disagreed with him – on war with Prussia in 1866, on defending the Papal States and on liberalising. Inclined to see things in black and white, she did not always share the outlook of a husband who thought in the finer shades of grey. Filon was not present at Council meetings and it seems unlikely that the empress would have described them to her son's tutor.

At the same time, Filon – who had a very good mind himself according to Victor Duruy – showed the utmost respect for Eugénie's intelligence. Here he is totally at odds with Pierre de La Gorce. 'Far sighted enough yet only intermittently, she was prone to violent fits of uneasiness and, increasingly disillusioned with her husband's judgement, as a mother she wanted to safeguard her son's inheritance', declared la Gorce. 'No doubt a woman of strong spirit, she was restless rather than resourceful, nervous, far too impressionable, simultaneously resolute and changeable, and when involved in policy-making caused as much damage by ill-judged enthusiasm as she did by her maternal intuition.'

It should be said that La Gorce did not attend Council meetings and had never even met the empress. Yet this Orleanist sympathiser's assessment has influenced all too many French historians.

Napoleon and Eugénie needed all the support they could find in the political climate that emerged after the Exposition Universelle, but the empress's foreign origins made her even more of a scapegoat – more than ever disliked as 'L'Espagnole'.

SEVEN

The Storm

REVOLUTION?

Admiral Jurien de La Gravière had joined the navy as a midshipman in 1828 when the Bourbons were still on the throne, but unlike most naval officers, who tended to be Legitimists, he had become a staunch Bonapartist. Napoleon used this shrewd Breton for difficult missions, such as ensuring that French and British warships cooperated during the Crimean War. (Queen Victoria says he was 'a quiet, gentlemanlike man who had always helped to keep matters straight between the two navies'.) He had nearly averted the Mexican adventure, by negotiating with Juarez.

By 1867 Jurien de La Gravière was seriously worried about the political situation in France. In November he wrote to the empress, insisting that she was the Second Empire's biggest asset and ought to play a key role in its government. 'You have no right to stand back when you could do so much to help,' the Admiral told her. 'We are in danger and you cannot be so remiss as to neglect us. The political experience that you have gained during a long apprenticeship of more than a dozen years must be used on behalf of us all.' That someone of Jurien's calibre should write like this shows just how much men at the centre of affairs respected Eugénie's capabilities.

Nor was the admiral exaggerating when he said there was danger. In January 1868 Lord Lyons, who had recently replaced Cowley as ambassador, reported, 'The discontent is great and the distress among the working classes severe' – there had been a bad harvest. He added ominously, 'the French have been a good many years without the excitement of a change'.

Republicanism had grown menacing, with constant demonstrations that turned into riots. Everyone knew that Napoleon was not well. The constitution loaded him with

190

responsibilities, but made no allowance for his ill health or death, while his ministers were mediocre – there was no one to replace Morny or Walewski. The rise of extremism was particularly alarming, a return to the revolutionary and atheist Jacobinism of 1793, Robespierre and Hébert being openly venerated in the wilder political clubs. There was also a threat from the royalist right. Early in 1867 Napoleon had grumbled bitterly to Lord Clarendon about Orleanist intrigues. 'The Duc d'Aumale [the Orleanist Pretender's uncle] is devoured by ambition and the spirit of revenge, and he is quite capable of accepting a republican ladder for climbing to power, of course with the intention of kicking it down as soon as he arrived there.'

When Lord Cowley paid a private visit to Napoleon at Fontainebleau, the emperor told the former ambassador that the countryside still supported the régime, but 'all the towns were against him'. In the spring of 1868 there were riots at Bordeaux, Toulouse and Montauban. 'Aged and much depressed' in Cowley's opinion, little by little the emperor gave ground. Censorship became less rigorous while socialist meetings were tolerated – they could be held in specified dancehalls so long as a policeman was present. Perceived as weakness, the concessions merely resulted in even worse riots.

Meanwhile, Henri de Rochefort was making the imperial family a laughing stock in his paper *La Lanterne*, whose title evoked the lampposts on which aristocrats had been lynched during the Revolution. Not even the Prince Imperial's dog Nero escaped his mockery, while he alleged that the empress used plaster-of-Paris for make-up. As Mme des Garets reminds us, Eugénie always took politics personally and could be deeply hurt by a sneering reference to her in a debate or in a hostile article. *La Lanterne* drew blood.

Among 'the infamous gibes with which Rochefort harried me', the one that upset her most appeared during the summer of 1868. Nearly forty years later, she still remembered it with resentment: 'Her Majesty the empress of the French presided yesterday at the Council of Ministers', wrote Rochefort. 'How surprised I should be if I learned that Mme Pereire had presided at the administrative council of the Crédit Mobilier' (her husband was the bank's chairman).

The insinuation that she was incapable of taking part in the country's government because she was a woman infuriated Eugénie.

The empress was even attacked by Bonapartists, or at any rate by Persigny. There had already been angry exchanges at Council meetings. (Once, when he remained grimly silent after a fierce argument, she observed, 'M. de Persigny, you aren't saying anything.' 'No, Madame.' 'Then you ought to stay at home instead of coming here and getting on my nerves.') She knew very well that behind her back he was always grumbling about 'the Spanish woman'. In November 1867 she had intercepted a letter from him to the emperor in which, after various blatantly insincere compliments – 'nobility of the Empress's mind', etc. – he complained of her presence at the Council of Ministers and of the 'detestable ideas' that she was constantly urging on them.

Losing her temper, Eugénie told her husband excitedly that she would never set foot in the Council again if she was going to be exposed to insults of this sort. 'Calm yourself,' said Napoleon in his usual quiet and gentle way. 'This new foolishness of Persigny is unimportant. It is my view that you should attend the Council of Ministers, and you will not cease to sit there. It is I who am master.' Although the empress was reassured, she nonetheless sat down and wrote 'a pretty strong letter' to Persigny, who prudently stopped coming to court.

The 'detestable ideas' included her conviction that, for the moment at least, a constitutional monarchy could not possibly work in France. Always more realistic than her husband, as well as more pessimistic, she saw only too clearly that the left had never forgiven Napoleon for shooting them down in 1851 and that it would never do so under any circumstances. His coup had erected a permanent 'barrier of blood'. In her opinion, his best solution would be for him to wait for the Prince Imperial to come of age in 1874, grant a constitution and then abdicate immediately. (By now both he and Eugénie were ready to contemplate abdicating in a few years time, even with eagerness, so long as the dynasty could be saved, which shows the extent of their weariness.) A new emperor with an unstained reputation might be able to attract the support essential for a viable constitutional monarchy.

'I was always opposed to the emperor proceeding any further with liberal reforms', she told Augustin Filon in 1903. 'In my opinion my husband ought to have stayed exactly where he was – political freedom should have been granted when his son succeeded to the throne.' When Filon asked what she thought was likely to have happened under so young and inexperienced a ruler, she replied, 'I would have relied with confidence on the innate generosity of the French nation.'

Nor did Eugénie fancy losing control of foreign policy at such a dangerous time, a prospect she dreaded, French chauvinism was not to be trusted, as could be seen only too easily from the luridly anti-Prussian articles that were appearing in the popular and now uncensored press. Among left and right alike, fashionable patriotism verged on xenophobia.

There was also a possibility, one which Eugénie found intolerable, that the ministers of a constitutional monarchy might abandon Rome and the embattled Pope Pius. Napoleon had withdrawn the French garrison at the end of 1866, but on the firm understanding that the Italian government would respect the city's independence. Early in October 1867, however, it was learned that Garibaldi had raised a band of volunteers with whom he intended to seize the city. Every French Catholic was outraged at the news, including Eugénie. 'Rome or death' was Garibaldi's melodramatic slogan – on hearing of it, she retorted, 'Death if they really want it, but certainly not Rome.'

The Council of Ministers, urged on by the empress, decided to send a relief expeditionary force to Rome without delay. On 3 October General Failly reached Mentana outside the city, where a hard fought battle was taking place between the Papal army (mainly French Catholics) and the Garibaldisti. His men arrived just in time to save the pope's troops from defeat, mowing down the poorly armed enemy with their new, long-range *chassepot* rifles. Many regarded the victory as a personal triumph for Eugénie.

In France, all the anticlericals, who included every socialist, were angered. The emperor Franz-Joseph's visit to Paris, to see the last days of the Exposition Universelle, coincided with the Roman crisis, and on his arrival at the Hôtel de Ville with Napoleon and Eugénie the three were greeted by booing, the air ringing with yells of

'*Vive Garibaldi!*' to the horror of the poor Metternichs. Fortunately, it was the only unpleasant incident in an otherwise successful visit.

From 1866 onwards the cost of living soared, and by 1868 many workers in Paris and other big cities were living on the edge of starvation. Inevitably they turned against the government, the opposition going from strength to strength. At the end of 1867 a well-organised confrontation with the police took place at the grave of Dr Baudin (whose sole distinction was to have been shot down on the barricades in 1851), ending in sixty-two arrests. A new socialist newspaper, *Le Reveil*, was founded in 1868 by Delescluze, an old enemy of Napoleon who had returned from serving a prison sentence in Guyana. Preaching the Jacobin gospel of 1792, it was far more dangerous than Rochefort's light-hearted *La Lanterne*, which was banned in the autumn – to resume publication in Brussels. At by-elections opposition deputies were returned with hugely increased majorities; among them was Leon Gambetta.

Napoleon III appeared to be losing control, although no one underestimated his resourcefulness. He was well aware that even if he managed to persuade the army to try and mount another *coup d'état* like that of 1851, it would almost certainly fail. Every aspect of their régime was under attack. When the news broke in 1868 that because of Baron Haussmann's megalomaniac management the finances of Paris were teetering on the brink of total bankruptcy, the opposition gleefully exploited the scandal, publishing a pamphlet which bore the inspired title of *Les Comptes fantastiques d'Haussmann*. Parisians had neither forgotten nor forgiven the way that they had been evicted from their houses during the capital's rebuilding.

During the prize-giving at the Lycée Bonaparte in August 1868, when the twelve-year-old Prince Imperial distributed the prizes, the son of General Cavaignac (a republican leader who had been arrested in 1851) refused to go up to the dais and accept his prize from the Prince. A few boyish shouts of '*Vive la République!*' rang out. The Prince was driven back to Fontainebleau in tears, where the court was in residence. His father was unconcerned. 'In any case Louis would one day have had to learn that there is such a thing as an opposition', he replied philosophically when Eugénie demanded the punishment of those involved. After dinner, when Octave Feuillet was sitting at a window he heard strange laughter which made him shudder. It was the empress. The 'terrible laugh' stopped, but then he heard it again. About an hour later, she joined those sitting in the garden, sniffing a large bottle of ether and muttering, 'My poor little boy!' Such fits of hysteria were rare – in Feuillet's letters she is usually calm personified – and it shows that she was on the verge of a breakdown.

On the whole, however, Eugénie appeared to be astonishingly self-controlled, and as handsome as always. If photographs reveal that she was ageing, she still cast a spell. Feuillet had written a few weeks earlier that none of the great beauties of French history had walked through the drawing-rooms of Fontainebleau 'with so graceful, so buoyant and so pleasing an air'. He added, 'She seemed twenty!'

The trouble was not confined to Paris. There was strike after strike in the industrial areas of France, always politically inspired. Frequently troops had to be sent in to restore order. As in the capital, demonstrators marched through the streets of provincial cities, shouting for a revolution and roaring out the banned Marseillaise – not from patriotism but because of its association with 1793.

Napoleon's tactics were to give the socialists their head until they terrified the bourgeoisie into rallying to him. But the tactics did not work. When a general election was finally held in 1869 the government candidates received four and a half million votes and the opposition parties five and a half million – although barely a million were for extremists. The main stream left polled two million and a half, the new 'third party' of former government supporters just over a million, 'Night after night large numbers would be arrested as rioters and revolutionists, and locked up in the prison of Mazas, or sent to the casemates of Fort Bicêtre', Elihu Washbourne, America's newly arrived minister, recalled. The atmosphere grew more and more explosive – the emperor could only pray that bourgeois France would turn to him in time.

Rioting in Paris was nearly out of control and *The Times* warned readers to expect another French Revolution at any moment. There were rumours that risings would take place all over Paris, so troops were billeted in the Tuileries. One evening Napoleon suggested to Eugénie that they ought to visit them. She refused, objecting, 'It will remind everybody of that dinner of October 1789, when Louis XVI and Marie-Antoinette were at the bodyguards' dinner party.' But she changed her mind and went to see them the next day.

'Everybody here is frightened without knowing why', Mérimée wrote to Doña Maria Manuela at about this time. 'It is a little like the feeling one has when the Commendatore [in *Don Giovanni*] is about to appear.' And in retrospect the more plain-spoken Alfred Verly, whose father commanded the Cent Gardes, wrote 'As if by instinct, one sensed that an explosion was coming. Everywhere there was indefinable menace.'

Filon conveys vividly the tense atmosphere at a gala evening in the Tuileries in 1869 with a riot going on outside. On this occasion a state dinner was followed by a play, a ball and then supper, in honour of Queen Sophie of Holland and Grand Duchess Marie of Russia.

> During the play telegram after telegram is delivered to the emperor, who does not open any of them, but continues to applaud the actors as if he does not have a care in the world. Everybody else is anxious and horribly ill at ease – many cannot help glancing at the windows that look on to the Place du Carrousel over which an infuriated mob is swarming. Waldteufel's orchestra is playing its most enchanting waltzes and five or six couples have ventured on to the dance floor – tonight, waltzing is an act of loyalty to the Empire. When the music stops we can hear the yells of the mob outside as they are charged by the police. There are many empty tables. Staying to supper is a sign of real courage.

Filon added, 'Every evening was more or less like this, over a period of many weeks. And all the time one could not help thinking of the scenes that had taken place in this same palace eighty years before, of another sovereign who had suffered the same agony of mind.' Eugénie's courtiers were remembering how the Swiss Guard had been massacred during the storming of the Tuileries in 1792, and what had happened to Marie-Antoinette.

The most violent of the riots occurred on the four evenings of 7–11 June, when it was not only the Tuileries that was under threat. Despite the detachments of cavalry that were patrolling the streets, many shops and houses in the more affluent areas of Paris had their windows broken, and well-dressed people were molested and robbed. Foreigners began to leave the city in droves. Just as Napoleon had foreseen, many of those Frenchmen who had voted against his government in the election now began to see him as France's only hope.

On the afternoon of 12 June, accompanied by Eugénie, the emperor deliberately drove from Saint-Cloud into Paris in an open landau, with no escort other than a single outrider. They went down the rue de Rivoli and the boulevard de Sevastopol towards the great boulevards which, as they knew, were packed with demonstrators – they might easily have been driving to their deaths. The crowd in the boulevards was so dense that the landau was forced to a snail's pace and at times had to stop altogether. When the couple were recognised by the mob, instead of lynching them on the spot it saluted their courage by giving cheer after cheer for the emperor and empress.

The rioting started to die down. For the moment it looked as if Napoleon had at last succeeded in re-establishing his authority. Troops ceased to patrol the Paris streets. 'After the quiet of the last two or three evenings, we may fairly conclude that the election riots of 1869 are over', Whitehurst reported on 14 June. However, he warned his readers that the 'affair . . . is only adjourned till the day when the Chamber is to open'. A fortnight later he wrote, 'The empress presided over a Cabinet Council yesterday. Nobody works harder than the empress, nobody has read much more, and nobody perhaps is now so interested in the politics of France.'

Then in August the emperor suddenly became alarmingly ill from his bladder complaint, so ill that he suffered attacks of delirium. Once again, the bourgeoisie lived in fear of revolution and, when there were rumours at the end of the month that he was dying, the bourse fell dramatically. Nobody believed the bland official statements that he was in no danger or that he was merely indisposed by a bout of rheumatism. He made a speedy recovery at the beginning of September, however, making very carefully judged public appearances.

The 'Sphinx of the Tuileries' decided that it was time to play his last hand. Aware that Eugénie would disapprove, he sent her out of France, as far away as possible.

OPENING THE SUEZ CANAL

The empress was to represent France at the official opening of the Suez Canal in November 1869. The idea for a canal through the isthmus of Suez, first conceived by General Bonaparte in the 1790s, had been revived in 1854 by the dynamic Ferdinand de Lesseps, whose success in raising the money to dig it owed a lot to the imperial couple. (Lesseps was Eugénie's cousin, his Grivégnée mother being Doña Maria Manuela's aunt.)

Eugénie badly needed a holiday. She knew that she was increasingly unpopular. What she did not know, however, was just how much she was hated by someone close to her, who pretended to be among her dearest friends. Princesse Mathilde told the Goncourts in August:

> The last time that I went to Saint-Cloud, she showed me her dresses for the trip to Suez. The whole journey means nothing more to her than a chance to make eyes at some Oriental potentate from her steamer – she has to have men round her the entire time, paying court . . . the heartless trollop. As you know, Spanish women have no idea of modesty. When she was ill with skin trouble – she's been of no use to the emperor for years because of her trouble, yes, she's got it there – the way she was prepared to show people, lifting up her skirts in front of everybody, was quite amazing. She's never been able to inspire affection in anybody, never shows the least sign of warmth, never even kisses her son. . . . You should hear what her ladies-in-waiting say about her . . . The woman just isn't French and doesn't like France or the French. The only time I've known her to be polite is when she's with foreign sovereigns. You ought to have seen her with the emperor of Austria!

Mathilde sneered at Eugénie's cult of Marie-Antoinette. 'Have you ever heard of anything so inane or so ridiculous or in such bad taste?' she asked the brothers. 'Do you know what she has in her bedroom? First, a portrait of her sister whom she hated and to whom she used to send insulting telegrams, so the emperor tells me. Then a portrait of Mérimée, one of Mme Metternich, a Sèvres bust of Marie-Antoinette, and a portrait of the little Dauphin. On her bedside table there's a copy of some book about Marie-Antoinette which she's never read because she never reads. She's not interested in anything.'

All too many of the French were prepared to believe lies of the sort spread by Princesse Mathilde. They help one understand why the 'Spaniard' was so much looking forward to her Eastern adventure.

In 1901 the empress told Maurice Paléologue of the 'frightful nightmare which I took with me from Paris', in a way that reveals her sense of near despair in 1869. (This is another instance where Paléologue's account carries conviction.) It was a gloomy but realistic assessment:

Abroad, a menacing Prussia and an ungrateful Italy, with all the other great powers resentful or ill-disposed towards us. At home, discontent and disaffection – a contemptible Press, thoroughly insolent and dishonest, unending strikes and violent demonstrations, the régime's foundations being undermined everywhere. Even the people who had the biggest stake in the dynasty's survival gleefully read Rochefort's *La Lanterne* each week, because a wind of insanity was blowing throughout France. What made matters even worse was that the emperor himself was ill, depressed and discouraged, and unable to see anything good in the future – there were only bad omens.

Eugénie set out for Venice from Saint-Cloud on 30 September, accompanied by forty ladies, gentlemen and servants, among whom were Paca's daughters, the dentist Dr Evans and the Abbé Bauer. She took her state papers with her, arranging to be kept informed daily, by special messenger and telegram, of what the Council had discussed. En route she visited Magenta, praying by moonlight on the battlefield for all those killed there in 1859.

Venice gave her a dazzling welcome, its palaces brilliantly illuminated, its canals lit by fireworks and gondolas with coloured lanterns. She was serenaded by waterborne orchestras, and cheered by a huge crowd in Piazza San Marco. Unfortunately, Cavaliere Nigra had warned Victor-Emmanuel that she was likely to raise important issues in casual conversation, even at dinner, so whenever she tried to discuss Rome the king changed the subject, going into ecstasies about her beauty. This added insult to injury since Eugénie was well aware that she was losing her figure and growing fatter in the face.

Then she boarded the imperial yacht, *L'Aigle,** to sail for Athens, where King George I proclaimed a public holiday and took her on a tour. Afterwards she told her entourage that she did not care for what she knew of the ancient Greeks: 'windbags living in a permanent state of civil war, revolution and intrigue, an impossible people to govern'. She may also have had in mind the modern Greeks, who had recently deposed King Otto.

Off Constantinople, after *L'Aigle* had failed to rendezvous in Besika Bay with the Turkish warship that carried the Grand Vizier and the French ambassador sailing past her in a dark night, next morning an entire fleet decked with bunting came out to welcome the empress. Enormous crowds thronged both sides of the Bosphorus. When the *L'Aigle* dropped anchor in front of the Beyler-Bey Palace on the Asiatic shore, which had been placed at her disposal, a magnificent barge rowed out to meet her. On the barge, seated on a red velvet dais, was the Sultan Abdul Aziz himself.

He had reason to be pleased to see her. Not only was she the wife of the man whom he saw as his most powerful ally, but she was Napoleon's special envoy. He knew that the Russians were furious at her visit – later, she commented, 'Now I've seen the Bosphorus I can see why the Russians want it so much.' Merely by coming to Constantinople before going on to Cairo he asserted his authority over the sultan's viceroy the khedive. He tried to kiss Eugénie's hand,

---

* A corvette of 1,400 tons, driven by steam and sail, she could do 15 knots and was manned by a crew of 180.

but she refused – clearly, he was an alarming host, a man of many moods. (One day he would kill himself with a pair of scissors.)

That evening the sultan's barge, manned by forty oarsmen, returned to bring Eugénie (in yellow silk) across the Bosphorus to a banquet in the Palace at Dolma Bagchtie. It was estimated that half a million people were watching, either from the shore or from a fleet of warships, steamers, yachts and innumerable caiques, all flying the flags of France and Turkey. Dr Evans, who was among the spectators, wrote:

In the barge, a graceful construction of polished cedar, and ornamented with gold, and massive silver and velvet, and richest fabrics – a dais or canopy of crimson silk had been erected, beneath the folds of which I saw the empress, as the barge drew near me, sitting alone in evening dress, a light mantilla over her head, wearing a diadem and many rich jewels, radiant and beautiful . . .

Eugénie found time to receive a deputation from the substantial French community at Constantinople, merchants and religious leaders. 'Their spokesman made a speech to which I had to reply, trembling like a leaf', she told Napoleon in a letter. (Even now, she had still not conquered her nervousness when speaking in public.)

There was a moment of unpleasantness when Sultan Abdul Aziz showed her round his harem. Seeing her son strolling arm-in-arm with an unveiled and unknown 'Frankish woman', the outraged Sultana Valida gave the empress a fierce punch in the stomach that almost knocked her down. A furious quarrel then erupted between mother and son. Fortunately, everyone burst out laughing.

After a week, the *Aigle* sailed on to Egypt, reaching Alexandria on 5 November. The khedive had tried to ensure a harmonious stay by rounding up ninety-seven of the city's most violent criminals, who had promptly been taken out to sea and thrown overboard in sacks weighted with stones. The canal was not to be opened for nearly a fortnight so Eugénie and her party took the train down to Cairo, which on the first evening was illuminated in her honour – a garish triumphal arch stood in front of the French consulate with the words, 'To the empress Eugénie from the French colony'. However, she insisted on remaining incognito, the khedive making sure that she was left in peace. She even attended an Egyptian wedding in Arab dress – a velvet waistcoat embroidered with mother-of-pearl and a burnous of gold and silver thread. The occasion reminded her a little of Spain, even the belly dancers, 'if perhaps more indecent'. She was genuinely fascinated by Egyptian antiquities and contemplated creating an Egyptian drawing-room when she returned to France, on the lines of her Salon Chinois.

After four days exploring the capital, she spent a fortnight sailing up the Nile on a dahabeeyah and visited the pyramids, a trip which had been organised by the great French Egyptologist, Auguste Mariette. It was probably the most relaxing holiday she had had since her marriage, full of interest but, above all, restful. Even so, unable to sleep one night, she went into Mme des Garet's cabin where they had a curious conversation about death. She did not blame the Egyptians for embalming their dead. 'I have never been able to accept the idea of total decay, which revolts me, especially since my sister's death', she told her young lady-in-waiting. 'But I don't suppose you've understood the Egyptian concept of death – at your age one doesn't think too deeply about the end of everything.' She added that in her opinion, 'the idea of survival which haunted the Egyptian mind for so many centuries gave them real grandeur as a people'.

Once again on board the *Aigle*, Eugénie reached Port Said very early on the morning of 16 November, the day of the canal's inauguration. Here she was warmly greeted by her cousin Ferdinand de Lesseps, whom she had been actively encouraging since 1865, often in the face of the most bitter opposition – he called her 'the canal's guardian angel'.

The actual opening of the canal, when a fleet of ships would pass through the new waterway, was to take place the following day. That evening, the empress gave a splendid dinner on the *Aigle* in preparation. During the night, however, the canal was blocked when an Egyptian corvette ran aground. The khedive threatened to have the officers impaled, but the efforts of 300 fellahin succeeded in refloating the boat.

In old age the empress recalled:

> The ceremonial opening of the canal took place at eight o'clock in the morning on 17 November, in the sea off Ismailia . . . There was a true Egyptian sky, that enchanting sunlight that has an almost hallucinating clarity. Fifty vessels, all flying their flags, were waiting for me at the entrance to Lake Timsa. My yacht, *L'Aigle*, took the head of this flotilla, and the yachts of the khedive, the Emperor Franz-Joseph, the Crown Prince of Prussia and Prince Henry of the Netherlands followed at barely a cable's length behind. The sight was one of such magnificence and proclaimed the grandeur of the French Empire so eloquently that I could scarcely control myself – I rejoiced, triumphantly. The frightful nightmare I had brought with me from Paris suddenly vanished, as if at the touch of some magic ring. For the last time I was convinced that a wonderful future lay in store for my son, and I prayed to God that He would help me with the crushing burden which I might soon have to shoulder if the emperor's health showed no improvement.

Eugénie represented France worthily. 'I can never forget her radiant figure as she stood on the bridge of the *Aigle*, while the imperial yacht slowly passed by the immense throng that had assembled on the banks of the canal', Evans remembers in his memoirs.

On 18 November the Khedive Ismail gave a great dinner and ball in a Palace at Ismailia which had been built for the opening. Before the dinner there was a display by dervishes holding burning coals between their teeth or swallowing scorpions. A keen westerniser, the khedive had imported row upon row of gilt chairs and marble-topped tables from Paris, while the meal, cooked by 500 chefs, was served by 1,000 footmen in red liveries and powdered hair. But since 6,000 guests had been invited, glittering with orders or in oriental robes, the palace was so crowded that they could not lift their arms to eat or drink, let alone dance. Accompanied by the Emperor Franz-Joseph and the khedive, Eugénie arrived at midnight in a spectacular diamond tiara and diamond-studded gown. The three drank a toast to the canal.

After the ball, Eugénie explored the Red Sea in the *Aigle*. Later, during an expedition on horses into the desert around Ismailia, her party was nearly overwhelmed by a howling sandstorm that blotted out the stars by which they were navigating. They were saved by the homing instincts of their horses who brought them safely back to Ismailia. She also made another short trip up the Nile, visiting Sakkarah and the Serapeum.

Then the *Aigle* left Egypt, taking her back to her 'nightmare'.

THE LIBERAL EMPIRE

Although Eugénie was alarmed at the prospect of the Second Empire being transformed into a constitutional monarchy, she decided during her Suez trip that nothing could stop Napoleon III from doing so. In a letter to the emperor, written on 27 October on her way along the Nile to Aswân, she explained her position to him. 'The only way forward is to go on with the concessions you have granted . . . it is essential to show the country that we are following ideas, not expedients.' She added, 'I don't believe in violence and I am convinced that we cannot mount a *coup d'état* twice in a reign.'

The 'Liberal Empire' was not forced upon Napoleon. He had been slowly feeling his way towards it for many years. At the very beginning of his reign, in 1851, he had promised that one day he would grant a constitution, and he had been making concessions since 1860 when, encouraged by Morny, he had issued a decree allowing free discussion in the Senate and Corps Législatif, giving the press permission to publish full reports of the debates. Nor did he surrender his powers in 1869 purely because of pressure from the opposition, and as the only means of saving his throne. Even if he was sorry to part with such faithful ministers as Rouher, as Theodore Zeldin observed, the liberal empire 'was not the victory of the opposition, but of a new party composed of both opponents and supporters of the old régime'. Nevertheless, the changeover to a constitutional monarchy was going to be a nerve-racking leap in the dark.

Recognising that there had been a complete regrouping of political forces in France, the emperor had waited for the emergence of a liberal majority that would accept his dynasty. He dared not try out a new system until this happened, which explains why the extremists thought they had him on the run and organised so many riots. Yet, far from being a defeat for him as so many observers thought, the 1869 elections had been a relief since they meant a viable solution.

Out of 300 deputies only about thirty red republicans of the Left wanted to overthrow the Second Empire. Most of the other republican deputies, many of whom were in any case conservatives, were prepared to keep Napoleon III as their sovereign. So were a majority of the Orleanist deputies, who in an ideal world might have preferred the Comte de Paris ('Philippe VII'). Not even Legitimists were ready to bring down the régime if it meant another revolution. Understandably, however, it was going to take months of negotiation between the various groupings before achieving a majority that could form a government.

Although it was widely suspected that Eugénie had deep reservations about a liberal empire, practically nobody except her husband understood what they were. At the same time, most politicians – and certainly the French public at large – overestimated her influence on the emperor. When the left demanded that the chambers should be summoned at the end of October, under the impression they were about to form a government, and Napoleon refused to do so until the end of the following month, many people blamed the empress. They were convinced that the date had been put back so that she could return in time to block the appointment of a liberal administration – perhaps, even, to urge her husband to launch another *coup d'état.*

In fact, Eugénie did not return until 5 December. Despite fears that there would be a revolution on 26 October and the left's threat to occupy the Corps Législatif, nothing happened. This was largely because the emperor made carefully judged public appearances to show that he was in control. The opening of the new legislature took place in the Salle des États at the Louvre on 29 November, when Napoleon received an ovation. Yet the atmosphere at the opening was not entirely pleasant. 'When our big carriage started back along the rue de Rivoli, it was surrounded by a vicious mob, bursting with hate, who hurled jeers and insults at us,' said Pauline in her memoirs. Obviously the crowd had recognised the Metternichs' black and yellow carriage as that of the empress's best friend. Pauline muttered to her husband, 'the Empire is over'.

On her return to France, Eugénie immediately fell under suspicion of being the leader of the 'Mamelukes' (so-called after the first Napoleon's faithful Egyptian bodyguard), authoritarian Bonapartists like Rouher, who were convinced that the only hope of salvation lay in a return to the 1851 régime – and, by implication, in a coup. Although they still fielded nearly ninety deputies out of the 300, and while she sympathised with their views, she realised that the Mamelukes' ideas would no longer work in the new political climate. By now, however, the 'Spanish woman' was generally considered to be a reactionary of the blackest dye.

There was an interregnum before the Liberals could take power, with the Marquis de Chasseloup-Laubat as minister-president of the Council, and although he drafted a constitution a ministry still had to be formed. There was also the question of who would lead it since there was a dearth of politicians with any experience of constitutional monarchy – many of the veterans from Orleanist days had been defeated in the recent elections.

The septuagenarian Adolphe Thiers, once Louis-Philippe's prime minister, was the obvious choice, but although his exclusion would make a dangerously spiteful enemy Napoleon still resented the way in which Thiers had sought to manipulate him in 1849–51, besides despising the old man as 'a mental, moral and physical coward'.* Certainly, no one in their right mind would have trusted this brilliant, treacherous little intriguer, a mini-Talleyrand. Nominally an Orleanist if by now really a conservative republican, he had only one abiding principle, his own prosperity. (The Musée du Louvre still displays the Collection Thiers, that monument to petit-bourgeois greed.) In any case, he would have tried to reduce the emperor to a cypher.

* This was partly because of Thiers's behaviour during the coup of 1851 – so craven that the police did not bother to arrest him.

Emile Ollivier was the man of the moment, a bespectacled lawyer from Marseilles in his forties, conceited, ambitious and glib to the point of oiliness, but who possessed an outstanding intellect and, very unlike Thiers, genuine integrity where money was concerned. He liked to think of himself as a new Mirabeau – the great tragic hero of 1789–90, who had hoped and failed to transform the *ancien régime* into a modern monarchy. Originally a hard-line republican 'irreconcilable', since 1860 he had believed firmly in the viability of a constitutional empire.

After discreet exploratory talks during the summer of 1869, Ollivier was informed by Napoleon that he was going to be the new government's leader when in October, wearing a false beard and without his spectacles, he paid a secret visit to Compiègne after dark. The Mamelukes laughed at this melodramatic meeting, which they wryly compared to Annas visiting the high priest Caiaphas by night, but the two men quickly established an excellent working relationship. The emperor began sending Ollivier state papers on a regular basis.

On 2 January 1870 it was officially announced that Emile Ollivier was to be the head of the empire's first elected government. He would scarcely be a prime minister, however, since the emperor would continue to preside over the Council of Ministers. Four of the new administration's ministers were former Bonapartist deputies, if definitely not Mamelukes, such as the Marquis de Talhouët-Roy, minister for public works, while the other four had been Orleanists, notably Comte Daru, who became foreign minister.

Many former opponents now accepted the Second Empire as the only form of French monarchy that was viable. The opposition's noisy violence helped them make up their minds. In March 1868 Whitehurst had observed how 'social fusion' was increasing. 'I could point out a dozen of the old Legitimist and Orleanist names which have been announced this year by the servants at the Tuileries.' Twelve months later he had explained to his readers that 'Every cry of "Vive la République!" rallies to the reigning dynasty everyone who has saved money, bought Rentes or taken shares.'

The court had changed. Filon tells us that people who had known it ten years earlier did not recognise it. The loose women had gone.

He quoted a conversation overheard in the Saint-Cloud smoking-room: 'Nothing but a boarding-school,' grumbled a gentleman, to which another replied, 'You mean a nursery.' The tutor explained that this was because of all the children in the château – the Prince Imperial, his friend Louis Conneau (the court doctor's son), the empress's nieces and Mme Walewska's two daughters. Even so, receptions at the Tuileries continued, especially for visiting sovereigns.

Reluctantly, Napoleon agreed to Ollivier's demand that the empress should no longer attend meetings of the Council of Ministers. The reason given to the press was 'to stop opinions which she does not hold being attributed to her, and so that she will not be suspected of possessing an influence to which she does not aspire'. There was an element of truth in this, but it is more likely that Ollivier was anxious that his government should not share in the 'Spanish woman's' unpopularity. And no doubt he remembered Rochefort's jibe about a woman being allowed to preside over the Council.

Eugénie had first met Ollivier in 1865, when as a keen supporter of penal reform he had encouraged her to visit the La Roquette prison. He had been so impressed by her intellect that he compared her to 'a heroine from Corneille', soon revised his judgement. At the end of December in the same year he had discussed the empress with Dr Libreicht, Doña Maria Manuela's occulist. 'We shared our impressions, which are very similar,' he noted in his journal. 'A passionate but not an affectionate nature, intelligent but without finesse, courageous, noble, but in a theatrical way and a bit of a Don Quixote – keener on doing good for the effect it produces than for any pleasure in it. Fickle, needs excitement.'

By 1870 he thoroughly disliked her, and not only because she was a political enemy: he realised her low opinion of him. If Paléologue can be believed, she thought he was nothing more than 'a clumsy Utopian, a pretentious wind-bag'. Although she had told him before her departure for Suez that she would no longer take an active part in politics and restrict her public activities to good works, he knew it did not stop her from criticising him in private to the Mamelukes and to her husband. Nor was he soothed by her pleasure at seeing him badly bitten by a pet monkey she had brought back from Egypt.

Meanwhile, the 'windbag' was full of bland reassurance about the political future. 'We are going to give the emperor a happy old age', Ollivier promised confidently. At first he and his administration seemed popular enough. His dismissal of Baron Haussmann as Prefect of the Seine was applauded, Haussmann's mismanagement of the capital's finances having provided the perfect excuse. He was even elected a member of the Académie Française, which until now had always been a bastion of opposition to the Second Empire and anybody connected with it.

Yet not all was well with the new régime. Although Ollivier was the government's leader, officially he was not even premier but merely minister of justice. When savaged in the Corps Législatif by Thiers, he cut an embarrassingly ineffectual figure. Strikes continued throughout the winter, some of them very serious indeed, troops shooting down strikers in self-defence more than once.

The Orleanist and the conservative republican deputies were horrified when Ollivier announced in April that, at the emperor's insistence, a plebiscite would be held to approve the constitutional reforms. The first plebiscite since 1852, this was a piece of old-fashioned, authoritarian Bonapartism and, adding insult to injury, was known to be the brain-child of Rouher, leader of the Mamelukes. Talhouët-Roy and Daru promptly resigned in protest. Extremist republicans did not object, however, since they were convinced that voters would reject the liberal empire.

There could have been no worse choice for Daru's successor as foreign minister than the arrogant and incompetent Alfred-Agénor, Duc de Gramont, who was appointed early in May. When a very young man he had been lured away from Legitimism by the emperor for decorative purposes at the Tuileries, and his career as ambassador at Rome and Vienna had begun as a reward for deigning to ornament the imperial court, in the hope that other Legitimists would follow suit. Almost excessively pro-Austrian, he had become the sworn foe of Bismarck, who despised him.

The impossible Bonaparte relations had caused yet another embarrassing scandal. This time it was not Plon-Plon but the even more dreadful Pierre Bonaparte, who was the culprit. On 10 January the 'Corsican wild boar', already credited with several murders in various foreign countries, shot in cold blood and at point-blank range an unfortunate journalist named Victor Noir, who had called on him to arrange a duel with Rochefort. 'Could anything more resemble a "rowdy" quarrel in a Far West drinking bar, than this deadly interchange of blows and shots in the salon of a Prince of the Imperial Family?' commented Felix Whitehurst. Noir's funeral at Neuilly was attended by 50,000 angry mourners and the army had to patrol the streets. Arrested, Pierre Bonaparte was tried in March at Tours, to avoid further disturbances in the capital. He was found not guilty, after a travesty of a trial. Although the emperor had not intervened to secure his acquittal, the whole episode brought discredit on the dynasty and the régime.

The plebiscite, which was held on 8 May 1870, asked every adult male in France to vote for or against the following resolution, phrased with deliberate ambiguity: 'The people approve the liberal reforms to the Constitution introduced since 1860 by the emperor with the cooperation of the great bodies of the State and ratify the Senate's decree of 20 April 1870.' Shortly before voting took place, the police discovered a plot to kill Napoleon at the Tuileries with explosives. Hundreds of socialists, all save a few of them innocent, were placed under arrest.

Even the emperor and Ollivier were astounded by the result of their referendum which resulted in over four times as many votes being cast in favour of the liberal empire as those against it – over 7 million compared with 1½ million. The socialists were confounded, leaders such as Gambetta thrown into despair. It was also a personal victory for the delighted Ollivier, who modestly hailed it as a French Königgrätz.

Had Napoleon III died at this moment of victory, he would have gone down in history as one of France's great hero-rulers, ranking with his uncle, with Louis XIV and with Henri IV in the national Pantheon.

'Sire, the country is behind you,' the president of the Senate assured him warmly at a triumphant ceremony at the Louvre. 'France has entrusted her liberty to your protection and to that of your dynasty.' Replying, the emperor told the assembly that he hoped to rally the honest men of all parties round the new constitution, to dispel any threat of revolution, to enlist everybody into the task of making France great and prosperous, and to see that education was available to all. 'We must, at the present time more than ever, look fearlessly forward to the future.' Whitehurst, who was present, tells us, 'Then his Majesty bowed, and there arose such a cheer as is seldom heard in Paris.'

When he returned to the Tuileries, Napoleon embraced the Prince Imperial, telling him, 'This has guaranteed your coronation – now we can look forward to the future, without fear.' 'Everything appeared to be reborn again,' is how Princess Metternich described the atmosphere.

'The ball of the *plébiscite* was the most splendid thing I ever saw,' said Mrs Moulton, who extolled the festoons of lanterns and coloured lamps that illuminated the Tuileries gardens, the hundreds of orange trees in tubs, adding 'there were about six thousand people invited, they said. It seemed as if all Paris was there.' 'After the *quadrille d'honneur* their Majesties circulated freely', Lillie tells us. 'Everyone was eager to offer congratulations to the emperor. Was it not the greatest triumph of his reign to have the unanimous vote of all France – this overwhelming proof of his popularity? As he stood there smiling, with a gracious acknowledgment of the many compliments, he looked radiantly happy. . . . As the emperor passed near me I added my congratulations, to which he replied, "*Merci, je suis bien heureux.*"'

On 1 June Whitehurst went to one of the smaller receptions given by Eugénie to celebrate her husband's triumph. 'The party was small, so not above eight or ten rooms were opened, and I should say that there were not more than five hundred people present,' he said. 'It was like going into the garden with Maud – there were so many flowers, the music was excellent, and when one heard the first valse echo through that glorious ball-room old times came back.' He did not know that it was to be the very last of her receptions.

Amid all the rejoicing, Eugénie remained uneasy. The strain of recent years had played havoc with her nerves so that her temper, never her strong point, was less under control than ever. Yet her judgement remained cool enough and, always more realistic than Napoleon if not so calm, she did not forget the barrier raised by the 1852 coup. Despite liberalisation, she knew that the republicans would try to bring him down should they see an opportunity. Ollivier, vain and incapable of taking advice, was not a man to inspire her with confidence, nor was the conceited, dandified Gramont. It might almost be said that if the French did not trust the empress, neither did she trust the French – although she would never have admitted it.

For the moment, however, what was worrying her much more than the political situation inside France was the threat from abroad.

THE 'SICK MAN OF EUROPE'

During the late nineteenth century, the 'sick man of Europe' was a phrase generally applied to the moribund Turkish Empire, whose decline sometimes threatened the peace between the great powers, but suited the Emperor Napoleon III. Only a handful of people realised that intermittently he became very ill indeed, although his courtiers were aware that he seemed to be ageing earlier than most men and suffered from occasional bouts of a mysterious disease, which he tried unsuccessfully to conceal from his wife. His health made Eugénie still more uneasy about the new liberal empire's viability.

She did not conceal her dislike of Emile Ollivier, 'Look at him,' she had said in February to Félix, the chief usher at the imperial court. 'Don't you have the impression that he thinks he's saved us?' During the same month she had grumbled bitterly, 'I do not understand what spell M. Ollivier is casting – the emperor seems to be in love with him.' Her disapproval was due to far more than resentment at the minister's attempt to exclude her from politics. She genuinely suspected that he was not the right man for a crisis, if one should occur, although he might be able to cope if Napoleon was there to take the real decisions.

Because of the alarming state of France's relations with Prussia, the senior generals, who had learned about the mysterious disease from court gossip, were beginning to worry about the possibility of the emperor being incapacitated if war broke out. In the Napoleonic state it was essential for the emperor to command his troops at the front – his absence would be unthinkable. What worried Eugénie even more was the thought of his being disabled during a crisis in foreign affairs.

Napoleon had first suffered from the illness in the autumn of 1864, when he had been at Chalons with the army for the annual manoeuvres. One night he had suddenly woken with acute pains in the abdomen, which were so agonising that he thought he must be dying. Baron Larrey, the imperial army's senior medical officer, identified what seemed to be a gallstone that was blocking the mouth of the urethra and causing an infection. Instead of removing the stone, Larrey merely dislodged it and the infection cleared. Napoleon ordered him to tell no one about the attack, not even the empress.

There were other attacks since then, almost annually. They usually began with a fluctuating fever and a severe headache, and culminated with excruciating pains. On each occasion the emperor was given Larrey's treatment (which consisted of little more than drinking vast quantities of water) and they had cleared fairly quickly, which meant that at one moment he would seem to be at death's door and a few days later would appear to be in normal health. Unfortunately the attacks became increasingly painful, so that he was forced to take either laudanum ('tincture of opium') or the recently patented chloral, or both – in those days they were the only effective painkillers – which inevitably left him comatose and incapable of concentration.

Eugénie did her best to discover precisely what was causing the attacks. One of the court medical team, Dr Conneau, who was a devoted and long standing personal friend of the emperor, could only think of such possibilities as rheumatism or cystitis. Other medical men suggested that it might be a heart condition, or diabetes. Eugénie learned to look out for such symptoms as blood in her husband's urine, spasms of the bladder and shooting pains. He himself could not tell her what it was, simply because he did not know; admittedly, if he had known, he would probably have kept it a secret.

When General de Montebello's wife, a close friend of the empress, fell ill in January 1870, the general suddenly noticed that Eugénie was carefully timing her visits to coincide with those of Mme de Montebello's physician, Augustin Nélaton, who was also one of the emperor's physicians. With a shock, Montebello realised that she was doing so in order to question Dr Nélaton about Napoleon's health.

In June, sensing that he was about to undergo yet another attack, the emperor decided that he wanted a fresh opinion on his malady. Accordingly, Germain Sée, a young professor of medical pathology at the University of Paris who was an expert on diseases of the bladder, came to examine him at Saint-Cloud on 19 June. Professor Sée found that he had a huge gallstone.

Six doctors met in secret on 2 July to discuss Sée's diagnosis. At first a Dr Fauvel argued eloquently that the cause was not a stone but in fact an abscess in the patient's bladder, while Dr Conneau was very much inclined to think that it was probably no more than a severe internal chill. In the end, however, all agreed with the professor's diagnosis. Sée insisted that an operation to remove the stone must take place urgently, adding that it ought to have been performed six months earlier. But Dr Nélaton, the most distinguished surgeon in France, disagreed, saying that they should wait until September and then reassess the situation. Since a majority of the doctors supported Nélaton, all that Professor Sée could do was give his report to Dr Conneau and ask him to present it to the emperor.

Later, a slanderous story was put about by Plon-Plon or by one of his allies, that Eugénie had not only intercepted and suppressed the report but that she had also withheld from Napoleon the doctors' unanimous opinion that the stone had made him incapable of riding a horse or of bearing the slightest physical fatigue. Her motive, claimed the slander, was to make certain that he either collapsed or died, so that she could be regent until her son came of age. In reality, she did not see the report or know that her husband was suffering from a gallstone until long after, while the doctors had never given any such opinion. Meanwhile, in early July, Napoleon suffered a particularly severe attack which almost totally incapacitated him for several days. He could not have fallen ill at a worse moment.

EIGHT

Downfall

A PRUSSIAN SPAIN?

A surprising number of distinguished men worshipped the empress. Among them were the imperial librarian, Octave Feuillet, the Austrian chancellor, Count von Beust, the Italian ambassador Cavaliere Nigra – even if Eugénie ranted at him more than once about Italy's designs on Rome – and Jacques Offenbach, although this may have been one of the maestro's jokes. The loyal Filon claimed romantically that Count Bacciochi shot himself 'to escape from the consuming tortures of a wild passion' for Eugénie, but he had really done so because of ruining himself on the stock exchange.

The most improbable of all was the Prussian ambassador, Count von der Goltz, who wrote the empress wistful letters of the utmost propriety. She kept them for the rest of her life, calling him, '*mon pauvre Goltz*'. In August 1866 Goltz tried in vain to persuade Bismarck of the benefits of a French alliance, but torn between his affections and his patriotism, while foreseeing war he tried, only once, to warn the empress. This was after visiting Berlin in 1868 when he wrote to her that German journalists in Paris were sending home reports which placed Napoleon III in the worst possible light and that the chauvinist tone of the French press was arousing hostility across the Rhine. A bit later the emperor grumbled to Cowley about rumours in the German press that he was preparing for a war and that when he lost it he would have to 'restore' Alsace and Lorraine to Germany, rumours that 'were doing incredible mischief'.

When Goltz became incurably ill in 1869 Eugénie had him installed in a pavilion in the park at Fontainebleau so that she could see he was properly nursed. 'One summer's evening we were sitting by the lake in front of the Chinese Drawing Room when a shadow –

a shadow, not a man, appeared,' recalled Filon. It was Goltz who, unable to speak, looked at the empress with 'the dumb devotion of a faithful dog'. He died shortly after.

In old age Prince Bismarck boasted that he deliberately provoked a war with France, to make the South German States unite with the North. In fact he blundered into one through tactless diplomacy. Even so, without Bismarck there would never have been a Franco-Prussian War.

Although Napoleon III was scarcely a great soldier, at least he tried to be a realist. 'He said that it was the superior military organisation of Prussia that had counted in the late war,' Cowley reported in December 1866. 'Austria, in fact, had been in the same position as he found himself during the war in Italy with a formidable army on paper, which dwindled to nothing when put to the test of activity.'

He had been seriously alarmed by reports from the French military attaché at Berlin, Baron Stoffel, who warned that highly trained officers and ultra-modern equipment gave the Prussian army overwhelming superiority. Already shocked by the Prussian performance at Königgrätz, the emperor welcomed the sweeping programme of military reform proposed by Marshal Niel, minister for war. Secret discussions during the annual staff conferences at Compiègne alarmed him still more. Niel, who died in 1869, always insisted that by itself even a stronger army was not enough and agreed with Eugénie on the need for an Austrian alliance – only a war on two fronts could defeat the Prussians.

Unfortunately, despite Königgrätz the new liberal France could see no reason for paying more taxes to improve an army that might be wasted on another Mexican adventure. Nevertheless, the army began to modernise early in 1868. It was equipped with a fine new breech-loading rifle, the *chassepot*, which was better than the Prussian 'needle-gun', and the first mass-produced machine-gun, the *mitrailleuse* (firing 150 rounds a minute), although the Corps Législatif refused to pay for artillery that would match breech-loading Krupp howitzers. Even so, having seen a demonstration of the rapid firepower of what he called 'the deadly Chassepots', Whitehurst was convinced that 'no infantry or cavalry could advance in the face of such a permanent and perpetual discharge of death'. By 1870 France was certainly much readier for war than it had been in 1859 – for war against an army of the same sort as itself.

As Napoleon realised very well, the daunting superiority of the Prussian army lay not only in its numbers, training and equipment, but also in its organisation. Its General Staff could supply commanders with information and advice throughout a battle, while it had learned how to use railways to rush men to the front. And as its commander-in-chief, in all but name, it had Moltke, who had been planning an invasion of France for the last ten years.

'Six railway lines were now available to bring the forces of the North German Confederation to the Rhineland – a total, in three weeks, of 300,000 men,' writes Sir Michael Howard. If Austria stayed put and the South German States fulfilled their treaty obligations, the total would be nearer half a million. 'Railway timetables were drawn up, so that every unit knew the exact day and hour that it would leave its barracks and reach its concentration area. Mobilisation and deployment would follow one another in a single smooth and exactly calculated operation. By July 1870 Moltke knew that he had under his hand one of the greatest engines of war the world had ever known; and he was openly impatient to use it.'

France's generals put their trust in their troops, now that they were armed with the *chassepot*. (General du Barail admitted in his memoirs that he told Marshal Canrobert, 'We beat Russia in the Crimea, Austria in Italy, and I most sincerely believe that these two campaigns have assured our supremacy in Europe.') They also hoped to find allies among the South German States, who had no wish to be absorbed by Prussia – the Grand Duke of Hesse informed General Ducrot that even a small victory by France would make all the South Germans go over to her side. Encouragingly, the Bavarians elected an anti-Prussian 'Patriot' government in the spring of 1870.

There was even a faint possibility the Austrians might help. During a visit to Paris in February 1870 Archduke Albrecht, their best general, proposed an alliance between Austria, France and Italy, but Franz-Joseph, who dared not risk losing a third war, would only say vaguely that if the French invaded South Germany 'as liberators rather than enemies' he might come in on their side. Some French generals thought an alliance of this sort had small chance of success, arguing that the Prussians could mobilise too quickly and that South Germans hated Frenchmen more than they did the Protestant Northerners.

The French did not appreciate that since the Dual Monarch's establishment in 1867 Franz-Joseph had become the prisoner of the Hungarians, who did not want him to become too powerful for them, as he undoubtedly would be if he defeated the Prussians. Budapest would never let him go to war with Berlin.

However, all this talk of a Franco-Prussian war seemed mere theorising in the weeks that followed the plebiscite. Even if the French and the Prussians disliked each other, there was no reason for war. 'The government has no cause for concern whatever', Emile Ollivier told the Corps Législatif when discussing foreign affairs. 'At no period has the maintenance of peace seemed more assured.' This was on 30 June. Three days later the French ambassador at Madrid telegraphed the Quai d'Orsai: 'A deputation has offered the throne of Spain to a Hohenzollern prince, who has accepted.' The prince was Leopold of Hohenzollern-Sigmaringen. He was not even a Prussian, only a remote kinsman of the Prussian king (they shared a mutual thirteenth-century ancestor) and in fact a close cousin of Napoleon III through the Beauharnais, but it made no difference to the French, who were convinced that Prussia was encircling France. The press erupted in hysteria.

Suddenly, in the words of the *académicien* L.-A. Prévost-Paradol, 'France and Prussia were hurtling towards each other like two locomotives on the same track.'

On 6 July the Duc de Gramont promised the Corps Législatif that France would not tolerate a Hohenzollern prince or any other Prussian prince on the Spanish throne: 'We shall know how to do our duty, without the slightest hesitation or weakness.' The emperor had asked Gramont to speak gently, but Ollivier told him to be as forceful as he liked. Privately the duke informed the Council that Leopold's accession 'means war.'

Gramont had made his statement after consulting the minister for war, General Leboeuf, who assured him that the French army was ready for hostilities. It was Ollivier who supplied the phrase, 'We shall know how to do our duty'. 'We have had enough of the humiliations that Prussia wants to inflict on us,' he informed the Austrian ambassador. 'La Valette and Rouher are no longer running French policy.' Undoubtedly he had judged the nation's mood correctly, and in the chamber Gramont's speech was greeted with cries of '*Vive la France! Vive l'Empéreur!*' even of '*A Berlin!*' Everyone agreed, on the left as well as on the right, including Gambetta. 'Rarely have we seen so much unanimity in the newspapers of all the various parties,' noted the *Figaro*.

Reading the foreign minister's statement to the Corps Législatif, Bismarck commented, 'this certainly looks like war'. Yet the Prussian chancellor had never intended to set a trap for Napoleon III, as many historians have suggested – and, indeed, as he himself would hint afterwards. Isabella II had abdicated in 1868 and for the last year Bismarck had been trying, in secret negotiations with the Spanish dictator Marshal Prim, to replace her by a Hohenzollern. However unwelcome a German king of Spain might be to the French, if they were presented with a fait accompli he saw no reason why they should go to war once Leopold had been safely installed by the Cortès. It was only by accident that news of the negotiations leaked out before the Cortès was able to give its approval.

The revelation that Bismarck had been intriguing in Spain outraged opinion throughout Europe. In London *The Times* called his scheme 'a vulgar and impudent *coup d'état* in total contradiction to accepted diplomatic practice in handling such matters'. It looked as if Prussia would have to back down, suffering considerable humiliation, while few, if any, observers expected there would be war.

On 7 July the Duc de Gramont sent a telegram to Count Benedetti at the French embassy in Berlin, instructing him to extract a promise at once from King William that he would arrange for Leopold to withdraw his candidature immediately. 'We have to know whether it is to be peace or a refusal which means war,' said the duke. 'If you can persuade the king to prevent the prince from accepting, it will be a great triumph and a great service. On his own initiative, the king will have guaranteed the peace of Europe. But if this does not happen, then there is going to be war.'

'The speech made by the Duke de Gramont in the Chamber stirred up the whole country into a war-fever which the feeble government of M. Ollivier could not control,' the Austrian diplomat Baron Vitzthum recalled later. Napoleon was the one man in Paris who kept his head and guessed at Prussia's military potential. He can scarcely have been reassured by the war minister Marshal Leboeuf, who on behalf of the French army claimed fatuously that in the event of a war lasting for a year, 'We won't need to buy a single gaiter-button.'

'If Prussia doesn't want to fight, then we shall have to give her a good kick up the backside, by going over the Rhine again and clearing the left bank [of Germans]', wrote Emile de Girardin in *La Presse* – and Girardin was no mere hack but one of the most influential journalists in France. The empress shared the general mood. When Prevost-Paradol, minister designate to the United States, came to Saint-Cloud for a farewell audience she gave him a warm welcome, knowing he had always said that a Franco-Prussian war was inevitable. 'We've got to go ahead,' Eugénie told him. 'France is on the verge of losing her place in the world – she has to fight or go under.'

On 7 July Gramont instructed Benedetti to obtain a categorical statement from the Prussian king, to the effect that he had ordered Prince Leopold to stand down. William, who had never liked the idea of the candidature, and who in any case did not want a war, politely declined. It was nothing to do with him, said the king – he did not object to Leopold withdrawing just as he had not objected to his accepting. Gramont's reaction, in a telegram on 9 July, was, 'If the King won't order the Prince of Hohenzollern to refuse, then it will be immediate war and within a few days we shall cross the Rhine.' On 11 July, in yet another frantic telegram, he told the ambassador that the ministry might fall because of popular excitement over the issue – however he did it, Benedetti must obtain William's formal undertaking.

Yet when Prince Metternich had seen the emperor on the day of Gramont's speech three days earlier, he had found him relaxed and optimistic. 'I must say that all this Spanish-Prussian affair seems to have been seized upon as an opportunity to score a diplomatic success and humiliate Prussia,' he reported, adding that the French thought they could bring it off without endangering the peace.

Ignoring both Eugénie and his ministers, Napoleon sent a secret envoy to Prince Leopold's father, imploring him to stop his son from accepting the Spanish throne. He also wrote to King Leopold II of Belgium, asking him to intervene with the Hohenzollern-Sigmaringen family. In addition, he told the French ambassador in London to ask the English foreign secretary Lord Granville to use his influence in Berlin and Madrid.

The emperor's diplomacy very nearly succeeded in avoiding a war. Horrified at the thought of starting one, and shaken by a stern letter from Queen Victoria, on 12 July Prince Leopold's father sent telegrams to Berlin, Madrid and Paris, announcing that his son had decided to decline the offer of the Spanish crown. When Napoleon read his telegram, he exclaimed delightedly, 'This is peace!'

Eugénie's reaction to the Hohenzollern-Sigmaringen telegram was very different, however. '*Qué verguenza!*' she cried in disgust – 'How shameful!' 'This renunciation just isn't good enough,' she continued furiously. 'The King of Prussia must guarantee that the candidature is never going to be repeated.'

This was also the reaction of the Corps Législatif. When Prince Leopold's withdrawal was announced, the deputies, especially those on the right, dismissed it angrily as a private message with absolutely no guarantee from Prussia that he might not change his mind. In a panic, Gramont informed the Prussian ambassador Baron von Werther that King William must write a formal letter 'of explanation' to the emperor, providing the necessary guarantee.

At this crucial moment Napoleon collapsed with an agonising attack from the stone in his bladder. The only possible relief from the pain was laudanum, which deprived him of the ability to concentrate.

Nevertheless, the duke insisted on seeing the emperor at Saint-Cloud, at 5.00 p.m. on 12 July. The only other person present was the empress. Since Ollivier had excluded her from Council meetings, she excluded him from the meeting that would decide whether there would be peace or war – a decision to be taken by herself and Gramont. The one account of the meeting is that given by Eugénie to Paléologue in 1906 and, despite Paléologue's unreliability, it is extremely convincing. First, she stressed how all the Second Empire's leading generals had promised her that in the event of war, despite some fierce fighting to begin with, the French would easily beat the Prussians:

Leboeuf, Canrobert, Ducrot, Vaillant, Frossard, Bourbaki, Lebrun, Gallifet – they all vouched for our victory . . . and what a victory. I think I can still hear them telling me, at Saint-Cloud: 'Never has our army been in better condition, better equipped, in better fighting mettle. Nineteen chances out of every twenty are in our favour. Our offensive in Germany will be so shattering that it will cut Prussia in two, and we shall swallow Prussia at one gulp . . . We'll soon find the way back to Jena.'

'Withdraw? Temporise? We could not possibly. We should have had the whole country rising against us . . . They were already taunting us with our weakness; a terrible remark had reached even our ears. "The Hohenzollern candidature is a second Königgrätz in the making." For years our ruthless enemies, Orleanists, Legitimists and republicans, had never wearied of flinging it in our faces.'

Eugénie explained to Paléologue that French national pride would not have tolerated further humiliation, and that she had fully agreed with Gramont's assessment of the situation, recalling how he put it:

Our differences with Prussia cannot be solved merely by the Hohenzollern candidate withdrawing. That is no sort of solution and it is never going to satisfy French public opinion – we should be blamed, and quite rightly so, for having been duped by Bismarck . . . I have just learned that the right wing in the Corps Législatif intends to question us closely about the guarantees we have demanded from King William – the guarantees to ensure that we shall never again be in danger of seeing a German prince reigning at Madrid. If we don't secure these vital guarantees, then France will have been humiliated and insulted in the eyes of all Europe. Every Frenchman will be infuriated, heart and soul, by the emperor's behaviour, and that would mean the end of the Empire.

By her own admission, Eugénie unhesitatingly agreed with the duke's policy, convinced that extracting public guarantees from Prussia was the sole means of saving the Second Empire. She claims that Napoleon 'raised no objection', although historians suspect he was too ill to say anything. 'All we discussed was the need to put an end to Bismarck's machinations,' she insisted. 'We had no desire for war. Even so, we weren't frightened of one either because, as I repeat again and again, our army appeared to be invincible, while we also counted on finding powerful allies.' Presumably by 'powerful allies' she meant Austria and Italy. No doubt, if the French army had done what its generals promised, Franz-Joseph and Victor-Emmanuel might have joined in on the emperor's side. But they would only march to the aid of a victorious France.

As a recently promoted career diplomat, a politician for just nine weeks, Gramont had no parliamentary skills and was unnerved by the fury in the Corps Législatif. The emperor or a veteran minister such as Rouher or La Valette might have defused the situation. But the duke could see no way out other than to humiliate Prussia.

'Yes, I fully approved Gramont's policy, and even gave him the full weight of my support when he came to see us,' was Eugénie's recollection, according to Paléologue. 'I was wrong to behave chivalrously (*d'être homme galant*) to the empress when I should have behaved chivalrously to France,' is Gramont's version – a far from chivalrous attempt to shift most of the blame on to Eugénie.

She explained her decision:

I had long been convinced that we were going along a doomed road, that the Liberal Empire was dragging us down into the worst sort of revolution, a revolution of mistrust. You may say I was thinking only of the Empire and not of France, but God is my witness that I never distinguished between France and the Empire. I simply could not conceive of French grandeur or French prosperity except under the Empire. And when my husband's health was becoming such a worry, I had to concentrate on handing over power to our son intact. . . . That is why I gave Gramont's policy such whole-hearted support.

Doubts have been cast on Paléologue's account of what Eugénie told him, especially by her admirers, and admittedly he is sometimes unreliable. Yet in this case he seems to be borne out by Emile Ollivier, who said, 'The war was wanted by the empress and [General] Leboeuf, forced on us by Bismarck.' General du Barail also claimed that she wanted war, because she thought it would be easy to win and wished the reign of 'Napoleon IV' to open in an atmosphere of military glory.

Within two hours of Gramont's discussion with Eugénie, Benedetti received a further cable. 'To make the renunciation certain,' instructed the duke, 'the King of Prussia must endorse it, guaranteeing that he is not going to renew the candidature. Please see the King at once and ask for a confirmation, which he cannot refuse unless he really does have some sort of reservation. Although the repudiation has become widely known, public opinion is so violent that we are not sure we will be able to control it.'

That day debates in the Corps Législatif and the Senate had been interrupted by yells of 'We've got to finish it!' In the evening crowds marched along the boulevards, singing the 'Marseillaise' and bellowing, '*A Berlin! A Berlin!*' Eugénie was far from being out of step with her people.

On 13 July Count Benedetti waylaid King William in the public gardens at Ems. An official sent a telegram for Bismarck to send, stating that the king had told Benedetti that Prince Leopold had promised to withdraw his candidature, and that there was nothing more to say. It was phrased with such moderation and courtesy that the Prussian chancellor and General von Moltke, hoping for war, were in despair. Bismarck shortened the telegram, however, distorting its message so as to seem insulting – Moltke commented approvingly, 'You make it sound like a trumpet call answering a challenge.' The doctored 'Ems Telegram' was then sent to Paris and released to the press.

Ironically, on 13 July the Council of Ministers' meeting at Saint-Cloud had second thoughts, voting against a proposal for immediate mobilisation. They were ready to water down Gramont's demand for guarantees.

The Ems telegram reached Paris the next day. 'Here is a man who has been slapped in the face,' Gramont told Ollivier hysterically. The crowds in the streets were screaming, '*Au Rhin!*' – 'To the Rhine!' At 4.40 p.m. the Council of Ministers agreed to a general mobilisation, yet delayed it again to discuss the possibility of a peace congress.

Afterwards, the duke claimed that Eugénie had put an end to the possibility by observing, 'I doubt that it will suit the chambers and the country.' Lord Malmesbury wrote: 'Gramont told me that the empress, a high-spirited and impressionable woman, made a strong and most excited address, declaring that "war was inevitable if the honour of France was to be maintained".' Although Eugénie was not present at the Council, she may perhaps have said something like this elsewhere. But it was Ollivier who killed the idea of a peace congress, telling the emperor – who was beginning to recover from his attack – 'If we laid the proposal before the chambers, they would pelt our carriages with mud and howl at us.'

That evening the Council decided there was no alternative to war. Next morning Ollivier addressed the Corps Législatif and the Senate, asking them to vote the money with which to fight. Some on the left denounced the war. "You have decided to shed torrents of blood over a mere form of words,' said Thiers. 'I accept the need for it with a light heart,' answered Ollivier. Not only the right and the centre was with him, but the left too. 'Thus by a tragic combination of ill-luck, stupidity and ignorance France blundered into war with the greatest military power that Europe had yet seen, in a bad cause, with her army unready and without allies,' is the verdict of Sir Michael Howard in *The Franco-Prussian War*.

Eugénie may not have said, 'It was I who wanted this war – it is my war', as Thiers alleged. She herself denied it. 'Never, do you hear me,' she supposedly told Paléologue, 'did that sacrilegious phrase, nor any like it, come from my lips.' Yet, like the Mamelukes, she expected a triumphant victory that would bring back a return to direct rule and true Bonapartism.

THE FINAL REGENCY

Most of the French did not take too seriously a war that was beginning in such gloriously sunny weather and with such catchy tunes. In any case, they believed their army was invincible.

They thought they were only fighting Prussia, which, despite Königgrätz, they still insisted on seeing as a second-rate power, and that the minor German states would join in on their side: they did not foresee that, contrary to expectation, every German would be against them, just as in 1813.

Paris was in holiday mood – and when the troops marched past they were cheered to the echo by men in shirt sleeves whose wives carried picnic baskets and whose children blew tin trumpets. Despite being banned as revolutionary, the 'Marseillaise' was sung on every street corner, while all the musc halls and bars rang with the chorus of some new patriotic song.

One of these choruses from the back streets, to an anti-Prussian song which for a time became almost as popular as the 'Marseillaise', ran:

> Oh Wilhelm, Oh you gross papa,
> We'll rub your nose in your own caca!

The Parisians were clearly in no doubt about who was going to win.

Yet it seems as if Eugénie very soon had second thoughts. Mrs Moulton had been asked to dine at Saint-Cloud on 17 July. When she and her husband arrived at the château, they were told by a chamberlain that the party had been cancelled but that all the same the empress would like them to stay for dinner. 'And stay we did,' says Lillie, 'and I never regretted anything so much in my life.'

The two Americans were the only guests other than members of the household. Lillie had never seen Napoleon III look so ill and tired. 'The emperor never uttered a word; the empress sat with her eyes fixed on the emperor, and did not speak to a single person. No one spoke. The emperor would receive telegram upon telegram; the gentleman sitting next to him opened the telegrams and put them before his Majesty. Every now and again the emperor would look across the table to the empress with such a distressed look it made me think that something terrible was happening.'

War with Prussia was officially declared on 19 July, although in reality France had been at war since the chambers had authorised the money for it four days earlier. When the Senate and Corps

Législatif came out to Saint-Cloud to offer a loyal address on 18 July, in striking contrast to the euphoric optimism in the press and in the streets Napoleon emphasised in his speech of thanks that 'We are entering upon a long and arduous war.'

Apparently the emperor's misgivings frightened Eugénie. 'A great country like France, so tranquil and prosperous, has embarked on a struggle which, even if it goes well, is bound to bring enormous destruction and misery,' she confided to a courtier at Saint-Cloud. 'France is fighting for her honour, but what a cataclysm there will be if the war goes against us. We have only a few cards to play. If we don't win, France will not only be humiliated and plundered, but will suffer the worst revolution that the world has ever seen.'

On 20 July Princesse Mathilde went to see Napoleon at Saint-Cloud. He greeted her in his study, his face ashen, his eyelids puffy, his eyes dead, his legs shaky and his shoulders hunched. 'Is it true you are taking command of the army?' she asked.

'Yes,' he replied.

'But you aren't in a fit state to command anything!' Mathilde burst out. 'You can't sit astride a horse, you can't even bear being shaken up in a carriage. How are you going to manage during the fighting?'

The emperor answered 'in a muffled voice' that she was exaggerating, and 'waved his hand in a gesture of resigned fatalism'.

Both he and the empress had decided that he had no other option than to lead the armies of France into battle. On 11 July, during a lucid interval from the stone and his laudanum, he had ordered that all three armies in any forthcoming German campaign must be under his personal command. After all, he was a Bonaparte. This was asking for trouble. 'The campaign of 1859 had shown his total incapacity for generalship even when in good health,' comments Sir Michael Howard.

On 26 July Eugénie was appointed regent for the third time. Two days later, accompanied by the fourteen-year-old Prince Imperial, Napoleon set out for the front. Much to the Parisians' surprise, he did not ride out from his capital at the head of the Imperial Guard, as he had in 1859, but instead took the train to his headquarters at Metz. Very few people were allowed to know of his illness.

227

Augustin Filon was among the small group of courtiers who saw the emperor and the prince off from the little railway station at Saint-Cloud. He watched Eugénie drive past with Princess Clothilde on their way back to the château. Both women were in tears, although the empress had managed to remain dry-eyed while making the sign of the cross on her son's forehead and telling him to do his duty. Another courtier, de Parieu, informed the tutor how when he had said to her that he thought the French would be wrong not to accept an offer of English mediation, if it materialised, she had replied, 'I think so too.' Clearly she was in a different mood from when she had discussed Prussian 'guarantees' with Gramont a fortnight before.

Filon became an extra private secretary to the empress, in charge of letters and telegrams in cypher. Although she was regent in name only, and did not attend Council meetings, he was struck by the determined way in which she worked at trying to persuade members of the opposition parties to support the war and also to gain allies among the European powers, even if Bismarck made this an unpromising task by publishing the emperor's demand for Belgium in 1866 in return for letting Prussia have a free hand in South Germany.

The new private secretary was surprised at how Ollivier and his ministers seldom if ever bothered to inform the regent of their decisions. In their eyes her job was awarding the Légion d'honneur. Throughout the war Eugénie was almost totally dependent on Napoleon's letters for news from the front; ironically this meant that she was better informed than any minister.

The French strategy was to invade Germany as quickly as possible with overwhelming superiority in numbers, striking either east across the Rhine or north into the Palatinate, and to win a crushing victory while the Prussian armies were still assembling. French generals were convinced that a spectacular success of this sort would immediately bring Austria into the conflict on their side – for weeks they refused to abandon their fantasies about Austrian intervention – and win over the South German states. Everyone, including even von Moltke, expected the campaign to be on German soil. Ollivier warned that French soldiers should not count on being given too warm a welcome by the Germans.

The chaos of French mobilisation and the incompetence of French staff work made such a plan out of the question. When the emperor's train deposited him at Metz, he found just over 200,000 troops instead of the 385,000 he had been promised. 'There was nothing anywhere but muddle, incoherence, delays, quarrels and confusion.' The railway system could not cope while not only were there insufficient troops, but inadequate food and ammunition.

'Nothing is ready here,' a horrified Napoleon wrote to Eugénie two days after his arrival. 'We don't have enough troops so I think we have lost our chance of invading.' His letter left her shattered, 'just as if my arms and legs had been broken'. A new chaplain who arrived at Saint-Cloud next day, the Abbé Pujol, saw the empress still deeply upset, weeping openly at dinner and drying her tears with a napkin. 'I'm good for nothing', she told him. 'A bad dispatch reaches me and I completely collapse. I am more of a wife and a mother than a regent, yet at the same time I long to give everything for France – I only want the good of France.' Some historians interpret this outburst as a symptom of mental breakdown, but it was probably due to frustration at being excluded from any useful role in government.

On 2 August an offensive was at last launched, 60,000 French troops occupying the hills overlooking Saarbrücken, two miles across the frontier, where they met with resistance from a mere handful of the enemy. Napoleon wrote to Eugénie how the Prince Imperial had picked up a spent bullet. 'He might have been strolling along the Bois de Boulogne,' wrote his father. 'Some men wept at seeing him so calm.' For most of the time the boy had been in the carriage from which the emperor 'directed' operations – any attempt by Napoleon to mount a horse caused the poor man agony.

The French press magnified the '*promenade militaire*' of Saarbrücken into a major advance during which the entire town had been burned to the ground after the annihilation of three Prussian divisions. Parisians were ecstatic at this first – and last – victory bulletin. Far from arousing admiration, however, Ollivier's publication of Napoleon's letter made the Prince Imperial a laughing stock in the republican papers, as '*l'enfant de la balle*' inanely frolicking on the battlefield.

The Prussian army, with their Bavarian and Württemberger allies were by now ready to attack. Superior railways enabled them to outnumber the French, while their officers, although no braver, were certainly much better trained. Above all, they had Helmuth von Moltke, whose roaming general staff acted as 'a nervous system' that enabled him to control and direct enormous bodies of men.

On 4 August the emperor was informed that the enemy had crossed the frontier into Alsace and seized the town of Wissembourg. On 6 August Crown Prince Frederick-William overwhelmed the French at Froeschwiller (Worth), capturing 4,000 prisoners with thirty cannon. If General von Steinmetz was not quite so successful at Spicheren on the same day, he forced General Frossard into withdrawing. The Germans had secured the initiative, cutting off Marshal Bazaine's troops from those of Marshal MacMahon.

These defeats were not catastrophic, but they put an end to any dreams of invading Germany or of acquiring allies. Franz-Joseph ordered the Austrian army to cease preparing for mobilisation. So did Victor-Emmanuel. 'Aha, the poor emperor!' commented the gentleman king (*Il re galantuomo*), 'I've had a lucky escape.'

THE REGENT TAKES CONTROL

'Towards noon on 6 August news of a great victory won by MacMahon spread like a train of gunpowder and central Paris gave itself up to an orgy of joy,' Filon recalled. It was said that 120,000 Prussians had been routed by 70,000 Frenchmen, who had taken 25,000 prisoners including the crown prince. Before the report was found to be a cruel trick by speculators to hoax the Bourse, the mobs sang the 'Marseillaise'. Even so, the crowd was in an ugly mood. 'We're in for a warm time tonight,' Pietri, the chief of police, told Filon.

If a little imprecise with dates, Filon's recollections are invaluable about what happened during the next four weeks, since he was at the empress's side the entire time. As soon as he returned to Saint-Cloud at 9.30 that evening, her equerry General Lepic brought a message from Ollivier that a revolution appeared to be imminent.

'Yes,' observed Eugénie. 'A conspiracy like Malet's' – referring to a republican plot to overthrow Napoleon I when he was away on campaign in 1810.

Lepic asked her to sign a decree drawn up by Ollivier, placing the capital under martial law. In addition, Ollivier implored her to 'return to Paris immediately with all the troops at her disposal'. Although Lepic warned her that the only men available were 160 men at the Guards Light Infantry Depot, she signed the decree and sent word to Ollivier that she would move back into the Tuileries next day. Then she went to bed.

Filon had hardly sat down when an urgent telegram that had just arrived from General Headquarters was brought in for him to decipher. 'Our troops are in full retreat,' he read, 'We must concentrate on defending the capital.' Almost as soon as he had deciphered it, another telegram arrived, announcing the defeats at Froeschwiller and Spicheren. It ended, 'All may yet be regained.' By now it was 11.30 p.m. The Marquis de Piennes agreed to tell the empress. 'Do you know what she said?' Piennes told Filon when he returned, looking pale. 'The dynasty is lost. We must think only of France.'

Within a quarter of an hour, fully dressed but without make-up, Eugénie came down to the drawing-room, where her ladies and gentlemen joined her. The Princess d'Essling burst into tears and cried, 'Oh, Madame!' The empress stopped her. 'No emotion, please. I'm going to need all my courage.' Jurien de La Gravière was more reassuring, saying, 'Well, after all, it might have been much worse.'

She left immediately for the Tuileries where she summoned a Council for 3.30 a.m., presiding as in the old days. Among those present were Ollivier, Eugène Schneider (president of the Corps Législatif) and the 'Mameluke' Rouher (president of the Senate). She told them of the two defeats, of the invasion of Alsace and Lorraine, of the threat to the capital.

Panic-stricken, Ollivier proposed a coup, arresting all left-wing deputies and banning every opposition newspaper. The empress refused. She also refused his demand that the emperor should return to Paris – in her view a commander-in-chief could not come home 'with the shadow of defeat hanging over him'. She refused, too, his request for General Trochu to be made minister of war, after hearing the hastily summoned general declare he would publicly attack the handling of the campaign. Nothing could be done until she had got rid of Ollivier. But she had asserted her authority as regent.

'When I reached the Tuileries at about one o'clock in the morning I was a completely different woman, no longer agonised, no longer weak,' Eugénie remembered. 'I felt calm and strong. I was lucid and resolved. And I was straining every nerve throughout that tragic night to revive confidence and courage in those around me.'

Filon lay down to sleep on a sofa. The palace furniture was covered with dust-sheets, which the regent would not let her staff remove. 'For the next month we led a totally Bohemian life,' he said. 'We ate and slept wherever, whenever and however we could, working on any table that happened to be free. In other words, we were camping in the Tuileries.' Mme Lebreton-Bourbaki, the empress's reader (and sister of the general commanding the Imperial Guard) made up a bed for herself next to Eugénie's dressing-room so that she could be called at once in case of an emergency.

'She was wonderful,' Ollivier commented after the regent had presided over the early morning Council. 'We were all deeply impressed.' It was an odd tribute from a man once so keen to ban her from meetings. That evening he sent a telegram to Napoleon, telling him France was loyal to the Second Empire: 'One or two wretches who shouted "*Vive la République!*" have been arrested by the people themselves.' Curiously, he did not mention the impending revolution of which he had warned Eugénie only the day before. 'We are all united and discuss policy in the Council in complete agreement,' he continued. 'The empress is in excellent health. She shows us a magnificent example of strength, courage and nobility of soul.' He may have been toadying, however, in order to save his government.

Pierre de La Gorce was not present during the dramatic scenes at Saint-Cloud and the Tuileries, and his asssessment of Eugénie's motives is more brutal, even if he uses polite phrases when referring to her, such as '*l'auguste infortunée*': 'Thoughts were running through the empress's head, which she did not altogether admit to herself,' he suggested:

She blamed the emperor for three failings in particular; he had grown old, he had turned into a liberal and he had been defeated. Since his position at home had been gravely weakened by his concessions, since he had been humiliated on the battlefield by his defeats, and since he was at the same time broken by the premature collapse of his health, what else should he do but disappear? In contrast, she was young, she was ambitious and she was a mother. She was also legally the regent. Thus was born her secret plan for France's future, for the empire's and for her son's, which had no place for the emperor who largely as a result of his own faults would be obliged to sacrifice himself.

This is no more than saying that Eugénie believed it might soon be time for Napoleon to abdicate in favour of the Prince Imperial – we know she had been thinking on these lines since 1866. What is intriguing is La Gorce's conviction that by now she was definitely planning to rule France herself, and in her own way.

On the evening of the day after her return to the Tuileries, she was sufficiently relaxed to write a confident letter to Paca's two daughters, whom she had sent home to Madrid as soon as bad news began to arrive from the front:

Everything remains quiet here although we can't be sure it's going to continue. A state of siege has been declared, all the dispatches have been published and the chambers have been recalled. Stay calm! For the time being that really is the most important thing we must do. The news from the troops is that we are still fighting. If we win a battle, then everything will be transformed. Be brave and don't worry about us. I'm in no way downcast despite the unpleasant moments I've been through since last night.

Ignoring Ollivier's angry protests and exceeding her constitutional powers, the regent insisted on recalling the two chambers. Quite apart from her own distrust of the man, she realised he had lost the chambers' confidence and that they would vote for a new government when they met on 9 August. She then asked a distinguished soldier and member of the Senate to form an administration, General Cousin de Montauban, Comte de Palikao, a scarred but vigorous septuagenarian who had led the expedition to China in 1860.

Palikao took over the now crucial portfolio of minister of war while the unlamented Gramont followed Ollivier into oblivion, replaced as foreign minister by the Prince de la Tour d'Auvergne. The new interior minister was an old acquaintance of the regent, Henri Chevreau, who had once helped her with emergency measures for the poor in Lyons. It was a cabinet chosen by Eugénie rather than by Palikao – 'I have to', she replied when Filon dared to point out that she had been acting in a revolutionary manner.

She issued a rousing proclamation. 'People of France,' announced the regent, 'the war has begun unfavourably for us. We have met with a reverse. But remain steadfast and let us repair the damage as soon as possible. There must be only one party among us, France, and only one criterion, the honour of our nation. I am here in the midst of you. Faithful to my mission and to my duty you will see me foremost in my post as leader in defending the flag of France.'

Palikao immediately set about making Paris ready to resist a siege, calling up every man between eighteen and twenty-five, together with all bachelors and widowers aged less than thirty-six. The already substantial war loan was doubled and banknotes replaced gold coins. Within three weeks Chevreau had succeeded in arming and equipping eighty new battalions of the National Guard, while 1,800 cannon were mounted on the fortifications, many borrowed from the navy. Bridges were broken down, railway tunnels blocked. No less than 35,000 cattle and 280,000 sheep were pastured in the Bois de Boulogne and in the gardens of the Luxembourg. A large number of the city's greatest art treasures were moved to Brest. Arrangements were put in hand for installing a provisional government at Tours in the event of Paris being cut off from the rest of the country. Much of the preparation was the result of suggestions made by the regent. Eugénie did her best to keep up morale, inspecting all Paris's military hospitals every day, besides establishing two more at the Tuileries – one inside the palace and another on the terrace.

Noisy and unhelpful criticism came from the left-wing in both chambers. One deputy wanted to revive the Revolutionary Committee of Public Safety of 1792 – another proposed that the Corps Législatif should take over the Regent's powers and replace Count Palikao by General Trochu. 'Unfortunately M. de Bismarck has a fourth army, which is inside Paris,' Prosper Mérimée observed bitterly. 'You see nothing here but drunken or dispirited crowds.' Yet there was also a new sense of resolution.

Although there was plenty of courage there was not much resolution in the French armies at the front. Having been advised to counter-attack from St Avold, the emperor was devastated when he learned on 7 August that the enemy had captured Forbach with its vital railway station and supplies for a French advance. Two days later, he received a telegram from Eugénie warning that he was about to be attacked by 300,000 Prussians and advising him to concentrate as many troops as possible on Metz. Although he managed to amass a respectable force, he had no idea of what to do next. In any case, he was in agony whenever he tried to mount a horse. He sent a cable to Eugénie, saying that he was handing over command and returning to Paris. 'Have you thought of all that might happen if you came back humiliated by two defeats?' she replied. He stayed with the army.

By now the regent was presiding twice a day over meetings of the Council. Never interrupting ministers, she always guided the discussion back to the point. 'Misfortune had tempered her spirit, freeing her from any feminine weakness or vanity, even from her obsession with the dynasty which she now considered doomed,' recalled an eyewitness. 'She thought only of the country, her speeches and her entire energies being concentrated only on saving France and securing an end to the Empire worthy of the name "Napoleon".' This, however, is an overstatement.

The emperor himself was quite ready to die, but he had to think of his troops. Dazed by pain and laudanum, he knew that he was no longer capable of commanding them – his appearance demoralised the officers who saw him. Accordingly, on 12 August he handed over supreme command of the armies of France to Marshal Bazaine.

François-Achille Bazaine appealed to left-wing politicians as a former ranker of peasant origins. Sir Michael Howard describes him: 'tiny malevolent eyes set in a suety, undistinguished face, the heavy bulldog jaw, the stout, flabby body sagging inelegantly on horseback'. The popular press had long been demanding his appointment. (One-third of French commissions were reserved for promotions from the ranks, unlike the Prussians whose senior officers were all noblemen.) And despite his appearance '*Notre brave Bazaine*' was certainly courageous, a former Foreign Legionnaire, a veteran of North Africa, the Crimea and Mexico, and a legend for his calmness under fire.

The marshal's trouble was that on the battlefield he was a little too calm, totally without imagination or aggression. Although a perfectly adequate commander up to brigade level, he was one of those officers who are born to obey orders, while during a military career of nearly forty years he had never once fought in a battle against an army that was as good as his own, let alone better, and when he did he would think in terms of defence and survival more than of winning a victory.

Bazaine's priority when he took over was to retreat as fast as possible, bringing the army of Lorraine from Metz to Verdun, and to join forces with Marshal MacMahon's army of Chalons. Moltke was determined to stop him. The Prussians attacked the French in a hard-fought action at Vionville-Mars-la-Tour on 19 August and, although a drawn battle, it made Bazaine more inclined to seek protection beneath the guns of Metz than to reach Verdun. He withdrew to a stronger defensive position on a line running from Gravelotte to Saint-Privat. When the enemy attacked two days later, they lost over 20,000 killed and wounded – 8,000 Prussian guardsmen being mown down by the *chassepot* rifles – while the French suffered less than 13,000 casualties.

The army of Lorraine had fought magnificently and deserved to win. If Bazaine had counter-attacked at the right moment, when the Prussians were very nearly defeated – some of the spike-helmeted regiments had been running for their lives – he might have won a great victory that would have won the war and changed the course of European history. But he did not issue the vital order, enabling the shocked German commanders to recover and regroup their troops.

The next day, abandoning his plans to link up with MacMahon's army, '*nôtre glorieux Bazaine*', retreated into Metz with his army of over 170,000 men, where they stayed until surrendering at the end of October. Their telegraph lines were swiftly severed by the enemy. Bazaine's cowardice meant that Moltke had cut the French armies in two.

Meanwhile, the bewildered Napoleon III and his son had reached the railway station at Verdun, from where they travelled on to Chalons, a journey that took them almost an entire day and night. The last part of the journey was in a 'train' consisting of a locomotive, one or two cattle wagons and a third-class carriage little better than a truck with wooden benches. It was not an ideal conveyance for a man tormented by a stone in his bladder 'the size of a pigeon's egg'.

At the great military camp of Chalons, normally so spick and span but now a muddy shambles, father and son saw trainload upon trainload of Marshal MacMahon's defeated troops arriving after being evacuated from Froeschwiller. Once among the pick of the French army, many were without rifles or equipment, and all were exhausted, filthy dirty and starving, collapsing on the ground in inert heaps as soon as they detrained. Other trains were depositing conscripts by the thousand, country boys who did not know how to march or shoot. Eighteen battalions of drunken, mutinous Gardes Mobiles (a sort of home-guard) added to the chaos. Clerks and workers from Paris who had hitherto escaped the call-up, but who had finally been given rifles, they were mostly republicans and hooted their sovereign whenever they caught sight of him, yelling '*Merde!*' instead of '*Vive l'Empereur!*' The officers of all these troops were too nervous to give them orders. Yet although MacMahon decided that the only thing to do with the Gardes Mobiles was send them back to Paris, within a few days he had turned his veterans and conscripts into a force with whom officers believed they could still win.

The emperor held a council of war with MacMahon, General Trochu and Plon-Plon. When he muttered 'I seem to have abdicated,' Plon-Plon told him, 'At Paris you abdicated the government, at Metz you abdicated the command. You can't possibly resume command. On the other hand, while resuming government will be hard and dangerous, what does it matter? If we're going to go down, let's do it like men.' He insisted that Napoleon should return to his capital with MacMahon's army and make Trochu military governor of Paris because he was so popular; 'You're the sovereign,' Plon-Plon reminded him when he said that he ought to consult the regent. 'And you must act at once.'

Trochu arrived at the Tuileries at midnight on 17 August, but Eugénie was unimpressed by the voluble Breton, whom she suspected of being an Orleanist, while Palikao pointed out the men and supplies would need to be re-routed on a railway system in chaos. Reluctantly confirming Trochu's appointment as military governor, she strongly objected to Napoleon returning. 'Imagine the emperor in this Palace, which has always been a trap,' she told the general. 'Either the army supports him, and there will be civil war between the army and the Parisians, or the troops abandon him and there will be revolution. Who benefits in either case? The Prussians.'

She cabled Napoleon, telling him to stay away from Paris – MacMahon must march to Bazaine's rescue. A message followed the telegram. 'If you return as a beaten man, you will be stoned,' she warned. 'Not just with stones but with dung.' Filon objected to her harshness. 'Don't you realise, I'm the first to feel what an awful position he's in?' she explained. 'The message you want to send wouldn't work, and he's doomed if we don't stop him.'

After the war, a legend grew up that by making her husband remain with the army, Eugénie had deliberately sent him to his doom because she wanted to keep power; but this is nonsense. 'The Council of Ministers and Privy Council were in complete agreement with her,' explained the veteran republican Jules Simon, no friend to the Bonapartes. 'They reached this decision for two reasons. First, what mattered above all to the empress was the personal danger that the emperor might run in Paris. Second, an inaccurate assessment of the risks run by MacMahon's army in advancing northward.'

Some historians criticise Eugénie for refusing to let the emperor's last army return to Paris, where it might have been more formidable under the city's guns. But the Parisians would have taken to the streets if MacMahon had not gone to Bazaine's aid. When the

Council learned he was blockaded in Metz, it endorsed Eugénie's decision, and MacMahon agreed when he received a message from Bazaine saying that he meant to break out in the direction of Ste Menehoud or Sedan. On 23 August, taking the emperor with it, the army of Chalons marched to Bazaine's relief.

THE ROAD TO SEDAN

When the war began Eugénie's old friend Prosper Mérimée, racked by asthma and bronchitis, and recovering from a stroke, had less than two months to live, but in his letters he gives vivid glimpses of her during these weeks. On 11 August he wrote to his old friend in London, Sir Anthony Panizzi, 'I saw the empress the day before yesterday. She is as firm as a rock, although she does not hide the horror of her situation. I don't doubt that the emperor is going to get himself killed, because he can only return victorious and victory is an impossibility.' He told another friend on 16 August, 'I have been to the Tuileries and spent a quarter of an hour with the empress. She has admirable courage. She sees the situation with the utmost clarity, and her calmness is truly heroic.' He wrote to Doña Maria Manuela on 24 August, 'I have seen the empress twice since our troubles began. She tells me that she never feels tired. If other people had as much courage, the country would be saved and not a single Prussian would get back across the Rhine.' Mérimée did not mention the change in her appearance. 'Her face was ravaged by worry and disappointment,' recalled one of her ladies, Marie de Larminat. 'Every trace of beauty had vanished from that pale countenance, which seemed as though furrowed with sorrow. I really thought that she would never smile again.'

'The empress had become the centre of everything, the soul of the defence and the government's real head,' claimed the devoted Filon. Yet although he was not exaggerating, there was precious little government. 'The dynasty that still reigns in France is commonly thought of as a thing of the past,' *The Times* commented on 12 August. There was no longer an emperor, only a beleaguered regent and, as Lord Lyons put it, Eugénie had 'much pluck, but little hope'.

Realistic observers, not merely alarmists, sensed that revolution was in the air. There was an attempt at an insurrection at La Villette in the Paris suburbs on 14 August, led by the veteran socialist Louis Blanqui. Although order was quickly restored, the incident was an omen. As Mérimée had already admitted to Panizzi. 'Even if we manage to drive the Prussians back across the Rhine, our situation will still be one of the utmost gravity. Whether an honourable or a shameful peace materialises, what government can possibly survive in the midst of this immense national uprising that has given us our armies and is wildly over-excited? We are hurtling towards a republic, and what a republic!'

Marshal MacMahon's army plodded resentfully north-east beneath drenching rain, along roads that were seas of mud, sleeping in the sodden fields, and urged on all the time by Palikao's telegrams from Paris. Food, wine and coffee were in very short supply. The troops lived as best they could off the country, robbing and looting any village they passed through on the march. Understandably, they resented bitterly the spectacle of Napoleon and his household riding by in snugly hooded carriages driven by powdered flunkeys, followed by a train of wagons that carried not only a field kitchen but silver plate and champagne. Although the emperor was closely escorted by watchful Cent Gardes, one enraged soldier had to be forcibly restrained from taking a potshot at him.

The emperor was not quite so comfortable as his troops imagined. An eyewitness told Paléologue many years later:

Growths on his eyelids sealed his eyes. His face was ashen, his back bent double. The least jolting by his carriage made him groan. He could only sit a horse at the cost of agonising stabs of pain. On one occasion he was seen to leave his carriage to lean his head against a tree, so terribly was he being tortured by the spasms of his bladder. During meals his ADCs saw him suddenly shaken by intense shivering, tears running down his hollow cheeks. Every morning when he rose, every evening when he arrived at the camping ground, his surgeon tormented him with a catheter.

His suffering was so intense that at times he thought he must be dying. In a state of physical, mental and moral collapse, he was aware that he had turned into a mere encumbrance.

For a short time the enemy lost sight of the army of Chalons, and General von Moltke was convinced that it must be withdrawing to the capital. Then, on 25 August the Prussian staff read *Le Temps* of two days before. Purchased by their spies in Paris, the paper obligingly informed them, 'At this very moment the army of MacMahon is going north to help Bazaine'. The cautious MacMahon, who had heard nothing further about Bazaine's promised break-out from Metz, was beginning to suspect that he was marching into a trap, but Palikao refused to let him change direction and go north instead of north-east. 'Should you abandon Bazaine', answered Palikao in response to his plea to do so, 'revolution will break out in Paris.'

Even Napoleon III had enough military knowledge to query the wisdom of going on to Metz, but by now no one bothered to listen to him. Later he wrote, 'Our march was the height of imprudence and very badly carried out.' On 27 August he sent the Prince Imperial north, with three aides-de-camp and a troop of Cent Gardes. He did not want him to learn any more about war – the fourteen-year-old had already seen three officers blown to shreds by Prussian shellfire, within yards of where he was having breakfast.

What remained of the Second Empire was embodied in the regent. 'I regard the Salic Law as a mistake,' Filon told Eugénie. 'Men will do much more for you than they would for the emperor.' Whatever she might say about the dynasty being doomed, she still hoped to save the throne for her son, refusing to despair or to leave Paris, as some ministers were urging. She read state papers or wandered through the empty Tuileries, sometimes changing her black for a beige woollen dress. The highlights of her day were the two Council meetings. Each time there was news of a defeat she sent one of her ladies to pray at the church of Notre Dame des Victoires. Few Parisians were aware of her courage. She was too realistic to expect them to accept 'the Spanish Woman' as another Joan of Arc, living as much in fear of the mob as she did of Prussians.

The histrionics of General Trochu, the new military governor of Paris responsible for Eugénie's safety, were a constant irritation. 'What would you do if the Regent was attacked?' he was asked. 'I should lay down my life on the steps of the throne,' was his reply. He also declaimed, 'That woman is a Roman.' When he harangued the Council on how to meet death, she broke in, '*Mon dieu*, General, one dies as best as one can!' Yet his posturing made this squint-eyed Breton the idol of Paris. But Eugénie distrusted him from the moment he arrived in the capital. Not only had he been appointed on Plon-Plon's recommendation but he was in touch with republican leaders such as Jules Favre and Jules Ferry. Sensing that the empire was tottering, they hoped for a constitutional take-over to avoid a revolution that might provoke a monarchist backlash. When the Corps Législatif rejected their demand for Palikao's replacement, they courted Trochu, who like many Orleanists had considerable sympathy with republicanism.

As late as 26 August Eugénie had written to her nieces in Madrid, 'it looks as if the Prussians will appear before Paris in the next few days, and if this really is the case then the siege will begin. Probably you will only be able to hear of me in the newspapers.' She added, 'I do not fear the crisis and still have hope.'

Nonetheless, walking in the Tuileries gardens one evening she remarked in terror that the red glow of the setting sun was making it seem as if the palace was on fire. She was eating almost nothing, taking only an occasional spoonful of soup, and would wake up looking even paler than usual, a ghastly, livid white, and shaking with cold from the effects of the chloral on which she had become dependent for a very few hours of sleep.

On 28 August she wrote to her nieces again. 'I can still write to you because it seems the Prussians have stopped advancing on Paris in order to attack the emperor's army in even greater numbers. You can imagine my state of mind. I am very uneasy and worried because there will be a big battle in a day or so. . . . Pray for us, children. God alone can give us strength to bear this dreadful ordeal.'

Eugénie waited anxiously for confirmation that MacMahon had relieved Bazaine. It was hoped that this would happen by 28 August at the latest, when there were rumours he had actually done so. But on 30 August the French suffered a fresh defeat at Beaumont, General de Failly's corps being almost wiped out after the Prussians took the French right wing by surprise. Many of the survivors mutinied. The news caused uproar and, already blamed for his failure at Froeschwiller, the wretched Failly was reviled in the press as a traitor. The empress sent a cable telling Napoleon to sack him – she did not realise that he no longer had the power.

Outmanoeuvred, Marshal MacMahon took his army to Sedan, a little town overlooking the River Meuse and ringed by hills, that was less than 10 miles from the Belgian border. He saw it as a natural stronghold where his men could rest briefly and then regroup. Moltke saw it differently. 'We've got them in a mouse-trap,' he told King William. The trap was sprung by nightfall on 31 August, the army of Chalons finding itself surrounded by two enemy armies, General Ducrot commenting famously, '*Nous sommes dans un pot de chambre et nous y serons enmerdés.*' Just over 100,000 bewildered French troops were encircled by a quarter of a million confident and superbly commanded Germans. Realising that disaster was imminent, the marshal advised Napoleon to escape while there was still time; but the emperor refused.

The Bavarians attacked over the Meuse at 4.00 a.m. before first light, on 1 September. The French objective was to try to hold off the enemy while as many of their troops as possible broke out of the encirclement. They were not helped by confusion over who was in command. MacMahon, badly wounded in the thigh early in the morning, was replaced by Ducrot, who in turn was replaced by General de Wimpffen.

The army of Chalons fought with the utmost gallantry, but by midday its encirclement was complete. From every hilltop massed batteries of the breech-loading Krupp howitzers were able to shell it with complete impunity, outranging and knocking out its artillery, setting fire to its munitions wagons which one after another began to explode, and decimating its troops. This time there was no need for wasteful infantry attacks against the *chassepots*.

In desperation and as a last resort, General Ducrot sent in his cavalry, with orders to hack a way out through the Prussian infantry, but the needle-guns were quite sufficient to mow down horsemen armed with sabres. When General the Marquis de Gallifet returned with the survivors of the death-ride, having left the ground in front of the Prussians piled high with his dead or dying comrades and their horses, Ducrot asked him to charge again. *'Tant que vous voudrez, mon general! Tant qu'il en restera un!'* Gallifet answered him unhesitatingly. ('As many times as you like, general! While a single one of us remains!') He then led two more magnificent but suicidal charges. Watching them from a hilltop the old Prussian king cried, *'Ah! les braves gens!'*

Finally, Gallifet – that ornament of the Tuileries and Compiègne – was beaten back a third and last time. As he rode away with the bare handful of his troopers who were still in the saddle, several Prussian officers ordered their men to cease firing and then saluted him with their swords.

For five hours Napoleon III did his best to get himself killed, riding to wherever he thought the fighting looked most dangerous, going as close to the front line as his staff would let him. His grey hair was freshly dyed, his moustaches were newly waxed and his face was rouged to disguise its pallor. His red képi gleamed with the gold braid of a marshal and he wore the grand star of the Légion d'honneur – he wanted to make as easy a target as possible for the Prussians. Afterwards a doctor commented that it must have needed almost superhuman self-control for him to stay on his horse for so long while he was in such dreadful pain.

Considerate as ever, he persuaded most of his staff to take cover behind a stone wall when he and three officers who refused to leave him rode into a particularly murderous artillery barrage. Amid the blinding smoke and the showers of earth, according to his aide-de-camp General Pajol* he remained motionless, waiting for a shell to hit him.

Smoking cigarette after cigarette, the emperor rode calmly into lethal barrages of this sort again and again, dismounting only once, when he got down to help fire a *mitrailleuse*. One of the three officers with him was killed by a direct hit, while the other two were both wounded by shell fragments, yet Napoleon himself remained

* Colonel of the Empress's Regiment of Dragoons.

unscathed. The enemy, who did not realise that 'the old fox' was present on the battlefield, unwittingly declined to give him a hero's death. 'That was a day when I was unlucky,' he later told Pajol.

Between 3.00 and 5.00 p.m. the army of Chalons disintegrated beneath the bombardment. 'I could never have imagined so frightful a disaster,' was how Napoleon later described it to Eugénie. 'Our troops began to run and tried to get back into the town. Since the gates were shut, they climbed over them. As a result the town was densely packed, jammed with vehicles of every description, while shells rained down on people's heads, killing men in the streets, ripping roofs off houses and setting the houses ablaze.'

Although General de Wimpffen wanted to fight on with the few troops still in formation, eventually the emperor ordered that a white flag be hoisted. He then sent an officer on his staff to the Prussian king with a short letter:

Monsieur mon frère,
   Not being able to die among my troops, it only remains for me to surrender my sword into your Majesty's hands. I am your Majesty's good brother.
   Napoleon

King William accepted the surrender in a courteous reply. Taken to William's headquarters, the emperor insisted that he was surrendering as a combatant, and as a prisoner of war was no longer the head of France's government.

He sent a telegram to the regent: '*L'armée est défaite et captive. Moi-même je suis captif*' ('The army has been defeated and is in captivity. I myself am a prisoner'). Then he wrote to her, explaining:

We went on a march that defied all principles of war and common sense. It was bound to end in disaster, and it did. I would far rather have died than witness such a shameful surrender, but in the circumstances it was the one way of saving 60,000 men from being massacred. If only that was the end of my torment! I am thinking of you, of our son, of our unhappy country. May God protect her. What will happen in Paris?

On 3 September Napoleon III was driven off to captivity in Germany, Bismarck observing, 'There goes a dynasty on its way out.'

THE FALL OF THE SECOND EMPIRE

Rumours of a great disaster reached Paris on 2 September, but Eugénie refused to believe them. 'The situation has changed a good deal,' she wrote to Paca's children that evening. 'I've heard nothing from the emperor for three days but I know there has been fighting during this time. Yesterday I did not even hear from Louis [the Prince Imperial]. There is no need for me to tell you my state of mind. If the silence continues, I don't see how I can go on.' Even so, she told them, 'We are preparing for the siege, determined to hold out for as long as we can and, if the city gives in, we shall continue fighting from somewhere else, because we must keep on till the end while there is still a single Prussian on French soil.' Always a Catholic fatalist, she added, 'I feel that what I am suffering at the moment may be to give me the strength that I shall need for even worse trials and to go on fighting.'

At about 5.00 p.m. the following day, the minister for the interior, Henri Chevreau, came into her drawing-room at the Tuileries, asking to speak to her alone. Then he told her Napoleon was a prisoner, producing the telegram. She fainted. 'You will lose your throne before the day is over,' he warned her when she regained consciousness. 'The governor of Paris is the one man who can save you. You must beg him to help you – let me give him the emperor's telegram.' Eugénie asked Chevreau to leave, telling him to do whatever he liked. For a moment she could not credit the telegram.

Filon had already heard. He went into the empress's study, where he found her secretary, Eugène Conti, who had also heard. Suddenly Eugénie came in. 'She was pale and terrible, her eyes were hard, gleaming with anger, her face distorted by emotion. She cried out, 'Do you know what they're saying? That the emperor has surrendered, that he has capitulated? Surely you don't believe it?' Then she broke into 'a torrent of incoherent and mad words'. Her listeners were appalled. 'What she said, Conti never repeated to anyone and like him I shall die without repeating it,' Filon informs us. Paléologue claimed to know what she said, although it is hard to see how. 'A Napoleon never surrenders!', Eugénie screamed, according to his version. 'He is dead. Do you hear me? I tell you he's dead, and they're trying to hide it from me.' Then, contradicting herself, 'Why didn't he kill himself? Why didn't he have himself buried under the walls of Sedan? Didn't he realise he was disgracing himself? What a name to leave to his son!' Even if Paléologue was guessing, this is probably very near the truth. Filon recalled that the empress's outburst lasted for five minutes, and that she then left the room. 'We remained there speechless and stunned, like men who had just survived an earthquake.'

A Council was summoned, but broke up at 8.00 p.m., without reaching any decision. Someone said that the emperor's old enemy, Adolphe Thiers, the wiliest politician in France, might have useful suggestions to make, but he had already refused to help when sounded out by Mérimée a week earlier. Eugénie sent for General Trochu, who said he was too tired, promising to come the following day. She went to bed at nine – there was nothing else she could do. From midnight until two in the morning crowds packed the Place de la Concorde, shouting 'Deposition!', and when Filon opened his window in the dark, he could hear the angry yells in the distance.

Next day, a Sunday, the empress heard Mass at 7.30 a.m. in the Tuileries chapel, so distracted that she wore a gold-fringed mauve shawl instead of her usual black. Only half a dozen people were at the service. 'Madame, nothing can be done in Paris,' Filon told her imploringly when it was finished. 'Leave this inferno, move your government to some town on the Loire and summon the Corps Législatif to meet there.' Eugénie replied dismissively: 'That means a civil war which would break the back of our fight against the Prussians, and for what purpose? If you don't have Paris, then you have nothing. No, I shan't leave.' She ended, 'I won't move, but I won't allow a shot to be fired.'

That morning, at 8.00 a.m. the regent presided over what was going to be her last Council. Everyone present was aware that on the previous night Jules Favre had proposed the deposition of the emperor in the Corps Législatif. The Bonapartist deputies had managed to resist the proposal and even Thiers, fearful of a revolution, had tried to dissuade Favre. But it was only a momentary respite until the Corps met again at one o'clock.

One minister, Duvernois, suggested launching a pre-emptive coup and declaring martial law. Since the entire French regular army was either in German captivity or bottled up in Metz, and as the garrison of the Tuileries numbered less than 200 men, his suggestion was understandably ignored. Finally it was decided to ask the Corps Législatif to form a new Council of Regency with full powers, but presided over by the empress. They all realised that there was little hope of the plan's acceptance.

As Henri Chevreau had said – and, as minister for the interior, he knew what Paris thought from the police reports – General Trochu was the one man who could save the situation. The military governor commanded the National Guard, that *'levée en masse'* of armed Parisians with whom he was enormously popular and an appeal by him to unite against the Prussians should have succeeded. Prince Metternich agreed with Chevreau. 'Had Thiers and Trochu come forward at this moment and supported the regency, they would probably have saved the Empire.' Thiers was certainly enough of an opportunist to have jumped onto Trochu's bandwagon.

Unfortunately, Eugénie had never bothered to conceal her dislike of the general. Afterwards, she admitted, 'I ought to have come to terms with that dangerous Tartuffe.' She certainly sent for him again on the morning of 4 September and at least one source says that he came, harangued her and then left in a hurry. According to Filon, however – and Filon was in the palace – he never appeared, but merely made the derisory gesture of promising to send an officer of the National Guard 'in uniform' to protect the Tuileries. Trochu, it will be remembered, was the man who had sworn he would die on the steps of the throne in the empress's defence.

In contrast, courtiers flocked to the Tuileries, not just the officers and ladies of the household, but members of the old and new nobility who had been in the habit of coming to court. 'They were not there to give advice,' said Filon, 'but to show their loyalty by being present and sharing the peril.' They knew very well how many courtiers had been slaughtered at the side of the Swiss Guard during the storming of the Tuileries in 1792.

'The news that reached us was terrible, our situation becoming worse every hour,' recalled Filon. 'By mid-morning the Place de la Concorde was full of National Guardsmen, armed with rifles, and clearly what they had in mind was the reverse of defending the Tuileries.'

At about midday a delegation of deputies arrived from the Palais Bourbon, led by two former ex-Orleanist imperial ministers, Comte Daru and Louis-Joseph Buffet. More reassuringly, it included two genuine Bonapartists, the Marquis de Pierres and the Comte d'Ayguesvives. They asked the regent to abdicate in all but name, by placing all power in the hands of the Corps Législatif, which would then appoint a provisional government – 'without prejudice to the dynastic question'. This solution, they informed the empress, would avoid an otherwise inevitable revolution. Eugénie told them:

The future of our dynasty no longer matters to me. I think only of France. My one personal concern is to fulfil all the duties imposed on me by my position, and the most obvious of these is not to desert my post. . . . As for the country's representatives, their duty is as obvious as my own – they must forget party quarrels and close ranks around me to form a rampart against invasion. The war's outcome lies in their hands.

However, if the Corps Législatif feels that I am a burden, or that the emperor's name has become a hindrance rather than a symbol of resistance, then you may declare us both deposed. I shall not complain because I will have quitted my post with honour instead of deserting it. . . .

I am ready to face any danger and follow the Corps Législatif to wherever it chooses as a last bastion from which to continue the war. Should further resistance become impossible, I think I could help to obtain better peace terms. Yesterday the ambassador of a great power offered to arrange mediation by neutral powers, based on two points – first, France's territorial integrity and, second, the Imperial dynasty's survival. My answer was that I would accept the first point but refuse even to consider the second. The dynasty's future is for this country alone to decide and I could never let a foreign power meddle with our internal affairs.

Daru assured the regent that, if she abdicated, 'Far from deserting your post, you will have shown the greatest courage in sacrificing yourself for everybody's sake and in saving France from the horrors of a revolution – a revolution when the enemy is at our gates.'

Well aware that Daru was right about the possibility of revolution, Eugénie said that she might abdicate if her ministers agreed with him. 'I insist on one thing, however,' she added. 'A house must be found for me so that I can stay and share our besieged capital's sufferings until the very end.'

Filon saw the delegation departing with bowed heads and gloomy faces, 'like mourners who have just thrown the last drops of holy water on a coffin'. As they left, each kissed the empress's hand. 'I could not help weeping,' Buffet, one of their leaders, recalled. 'I was in the presence of a great and selfless personality.' A reserved, austere man, who was not given to superlatives, he told Paléologue how much he had admired her strength, her patriotism and her calmness.

Meanwhile, the revolt had broken out, encouraged by General Trochu. Hooting the police, mobs marched along the boulevards to the Palais Bourbon, where the Corps Législatif sat debating the problem of the regency. The general replaced the troops outside by National Guards, who immediately allowed a cheering horde to storm into the chamber. When the deputies sent to Trochu for help, his reply was, 'General Palikao has tried to break me during these last few days, and he has succeeded – it is too late to ask me.'

'This is not the right place to proclaim the Republic,' Jules Favre shouted above the din. 'It has to be done at the Hôtel de Ville.' Here, fighting off attempts by extremists like Louis Blanqui to start a socialist revolution, Leon Gambetta proclaimed the Third Republic from a window. Invited to become President, Trochu accepted with alacrity.

During the empress's meeting with the delegation, frantic messages came from Henri Chevreau, warning her that the situation was deteriorating. Finally the minister arrived in person from the Palais Bourbon, crying 'All is lost, Madame!', at which Eugénie inquired acidly, 'Do you mean that poor General Trochu has been killed?' He explained what had happened, telling her that regular troops were throwing down their arms. Paris was in the hands of the National Guard, who wanted revolution, and soon there would be an attack on the Tuileries. Telling himself, 'The end of the drama is not far off,' Filon ran to his room to get his revolver.

By now it was mid-afternoon, a beautiful sunny day. Inside the gloomy palace with its dust-sheeted furniture everyone begged the empress to escape while there was still time, but she refused. From the windows a vast crowd could be seen, stretching back to the Place de la Concorde, 'nothing but heads and bayonets'. It knew that Eugénie was inside because the imperial standard was still flying. The crowd, eventually 200,000 strong, chanted angrily, '*Déchéance!*' '*Déchéance!*' – 'Deposition!' It surged against the palace railings, tearing down the gold eagles, before pushing them over.

General Mellinet, commanding the Tuileries' garrison, pleaded for permission to open fire – otherwise the mob would break in within minutes. 'No bloodshed,' insisted Eugénie. 'I won't allow it at any price – I would prefer the dynasty to perish rather than lose a single French life.' When he asked if his men could merely use their rifle butts, she replied, 'General, not even rifle butts.' She did not want the garrison to suffer the fate of the Swiss Guard, butchered for trying to defend Louis XVI and Marie-Antoinette. Yet Eugénie refused to leave the Tuileries. Why? Despite her offers to abdicate and her claims to be no longer interested in 'the future of the dynasty', the only possible explanation is that by staying she hoped through some miracle to save the throne for the Prince Imperial. At least she knew he had not been captured at Sedan and was near the Belgian border: she told Filon to send a telegram to the boy's aide-de-camp – 'Leave immediately for Belgium.'

At the same time, Eugénie was terrified of suffering an even worse fate than her heroine Marie-Antoinette. 'I wasn't frightened of dying,' she said later. 'What did frighten me was the thought of falling into the hands of viragos, who would defile my death in some grotesquely revolting way, who would try to humiliate me as they killed me. I could already imagine them lifting up my skirts and hear savage laughter. . . .' Some people in the crowd outside the Tuileries thought of Marie-Antoinette, too, like Lord Ronald Gower.

'It seemed as if 1792 had come back,' he wrote in his memoirs. 'Had the empress been found there and then, her life would not have been worth a moment's purchase.'

Beyond question, the mob's only motive for storming the palace was to lynch '*l'Espagnole*' – there were even cries of '*A la guillotine*'. 'No one who has not heard it can realise the horror of . . . the roar of a crowd that has only one desire – to tear you to pieces,' Eugénie admitted long afterwards.

In the end courtiers managed to convince her that she would fall into the mob's hands if she stayed and – at best – be made to abdicate. 'You would sacrifice the rights with which you are entrusted,' someone argued. 'But by escaping, wherever you go you will keep them.'

After taking a morsel of bread – she had not eaten since breakfast – and putting on her hat, she said goodbye to her ladies, embracing them. Only her reader, Mme Lebreton-Bourbaki, went with her (eventually giving Filon a full account of their adventures). Ordering General Mellinet to withdraw his troops from the palace immediately everybody else had left, she slipped away through a small passage behind her bedroom. Five men accompanied the two women – Prince Metternich, Cavaliere Nigra, Admiral Jurien de La Gravière, Eugène Conneau and Eugène Conti.

Eugénie had hoped to leave in a small carriage standing at a side entrance, then realised they would be seen. Instead, they decided to go out through the adjoining Louvre, which was closed because of the war. Finding the door locked, however, they thought of leaving through an underground passage that led from the kitchens to the Seine. But by now the mob was breaking in. Jurien de La Gravière rushed off to see if he could delay the pursuit while the little party fled back to the first floor.

In the nick of time a servant appeared with a master-key which opened the door into the Louvre. They hurried through the empty galleries, a museum attendant leading the way. The walls were largely bare, most of the pictures having been taken to Brest for safe-keeping, but Gericault's *Radeau de la Méduse* was still hanging in the Salle des Sept Cheminées and, glancing briefly at the scene of nightmare shipwreck, Eugénie murmured 'How strange!'

Halfway through the Louvre, she ordered Conneau to go back and make certain that anyone left in the palace was told to escape, reminding him to take off his elaborate uniform before venturing into the street. He kissed her hand. While descending the massive staircase into the Egyptian gallery, she also ordered Conti to leave her, embracing him.

The side doors were locked so that the only way out was through the main entrance, opposite the church of Saint-Germain l'Auxerrois. A crowd was surging past on its way to the Tuileries, howling '*A mort! A mort! A bas l'Espagnole!*' ('Death! Death! Down with the Spanish woman!') The four waited for a bit in the doorway, Eugénie on Nigra's arm, Mme Lebreton on Metternich's. Nigra asked the empress if she was afraid. 'Not a bit,' she answered. 'Why ask? You're holding my arm and you don't feel it trembling.' The men wanted to wait longer but, saying 'One has to be bold,' she stepped into the street.

Metternich had gone off to find a cab, when a lout of about eighteen or twenty recognised Eugénie and shook his fist at her, yelling to the crowd, 'Here's the empress', but nobody could hear him because of the uproar. Then Nigra saw a *fiacre*, hailed it and pushed in the two women. The youth came back, shouting, so Nigra grabbed him, holding on until the cab disappeared in the direction of the rue de Rivoli.

FLIGHT

Early on the sunlit evening of Sunday 4 September 1870, Dr Thomas W. Evans returned to his home in Paris. He had been deeply saddened by the news from Sedan. A tubby little man with comical mutton-chop whiskers, at forty-seven he was one of the most successful dentists in the world and owed a lot of his success to the emperor's friendly patronage. He had spent the morning with his young nephew Dr Edward A. Crane, making the new American hospital ready for the trainloads of wounded troops that were expected to arrive at any moment.

Evans had arranged to meet his nephew again later in the day, at 4.00 p.m. at his office in the rue de la Paix, and then go for a drive in the Bois de Boulogne. On the way to his office in his light American carriage, he had come across groups of men shouting '*Vive la République!*' who seemed to be marching towards the Palais Bourbon. At the office Crane had told him he had heard that a large mob was invading the Tuileries gardens, but that it appeared to be fairly harmless, singing and dancing. However, from the office balcony of the rue de la Paix they had then seen that the ever-growing crowds were being joined by soldiers, while shopkeepers were tearing down the crowned gold 'N's that denoted imperial custom. Uncle and nephew had driven back to Evans's house in a melancholy mood.

Reaching the house in the avenue de l'Impératrice at 6.00 p.m., the dentist handed the reins to his nephew and got down to order their dinner before going on to the Bois. When he came in, a servant informed him that two mysterious ladies were in his library. 'They haven't given their names and won't say why they've come,' he was told. 'But they seem very anxious to see you and have been waiting for more than an hour.' After ordering dinner, Evans went up to see them. Both in black, heavily veiled, one was standing and the other was seated, wearing a smart little bowler hat with a heavy veil. The lady in the bowler raised her veil. It was the Empress.

After leaving the Louvre, their *fiacre* had gone at a snail's pace through the dense crowds in the rue de Rivoli. In any case, it was a slow vehicle with four wheels, pulled by a single horse – a cab of the type the English called a 'growler'. When a ruffian stuck his head through the window, yelling '*Vive la Nation!*' he did not recognise Eugénie, who had lowered her veil and covered her mouth with her hand. After he had gone, she calmly pointed out to Mme Lebreton the shopkeepers pulling down the imperial warrants, commenting 'They don't waste much time, do they?'

The only money they had with them was 500 francs in Mme Lebreton's handbag (about £20) while they did not know where to go. Mme Lebreton had told the driver to take them to the house of a friend in the boulevard Malesherbes. She paid off the cab when they got there, only to find that the friend was out. Hailing another cab, they drove to Monsieur de Piennes in the avenue de Wagram. He too was out and his servant, who would not even open the door, refused to let them come in and wait. Eugénie had thought of going to Mr Elihu Washbourne, the United States minister, but did not know his address. Then she had remembered her American dentist.

'I have come to you for protection and assistance,' she told Dr Evans, who at once offered to help in any way that he could.

'You see, I am no longer fortunate,' she continued, her eyes filling with tears. 'The evil days have come, and I am alone.' She asked him to help her escape from Paris and go to England as soon as possible, producing a passport obtained from the British Embassy a short time before by a courtier who had anticipated disaster. This transformed the empress into an English invalid being taken home by her doctor and her brother.

Eugénie revived after a meal, surprising Evans by her calmness. He could not avoid thinking of what had happened to Marie-Antoinette. Yet Eugénie knew very well that, if she was caught, General Trochu's 'provisional government' might put her on trial as a scapegoat – or she might be lynched by a mob.

At 5.30 the next morning, just before sunrise, they set out for the Norman coast in the dentist's landau. He pretended to be the invalid's brother, while Crane was her doctor and Mme Lebreton her nurse. They had no trouble in leaving Paris. The empress joked how only a few days ago she had been saying, 'I will never leave the Tuileries in a cab, as Charles X and Louis-Philippe did. Well, that's just what I've done.' And she began to laugh.

Hiring new carriages several times, they drove for twenty-four hours, with nothing to eat but bread and sausage which the fugitive sliced with her penknife. The party finally had a coarse meal at a wretched little inn at La Rivière, where they spent the night. When Eugénie saw her bedroom, she burst out laughing at its squalor. Mme Lebreton broke down. 'Oh, mon Dieu! Mon Dieu!' she lamented. 'Madame, how can you laugh in this sad situation?' From La Rivière they travelled to Lisieux by train. At La Rivière station the empress became really frightened when the stationmaster leered at her maliciously – she thought that the man had recognised her.

When they arrived at Lisieux it was pouring with rain. Evans went to look for a carriage to take them on to Deauville, leaving the empress sheltering in a shop doorway. Only the previous year he had seen her being rowed across the Bosphorus blazing with jewels, he reflected. Now, looking at the bedraggled, rain-sodden woman in the doorway, he wondered if he was dreaming. The dentist told himself with pride, 'her existence is known but to two men – and those two are Americans'.

Eventually on 6 September, they reached Deauville without incident at about 3.00 in the afternoon. Mrs Evans had been staying here for some weeks, at the Hôtel du Casino. Fearing that a description of his party might have been sent to every French seaport and that the hotel was being watched by the police, Evans smuggled Eugénie into his wife's rooms through the hotel garden. After greeting her hostess, she collapsed exhausted into an armchair, exclaiming, 'My God, I'm safe!' She did not know that the most frightening part of her escape still lay ahead of her.

Going off to search for a boat in which to cross the Channel, Evans and Crane saw a beautiful English yacht in the harbour, the *Gazelle*. The owner, Sir John Burgoyne, a baronet and a former officer of the Grenadier Guards, was only too pleased to show them over the vessel – 42 tons and 60 feet long, with a crew of six. He told them that he hoped to sail from Deauville the next morning. When Evans explained why he was in the port and asked him bluntly if he would take the empress over to England, Sir John's manner changed and he replied coldly, 'I regret, gentlemen, that I am unable to assist you in this matter.' Furious, Dr Evans informed him that in America, 'every man will run any risk for a woman, and especially for a lady in danger'. Pointing towards a small schooner in the harbour, he added that he was sure she was a craft which would do just as well as Burgoyne's yacht. Sir John then said he was by no means sure that he would be able to leave Deauville in the morning, because of heavy seas and a stiff north west wind. Indicating the other boat that Evans had mentioned, he added, 'That little schooner, in such weather as we shall probably have, would be very likely to go to the bottom.' Dr Crane then joined in, imploring the baronet to change his mind. Finally, Sir John referred the matter to Lady Burgoyne. She immediately overruled her husband and invited the empress to come on board that night.

There was a secret and at first even cheerful supper in Mrs Evans's rooms, Eugénie laughing loudly at the improvised meal. 'What does it amount to, this Revolution in Paris?' she demanded. 'It can't change the past and the future is in God's keeping.' But then she took a locket with a miniature of the Prince Imperial out of her pocket, looked at it and burst into tears. Mrs Evans insisted that she lay down on her bed.

At midnight, wading through the moonlit puddles left by the rain, which by now had stopped, the empress, Mme Lebreton and Evans stole out of the hotel across the gardens. The path to the harbour had turned into a quagmire so that by the time they reached the yacht, as Eugénie recalled, 'Our shoes were soaked and our clothes bespattered with mud.' On board the *Gazelle*, Sir John kissed the empress's hand and Lady Burgoyne curtsied – she also gave up her cabin to the two women and had hot punch served to them.

Suddenly they heard shouts of '*Vive la République!*' '*Vive la Nation!*' and hoarse voices singing the 'Marseillaise'. Taking Dr Evans up on deck, a nervous Sir John told the dentist that he had always suspected that the empress was being followed by police spies. However, the shouts and the singing were from some rowdy passengers who had just got off the Paris train. At about 11.30 p.m. there was another alarm when a young Russian, whom Sir John knew only slightly, appeared out of the blue and despite it being so late, asked if he and a friend could see over the boat. They were shown everything – except Lady Burgoyne's cabin.

Ironically, contrary to the fears of Burgoyne and Evans, the new government of France was not interested in finding the empress and had given no instructions about her to the police.

Next morning at just after 7.00 a.m. the *Gazelle* sailed out from Deauville. Despite a rough sea and a little rain, the yacht made good headway until, towards one o'clock, a violent squall blew up. The wind veered round, almost dead ahead, and the spinnaker boom was lost. All hands were summoned, reefing sails, battening down hatches. The wind increased steadily. Sir John wanted to take refuge in the nearest French harbour but was shamed into sailing on, as he put it, by Eugénie's 'cool courage and a consideration for others that won the esteem of everyone on board'. The gale worsened, however, and the sea ran higher and higher. At 6.00 p.m. the Isle of Wight was sighted, but by then the storm appeared to offer very little hope that they would ever reach port. 'The gusts of wind became still more frequent and the rain fell in torrents, accompanied by vivid flashes of lightning and sharp thunder,' wrote Dr Evans. 'The yacht reeled and staggered in the wild sea that swept over her deck.'

Mme Lebreton spent the whole night on her knees, saying her rosary. There was a dreadful moment when someone shouted an alarm, mercifully false, 'We're aground!' (If true, it would have meant that the boat had struck a rock and would soon break up.) 'What are they saying?' screamed the poor woman, who did not understand English. 'We're nearing land,' the empress answered dryly, although she herself expected to drown at any moment. 'The little boat was jumping on the waves like a cork', she remembered. 'I really thought we were lost.' Afterwards, she confided in Evans that if they had sunk, since no one knew where she was, no one would ever know what had happened to her – 'there could not have been a more welcome grave'.

Towards midnight, however, the gale at last began to lessen and at 4.00 a.m. on 8 September the battered *Gazelle* limped into Ryde harbour. Here they learned that during the same storm their host's cousin, Commander Sir Hugh Burgoyne RN, had gone down with his ship HMS *Captain* off Finisterre, together with the entire crew of 500 officers and men.

The best hotel in Ryde, next to the jetty, would not admit such impossibly shabby people, on foot and without even hand-luggage, so they had to walk up George Street until they came to the clearly very inferior York Hotel. Here Evans booked accommodation in the names of 'Mr Thomas and sister, with a lady friend', which he wrote on a bit of paper. The landlady was barely civil, giving them tiny bedrooms at the top of the house.

When he knocked on the former empress's door a few hours later, he discovered her reading an English Bible, which she had found by her bed. It had fallen open at Psalm 23, 'The Lord is my Shepherd: I shall not want.' He was able to tell her that, according to the morning papers, her son the Prince Imperial had also reached England.

EPILOGUE

After the Empire

RESTORATION?

Sedan was a defeat even more bitter than Waterloo. Although the war was far from over, it delivered France into the hands of Prussia, and generations of Frenchmen have never forgiven Napoleon III for their country's humiliation. Yet during the shabby régime that followed, many regretted the Second Empire. For the next few years the possibility of a Bonapartist restoration can never have been very far from the empress's thoughts, and with reason.

After a dramatic reunion with the Prince Imperial in Hastings, at the Marine Hotel on Eastern Parade, mother and son stayed on the Sussex coast for the next fortnight. Filon, who appeared out of the blue on 12 September, was shocked to see them in such 'modest apartments', if impressed by the way in which the empress adapted to 'private life'. Before the end of the month, however, they had moved into Camden Place at Chislehurst in Kent. Just outside the village, and only twenty minutes by train from Charing Cross station in London, this had been found for them by the tireless Dr Evans. If scarcely imposing, it was a nice enough Georgian gentleman's mansion, built in red brick. (Today it is the clubhouse of Chislehurst Golf Club.)

Eugénie was pleasantly surprised by the arrival of her former *maître d'hôtel* from the Tuileries, together with the palace butler and even the principal chef – whose cuisine made a welcome change from the food they had endured at English seaside hotels. Fortunately, money was not a problem. Although the new government had at once confiscated all imperial assets in France, Pauline Metternich had smuggled the empress's jewellery out of the Tuileries in August and sent it to London in a diplomatic bag –

even if she dropped Eugénie when she lost her throne. In any case, Doña Maria Manuela was prepared to help, while Napoleon still owned his mother's house in Switzerland, Arenenberg.

Eugénie was soon joined by the amiable Duc de Bassano, her former grand chamberlain, and by Marie de Larminat, one of her favourite readers. Together with Mme Lebreton and other refugees, these diehards formed a little court in exile at Camden Place, which quickly became too crowded for comfort. Eugène Rouher, the leader of the Mamelukes, who settled at Richmond was a frequent visitor. Having asked the empress for permission, Filon went back to enlist in the French army – to be arrested, held in prison for weeks with every likelihood of being shot, and then expelled from France.

Since the empress had never abdicated, technically she was still regent, although her authority was recognised only by Marshal Bazaine and the remnant of the imperial army besieged in Metz.

Intending to discuss the situation, Plon-Plon turned up unexpectedly at Chislehurst, the first of his many unwelcome visits. Characteristically, he began by informing Eugénie that 'Palikao's government was a ministry of imbeciles'. Understandably she lost her temper, telling him sharply that the general and his ministers had been good and faithful friends, loyal to the very end. 'Monseigneur, for eighteen years we have watched you criticising the Empire,' she reminded the prince. 'You and your friends have never ceased trying to undermine it, and you are continuing to behave in just the same way even though the empire has fallen. No doubt had you been in Paris on 4 September, presumably you could have told us just what we ought to have done. But you were not there, as you have never been at any really dangerous moment, on all too many occasions.' This brought their discussion to an end, Plon-Plon storming out in a fury.

Meanwhile, a mysterious Monsieur Regnier, of whom nothing was known, had tried to call on her while she was still at Hastings, eloquently explaining to Filon his scheme for her restoration. Sensing that there was something wrong about the man, she had refused to see him. Regnier was almost certainly a double-agent, employed by Russia as well as Prussia, since both powers hoped to avoid recognising the 'revolutionary' government. Evans said that he possessed a Prussian passport, obtained from the embassy in

London, which enabled him to pass through the enemy lines. (Later he would be condemned to death in absentia as a spy by a French military tribunal during Bazaine's court martial.)

Whoever he may have been working for, Regnier was undoubtedly a very skilful operator. For a time he even succeeded in giving the impression that he had tricked Bismarck into believing he was the empress's personal representative – he was supposed to have done so by showing him a postcard of the Marine Hotel at Hastings signed by the Prince Imperial, which he had obtained from the gullible Filon. Bismarck sent him to Metz with a proposal that Marshal Bazaine should immediately ask for an armistice and then restore Napoleon III, who would negotiate peace with Prussia. The glib Regnier impressed the marshal so much that he at once dispatched General Bourbaki, commander of the Imperial Guard (and Mme Lebreton's brother), through the Prussian siege lines, disguised as a doctor from the Red Cross, to Chislehurst in order to obtain the empress's agreement. When he arrived there, an amazed Eugénie explained to the general that she knew nothing about Regnier's activities or about the proposal, which she dismissed out of hand. Too bewildered and inarticulate to explain the proposal properly, poor Bourbaki went back to France, hoping to rejoin his men.

After finally meeting and questioning Regnier, and although the meeting confirmed her distrust of the man, she became more interested in his ideas, especially when General Boyer, chief of staff of the French army of the Rhine, arrived from Metz on 22 October with a new, detailed plan which had the Prussian chancellor's full approval.

General Boyer had seen Bismarck, who had specifically stated that the plan's primary purpose was 'for the army of Metz to remain faithful to its oath and become the champion of the imperial dynasty', and who had then given him a safe conduct through the Prussian lines. Boyer also brought letters from Bazaine and General Frossard, who both implored Eugénie to accept the Prussian conditions for peace, whatever they might be, 'in order to save the country which will otherwise be utterly destroyed by prolonging the present situation'.

261

The plan was that after an armistice, Marshal Bazaine should march on Paris and proclaim the empress as regent, whereupon she would summon the illegally dissolved Corps Législatif and Senate, and negotiate a peace treaty – the terms of which would be decided later. All the officers had stayed loyal to the emperor and the army would certainly obey them, Boyer assured her, but, haggard and visibly weak from starvation, he added that she must accept Bismarck's offer as quickly as possible, since no more than two days' rations had remained when he left Metz.

However, the general was unable to give Eugénie any information about what Prussia's conditions were likely to be, nor could she obtain the slightest idea of them despite visiting the Prussian ambassador in London and cabling desperate appeals to King William. Then Bismarck informed her in a telegram that he wanted Bazaine to launch a '*pronunciamento*' of the sort that had recently taken place in Spain. Well aware that every Frenchman, whether Bonapartist, republican or royalist, was united against the invaders, she saw at once that a coup would alienate the Empire's remaining supporters by starting a civil war which, as the Prussian chancellor obviously hoped, would weaken France's resistance.

Bismarck made a serious misjudgement in assuming that he was dealing with a woman who would seize any chance of regaining her throne. Realising the scheme was a trap, she refused to have anything more to do with it, saying that she was not going to give the Prussians a 'blank cheque'. It was a bitter disappointment – she had genuinely believed that she could obtain better terms than the 'Government of National Defence' at Tours.

On 27 October Bazaine and his starving army surrendered unconditionally – the entire French regular army had now been taken prisoner. With it disappeared the last vestige of imperial authority and France's only government became the one at Tours. Yet the emperor thought Eugénie had been right to refuse Bismarck's offer. 'I am in complete agreement with you, and the letters I have written, and which crossed with your last one to me, will show you how well we understand each other, body and soul,' he wrote from his captivity. 'It is a thousand times better to live in obscurity and poverty than to owe our position to abandoning our self-respect and our country's best interests.'

After Sedan, Napoleon had not heard from his wife for over a fortnight. Then three letters reached him on 17 September, the first of many. 'My heart breaks to see from your letters how deeply wounded you are,' he told her on 6 October. 'From our past grandeurs, nothing remains of what once separated us,' she wrote to him after Metz surrendered. 'We are more attached to each other, a hundred times more attached, because of our sufferings and all our hopes have become one in the dear young person of Louis. The darker the future, the more we shall feel the need to support each other. . . .'

'You and Louis mean everything to me,' she would tell him later. 'You take the place of family and country. France's misfortunes move me to the depths of my soul, yet not for one moment do I miss the brilliance of our past life. Simply to be together again, that is all I wish for. My poor *cher ami*, if only my devotion to you could make you forget just for an instant the trials that you have endured with such greatness of soul. Your long, admirable suffering reminds me of Our Lord.' Some historians have marvelled at Eugénie's 'inconsistency' in transforming the man whom she had accused of being a coward, because of his surrender at Sedan, into a martyr. They recall how violently she had abused him in that dreadful outburst at the Tuileries in front of Filon and Conti. Yet she remained devoted to him for the rest of his life.

Meanwhile, Napoleon was being treated with almost too much consideration by his Prussian captors. No less disagreeable prison could be imagined than Wilhelmshöhe near Cassel, with its beautiful park and lake – King William used it as a favourite summer residence. Once the palace of the emperor's late uncle Jerome, as king of Westphalia under the First Empire when it had been called 'Napoleonshöhe', it even contained a portrait of the prisoner's mother, Queen Hortense. Nor could any jailer have been politer than its military governor, General Count Monts. The imperial staff included not only his aide-de-camp but such stalwarts as his cousin Prince Joachim Murat and his old friend Dr Conneau – and also his hairdresser from the Tuileries, M. Caumont. The attacks from his stone ceased, for the time being, and there was a definite improvement in his health.

The Prussians were not entirely altruistic, however, keeping a careful account of the cost of the emperor's upkeep and eventually sending the bill to the government of the Third Republic, and extracting full settlement. Moreover Napoleon's treatment made an embarrassing contrast to that of most French prisoners of war, some of whom died from exposure in the open cattle trucks in which they were taken to prison camps. Dr Evans, who visited the camps, was horrified by their sufferings during the terrible winter of 1870/1, when 20,000 died from disease. The emperor did what he could, sending money to buy them proper clothing.

The authorities had no objection whatever to the empress visiting Napoleon at Wilhelmshöhe. Dressed in deep black, she arrived on 30 October, having travelled through Belgium. Her husband met her on the palace steps, coldly formal – a little to her alarm – but then there was a highly emotional reunion when they were in private. She stayed with him for four days before returning to England.

General Monts was fascinated by Eugénie, noticing that her obvious exhaustion seemed to add to her distinction. As a good Lutheran he observed patronisingly, in a book written many years afterwards, that he was convinced her sufferings had purged her of all traces of frivolity. The forcefulness of her manner made him feel sure that she had always influenced her husband's policies, and 'was accustomed to having the last word'. He also claimed that she spoke to Napoleon not as an equal but as a grown-up talking to a child, which must have been a figment of his imagination.

The emperor did not forget the feast of St Eugénie, 15 November. 'I hope that you received, yesterday and today, my little flowers,' he wrote. 'They are not very beautiful, but I could not find any others. My thoughts are with you and I suffer from being far away from you on this day more than any other.'

'What matters above all else is seeing you again,' she wrote back with renewed affection. 'These long days of exile are so sad for me. . . . I am quite sure God will give us happier days, but when? I cannot tell. Yet my tenderness and love for you continue to grow. I would make any sacrifice to make life happier for you, and the more everything looks dark, the more we should remember that all things have an end, both good and bad.'

Eugénie informed Doña Maria Manuela on 16 November:

The events through which we are living have broken my heart. I cannot get used to the idea of France being in ruins and miserable, even less to the idea that in her day of trial I am not there. In England they are beginning to see that nowadays Prussia and Russia rule the world. I only hope it is frightening enough to shake them out of their apathy . . . All that matters is saving France, no matter how or by whom. As for us, the world is big enough for us to hide our misfortunes somewhere, even if we are not allowed to save our country.

Even so, it is clear that Eugénie still regarded herself as regent. She had complained to Monts that if only his king had given them back the army in Metz, 'it would have let us make an honourable peace and restore order in France'. Yet even had the Prussians done so, this was wishful thinking. A scheme she proposed in a letter to Wilhelmshöhe in December, when Paris was besieged and starving, was no less unrealistic. She would go to a city in the French provinces, summon the Corps Législatif and negotiate a peace. The Prussians were bound to offer her better terms than to the Tours government, and she would submit them for approval in a plebiscite.

Horrified, Napoleon forebade the scheme by return of post. (So much for Monts's view of their relationship.) 'We cannot take such risks, which might end in ridicule and being arrested by four *gens d'armes*', he told her. Even if they did not, any peace was going to be disastrous for France. 'After the position we have held in Europe, all our actions must bear the hall-mark of dignity and grandeur.' Eugénie abandoned the scheme – it was her last attempt to take control.

On 30 November Camden Place was honoured by a visit from Queen Victoria. 'At the door stood the poor empress in black, the Prince Imperial and, a little behind, the Ladies and Gentlemen,' the queen noted in her diary. 'She looks very thin and pale, but still very handsome. There was an expression of deep sadness on her face, and she frequently had tears in her eyes.' As for the Prince Imperial, he was 'a nice boy but rather short and stumpy. His eyes are rather like those of his mother, but otherwise I think him more like the emperor.' Victoria's summing-up was, 'a sad visit and seemed like a strange dream'.

She invited Eugénie to come and see her at Windsor the following week. 'What a fearful contrast to her visit here in '55', thought the queen. 'Then all was state and pomp, wild excitement and enthusiasm – and now? . . . The poor empress looked so lovely in her simple black, and so touching in her gentleness and submission.'

For thirty years their friendship was to grow closer and closer, always unclouded. Yet no two women could have been more different. Filon, who compares them in his memoirs, said that as time went by the contrast grew even more striking. Since he knew her better, his comparison sheds more light on Eugénie than on Victoria:

> The Queen was hard-working and methodical, keen to store facts in her brain and arrange them neatly; impulsive like all her race, the empress was incapable of keeping to a regular routine, quick at seeing truths that might escape more experienced eyes, yet then losing sight of them after much reflection and discussion: one woman was very reserved, the other highly indiscreet, but both were incapable of deceit; they had reached an age when one values sincerity more than anything else.

Meanwhile, the Prussians routed the last makeshift armies of France, plundering and burning. Among the casualties was the lovely château of Saint-Cloud, which went up in flames. On 18 January King William of Prussia was proclaimed Emperor William I of Germany by his fellow rulers in the hall of mirrors at Versailles – the new Germans were unaware they had set out on a road which was going to end in two world wars. Napoleon realised it immediately, however, prophesying that eventually Europe would have to crush Prussia.

After an armistice between France and Germany was signed in February 1871 a general election was held in order to produce a National Assembly that would ratify the peace terms. These were draconian, having been designed by Bismarck to crush France for the next hundred years. All of Alsace and most of Lorraine were to be handed over to Germany while a war indemnity of 5,000 million francs would have to be paid to Berlin. Out of 650 deputies elected to the new National Assembly, only 30 were Bonapartists while nearly 400 were Legitimists or Orleanists and, when it met at Bordeaux on 1 March, besides endorsing the peace terms the Assembly formally confirmed the deposition of Napoleon III.

Starved in a terrible siege, humiliated by the Prussian army's triumphant ceremonial entry into the city and infuriated at the election of so many monarchist deputies, on 18 March Paris erupted in the revolution which Napoleon and Eugénie had so much feared during the last years of their reign, proclaiming itself an independent republic, the Commune: a fatal mistake had been made in allowing National Guardsmen to keep their rifles, since they now became a citizen army.

Flying the red flag, the Commune was a conscious attempt to repeat the Jacobin Revolution of 1792, reviving the revolutionary calendar and replacing *'monsieur'* with *'citoyen'*. Right-wing newspapers were shut down, churches and rich men's houses pillaged, and banks and insurance companies forced to contribute to the régime. Hundreds of innocent people were thrown into prison, merely on suspicion of being enemies of the revolution.

From Versailles, Thiers, now President of France, ordered a second siege of Paris which lasted from 2 April until 21 May. The *communards* shot their hostages in batches, among them a group of seventy who included the archbishop of Paris, besides murdering dozens of monks and priests. A detachment billeted themselves in Eugénie's orphanage, raping the children and leaving many of the girls pregnant. When government troops stormed in, during the ensuing 'Bloody Week' fire-bombers (often women called *'pétroleuses'*) destroyed the Tuileries, the Palais Royal and the Hôtel de Ville – the Louvre was saved only just in time. Led by General de Gallifet, Thiers's men shot over 17,000 *communards* in seven days, 40,000 more being tried and either shot or transported.

Among those transported was that scourge of the Second Empire, Henri de Rochefort, who had been one of the Commune's leaders but he soon escaped from his prison settlement in New Caledonia.

Always unbalanced, he then became not only an extreme Legitimist but a fanatical anti-Semite.

Released from captivity, Napoleon III landed at Dover on 20 March 1871, two days after the revolution had broken out in Paris. In tears, Eugénie met him on the quay while the English crowd cheered. He quickly settled down to life at Camden Place, and despite the sadness of exile this was the most serene period of his marriage. The empress's jewels (sold to the Rothschilds for over £150,000), together with her money in Spain provided an adequate income, and she was an excellent manager. He may have also had secret funds.

Queen Victoria came to see the ex-emperor soon after his arrival, admiring the way in which 'he bore his terrible misfortunes with meekness, dignity and patience'. She says he had 'grown very stout and grey and his moustaches are no longer curled or waxed as formerly, but otherwise there was the same pleasing, gentle and gracious manner'. (One wonders if the Prince Consort, had he lived, would have been quite so welcoming.) Eugénie told Paléologue how much she owed to the queen: 'You would never believe all the delicate attentions she lavished upon us in those first cruel days of our exile. She always treated us as sovereigns, just as in the days when we were allies of England; one day she said to me: "you no longer have the sovereignty of power; but you have a still higher sovereignty, that of misfortune". Her visits to Chislehurst did us so much good.'

Another visitor to Chislehurst was Dr Evans, who found Napoleon more worried about the miseries of France than his own misfortunes. He was also impressed by the 'kindly way' the emperor spoke of the men who were running France. Evans did not realise that he was already planning to win them over when he regained his throne.

Germany was now the leading European power in Europe, while France was becoming second-rate. Plenty of Frenchmen resented the prospect. Moreover, France was not just Paris and many people had been horrified by both the Commune and its repression. At the same time, a majority of deputies in the Assembly felt there was something undignified about a republic. While most of them were monarchists, their candidates handicapped them. The Comte de

Chambord was a charismatic and unmistakably regal personality, but as a romantic who lived in the Middle Ages he was incapable of making the compromises that were needed. If highly intelligent, his rival the Comte de Paris was dull and uninspiring. In any case there was a long-standing vendetta between Legitimists and Orleanists.

Even the republicans were divided into left and right, conservatives fearful of revolution such as Thiers, or radical fire-brands like Gambetta. Meanwhile the government was dominated by Orleanist aristocrats, who were unable to restore their pretender. Nobody was satisfied with the situation.

Crushed by war and the indemnity, the French were beginning to miss the prosperity they had known under Napoleon III. While the army blamed the emperor for failing to prepare adequately for hostilities in 1870 and for appointing commanders such as Bazaine, they recognised his bravery on the battlefield, dismissing smear stories about 'the Coward of Sedan'.

The British ambassador Lord Lyons was convinced that the emperor still enjoyed widespread support. His assessment was borne out by an agent of the Rothschild family in Paris, known only by his initials 'C. de B.', who in October 1871 reported that a group of senior French bureaucrats had secretly carried out a political survey. They estimated that if France had the opportunity of choosing its rulers, 1 million would vote for the Comte de Paris, 2 million would vote for a republic, 2 million would vote for the Comte de Chambord – and 3 million for the emperor.

No doubt this may have been wishful thinking by the bureaucrats, who were probably closet Bonapartists – the administration was full of them – yet C. de B., a self-confessed Orleanist, reluctantly put Napoleon's chances even higher, and believed that he could secure 5 or even 6 million votes in a plebiscite. C. de B. also claimed that in the capital's salons, 'the possibility of a Bonapartist restoration is the one topic of conversation'.

Eugène Rouher, the old 'Mameluke' and former president of the Imperial Council of State, was elected to the Assembly for a Corsican constituency in February 1872, leading a small but vigorous group of about thirty Bonapartist deputies. He had already founded *La Situation*, one of several newspapers that supported

Napoleon III. A network of Bonapartist clubs busily distributed large quantities of leaflets and photographs.

Among the propaganda photographs was a carte-de-visite-sized re-enactment of Eugénie escaping from the Louvre. About to enter the *fiacre* outside the main entrance, she is shown with Mme Lebreton and flanked by Prince Metternich and Cavaliere Nigra, as she graciously says goodbye to Conti and Lieutenant Conneau, who are seen kissing her hand; a fifth man holds open the cab door. (In reality, as we now know, she had already made Conti and Conneau leave her, while there was no fifth man.) The photograph is of course a montage, the faces having been superimposed over those of the actors who replayed the scene. It was produced by 'M. le Cte Aguado' – Olympe Aguado, once the imperial court's photographer.

The emperor had been plotting his return to France ever since his surrender at Sedan. His light had been seen burning all night throughout his enforced stay at Wilhelmshöhe, and there were even rumours that he had been in touch with Regnier during the abortive negotiations for an armistice at Metz. He was undoubtedly in close contact with his leading supporters in France, not merely with Rouher and his friends, but with senior army officers who might help him launch a coup. Bonapartist agents were constantly slipping in and out of the Channel ports.

Just how seriously M. Thiers's government regarded the possibility of a Bonapartist restoration could be seen from the large number of French spies who swarmed around Camden Place, much to the locals' amusement. One of them installed himself with a telescope in the windmill on Chislehurst Common while others actually climbed trees overlooking the house. Frenzied attempts were made to identify every visitor, lists of names being sent regularly to Paris. A valet was bribed lavishly to steal important-looking papers from Napoleon's desk.

When Eugénie went to Spain in September 1871 to stay with Doña Maria Manuela, quite innocently the emperor and the Prince Imperial travelled down together to Torquay for a holiday. To their surprise, they frequently found themselves being cheered in the streets, with shouts of '*Vive L'Empéreur!*' a reception that was zealously noted by republican spies. Did the people of Torquay know something that they did not, they wondered? In France, newspapers began to talk of an imminent attempt by Napoleon, who was said to be about to sail from Torquay with an expeditionary force, his destination being the sea port of Rochefort, where troops and police were put on full alert. Secret agents were urgently dispatched from Paris to Spain with orders to shadow the empress wherever she went, since she was clearly involved in what the press was by now calling the 'descent from Torquay' – obviously she was about to launch a simultaneous rising across the Pyrenees, from an as yet unidentified base in the Basque country.

Republican hysteria over the 'descent from Torquay' delighted the emperor, encouraging him to spread rumours of other imaginary risings. At the same time, however, he was hatching a real and very formidable plot. He wanted to re-establish the throne for the sake of his son, and he was confident he would succeed, telling the boy, 'If the Empire has lost fifty per cent of its prestige, it still has the other half.'

During the autumn of 1872 the watcher in the windmill on Chislehurst Common must often have had the thrill of sighting Plon-Plon through his telescope. The self-proclaimed republican was enthusiastically helping to plan the restoration of the Second Empire. By the end of the year a detailed programme for a coup had been decided, which can to some extent be reconstructed. Timed for 20 March 1873, it was full of striking and no doubt deliberate echoes of Napoleon I's return from Elba in 1815.

Like his uncle, the emperor would discreetly slip away from exile, in a yacht from Cowes where he was going to convalesce after an operation. Crossing to Belgium, he would join Plon-Plon in Switzerland. They would then enter France across Lake Annecy, making for Lyons, where General Bourbaki was the garrison commander. From here, acclaimed by Bourbaki's troops, the emperor intended to march to Paris, where Marshal MacMahon would already have won over the key officers in the army. Any deputies opposed to the restoration – which meant most of them – were to be removed at bayonet point from the National Assembly, forced on to a train and incarcerated in the Saint-Cloud tunnel during the coup's consolidation.

Since both the Tuileries and Saint-Cloud had been burned down, the emperor and empress would use the Louvre as their principal palace. Rouher's new administration was to include the Comte de Kératry (minister for the interior), MacMahon (minister for war) and Fleury (governor of Paris). Foreign governments, who had been secretly sounded out, made no objections.

The plan had serious weaknesses. Far too much depended on Bourbaki and MacMahon. Although brave enough and a fine leader, the general was notoriously stupid, while if the marshal was a monarchist he was more inclined to favour Legitimism, and in any case he was an unimaginative man, too fond of army regulations, who did not care for political gambles. The most obvious weakness, however, was Napoleon's poor health.

Everybody felt that Chislehurst was bad for him. 'These fogs are the cause of all my discomfort,' he told a German visitor. 'A fortnight of brilliant sunshine such as we enjoyed at Wilhelmshöhe, and I should be cured.' Eugénie disliked it just as much. 'In this foggy weather I feel like a fish in an aquarium,' she wrote to Maria Manuela in November. 'At any rate, that's how it seems when I look out of the window; everything looks as if it is yellow, just like the water in which we put some miserable fish. . . .' Nor did it help matters that while she loved fresh air, the emperor loved central heating, as hot as possible. Yet nothing disturbed the serenity of these last years together. 'If you could have seen him at Chislehurst,' she recalled. 'Never a word of complaint or blame or recrimination.' He was helped by his stoicism and his humour. When a dissenting minister invited him to a lecture proving he was the Antichrist he sent Filon, listening to his report with wry amusement.

In December 1872 Napoleon received a German journalist from Cassel, Mels Cohen, who had interviewed him during his time at Wilhelmshöhe and had been impressed by his forecasting the Commune – 'horrible things will happen in France after the peace'. This time he told Cohen that the republic was a disease that must be eradicated. 'The Empire will be re-established, that is certain,' he prophesied confidently. 'M. Thiers knows that at a single word from me the flag of the Empire would be raised in fifty places at once, from one end of France to another, and the Army would recall as if by magic its ancient battle-cry at Malakoff and Solferino.' He then added, as if to deny any intention of a coup, 'M. Thiers knows also that I will never speak that word.'

Napoleon carefully concealed his intentions. Although Dr Evans was convinced that the empire was going to be restored, he was naively sure that the emperor would do nothing to hasten the process. 'Those persons who imagine that the emperor was at this time conspiring to overthrow the French Republic, and intriguing to recover his throne, are greatly mistaken,' Evans stated sternly in his memoirs.

Dr Evans never knew of Napoleon's worries about staying on a horse when he rode into Paris at the head of his troops, or that he practised every day on a wooden horse, commissioned by Eugénie from a sculptor and smuggled into Camden Place.

Although the emperor began to suffer from the gallstone again in September 1872, he insisted that he was going to go on with the coup when Plon-Plon saw him in early December. 'The worst that can happen to me is being shot like poor Emperor Maximilian,' he said. 'Better than dying in bed, in exile'. Shortly afterwards, as a test of his fitness, he tried to ride over to the Woolwich Military Academy, a few miles away, which the Prince Imperial had just entered as a cadet. The pain was so dreadful, however, that he had to dismount after less than a mile. The jolting carriage in which he came home made it worse and he spent three days in bed with a fever, in agony. Reluctantly, he summoned specialists from London. Evans commented, 'he was at last compelled to give up all exercise, rarely leaving the house'.

Filon confirms that after the loss of their throne Eugénie had given back to her husband all her old affection, especially when she learned how bravely the man branded as a coward by his enemies had behaved at Sedan. He explains that she had completely forgotten her terrible outburst on receiving his telegram after the battle, just as a man forgets a fit of madness. 'It is my duty to say that during those last hours of married life, perfect sympathy existed between the emperor and empress.'

'I have been worried to death about the emperor,' Eugénie – who had never seen Professor Sée's report – wrote to her mother on 30 December. 'He has at last agreed to be examined and the examination showed that he has a stone. He will have a first operation the day after tomorrow, and I profoundly hope that having undergone so much awful pain he will get better and eventually be completely cured. I am praying for this and am sick with worry.'

There were two excruciating operations, which Napoleon bore with his usual patience. A third was to be performed on 9 January, but at 10.25 a.m. that day it was realised that he was deteriorating fast and a priest was summoned to give him the last Sacraments. He died twenty minutes later – after muttering to Dr Conneau, 'We weren't cowards at Sedan, were we, Conneau?' Eugénie whispered, '*C'est impossible!*' again and again. Then she flung herself across the bed, weeping.

In Napoleon's will he had told his son to 'make himself thoroughly familiar with the writings of the Prisoner of St Helena, and study the emperor's decrees and letters . . . the spirit of my glorious uncle has always inspired and sustained me'. As for his wife, 'I hope that my memory will be dear to her and that when I am dead she will forgive me whatever sorrows I may have caused her.' It was a belated apology for his unfaithfulness.

Eugénie was too overcome to attend the funeral at the little Catholic church in Chislehurst, when the Prince Imperial walked behind the hearse at the head of the cortège. There was a crowd estimated at 17,000 while the mourners included all the famous names of the Second Empire – among them Plon-Plon, Fleury, Rouher, Haussmann, Palikao, Bourbaki, the duc de Gramont and Marie-Anne Walewska. There were two marshals of France, seventeen generals and twenty-seven ex-ministers, together with a hundred who had been senators or deputies during the reign. Lord Cowley was there, while Queen Victoria was represented by the Prince of Wales and the Duke of Edinburgh. Marshal MacMahon was absent, however, and so was Princesse Mathilde.

The emperor might not have succeeded in launching his last coup, yet even so his son was greeted with shouts of '*Vive L'Empéreur! Vive Napoléon IV!*' as he left the church.

The crowd, as well as Eugénie, knew that the Second Empire was not dead yet.

Epilogue: After the Empire

In March 1874 the Prince Imperial celebrated his eighteenth birthday. Had the Second Empire survived, this would have been the moment when his father abdicated to make way for 'Napoleon IV'. He possessed all the right qualities and his mother can scarcely be blamed for believing that one day her son might go home in triumph.

A royalist challenge which at the time appeared extremely serious, causing considerable alarm at Chislehurst, had receded. In the previous autumn the Legitimist pretender, the childless Comte de Chambord had recognised the Orleanist pretender, the Comte de Paris, as his successor; in October the president of the National Assembly had promised its overwhelmingly royalist majority that the Bourbon monarchy would be restored within three weeks.

'Henri V' would only return on his own terms, however. A man of inflexible principles who seemed to have stepped straight out of a novel by Sir Walter Scott, he embodied the old France and refused to return unless the white standard of the *ancien régime* came with him and replaced the tricolore. This single issue prevented an otherwise certain restoration – the pope commenting, 'Whoever heard of a man giving up a throne for a napkin?' In any case, the royalists' peasant supporters were deserting them, even in the Vendée, alarmed by rumours that a king might bring back feudal dues and clerical tithes.

French royalism should not be dismissed too lightly. It enjoyed a large following among intellectuals, especially historians, until the Second World War. During the late 1870s, however, after Chambord's political suicide, the only possible form of monarchy for France was Bonapartism. It was quite clear that many royalists could be won over, just as they had been under the Second Empire – anything was better, in their eyes, than a republic.

A large number of the French people thought the new republican régime too undignified for a great European nation with a long, glorious history. It lacked the still potent magic of monarchy. Even on the left many found themselves sympathising with the gibe, '*Que la république était beau sous l'empire*' ('How beautiful the Republic was under the Empire'). Despite being blamed for the suffering and humiliation it had brought upon France in 1870–1, Bonapartism remained a viable political creed, so long as it possessed a really able

275

leader. It stood for the reconciliation of the old France and the new, unlike royalism or republicanism. At the same time, in a harsher economic climate, the Second Empire's prosperity was recalled with nostalgia. Should the Third Republic fail, then the empire was the only possible alternative.

'If the people wanted to bring back a dynasty, that is the one dynasty they would choose,' admitted Adolphe Thiers who prided himself on his realism, even if he thought the republic was likely to last for a long time. He added, 'The Napoleons are genuine democrats'.

When the Prince Imperial (who called himself the 'Comte de Pierrefonds') had left the church after his father's funeral the crowd had cried, '*Vive Napoléon IV!*', but he had told them to cry '*Vive la France!*' instead. On his eighteenth birthday 6,000 people came to Chislehurst to cheer him. Among them were fourteen deputies from the National Assembly, sixty-five former imperial prefects and a large number of retired army officers – there should have been plenty of serving officers too, but the republican government had promised them they would be cashiered if they crossed the Channel. Still more significant, was a large group of Parisian workmen. Again, there were cries of '*Vive Napoléon IV!*', and again he showed restraint.

After this triumphant demonstration many observers began to think that the Prince Imperial's restoration was only a matter of time. However, he himself had recently assured a French journalist that under no circumstances would he contemplate mounting a *coup d'état*, quoting his father as saying that his own coup had always been a millstone round his neck. Only when France was threatened by 'anarchy' (or revolution) and needed him, was he going to return. He owed at least some of his realism to his mother, who knew just how much the world had changed in the last thirty years.

The empress had very mixed feelings about a restoration. 'I have to admit that the thought of making any move towards regaining the crown of France, a crown of thorns, leaves me cold,' she confided to Doña Maria Manuela in March 1876. 'I think that France is quite ungovernable unless her vanity and self-love are satisfied.'

Meanwhile, Plon-Plon's behaviour was more deplorable than ever. As soon as Napoleon III died, he demanded that Eugénie should hand the boy over to him for his education, infuriating both mother and son. In the election of 1876 he stood against Rouher, splitting the Bonapartists into conservatives and semi-republicans. The prince was bitterly opposed to Plon-Plon's peculiar version of Bonapartism, telling his supporters that 'Prince Napoleon stands as a candidate. . . against my wishes.' In any case he loathed the man.

He was well aware that the bulk of the vote in favour of the liberal empire had come from the peasants, who on the whole were conservative and Catholic, even if they did not always trust their priests. It had never come from free-thinking intellectuals. He remembered the advice in his father's will, to familiarise himself with the writings of the prisoner of St Helena, 'so that when the time comes he will not forget that the ordinary people's cause is France's cause'. Most of these 'ordinary people' were peasants.

Always a realist, Eugénie was horrified by the rift between her son and his cousin. She realised that it was a feud which might alienate valuable supporters. Plon-Plon was ageing but his followers included one or two brilliant young men (notably the future historian Frédéric Lemasson) and their loss could seriously damage her son's cause. But in this instance Louis refused to take her advice.

In 1872 the prince had entered the Royal Military Academy at Woolwich. 'The Shop', as cadets called it, was in Kent and in those days just outside London, a place where they were trained for entry into the artillery or the engineers. He desperately wanted to become a gunner in the footsteps of the first Bonaparte. Cheerfully accepting the inevitable horseplay and ragging, he got on well with his fellow cadets and made several good friends.

The Duke of Cambridge, the commander-in-chief, was present at his 'passing out' at Woolwich in February 1875 and was impressed by the cadets' drill. 'The Prince Imperial drilled them remarkably well when called upon,' he wrote in his diary. 'The Empress Eugénie was present throughout the day. . . . The Prince Imperial took the 7th place in the List, a most excellent position for a Cadet 11 months younger than the greater portion of his class, and who had to study in a foreign language.' The duke also noted that he took first place in riding and fencing.

Although 'Louis' was an only child, Eugénie was a surprisingly unpossessive mother. (Admittedly this is not the impression that one has from Tissot's portrait of the two in which, heavily middle-aged and bursting with pride, she stands beside her son in his pillbox cap.) When he discussed politics with key supporters such as Rouher, she kept out of sight and never tried to interfere, while she made him financially independent with a generous settlement.

The British royal family's friendship was a constant encouragement. Victoria had already written, 'For the peace of Europe, the Queen thinks that it would be best if the Prince Imperial were ultimately to succeed.' She had the young man to stay at Osborne where she took a great fancy to him – he was said to be the only person other than John Brown who was not frightened of her. The Prince of Wales invited him to receptions at Marlborough House and took him to his club next door in Pall Mall, the Marlborough. (Until the end of his life the future architect of the 'Entente Cordiale' between Britain and France thought that Bonapartism was the form of government best suited to the French.)

Earlier biographers – some of them extremely well informed, such as Roger Sencourt – were convinced that Eugénie and Victoria hoped Louis would marry the queen's youngest daughter, Princess Beatrice, despite the difference in religion. Certainly he met her a good deal, since she accompanied her mother on the latter's visits to Camden Place, but her son Lord Carisbrooke told Harold Kurtz that there was no truth in the story of an intended marriage and that she had never been in love with the Prince. In any case, he was in no hurry to marry – a wife might hinder his activities as pretender. There were also rumours that he had his eye on a German or Swedish princess, but he told Filon they were untrue.

The French left tried to discredit the former empress with a smear campaign, a socialist newspaper pretending it had seen evidence that Don Cipriano had died three years before she was born so that she must be illegitimate. When Maria Manuela sued the paper in the Paris courts, she won the case but was awarded derisory damages.

There were attempts by the French press to discredit the prince too, with allegations that he was a dismal young man, repressed and joyless. In reality, he was tall, vigorous and strikingly handsome, noticeably cheerful and with a quick, enquiring mind – he even read Karl Marx. Although he concealed it, he was deeply religious, while he had an intimation that he would die violently and drew a strange, haunting sketch of a young hero being received by the Angel of Death. He got on well with his mother, who was understandably proud of him. 'I don't know why everybody grumbled about Camden Place,' she later told Mme Filon. 'For me it was heaven.' Filon commented, 'Those four years, 1875 to 1879, were happy years for her, probably almost the happiest of her entire life.'

As a devout Catholic, in 1876 the prince visited Rome where he saw the pope, old Pius IX, who told him he hoped that he would soon be restored to the French throne, for the sake of both France and the Church. When he visited Sweden two years later, he was treated as a reigning sovereign. He spent much of his leave in Switzerland at Arenenberg, once Queen Hortense's château, with his mother, and brother officers from his regiment.

He was eager to see some fighting and in 1878 was advised by Baron Stoffel to join the army of Austria-Hungary, then preparing to occupy Bosnia-Herzegovina. Eugénie disagreed. 'You'll spend all your time in an Austrian garrison, playing billiards and making love to an Italian singer,' she warned. 'If there's a war, you'll find yourself fighting the poor Turks, who are France's allies. And politics in the Balkans change so fast and unexpectedly that it might even mean your fighting against the Russians, whose Tsar spoke to you like a father at Woolwich four years ago.' However, when the prince applied to the Austrian authorities, Franz-Joseph politely refused his request.

The empress watched French politics, closely. She understood why Marshal MacMahon was so inadequate as president, 'standing for nothing, supported by nobody', prophesying his outmanoeuvring and downfall. She also saw that the key republican was Gambetta and, unlike most observers, she appreciated that what he wanted was power to build his sort of France. In her opinion he was her son's greatest rival.

Eugénie had no time for romantic conservatives, blinkered by tradition. 'Your view of the world is straight out of the Middle Ages,' she wrote to Doña Maria Manuela in 1876. 'Someone of real ability has to have on his side what you call the Popular Hydra, because no one can resist it any longer. The kings, princes and nobles have weakened each other too much down the centuries so that even when they ally it is no use. We have to deal with new forces.'

Nor was Eugénie surprised when during the following year North America had to call in troops to break strikes. 'I see that you are worried about what is happening in the United States,' she remarked to her mother. 'The railroad strikes and the accompanying violence are certainly very serious, but they do not surprise me, and I'm sure they will find imitators in Europe. The more civilisation progresses, the hollower it becomes and the easier to destroy, and – don't let us deceive ourselves – today's problems are much more social than political.' Like her late husband, she knew that western society's greatest challenge lay in satisfying its working classes.

The prince derived his political views from his mother, although he was already much more cynical. Noting the far from revolutionary programme of the republicans who took over from Marshal MacMahon, he told a friend, 'After ten years of a régime like this, France will be ruled like the United States, by a clique of politicians who have failed in other careers, whose game lies in exploiting their popularity.'

In 1879 war broke out with the Zulus. The prince's regiment stayed at Aldershot, but he was determined to see active service at the front. 'I'm always being reminded that the Orleans princes have seen plenty of fighting while I've seen none,' he told Eugénie when she tried to dissuade him. Those who did the reminding were republican and royalist papers in Paris, who sneered that he had deserted the French army before Sedan and had grown into a colourless imitation of an Englishman. Threatening to resign his commission and enlist as a private, he pestered the queen and the Duke of Cambridge as commander-in-chief, so eloquently that in the end he was allowed to go out as an observer attached to the staff.

He sailed from Southampton on 27 February 1879. Eugénie had travelled down with him, on a special train supplied by the queen, to say goodbye at the boat. Joining General Lord Chelmsford's army at Durban, he was under Chelmsford's quarter-master, Colonel Harrison, with orders that he was to be treated like any other young staff officer except that he must always have an escort. He enjoyed sleeping under the stars and skirmishing, charging a party of Zulus sword in hand.

He also helped to capture a kraal. The enemy, ferocious opponents, had just wiped out a British force at Isandhlwana.

'I should hate to be killed in an obscure skirmish,' he told a French journalist. 'Dying in a big battle would be all right, the hand of providence. But not in a mere skirmish.' The journalist, Paul Deléage, was amazed at how different he was from the caricatures in the French press. 'This was not some little princeling, but an impressive and commanding personality gifted with enormous charm, and a complete Frenchman.'

All the odds were on the young man coming home safe and sound, but his mother's intuition gave her no peace. 'I've lost all confidence and expect only bad news,' she lamented to Maria Manuela on 9 April. A month later she declared, 'I shall end up mad if this awful uneasiness goes on torturing me.'

On 1 June Harrison encamped at Itelezi Ridge, sending out a scout party of six troopers under a Lieutenant Carey. The prince rode with them. There was no sign of the enemy and about noon they halted at a deserted kraal, dismounting for a brief rest. Suddenly shots rang out and over forty Zulus appeared from the long grass a few yards away. Remounting in panic, the party rode for their lives, two being killed by Zulu bullets. As the prince remounted a strap broke and he fell to the ground, his horse bolting.

A trooper who had hidden in the rocks nearby watched what took place. The prince got up and made a run for it, but after a quarter of mile realised he had no chance. Turning, he drew his revolver and advanced to meet the Zulus, who threw assegais at him. Moving his revolver to his left hand and picking up an assegai with his right, he continued to walk towards them. In a moment he fell dead beneath a hail of assegais – when found, he had seventeen wounds, all in front. Later the Zulus said, 'he died like a lion'.

The news did not reach England until 19 June. Informed by the telegraph office, Queen Victoria sent Lord Sydney to break it to the empress before she learned from the newspapers. She did not cry, but sat down staring into space. For over a month she sat in a darkened bedroom, refusing even to go into the garden. When the body came home, she rushed down the stairs and embraced the coffin, staying with it until dawn without a word or a tear.

The Queen, who visited Camden Place almost weekly, wanted a monument to the Prince placed in Westminster Abbey. When the idea was rejected by the House of Commons, she had a fine funeral effigy set up in St George's Chapel, Windsor. (A statue erected at Woolwich is now at Sandhurst.) She attended the requiem at the Catholic church at Chislehurst, together with the Princess of Wales and Princess Beatrice, while the Prince of Wales, the Duke of Connaught and the Duke of Cambridge were among the pallbearers. The prince was given full military honours, officers marching with sabres reversed to the beat of muffled drums. The crowd was estimated at 40,000. But Eugénie stayed in her darkened room, where Victoria visited her.

In his will the Prince Imperial excluded Plon-Plon from the succession – 'when I am dead, the work of Napoleon I and Napoleon III falls on the eldest son of Prince Napoleon'. Eugénie tried to stop the will becoming widely known, aware that it would split the party irretrievably. Rouher published the will, however, and from now on there were two Bonapartist parties, those of Plon-Plon and Prince Victor Napoleon – a father and son who hated each other. Although Eugénie treated Victor Napoleon as emperor of the French, and for a time did not altogether despair of a restoration, she realised that now there was very little hope for Bonapartism.

Eugénie had prayed so long and fervently for her son's return that for a moment she questioned if there was any point in praying for anything. In the end, however, she decided that his death might have been providential. 'But I often say to myself, rather he is dead than think of him as an emperor,' she confided to a friend. 'To think of *his* perhaps going through it all – *de passer par là où j'ai du passer . . . ah!*' She wished she had never given birth to him, telling Victoria that his parentage was fatal. 'Because of my race, I bestowed the quixotic gift, that readiness to sacrifice everything for an ideal, while the emperor bequeathed the traditions of his family. And in the mid-nineteenth century when materialism is engulfing us!'

She wore black for the rest of her long life and would sometimes say, 'I died in 1879.'

A LONG TWILIGHT

'I am alone now,' Eugénie wrote to her blind old mother at Madrid early in September 1879, 'in a country where I am forced to live and die.' She described herself as 'truly crushed'. For the moment the English were sorry for her, she said but their sympathy would soon fade. One day there would be an obituary in *The Times*, then it would all be over. 'Not a single friend to pray at my tomb,' she prophesied. 'Alone in life – alone in death.' Within two months Doña María Manuela, too, was dead, leaving the bulk of her considerable fortune to her daughter.

In March 1880 the empress went on what she called 'a pilgrimage' to South Africa, to retrace her son's last weeks. On Queen Victoria's instructions a British general accompanied her, Sir Evelyn Wood, together with two of the prince's closest brother officers, Lieutenants Bigge and Slade of the Royal Artillery, while at Capetown she was the guest of the governor, Sir Bartle Frere. Even so, the journey meant a trek of several weeks through the veldt by wagon, sleeping in tents that were nearly blown away by storms. She spent the night of the anniversary of Louis's death kneeling in prayer by the cross placed where he had fallen in the little valley – when her candle flickered, she believed that he was there with her.

On the way back the party passed by the battlefield of Isandhlwana, which was still littered with British bones, and at Eugénie's suggestion they spent a day burying them, shovelling earth over as many as they could, she herself wielding a spade. After the trip Evelyn Wood remained a friend for life while she took a personal interest in the career of Arthur Bigge, whom she considered to be exceptionally able, and on her recommendation the queen made him her assistant private secretary. Her judgement did not fail her – Bigge ended as private secretary to King George V, who created him Lord Stamfordham.

In September 1881 the empress moved into a new and much larger house in Hampshire, Farnborough Hill, which had been built in the 1860s for Longman the publisher, on a knoll overlooking the minute but fast-growing town of that name near Aldershot. She made it even bigger, so that eventually it needed more than twenty servants to run it. (Nikolaus Pevsner described it as 'an outrageously oversized chalet with an entrance tower and a lot of bargeboarding'). This was to be her final home.

One of the main reasons why Eugénie moved to Farnborough was her wish to create a worthy resting place for the emperor and the Prince Imperial. During his reign Napoleon had prepared a tomb for himself in the crypt of the abbey of Saint-Denis with the kings of France, and until 1879 she had confidently assumed that he would be reinterred there, after her son's restoration. The little Catholic parish church at Chislehurst was obviously quite inadequate, and if the British had honoured the prince by placing a monument to him in St George's Chapel, then in her view the French must do as well. Moreover, as a Spaniard, she set a particularly high value on praying for the dead.

Unable to enlarge the mortuary chapel at Chislehurst, she had found a site at Farnborough where she could build a great church dedicated to St Michael, patron saint of France, with a crypt in which their bodies and her own would lie. There would also be an abbey of monks to pray for their souls. The site was on another knoll, opposite Farnborough Hill, separated by the London to Southampton railway line. She would have liked Viollet-le-Duc as architect but, anxious not to upset his new republican masters, he declined. Instead she employed another Frenchman, Gabriel Destailleur, who had remodelled the château de Mouchy for Anna Murat and designed Waddesdon for the Rothschilds. There is a story that she showed him just what she wanted by tracing the church's outline on the turf with her walking-stick.

Destailleur proved an inspired choice, producing a most beautiful building, admired even by Pevsner, which Ronald Knox described as 'France transplanted into England'. It is late French Gothic, *flamboyant*, with swirling tracery, ogee arches, flying buttresses and soaring gargoyles, crowned by a small Baroque dome that is a copy of the dome over the Invalides. Bonaparte eagles and bees abound, even in the Romanesque crypt where there is royal as well as imperial symbolism, with a high altar dedicated to St Louis, to proclaim the Bonapartes' claim to be the 'fourth dynasty' and the legitimate successors of the Bourbons as rulers of France. The two bodies were moved here from Chislehurst in 1888 and placed in red granite sarcophagi, a present from Queen Victoria. Four White Canons (Premonstratensians) were installed in the abbey next door. Often curiously ill at ease with priests, Eugénie soon fell out with the canons, who seem to have been a boorish and uncouth group and whose prior was in any case a republican. Eventually they left, leaving the abbey in a state of squalor.

The empress was on far better terms with their successors. These were a community of scholarly Benedictine monks led by Dom Cabrol, former prior of Solesmes, who had been forced to leave their native land by a growing climate of anticlericalism. They brought with them a tradition of superb Gregorian chant and liturgy that made services in the church worthy of an imperial foundation. As well as a roll of priceless silk that had been presented to her by Sultan Abdul Aziz Eugénie gave them her wedding dress, with which to make vestments. (They are still preserved at the abbey.) Nonetheless, although she attended a monthly requiem Mass in the church, besides the great requiems on each anniversary, normally she preferred to hear Mass in the private chapel at Farnborough Hill.

In 1881 the French authorities allowed her to travel through France so that she could attend the inauguration of a monument to Napoleon III in Milan. On the way back she stayed discreetly in Paris with the Duchesse de Mouchy (Anna Murat) and went to Fontainebleau where, despite an ecstatic greeting from the staff, she wept on seeing again the rooms which had been her son's. She was almost as upset when she saw what the Prussians had done to her beloved Saint-Cloud.

Two years later she went back to Paris after Plon-Plon's ludicrously inept attempt at a coup. He had plastered the capital with posters demanding a referendum to decide if France should become an empire again – with himself as emperor – and, promptly arrested by 'four gendarmes', was immured in the Conciergerie. Before the '*César déclassé*' was released and expelled from France, Eugénie rushed over to Paris to see if she could help, her main reason, however, being to try and unite the two branches of the Bonapartist party.

Afterwards Queen Victoria congratulated her on her courage. 'You know how great are the affection and friendship which I feel for you,' wrote the queen, 'and you will, I hope, understand that for a few hours I have been feeling anxious for you.' Someone who still insisted on styling herself 'Empress Eugénie' – although never 'empress of the French' – might easily have joined Plon-Plon in the Conciergerie.

Even so, informally if not officially, her relations with the Republic grew more relaxed as the years went by. Despite the French crown jewels being put up for public auction in 1887, a large number of priceless possessions were restored to her. Among them were the Golden Rose, paintings by Winterhalter (including that of herself with her ladies), by Mme Vigée-Lebrun (of Marie-Antoinette and of the dauphin) and by David. Also returned were her collections of Louis XVI furniture and Sèvres porcelain from Compiègne, and the Gobelin tapestries of Don Quixote from the Villa Eugénie. Farnborough Hill became an imperial palace in more than just a nostalgic sense.

Enthusiastically enlarged by Destailleur, the architect of the abbey church who added turrets, gables and huge chimneys, what had originally looked like some sort of cross between a big Swiss chalet and a Scottish hunting lodge was slowly transformed into a vast French château. An undeniably eccentric building, which to Lucien Daudet appeared like 'a fantastic village', its elaborate roofs were at different levels and it had an incongruous little clock tower. Inside, Destailleur extended the main gallery by constructing a 'cloister in the Renaissance style' that was paved with a marble terrazzo, and added a large, glass-roofed courtyard. The kitchen wing was also extended, to provide accommodation for the staff, while there was an entire new annexe of three storeys. Today the building houses a girl's school, originally founded as a convent school with Eugénie's encouragement and still forming a tenuous link with her.

In the empress's time there were several great drawing-rooms, including a Salon d'Honneur, a Salon des Princesses, a Salon des Dames and a Salon des Greuzes – each of them named according to the paintings they contained. Another room re-created the Prince Imperial's study at Chislehurst in every detail, with his clothes, his swords and guns, and his books; it was a cross between a museum and a shrine.

A phantom imperial court shared Eugénie's exile here, one or two of its members spending the rest of their lives with her at Farnborough Hill – notably the veteran secretary Franceschini Pietri. Luncheon was at one o'clock, dinner at eight, and the rosary was said in the chapel at five. She almost invariably went to bed before eleven, the tiny household bowing and curtsying to her when she retired and she herself curtsying in response, as if they were all still at the Tuileries. There were plenty of visitors. Most of them were young relatives from Spain or former courtiers from France, such as Anna Murat, Jurien de La Gravière, Mme Carette or even Mme de Gallifet, although not her husband, the hero of Sedan. (The general had accepted the new régime and eventually became the Third Republic's minister for war.)

The most faithful visitor was undoubtedly Queen Victoria. Few could equal the delicacy of this fearsome old lady, who wrote often, always in French, inviting the empress to Windsor or Osborne, or to her Scottish castles. As time passed, they grumbled to each other about the infirmities of advancing age, Eugénie's being rheumatism and bronchitis which, privately, she blamed on the English weather. The queen told her to stop calling her 'Your Majesty' or 'Madame' – 'Why not "sister" or "friend" – that would be so much more pleasant.' Neither would precede the other through a door, gently remonstrating. '*Après vous, ma soeur.*' Eugénie's manner towards Victoria was not unlike that of 'an unembarrassed but attentive child talking to its grandmother', said Ethel Smyth, who saw them curtsy to each other. 'The movement of the Queen, crippled though she was, was amazingly easy and dignified; but the empress, who was then sixty-seven, made such an exquisite sweep down to the floor and up again, all in one gesture, that I can only liken it to a flower bent and released in the wind,' Ethel tells us. They shared similar views on foreign affairs, Victoria becoming increasingly pro-French, a development which an angry Bismarck attributed to Eugénie.

Other sovereigns besides Queen Victoria treated her as an equal. In 1888 alone she was visited at Farnborough by King Oscar of Sweden, King Luis of Portugal, the Crown Prince of Italy and Empress Frederick of Germany, who still remembered with pleasure her visit as the young Princess Royal to Eugénie in Paris over forty years before. Kaiser William II would come in 1894.

In 1892 Eugénie built a villa at Cap Martin between Monte Carlo and Menton, where she was to spend many winters: the Villa Cyrnos ('Cyrnos' is Greek for Corsica). En route she usually stayed in Paris at the Hotel Continental, because it stood opposite the site of the Tuileries, overlooking the gardens where the Prince Imperial had played as a little boy – on one occasion a gardener scolded her for picking a flower. During her stay here in 1894 she went to see the dying Victor Duruy in his flat, toiling up eight flights of stairs.

Eugénie had renewed her friendship with Empress Elizabeth of Austria, by now a melancholy, slightly unbalanced wanderer, and became one of the few people in whom Elizabeth would confide. She often wrote to Eugénie, especially after her son Crown Prince Rudolph shot himself and his mistress at Mayerling in 1889. Later, she sometimes stayed with her at the Villa Cyrnos.

In the late 1890s Eugénie regained her energy, learning to ride a bicycle when she was over seventy and exploring the shores of the Mediterranean each summer in her steam yacht, *Thistle*. This had six cabins but anybody unwise enough to accept an invitation to go for a cruise regretted it, since the boat rolled horribly. Their hostess did not even notice and had lost none of her taste for stormy weather, having herself tied in a chair to the mainmast when rounding the Mull of Kintyre in a high sea.

She watched events in France but took no part in politics although she still thought that a Bonapartist restoration was not impossible – the Third Republic was riven by scandal and royalism was in steep decline, while Plon-Plon had died in 1891. However, Prince Victor Napoleon, whom she regarded as emperor, proved to be an ineffectual pretender. She became a fervent Dreyfusard, convinced that Captain Dreyfus had been wrongly convicted of spying for Germany, and if she did not speak out publicly she quarrelled bitterly with Anna Murat for saying he was guilty. She was outraged when the maniac Edouard Drumont claimed in *La Libre Parole* that she was anti-Semitic, writing an indignant letter of denial.

'I feel even more than ever a foreigner, alone in this land,' she lamented when Queen Victoria died in 1901. 'I am very saddened and discouraged.' Yet Edward VII was fond of her too, writing, 'I knew how deeply Your Majesty would sympathise with us in our grief. Our dear mother was deeply attached to you.' Queen Alexandra often visited Farnborough, generally without warning.

Maurice Paléologue first met Eugénie at the Hôtel Continental in 1901. 'Despite her seventy-five years, she retains traces of her former beauty,' he said. 'The quick, deep-set eyes shine with a steely, sombre fire and you notice her make-up, the pencilled eye-shadow underlining the rims of the faded eyelashes. Her straight back and upright shoulders do not touch the back of the arm-chair.' Among the books she was reading he saw one of the volumes of Sorel's massive *L'Europe et la Révolution Française*.

Other sovereigns as well as King Edward continued to treat Eugénie with deep respect. She was invited to Austria in 1906, staying at Ischl. Franz-Joseph met her at the station and at dinner wore the star of the Légion d'honneur with Napoleon III's head given to him by the emperor long ago; she looked magnificent, her white hair crowned by a jet tiara, recalled an English friend who was present. Yachting in the Norwegian fiords in 1907, she encountered a German cruiser carrying the kaiser, who came on board the *Thistle* and behaved with the utmost courtesy. (Paléologue's account of their meeting should be treated with caution.)

Eugénie was ageing well, climbing Vesuvius when she was eighty and sailing with Sir Thomas Lipton on board his famous, ocean racing yacht *Erin* on at least one occasion. She never tired of travel, her cure for depression, and set out for India on a liner in 1903, although illness forced her to turn back at Ceylon. She welcomed new inventions with enthusiasm. Meeting a young scientist called Marconi, she lent him *Thistle* to try out his experiments between Nice and Corsica. When his system of wireless communication was established in Canada, she was the first person after Edward VII to whom he transmitted a message. She also became interested in the use of radium as a medicine and was fascinated by aviation, reading everything available on the subject – in 1908 she went to a flying display at Aldershot by Colonel Cody, being photographed with him. She even went to the cinema.

Always practical, Eugénie installed a wireless on her yacht, as well as electric light and a telephone at Farnborough Hill. She also acquired a gramophone, which Filon thought 'one of the most perfect I ever heard'; she told him, 'it enables me to listen to entire operas without leaving my home'. She bought a car, too, a large black and green Renault, engaging a somewhat erratic chauffeur to drive it – on one occasion the vehicle and its passengers had to be rescued from a ditch by a steam roller, while in 1913 he was fined for speeding although his employer disliked going at speed.

Speaking noticeably poor English with a strong accent – she invariably dropped her 'h's – Eugénie made comparatively few close English friends. Among them, a little surprisingly, was the colourful Ethel Smyth, whom she first got to know in 1891 and who spoke excellent French. A lesbian (and a future admirer of Virginia Woolf), Ethel would cycle to Farnborough Hill in tweed knickerbockers, changing into a dress in the shrubbery. None of this bothered Eugénie. What interested her was that Miss Smyth was a composer and, always eager to overcome 'sex-prejudice', she did everything she could to further her career, even arranging for her to sing before Queen Victoria. In Ethel's memoirs Eugénie emerges as a delightful old lady, if also a fierce one, who when arguing would sometimes bang the table until the glasses rattled.

Predictably, Eugénie approved of the suffragette movement. Despite deploring violence, she ignored Ethel's prison sentence for smashing an MP's window and was keen to meet 'the Militant Leader'. When Mrs Pankhurst came to lunch, they took to each other immediately, and Ethel was asked to bring her as often as possible.

Ethel Smyth's account of Eugénie, largely ignored by French historians, is telling. 'Many are under the impression that certain of her qualities were only acquired in old age,' wrote Ethel. 'But in 1891 she was a great deal nearer to "les événements", as she always called the downfall of the Second Empire than in 1918.' (People had been saying that time had mellowed the empress.) While describing her as the kindest person she had ever met, Ethel admits that Eugénie lacked 'poetic imagination' and suffered from an 'extremely halting and uncertain sense of humour'. What impressed her most was the way – 'betrayed, falsely accused, vilified – the *feet too small to believe !!*

empress has attacked no one, nor uttered a single word in her own defence'. 'Can anything transcend the dignity of that long, iron silence?' asked Ethel.

Isabel Vesey, like Ethel the unmarried daughter of a retired army officer who lived nearby, but a very different personality, became no less of a friend. Eugénie particularly enjoyed her company, inviting her to stay at Cap Martin and for cruises. Isabel remained devoted to the empress for the rest of her life, her diaries and reminiscences in *The Times* complementing Ethel's memoirs. She was a guest on *Thistle* when the kaiser came on board at Bergen in 1907, and noticed how Eugénie 'rather liked him', and said 'he is always most agreeable and charming to her'. Her liking is understandable – he went out of his way to treat her as if she was still empress of the French. Isabel also tells us that when Eugénie gave a young girl a pair of her own shoes, they proved to be too small, although the child only wore size 3.

Another English friend, loyal if scarcely close, was the general who had gone to South Africa with her, and who often came to play tennis at Farnborough Hill in top hat, frock-coat and white flannel trousers. 'She would enjoy the ludicrousness of dear Sir Evelyn Wood falling on his knees before her on the gravel path, and kissing her hand in the costume he adopted.'

Predictably, Eugénie remained unpopular in France among republicans, who with relentless unfairness accused her of being responsible for 1870. In 1907 Ferdinand Loliée published the first of his poisonous books. There was even antagonism on the right, and not just from royalists. 'The emperor's death and the awful tragedy in Zululand should have aroused sympathy for the empress, so sorely tried as wife and mother,' Jean Guétary, one of Napoleon III's earliest apologists, had written two years earlier. 'It did not.' But although a Bonapartist Guétary was also a bigoted anti-Dreyfusard, outraged at Eugénie having sent a letter of enthusiastic support to Colonel Picquart, the officer who established Dreyfus's innocence. Even so, Guétary reminded his readers that those most eager for war in 1870 had been the deputies and journalists of the left: Eugénie certainly possessed at least some French admirers among those still faithful to the dynasty.

The son of a famous writer and one of Marcel Proust's young friends, Lucien Daudet was a homosexual dilettante who was fascinated by the Bonapartes and had great charm, and after presenting himself to Eugénie unintroduced at the Villa Cyrnos in 1899, having arrived on a bicycle, he became almost an adopted son. He brought Jean Cocteau to see her. 'The eyes remained a heavenly blue although their keenness had been diluted,' observed Cocteau. 'A whole sea of blue water looked into you.' He also noticed her deep Spanish laugh, which 'conjured up the bull-ring'. Sadly, Daudet never presented Proust, who might have immortalised her in the way that he did Princesse Mathilde.

In 1911, with Eugénie's grudging permission, Lucien published *L'Impératrice Eugénie*. The first objective study of her and one of the best, it is an odd, haunting book that stresses the poignancy of her existence, but as a collection of impressions and vignettes rather than a biography it tends to be overlooked, especially by English biographers. Clearly she had told him a good deal about herself, for example how in South Africa a smell of verbena led her to the place where her son had died – it had been his favourite scent. Like Ethel, Daudet is at pains to stress that she is neither frivolous nor a bigot. 'She hates prejudice . . . in her eyes Catholics, Jews and Protestants are equal members of humanity.' He mentions her love of handsome people – 'for her, as for the Greeks, beauty, intelligence and goodness are inseparable'. While she has few illusions about mankind, she detests cynicism.

The empress gave '*le petit Lucien*' some good advice in return. 'Never waste time dramatising life', she warned him. 'It's quite dramatic enough without it.'

In 1910 she revisited Compiègne, discreetly joining a guided tour. However, when it reached the Prince Imperial's bedroom she nearly fainted and, asking for a chair and a glass of water, raised her veil. Realising who it was, the guide informed the *conservateur* and they let her stay in the room by herself for ten minutes. Yet she lived firmly in the modern world. 'Mr Marconi was thunderstruck at her grasp of wireless telegraphy,' Ethel remembered, 'and later on the officers of the Royal Aeroplane factory were amazed at her knowledge of their particular subject.' She planned to go up in an aeroplane but was prevented by the First World War.

If Paléologue may be believed, Eugénie told him in June 1912, 'There is a lot of electricity in the air. Don't you think a storm is brewing . . . the most serious problem I can see in European affairs is the antagonism between England and Germany.' She added, 'The danger of war is no longer in doubt.' In January 1914, just before he left to take up his post as ambassador to St Petersburg, she warned him, 'Something is rotten in Russia.'(As long ago as 1876 she had written to her mother that 'In Russia the nobility is corrupt and the court without morals, and the people know it.')

When the war broke out in 1914 she realised it would be long and bitter, giving her yacht *Thistle* to the Royal Navy and turning a wing of Farnborough Hill into a small hospital, which she maintained entirely out of her own pocket. Ethel was staggered to learn what immense sums she gave to hospitals in France, in strict secrecy. She also took in Prince Victor Napoleon and his wife and children when they had to flee from Belgium.

'The spirit of France is beyond all praise and gives one confidence,' she wrote to Lucien Daudet when the Germans were advancing on Paris in August. From the start she hoped fervently for the recovery of Alsace-Lorraine, and Ethel Smyth recalled what a comfort she was at dark moments, 'so sane and unshakeable was her faith in ultimate victory'. The empress believed firmly that, together, France and England were unbeatable. She never indulged in xenophobia, however, rebuking anyone who referred to 'Les Boches'.

Franceschini Pietri, who as the emperor's secretary had ridden with him during the 1870 campaign, died in 1916 and was buried as he wished, near the stair down to the crypt of Farnborough Abbey – so that the empress would pass him on her way to pray at the tombs of her husband and her son.

Augustin Filon passed away in the same year. He had settled in Croydon, supporting himself by writing until he went blind, and left a book to be published after Eugénie's death – *Souvenirs sur l'Impératrice Eugénie*. For Filon

the empress is a true Frenchwoman and a great one . . . those who know her well refuse to see her as no more than the embodiment of the Second Empire's elegance and glitter . . . in reality she had been a convinced idealist in a cynically materialist society. . . . Just a glance at one of her notebooks, in which she jots down reactions to what she is reading or to a stimulating remark, would show you how wide was the gap in sympathy and outlook that had existed between herself and most of the people who then surrounded her.

A warning that the Germans might bomb Farnborough Hill in error, as it was next to the Royal Aerodrome Factory, exhilarated her. 'If they come', she told Ethel, 'then at least we shall be in the front line.' Ethel suspected that her own terror increased the empress's pleasure at the prospect.

Learning in 1917 that the Allies considered Alsace-Lorraine to be part of Germany, she sent the French government a letter written to her by William I in 1871, in which he admitted that the provinces had been annexed purely for strategic reasons and not because their inhabitants were seen as Germans. The letter convinced the Allies that Alsace-Lorraine must be returned to France. It was her last and most effective intervention in foreign affairs.

Eugénie was shrewd enough to guess that conditions in Germany were very bad indeed when the German army postponed its offensive in the summer of 1918. Realising it was beaten, she foresaw that the kaiser would have to abdicate and that many other crowned heads would have to go with him. She was horrified by the dissolution of Austria–Hungary, and by the Treaty of Versailles although she took it down to the crypt to read to the emperor in his tomb. 'I see in every article of this peace a little egg, a nucleus of more wars. . . . How can Germany earn the money to pay?' She also prophesied that if England was not careful 'Ireland will become a second Bohemia.'

Nonetheless, she was elated by the Allies' victory, believing that God had let her live so long in order to see Alsace-Lorraine restored to France. In 1919 King George made her a Dame Grand Cross of the British Empire in recognition of her war work, sending the Prince of Wales and the Duke of York (Edward VIII and George VI) to Farnborough to present her with the insignia.

In December 1919 Eugénie returned to Cap Martin, stopping en route in Paris at the Hôtel Continental, where Paléologue called on her. He was shocked by her appearance. 'Eyes sunk deep in their sockets, eyeballs glassy and staring', he wrote. 'Her neck is fleshless, her hands are the hands of a skeleton.' She was, after all, ninety-three. 'Yet I could see at once that even now this pitiful frame was ruled by a vigorous, tenacious, proud spirit.' Still defending the Second Empire, she asked him, 'Don't you agree that the World War completely justifies my view that [Imperial] France remained capable of putting up a fight after Sedan?' She said she was looking forward to revisiting Spain the next spring. 'Nowadays I am just a very old bat. But, as butterflies do, I still feel I must fly towards the sun. Before death takes me, I should like to see my Castilian sky for a last time.'

Lucien Daudet also called on the empress. He, too, had not seen her since 1914, yet she made him feel it had only been the previous week. She told Lucien about her forthcoming trip to Spain. 'Do you know, I wanted to go by aeroplane, but people might have said I was a crazy old woman.' Someone else who met her during that winter was the Duchess of Sermonetta, a smart young Roman. She realised that Eugénie had not lost her sense of fun when she said she had three hats, '*Trotinette*' for walks, '*Va t'en ville*' for shopping and '*La Glorieuse*' for grand occasions. She offered to lend *La Glorieuse* to the duchess.

In June 1920 the empress went to Spain by sea, sailing from Marseilles to Gibraltar. When her boat put in to Algeciras the warships in the harbour, Spanish and British, gave her a sovereign's salute of twenty-one guns, which thrilled her as she had not been so greeted since her expedition to Suez over fifty years earlier. Looking like a ghost, she was driven to Madrid where she stayed with her great nephew Alba in the Liria Palace.

Since no doctor, British or French, had dared give chloroform to someone so frail, Eugénie remained half blind from cataracts. However, a Spanish doctor performed the operation without an anaesthetic, restoring her sight completely. As a result she thoroughly enjoyed herself, even going to a bullfight. 'I've come home,' she declared happily, and she even spoke of going up in an aeroplane at last when she got back to England, now that she could see properly again. But on 10 July she suddenly felt exhausted and in pain, and had to be put to bed without undressing. It quickly became apparent that she was failing. Having received the last sacraments, she died very peacefully at 8.30 the following morning – in a room that had once been her sister Paca's bedroom, and in Paca's old bed. Her last words were, 'I am tired – it is time that I went on my way.'

The coffin was taken to the station in the king of Spain's state coach, with an escort of halberdiers and footmen carrying tapers. Accompanied by the Duke of Alba and another great nephew, the Duke of Peñaranda, the body of the last empress of the French travelled back by train and ferry to her English home. If unacclaimed by her former subjects, it was received with fitting pomp at Farnborough, drawn from the station on a gun-carriage escorted by cavalry to the abbey church. Here it lay in state for two days, draped in a blue imperial pall which bore the golden eagles and golden bees of the Bonapartes.

The congregation at the funeral on 20 July included George V and Queen Mary, Alfonso XIII and Queen Ena of Spain, and Manuel II of Portugal and the Portuguese queen mother, together with Prince Victor Napoleon, the Bonapartist pretender, and his wife. The Third Republic had protested on learning that the empress would be given a twenty-one gun salute, and, while it did not fire the salute, a battery of Royal Horse Artillery remained drawn up outside the abbey throughout the service. Although the band played the 'Marseillaise' instead of 'Partant pour la Syrie' (no one remembered how to play it), many people in the packed church bore famous Second Empire names, as the children or grandchildren of her courtiers – Murat, Bacciochi, Primoli, Walewski, Bassano, Bassompière, Clary, Girardin, Fleury. Ethel Smyth and Lucien Daudet were there too. Cardinal Bourne, archbishop of Westminster, celebrated the Mass for the Dead, the monks chanting the *Dies Irae*, and Abbot Cabrol gave the address. Finally, wearing a nun's habit, she was laid to rest.

Eugénie's body still lies with those of Napoleon III and the Prince Imperial in the abbey crypt at Farnborough, where the monks continue to sing an annual requiem for their souls. To those who know and sympathise with her story, the shrine is a place of extraordinary poignancy, her presence almost tangible.

Smyth, Daudet and Filon testify to the empress's integrity. Human beings of her type do not change so very much and it is clear that during her reign she was already the person whom they knew in exile. Yet France rejected her even before Sedan, as a foreigner and as a woman who dared to covet power. Nevertheless, more than a few contemporaries thought of her as a character out of a play by Corneille, whose women are embodiments of stoicism and endurance, driven by love, honour and duty, and Admiral Jurien de La Gravière often compared her with Chimène in Le Cid.

Her best epitaph, however, is a dedication found by Ethel in a copy of Lord Rosebery's *Napoleon I: the Last Phase*, which the author had presented to Eugénie:

> To the surviving Sovereign of Napoleon's dynasty
> The empress,
> who has lived on the summits of splendour, sorrow
> and catastrophe
> with supreme dignity and courage.

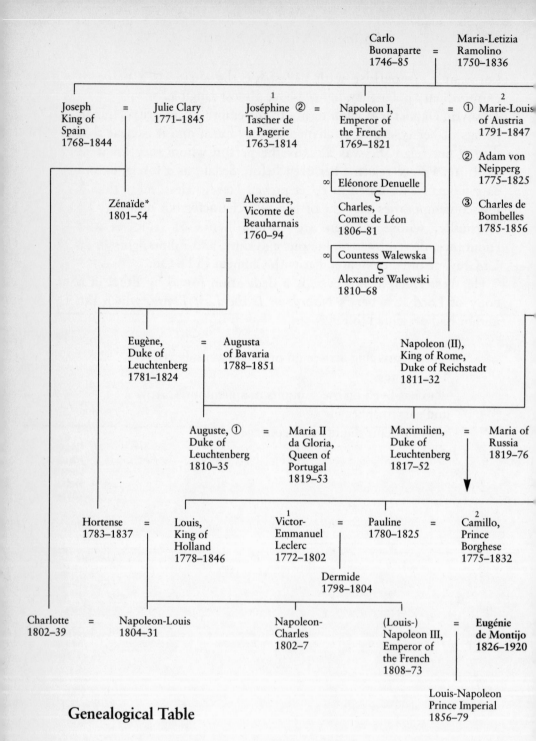

Genealogical Table

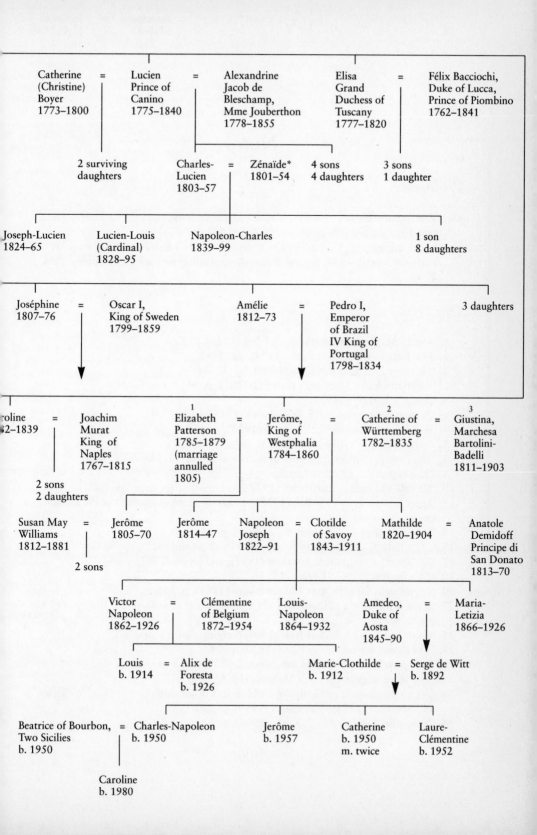

Catherine (Christine) Boyer 1773–1800 = Lucien Prince of Canino 1775–1840 = Alexandrine Jacob de Bleschamp, Mme Jouberthon 1778–1855

Elisa Grand Duchess of Tuscany 1777–1820 = Félix Bacciochi, Duke of Lucca, Prince of Piombino 1762–1841

2 surviving daughters

Charles-Lucien 1803–57 = Zénaïde* 1801–54   4 sons 4 daughters   3 sons 1 daughter

Joseph-Lucien 1824–65   Lucien-Louis (Cardinal) 1828–95   Napoleon-Charles 1839–99   1 son 8 daughters

Joséphine 1807–76 = Oscar I, King of Sweden 1799–1859

Amélie 1812–73 = Pedro I, Emperor of Brazil IV King of Portugal 1798–1834

3 daughters

roline 2–1839 = Joachim Murat King of Naples 1767–1815

1
Elizabeth Patterson 1785–1879 (marriage annulled 1805) = Jerôme, King of Westphalia 1784–1860

2
Catherine of Württemberg 1782–1835

3
Giustina, Marchesa Bartolini-Badelli 1811–1903

2 sons 2 daughters

Susan May Williams 1812–1881 = Jerôme 1805–70

Jerôme 1814–47

Napoleon Joseph 1822–91 = Clotilde of Savoy 1843–1911

Mathilde 1820–1904 = Anatole Demidoff Principe di San Donato 1813–70

2 sons

Victor Napoleon 1862–1926 = Clémentine of Belgium 1872–1954

Louis-Napoleon 1864–1932

Amedeo, Duke of Aosta 1845–90 = Maria-Letizia 1866–1926

Louis b. 1914 = Alix de Foresta b. 1926

Marie-Clothilde b. 1912 = Serge de Witt b. 1892

Beatrice of Bourbon, Two Sicilies b. 1950 = Charles-Napoleon b. 1950

Jerôme b. 1957

Catherine b. 1950 m. twice

Laure-Clémentine b. 1952

Caroline b. 1980

Notes

Prologue

xiv. 'She cannot really . . .': 'Elle n'aura pas été véritablement un caractère, ayant trop femme pour cela', Loliée (1907a), p. 404.

xiv. wider influence': One of Loliée's disciples was Ferdinand Bac, who, as a (natural) grandson of Jerome Bonaparte, sympathised with her enemy Plon-Plon.

One

1. 'On 28 May an earthquake . . .': Filon (1922), p. 9.
1. 'Her father's name . . .': Filon (1894), pp. 51–2.
2. 'the story . . .': Jean des Cars (2000), pp. 17–18.
2. 'Kirkpatrick of Closeburn': Burke (2000), I, p. 787.
4. Llanos y Torriglia (1932).
4. 'Among her guests . . .': S.T. Williams (1935).
4. 'It did them no harm . . .': Primoli (1923).
5. 'Screaming . . .': Alba (1941), p. 5.
5. 'The Paris . . .': A good account of the city at this date is Mansell (2001).
8. 'In a report . . .': *Lettres familières*, I, p. 235.
10. 'He told the girls . . .': Arbeley (1932).
13. 'Later known as . . .': F. Bac (1928b) (a subtly partisan account of the author's uncle).
16. 'In a postscript . . .': *Lettres familières*, I, p. 22.
17. '. . . a lady of very easy virtue indeed': Fleischmann (1923), pp. 46–83.
17. '. . . abortive coup': F.A. Simpson (1923); and Smith (1982).
20. 'As a hostess . . .': A. Revesz (1953).
20. '. . . an ugly, fat little man': Malmesbury (1884), p. 285.
21. 'If the handsome . . .': Smyth (1921), p. 32; Kurtz (1964), p. 27; Ridley (1979) pp. 169–71.
23. 'From here . . .': J. Richardson (1969) (verging on hagiography).
26. 'The dinner for four . . .': Filon (1920), p. 24.
26. 'In September . . .': *Lettres familières*, I, p. 37.
31. 'The more respectable . . .': Maurois (1956).
34. '. . . at the château of Compiègne': Hübner's dispatch to Count Buol, Wellesley and Sencourt (1934); Viel Castel (1884), p. 130.
36. 'Now it so happened . . .': Kurtz (1964), p. 42.

Notes

40. 'So today . . .': The emperor's letter of proposal is in the Alba archives at Madrid.
41. 'Cowley mentions . . .': Cowley, in Wellesley (1928), p. 17.
41. 'He explained to . . .': *Oeuvres de Napoléon III*, III, pp. 357–60; Queen Victoria thought the speech 'in very bad taste', *Journal*, 24 January 1853.
42. 'A marriage . . .': Wellesley and Sencourt (1934), p. 17.
43. 'She tried to explain . . .': *Lettres familières*, p. 53.
43. 'in white velvet . . .': Bac (1928a); Lady Augusta's letter to the Duchess of Kent, transcribed by Queen Victoria into her *Journal*; *The Times*, 31 January 1853; Hübner (1904), I, p. 105.

Two

45. 'I once held . . .': Haussmann (1890–3), I, p. vii.
46. 'Despite being . . .': Bluche (1981).
46. 'The Second Empire . . .': Zeldin (1973), I, pp. 552–8.
47. 'From the start . . .': Fould (1867). Fould's elder brother, Benoît, founded the banking house Fould et Cie.
47. 'The emperor's . . .': Christophe (1951); Zeldin (1973), I. p. 549.
48. 'Eugénie . . .': Persigny (1896).
50. '. . . the Imperial household': *Almanach Impérial*; Verly (1894), pp. 100 ff.
50. '. . . the *Cents Gardes*': Verly (1894).
50. '. . . the Guides': Fleury (1897–8), I, p. 226.
51. 'Hübner saw . . .': Hübner (1904), I, p. 143.
52. 'Emile Ollivier . . .': Ollivier, *Journal*, 22 February 1853.
52. 'Eugénie had her own household . . .': *Almanach Impérial* and Verly (1894).
52. 'In secret . . .': Mrs Moulton caught her smoking one in her bedroom; Hegermann-Lindencrone (1912), p. 94.
54. 'When she told him . . .': Viel Castel (1884), II, p. 199.
54. 'All this was known . . .': Bouchot (1896); Carette (1888–91); Whitehurst (1873); Vizetelly (1912).
55. 'An invitation . . .': Hegermann-Lindencrone (1912), pp. 25–31.
56. '. . . not so *petit*': Hegermann-Lindencrone (1912), p. 31.
56. 'Certainly there were . . .': Crane (ed.) (1905), I, p.135; Gower (1883), I, p. 295
59. 'Even in winter . . .': Murray (1864); Clouzot (1925).
59. 'Gentle, peaceful days . . .': Filon (1920), pp. 61–2.
60. 'Traditional French hunting . . .': Metternich (1922), p. 97.
62. 'Octave Feuillet . . .': Feuillet (1894), pp. 346–66.
64. 'It was the carefully . . .': Wellesley and Sencourt (1928), p. 141.
65. 'A few years later . . .': Hegermann-Lindencrone (1912), p. 96.
69. 'One night . . .': Hegermann-Lindencrone (1912), p. 110.
69. 'She made friends . . .': Hegermann-Lindencrone (1912), pp. 141–2; Thomas (1911).
72. 'It was a sport . . .': Barthez (1912), pp. 84–8.
72. 'A barely credible . . .': Barthez (1912), pp. 175–82.

Notes

74. 'The household . . .': Metternich (1922), pp. 28–39.
75. '. . . a compact crowd': Whitehurst (1873), II, pp. 24–32.
75. 'His description . . .': La Gorce (1894–1905), I, p. 130.
77. 'His best organised . . .': De Luz (1931); Osgood (1960); Zeldin (1973), I, pp. 412–13.
79. '. . . the scourge of the Imperial family': Hübner (1904), I, p. 310.
79. 'She adds . . .': Bicknell (1893), pp. 64–5.
80. 'He hated . . .': Paléologue (1928), p. 59.
80. 'A few were respectable . . .': Filon (1920), p. 74.
82. 'The emperor . . .': Guest (1952), Queen Victoria, *Journal*, 16–21 April 1855; *The Times*, 16–21 April 1855; Malmesbury (1884), II, pp. 18–20.
83. 'Everybody raved . . .': Disraeli, letter of 1 May 1855 to Mrs Brydges Williams, Monypenny and Buckle (1910–20), IV, p. 5.
84. 'On 18 August . . .': Queen Victoria, *Journal*, 18–27 August 1855; Viel Castel (1884), III, pp. 175–7; Fleury (1897–8), I, pp. 183, 184.

Three

89. '. . . beauty of their own sex': Sencourt (1931), p. 211.
89. 'How can you call . . .': Ollivier (1961), II, 8 July 1867.
89. 'After twenty-two hours . . .': Hübner (1904), I, p. 403; *The Times*, 17 and 18 March 1856; Viel Castel (1884), III, p. 213.
92. '. . . I am a foreigner': Kurtz (1964), p. 67.
93. 'When my mother . . .': Filon (1920), p. 11.
94. 'It was one . . .': Clouzot (1925), Clouzot (1939); E. Rouyer (1867); Carette (1888–91), I, pp. 133–46.
96. 'The best place . . .': Moulin (1967); Gaillemin (1990); Cornforth (2002).
98. '. . . loot from the Summer Palace': first displayed in a memorable exhibition in Paris, which aroused widespread interest; *Gazette des Beaux Arts*, Paris, 1861.
98. 'A smaller room . . .': *Connaissance des Arts*, No. 479, January 1992.
99. 'An Empress Dresses': For this chapter Blum and Chassée (1931); Cabris (1901); Uzanne (1898); particularly important are Professor A. Ribeiro, 'Fashion in the work of Winterhalter', in Ormond and Blackett (1987), and Byrde (1992).
99. 'In a letter . . .': Barthez (1868), p. 95.
101. 'There is an acme of dressing . . .': Taine (1867), pp. 23–4.
102. 'Unseen since 1830 . . .': Bapst (1889); Vever (1906–8); Bury (1991).
103. 'When the . . .': De Marley (1980).
105. '. . . the bustle': Whitehurst (1873), II, p. 85.
107. 'Have you ever . . .': Wellesley and Sencourt (1928), *Paris Embassy*, p. 111.
108. '. . . sent to the Mazas prison': yet Dr Barthez thought that to some extent she still believed in Home: Barthez (1912), p. 164.
109. 'This was . . .': Clotilde de la Bedoyère, Fleischmann (1923), pp. 312–14.
109. 'Virginie . . .': Decaux (1953).
110. 'Her vain, venal husband . . .': Ornano (1958).

302

112. '. . . photography': by photographers such as Gustave le Gray.
113. 'Almost without warning . . .': Malmesbury (1884), II, pp. 239, 283.
116. 'She told the Walewskis . . .': Wellesley and Sencourt (1928), p. 273.

Four

117. 'As they arrived . . .': Pack (1958).
120. 'The campaign . . .': Dunant (1863).
122. 'It was a letter . . .': Comte Fleury (1920), II, pp. 29–30
124. '. . . a shirt of Nessus': Paléologue (1928).
124. '. . . a decorative sovereign': Loliée (1907b), p. 205.
125. 'This transformation . . .': Zeldin (1973), I, pp. 552–7.
127. 'The work people . . .': Senior (1880), 19 August 1861.
127. 'According to . . .': Murray (1864), p. 48.
128. 'The emperor's . . .': Haussmann (1890–3), II, pp. 1 ff.
130. 'Pauline's husband . . .': Salomon (1931).
144. 'He probably thinks . . .' – Filon (1920), p. 68
146. 'Shortly after . . .': Filon (1920), p. 69.
146. '. . . the cholera scares of the 1860s': 'The empress spent the day visiting those who have contracted cholera at the Beaujon, Lariboisière and Saint-Antoine hospitals. She went into the wards where victims are being nursed, going to bedsides, asking questions and encouraging patients, in a spirit worthy of a Sister of the Poor', *Gazette Nationale*, 23 October 1865.
150. 'Jacques Offenbach . . .': Krackauer (1937); Harding (1980); and Faris (1980).
153. 'The irony . . .': Krackauer (1937), p. 16.

Five

133. 'Eugénie showed . . .': Lavisse (1895).
134. '. . . one third those of men': quoted by Zeldin (1973), I, p. 345.
135. 'The painter . . .': Klumpke (1999), p. 169.
136. 'Despite her . . .': Sand's novel *Malgrétout* was serialised in the widely read *Revue des Deux Mondes* in February and March 1870.
136. 'Eugénie was . . .': Rollet (1988).
137. 'The emperor . . .': d'Hauterive (1925).
139. 'There were two sorts . . .': Maritain (1930); Daniel-Rops (1965).
139. 'I was something . . .': Paléologue (1928), p. 58.
139. '. . . the pope should stay in Rome': the emperor's anonymous pamphlet, *Le Pape et le Congrès*, outraged French Catholics, including Gallicans and even Viel Castel (1884), V, pp. 245–51.
142. 'Soon the water . . .': Lasserre (1892).
143. 'The Revocation . . .': Eugénie to Doña Maria Manuela, *Lettres familières*, II, p. 57.
148. 'Clearly Eugénie . . .': Berlioz (1972), p. 620.
148. 'In November 1864 . . .': Clarette (1882).

Notes

149. '. . . Ambroise Thomas': Moulin (1967), p. 63.
149. 'The bourgeois . . .': Flaubert (1926–30).
150. 'Many of them . . .': Filon (1920), pp. 54–5.

Six

156. 'Shall America . . .': Anon, *Lettres sur les États-Unis d'Amerique*, Paris, 1862.
157. 'The concept of a Catholic monarchy . . .': This did not mean she was hostile to the United States, whatever Nancy Nichols Barker (1965) may say.
157. 'Early in 1866 . . .': The classic narrative account is still Count Corti (1928); Parkes (1960).
161. 'The emperor assured . . .': Zamoyski (1987), p. 284.
162. 'Historians . . .': the report of the conversation is in *Il problemo veneto e l'Europa*, Venice, 1966–67. For the diplomatic context, Taylor (1954).
163. '. . . the crisis over Schleswig-Holstein': Bismark said that only the Prince Consort, a German professor and Bismarck understood the problem, but the prince had died, the professor had gone mad and he himself had forgotten.
165. 'Really, Eugénie . . .': Viel Castel (1884), VI, p. 132.
166. 'We are hastening . . .': Viel Castel (1884), VI, p. 332.
166. 'My God . . .': Barthez (1912), p. 254.
169. 'The consternation . . .': Wellesley and Sencourt (1934), p. 284.
171. 'Drouyn resigned . . .': Harcourt (n.d.), p. 310.
171. 'But Eugénie . . .': Wellesley and Sencourt (1934), pp. 306–12.
174. '. . . a more adroit courtier': Smyth (1921), p. 34.
175. 'I am thinking with terror . . .': *Lettres familières*, I, p. 83.
175. '. . . going to die on the scaffold': Hübner (1904), I, p. 320.
176. 'Eugénie bought everything . . .': Barbara Scott, 'In the Shadow of Marie-Antoinette', *Country Life*, 6 December 1979.
178. 'It really is quite extraordinary . . .': Filon (1920), p. 78.
178. 'For everyone . . .': La Gorce (1894–1905), V, p. 151.
180. 'Clearly, Lillie Moulton . . .': Hegermann-Lindencrone (1912), p. 154.
180. '. . . a Winterhalter': Whitehurst (1873), I, pp. 289–90.
184. 'When squadron on squadron . . .': Sencourt (1931), p. 204.
186. 'Meeting the empress . . .': Daudet (1911), p. 45.
186. 'Within a week . . .':Vandam (1897), p. 319.
187. '. . . she never forgave him': Guétary (1905), p. 278.
189. 'One can dismiss . . .': Ducamp (1949), I, p. 146.
189. 'No doubt a woman . . .': La Gorce (1894–1905), V, p. 149.

Seven

190. 'We are in danger . . .': Jurien's letter; Kurtz (1964), pp. 223–4.
191. 'Among the infamous jibes . . .': Paléologue (1928), p. 79.
192. '*Alors, vous auriez mieux fait de rester chez vous, au lieu de venir agacer mes nerfs ici*', Wellesley (1928), p. 294

192. '. . . the barrier of blood': while Eugénie regretted the *coup*, she saw it as having been unavoidable.
193. '. . . Franz-Joseph's visit': Metternich (1922), p. 171.
194. 'After dinner . . .': Feuillet (1894), p. 352.
196. 'Everywhere . . .': Verly (1894), pp. 118–19.
198. 'The last time . . .': Jules and Edmond de Goncourt, *Journal*, Paris, 1989.
202. '. . . the great French Egyptologist': An expert on hieroglyphics, Mariette Bey had helped to discover the Serapeum of Memphis.
204. 'In a letter . . .': Pincemaille (2000), p. 14, quotes this letter at some length.
207. '. . . the only form of French monarchy' Almost ninety years later, it inspired the constitution of General de Gaulle's Fifth Republic, a republican monarchy.
209. 'There could have been . . .': Grunwald (1951).
210. 'Could anything . . .': Whitehurst (1873), II, p. 288.
211. 'It was like . . .': Whitehurst (1873), II, p. 347.
212. 'Only a handful . . .': C. James, *Des causes de la mort de l'empéreur*, 1873; also Bresler (1999), pp. 404–15.

Eight

216. 'He had been . . .': La Gorce (1894–1905), VI, pp. 129–30; Howard (1961), pp. 38, 44–5.
217. 'Six railway lines . . .': Howard (1961), p. 24–6.
218. 'The French did not . . .': Namier (1958), p. 142.
222. 'Eugenie explained . . .': Paléologue (1928), p. 150.
225. 'Thus by a tragic . . .': Howard (1961), p. 57.
229. 'Nothing is ready . . .': 'Lettres à l'Impératrice Eugenie (1870–71)', *Revue des Deux Mondes*, 15 July 1929.
229. 'I am good for nothing . . .': Abbé Pujol, 'Les Derniers Jours de Saint-Cloud', *Revue des Deux Mondes*, 15 July 1929.
230. 'The Regent Takes Control': For this chapter, see Duc d'Abrantès, *Essai sur la Régence de 1870*.
235. 'Accordingly . . .': Howard (1961), pp. 134–5.
238. '. . . a legend grew up': A modern historian refutes this by quoting the republican Jules Simon (*Souvenirs du quatre Septembre*, Paris, 1874). 'The Council of Ministers and Privy Council were unanimous in agreeing with her. There were two reasons for their decision. First, and which counted most with the empress, the personal danger the emperor would run in returning to Paris. Second, a failure to appreciate what MacMahon's army was risking in marching north.' W.C.H. Smith, *Eugénie, L'Impératrice et femme*, p. 371.
239. 'Her face was ravaged . . .': Garets (1928), I, p. 205.
242. 'She was eating . . .': Garets (1928), I, p. 204.
243. '. . . I do not fear the crisis': *Lettres familières*, I, p. 228.
243. '. . . in a mouse-trap': Howard (1961), p. 207.
246. 'She was pale and terrible . . .': Filon (1920), p. 139.
247. 'Paléologue claimed . . .': Paléologue (1928), p. 217.
252. 'Had the empress. . .': Gower (1883), I, p. 371.

253. 'Flight' For this chapter, Crane (ed.) (1905).
259. '. . . the club house of Chislehurst Golf Club', whose members wear a tie with the imperial eagles.
264. 'General Monts . . .': H. Welschinger, 'La Captivité de Napoléon III', *Revue des Deux Mondes*, March–April 1910.
264. 'These long days . . .': 'Lettres à l'Impératrice Eugénie', *Revue des Deux Mondes*, September 1930.
265. 'The events through which . . .': *Lettres familières*, II, p. 7.
266. 'Yet no two women . . .': Filon (1920), p. 255.
268. 'Her visits to Chislehurst . . .': Paléologue (1928), p. 237.
269. 'The Comte de Chambord . . .': Halévy (1937), pp. 62–8.
272. 'The Empire will be . . .': Wellesley and Sencourt (1934), p. 375.
274. 'Eugénie was too overcome . . .': Filon (1920), pp. 283–6.
275. 'French royalism . . .': Osgood (1960).
276. 'The Napoleons are genuine democrats': quoted in Crane (ed.) (1905), p. 617.
276. 'I have to admit . . .': *Lettres familières*, II, p. 52.
278. 'Certainly he met her . . .': Kurtz (1964), p. 289.
279. 'Those four years . . .': Filon (1920), p. 302.
279. 'Your view . . .': *Lettres familières*, II, p. 60.
280. 'After ten years a regime like this . . .': Even so in 1877 the Bonapartists won 105 seats, more than the Legitimists and Orleanists combined. Zeldin (1973), I, p. 564.
281. '. . . he died like a lion': The most recent study is Phillips (1999).
283. 'Alone in life . . .': *Lettres familières*, II, p. 115.
283. '. . . a new and much larger house': Mostyn (1999).
284. '. . . she employed another Frenchman': For Destailleur see Hall (2002), p. 45.
285. 'Four White Canons': W.H.C. Smith (2001).
287. '. . . curtsy to each other': Smyth (1921), p. 108.
288. 'Eugénie had renewed . . .': Kurtz (1964), pp. 352–3.
289. 'Maurice Paléologue first met . . .': Paléologue (1928).
290. 'When Mrs Pankhurst . . .': Smyth (1921), p. 58.
291. 'But although . . .': Guétary (1905), p. 279.
292. 'She hates prejudice . . .': Daudet (1911), p. 97.
293. 'She never indulged . . .': Daudet (1935), p. 252.
294. 'She realized . . .': Sermonetta (1929), p. 133.
297. 'Her best epitaph . . .': Smyth (1919), II, p. 243.

Sources and Bibliography

This book is a reinterpretation rather than a definitive study so it is largely (but not entirely) based on printed sources. For those who wish to consult the unpublished material, the principal collections are: the Alba Archives, Liria Palace, Madrid (letters to Doña Maria Manuela and the Alba family; the Archives Nationales, Paris (Archives Napoléon – A.N. 43, A.P.– for letters between the emperor and Eugénie, and between Eugénie and the Prince Imperial); the Royal Archives, Windsor Castle (for Queen Victoria's *Journal*, and letters between the queen and the empress); and the Public Record Office, Kew (for Foreign Office papers).

Primary Printed Sources

Duke of Alba and G. Hanoteaux (eds), *Lettres familières de L'Impératrice Eugénie*, Paris, 1935.

Papiers et Correspondance de la Famille Impériale. Papiers sauvés des Tuileries, Paris, 1871–72.

Les Papiers Secrets du Second Empire, Brussels, 1870.

L'Impératrice, notes et documents, Paris, 1877.

Oeuvres de Napoléon III, Paris, 1856–69.

'Lettres à l'Impératrice Eugénie (1870–1871),' *Revue des Deux Mondes*, Paris, September 1930.

M. Parturier, P. Jusserand and J. Mallon (eds), *Correspondance Générale*, Toulouse and Paris, 1931–61.

A.C. Benson, Viscount Esher and Gr E. Buckle (eds), *Letters of Queen Victoria*, 1854–1901 (London), 1907–32.

Les Origines Diplomatiques de la Guerre de 1870–71, Paris, 1910–32.

Correspondence, Memoirs, Contemporary Studies

Abrantès, duc d' (1879), *Essai sur la Régence de 1870* (Paris).

Almanach Impérial pour MDCCCLXVIII (1868), (Paris).

Ambès, Baron d' (C. Simond and M.C. Poinsot eds) (1910–11), *Mémoires inédites sur Napoléon III: Le Mémorial de Chislehurst* (Paris).

Bapst, G. (1889), *Histoire des joyaux de la couronne de France d'après des documents inédits* (Paris).

Barail, General du (1896), *Mes Souvenirs* (Paris).

Baroche, Mme Jules (1921), *Le Second Empire, Notes et Souvenirs* ed. F. Masson (Paris).

Barthez, E. (1868), *La famille Impériale à Saint-Cloud et à Biarritz* (Paris).

—— (1912), *The Empress Eugénie and her Circle* (London).

Beaumont-Vassy, Vicomte de (1868), *Les Salons de Paris et la Société parisienne sous Napoléon III* (Paris).

—— (1874), *Histoire intime du Second Empire* (Paris).

Bellanger, Marguerite (1882), *Confessions, Mémoires anecdotiques* (Paris).

Berlioz, H. (1972), *Correspondance, générale d'Hector Berlioz*, vol V (Paris).

Bicknell, A.L. (1893), *Life in the Tuileries under the Second Empire* (New York).

Bigelow, J. (1909), *Recollections of an Active Life* (New York).

Bouchot, H. (1896), *Les Elégances du Second Empire* (Paris).

Bouscatel, Edouard (1872), *L'Impératrice et le quatre Septembre* (Paris).

Cabris (1901), *Le Costume de la Parisienne au XIXe siècle* (Paris).

Cabrol, Abbot Fernand Michel (1920), *L'Impératrice Eugénie: Discours prononcé à ses funerailles le 20 Juillet 1920* (London).

Carette, Mme (1888–91), *Souvenirs intimes de la Cour des Tuileries* (Paris).

Cassagnac, G. de (1879–82), *Souvenirs du Second Empire* (Paris).

Castellane, Comte V. de (1895–7), *Journal du Maréchal de Castellane 1804–1862* (Paris).

Chevreau, L. (1998), ed. J. Dumont de Montroy, *Souvenirs de Léon Chevreau 1827–1910: Préfet du Second Empire, Deputé de l'Oise* (Paris).

Clarette, J. (1882), *Peintres et Sculpteurs* (Paris).

Cocteau, J. (1951), *Oeuvres Complètes*, vol XI (Paris).

Crane, E.A. (ed.) (1905), *The Memoirs of Dr Thomas W. Evans: Recollections of the Second French Empire* (London).

Cuvellier, B. (January 1908), 'The Empress Eugénie Today', *The London Magazine* (London).

Daudet, L. (1911), *L'Impératrice Eugénie* (Paris).

—— (1935), *Dans l'Ombre de L'Impératrice Eugénie* (Paris).

Deléage, P. (1879), *Trois mois chez les Zoulus et les derniers jours du Prince Impérial* (Paris).

Ducamp, Maxime (1949), *Souvenirs d'un demi-siècle* (Paris).

Dunant, J.H. (1863), *Un souvenir de Solferino* (Geneva).

Feuillet, Mme Octave (1894), *Quelques années de ma vie* (Paris).

—— (1896), *Souvenirs et Correspondance* (Paris).

Filon, A. (1894), *Mérimée et ses amis* (Paris).

—— (1912), *Le Prince Impérial* (Paris).

—— (1920), *Souvenirs sur L'Impératrice Eugénie* (Paris).

Flaubert, G. (1926–30), *Correspondance* (Paris).

Fleury, General Comte (1897–8), *Souvenirs* (Paris).

Fleury, Comte M. and Sonolet, L. (1911–13), *La Société du Second Empire* (Paris).

Fould, A. (1867), *Journaux et discours* (Paris).

Garets, Comtesse des (1928), *Auprès de l'Impératrice Eugénie* (Paris).

—— (1929), *L'Impératrice Eugénie en exile* (Paris).

Gower, Lord R. (1883), *My Reminiscences* (London).

Sources and Bibliography

Gramont, Duc de (1872), *La France et la Prusse avant la Guerre* (Paris).

Guétary, J. (1905), *Napoléon III, un grand méconnu* (Paris).

Harcourt, Comte d' (n.d.), *Les Quatres Ministères de Drouyn de Lhuys* (Paris).

Hauterive, E. d' (1925), *Napoléon III et le Prince Napoléon* (Paris).

Haussmann, Baron G.E. (1890–3), *Mémoires du Baron Haussmann* (Paris).

Hegermann-Lindencrone, L. de (1912), *In the Courts of Memory 1858–1875* (London).

Hérisson, Comte d' (1891), *Les responsabilités de l'année terrible* (Paris).

—— (1892), *Journal d'un officier d'ordonnance* (Paris).

Hübner, Baron (1904), *Neuf ans de Souvenirs d'un ambassadeur d'Autriche à Paris* (Paris).

Imbert de Saint-Amand, A.L. (1897), *Napoléon III et sa cour* (Paris).

Jerrold, W.B. (1871), *At Home in Paris: at Peace and at War* (London).

—— (1874–82), *The Life of Napoleon III* (London).

La Gorce, P. de (1894–1905), *Histoire du Second Empire* (Paris).

Lasserre, H. (1892), *Notre Dame de Lourdes* (Paris).

Llanos y Torriglia (1932), *Maria Mannela Kirkpatrick, Contesa del Montijo* (Madrid).

Legge, E. (1910), *The Empress Eugénie 1870–1910* (London).

—— (1916), *The Empress Eugénie and her Son* (London).

Malmesbury, Earl of (1884), *Memoirs of an ex-Minister* (London).

Maugny, Comte de (n.d.), *Mémoires* (Paris).

Maupas, C.E. de (1884–5), *Mémoires sur le Second Empire* (Paris).

Metternich, Princess (1922), *Souvenirs* (Paris).

Monts, Count (1909), *Napoleon III auf Wilhelmshöhe* (Berlin).

Monypenny, W.F. and Buckle, G.E. (1910–20), *Life of Benjamin Disraeli, Earl of Beaconsfield* (London).

Murat (1910), *Princess Caroline, My Memoirs* (London).

Murray, J. (1864), *A Handbook for Visitors to Paris* (London).

Ollivier, E. (1895–1915), *L'Empire libéral* (Paris).

——, eds T. Zeldin and A. Troisier de Diaz (1961), *Journal* (Paris).

—— (1921), *Lettres de l'exil* (Paris).

Ollivier, Mme Emile, ed. A. Troisier de Diaz (1970), *J'ai vécu l'agonie du Second Empire* (Paris).

Paléologue, M. (1928), *Les Entretiens de l'Impératrice Eugénie* (Paris).

Palikao, Comte de (1871), *Un ministère de la Guerre de vingt-quatre jours* (Paris).

Peat, A.B. North, ed. A.R. Waller (1903), *Gossip from Paris during the Second Empire: Correspondence (1864–1869)* (London).

Persigny, Duc de (1896), *Mémoires* (Paris).

Primoli, Comte (October 1923), 'L'enfance d'une souveraine', *Revue de Deux Mondes* (Paris).

Rouyer, E. (1867), *Les Appartements privés de S.M. l'Impératrice au Palais des Tuileries décorés par M. Lefuel, architecte de SM. L'Empéreur . . .* (Paris).

Rumbold, Sir H. (1902), *Recollections of a Diplomatist* (London).

Sand, George (February–March 1870), 'Malgrétout', *Revue de Deux Mondes* (Paris).

—— (1882–4), *Correspondance 1812–1876* (Paris).

—— (1904), *Souvenirs et Idées* (Paris).

Senior, N. ed. M.C.M. Simpson (1880), *Conversations with Distinguished Persons during the Second Empire from 1860 to 1863* (London).

Smyth, Ethel (1919), *Impressions that Remained* (London).

—— (1921), *Streaks of Life* (London).

Taine, H. (1867), *Notes sur Paris. Vie et opinions de M. Frédéric-Thomas Graindorge* (Paris).

Tascher de la Pagerie (1894), *Comtesse Stephanie, Mon Séjour aux Tuileries* (Paris).

Thouvenel, L. (1889), *Le secret de l'Empéreur* (Paris).

—— (1903), *Pages de l'Histoire du Second Empire* (Paris).

Ticknor, G. (1876), *Life, Letters and Journals of George Ticknor* ed. G.S. Hillard (Boston).

Tocqueville, A. de (1948), *Recollections* (London).

Uzanne, Octave (1898), *Fashion in Paris. The Various Phases of Feminine Taste and Aesthetics from 1797 to 1897* (London).

Vandam, A. (1897), *An Englishman in Paris* (London).

—— (1897), *Undercurrents of the Second Empire* (London).

Verly, A. (1894), *Souvenirs du Second Empire* (Paris).

Vever, H. (1906–8), *La Bijouterie française au XIXe siècle (1800–1900)* (Paris).

Viel Castel (1884), Comte Horace de, *Mémoires sur la règne de Napoléon III* (Paris).

Villemessant, H. de (1873), *Mémoires d'un journaliste* (Paris).

Vizetelly, H. (1893), *Glances Back through Seventy Years* (London).

—— (1912), *The Court of the Tuileries 1852–70* (London).

Washbourne, E.B. (1869–1877), *Recollections of a Minister to France.*

Wellesley, F.A. (1928), *The Paris Embassy during the Second Empire* (London).

Wellesley, Sir V. and Sencourt, R. (1934), *Conversations with Napoleon III* (London).

Whitehurst, F.M. (1873), *Court and Social Life in France under Napoleon III* (London).

Later Studies

Alba, Duke of (1941), *The Empress Eugénie* (Oxford).

—— (1947), 'La Emperatriz Eugenia', *Boletin de la Real Academia de Historia*, CXX (Madrid).

Arbeley, P. (31 December 1932), 'Un dernier amour de Stendhal: Eugénie de Montijo', *La Revue Hebdomadaire*.

Augustin-Thierry (1935), A., *Le Prince Impérial* (Paris).

Austin, J. (1990), *L'Impératrice Eugénie* (Paris).

Bac, F. (1928a) *Le mariage de l'Impératrice Eugénie* (Paris).

—— (1928b), *La Princesse Mathilde* (Paris).

—— (1930), *La Cour des Tuileries sous le Second Empire* (Paris).

—— (1932), *Napoléon III inconnu* (Paris).

Barker, N.N. (1967), *Distaff Diplomacy: The Empress Eugénie and the Foreign Policy of the Second Empire* (Texas).

Bapst, G. (1889), *Histoire des joyaux de la couronne de France d'après des documents inédits* (Paris).

Bertault, J. (193?), *Napoléon III secret* (Paris).

Bertin, C. (1982), *La dernière Bonaparte* (Paris).

Bluche, F. (1981), *Le Bonapartisme* (Paris).

Blum, A. and Chassée, C. (1931), *Les Modes au XIXe siècle* (Paris).

Bourachot, C. (1994), *Bibliographie critique des mémoires sur le Second Empire* (Paris).

Bresler, F. (1999), *Napoleon III* (London).

Burke (2000), *Landed Gentry of Great Britain* (London).

Bury, S. (1991), *Jewellery, 1789–1910 – the International Era* (London).

Bushell, T.A. (1974), *Imperial Chislehurst* (Chesham).

Byrde, P. (1992), *Nineteenth Century Fashion* (London).

Cars, J. des (2000), *L'Impératrice Eugénie* (Paris).

Castelot, A. (1973–4), *Napoléon Trois* (Paris).

Christophe, R. (1951), *Le Duc de Morny* (Paris).

Clouzot, H. (1925), *Des Tuileries à Saint-Cloud, L'Art décoratif du Second Empire* (Paris).

—— (1939), *Le style Louis Philippe Napoléon III* (Paris).

Cornforth, J. (14 November 2002), 'How the Empress dressed the Château', *Country Life*.

Corti, E.C. Count (1928), *Maximilian and Charlotte of Mexico* (London).

Daniel-Rops, H. (1965), *L'Eglise des Révolutions* (Paris).

Dansette, A. (1972), *Du 2 septembre au 4 septembre* (Paris).

—— (1961–76), *Histoire du Second Empire* (Paris).

Decaux, A. (1953), *La Castiglione, le coeur de l'Europe* (Paris).

De Marly, D. (1980), *Worth, Father of Haute Couture* (London).

Desternes, S. and Chandet, H. (1957), *Louis Prince Impériale* (Paris).

—— (1961), *Napoleon III: homme du XX siècle* (Paris).

—— (1964), *L'Impératrice Eugénie intime* (Paris).

Diaz-Plaza, F. (1992), *Eugenia de Montijo, Emperatriz de los Franceses* (Madrid).

Dictionnaire de biographie Française (1932) (Paris).

Dufresne, C. (1986), *L'Impératrice Eugénie* (Paris).

Faris, A. (1980), *Jacques Offenbach* (London).

Fleischmann, H. (1923), *Napoléon III et les Femmes* (Paris).

Fraser, Sir W. (1895), *Napoleon III* (London).

Gaillemin, J.L. (February 1990), 'Château de Compiègne', *The World of Interiors* (London).

Girard, L. (1986), *Napoléon III* (Paris).

Giraudeau, F (1895), *Napoléon III intime* (Paris).

Grunwald, C. de (1951), *Le Duc de Gramont* (Paris).

Guedalla, P. (1922), *The Second Empire* (London).

Guérard, A. (1924), *Reflections on the Napoleonic Legend* (London).

—— (1945), *Napoleon III* (London).

Guest, I. (1952), *Napoleon III in England* (London).

Haléry, D. (1937), *La République des Ducs* (Paris).

Hales, E.E.Y. (1954), *Pio Nono* (London).

Sources and Bibliography

Hall, M. (2002), *Waddesdon Manor* (London).

Harding, J. (1980), *Jacques Offenbach: a biography* (London).

Hermant, A. (1942), *Eugénie, Impératrice des Français* (Paris).

Horne, A.A. (1965), *The Fall of Paris: The Siege and the Commune* (London).

Howard, Sir M. (1961), *The Franco-Prussian War* (London).

Katherine, J. (1939), *The Prince Imperial* (London).

Klumpke, A. (ed.) (1999), *Rosa Bonheur: The Artist's (Auto)biography* (Michigan).

Krackauer, S. (1937), *Jacques Offenbach, ou le secret du Second Empire* (Paris).

Kurtz, H. (1964), *The Empress Eugénie* (London).

Lachnitt, J.C. (1997), *Le Prince Impérial* (Paris).

Lavisse, E. (1895), *Un Ministre, Victor Duruy* (Paris).

—— (1912), *Souvenirs* (Paris).

—— (March, 1929), 'Correspondance avec le Prince Impérial', *Revue des Deux Mondes*.

—— (1921), *L'Histoire de la France contemporaine*, vols VI and VII (Paris).

Lecomte, G. (1937), *Napoléon III: Sa Maladie, Son Déclin* (Paris).

Lenz, T. (1995), *Napoléon III* (Paris).

Llanos y Torriglia, F. de (1932), *Maria Manuela Kirkpatrick Condesa del Montijo* (Madrid).

Loliée. F. (1907a), *La Fête Impériale: les femmes du Second Empire* (Paris).

—— (1907b), *La vie d'une Impératrice: Eugénie de Montijo* (Paris).

Luz, P. de (1931), *Henry V* (Paris).

Mansell, P. (2001), *Paris between Empires, 1814–1852* (London).

Maritain, J. (1930), *La Politique ecclésiastique du Second Empire* (Paris).

Maurois, A. (1956), *Miss Howard: la femme qui fit un empéreur* (Paris).

Minc, A. (1997), *Louis Napoléon revisité* (Paris).

Mostyn, D. (1999), *The Story of a House: A History of Farnborough Hill* (Farnborough).

Moulin, J.M. (1967), *Le Château de Compiègne* (Paris).

Namier, Sir L. (1962), *Vanished Supremacies* (London).

Ormond, R. and Blackett, C. (eds) (1987), *Franz Xaver Winterhalter and the courts of Europe 1830–70*, National Portrait Gallery exhibition catalogue (London).

Ornano, Comte (1958), *Le Comte Walewski* (Paris).

Osgood, S. (1960), *French Royalism under the Third and Fourth Republics* (The Hague).

Pack, G. (1958), *The Bombs of Orsini* (London).

Parkes, H.B. (1960), *A History of Mexico* (Boston).

Phillips, W.P. (1999), *The Death of the Prince Imperial in Zululand, 1879* (Hampshire).

Pincemaille, C. (2000), *L'Impératrice Eugénie: De Suez à Sedan* (Paris).

Plessis, A. (1973), *Nouvelle Histoire de la France contemporaine*, vol. IX (Paris).

Raitt, A.W. (1970), *Prosper Mérimée* (London).

Revesz. A. (1953), *Un dictador Liberal* (Madrid).

Richardson, J. (1969), *Princesse Mathilde* (London).

Ridley, J. (1979), *Napoleon III and Eugénie* (London).

Rollet, H. (April 1988), 'Le feminisme de l'Impératrice Eugénie', *Souvenir Napoléonien*.

Sainte-Fare Garnot, N. and Jaquin, E. (1988), *Le Château des Tuileries* (Paris).

Salomon, H. (1931), *L'Ambassade de Richard de Metternich* (Paris).

Schneider, L. (1923), *Offenbach* (Paris).

Seguin, P. (1990), *Louis Napoléon le Grand* (Paris).

Seignobos, C., *Le second Empire (1848–59)* in vol. VI, *Histoire de la France contemporaine* (ed. E. Lavisse).

Sencourt, R. (1931), *The Life of the Empress Eugénie* (London).

Sermoneta, Duchess of (1929), *Things Past* (London).

Simpson, F.A. (1923), *Louis Napoleon and the Recovery of France* (London).

Smith, W.H.C. (1982), *Napoléon III* (Paris).

—— 'L'Impératrice Eugénie' in *Dictionnaire du Second Empire*.

—— (1998), *Eugénie Impératrice des Français* (Paris).

—— (2001), *The Empress Eugénie and Farnborough* (Hampshire County Council).

—— (n.d.), *Eugénie: impératrice et femme*.

Stoddart (1906), *The Life of the Empress Eugénie* (London).

Taylor, A.J.P. (1954), *The Struggle for Mastery in Europe 1848–1914* (Oxford).

Thomas, L. (1911), *Le Général de Galliffet* (Paris).

Tschudi, C. (1900), *Eugénie Empress of the French* (London).

Tulard, J. (ed.) (1995), *Dictionnaire du second Empire* (Paris).

Vautel, C. (1946), *Le Prince Impérial* (Paris).

Verner, W. (August 1920), 'The Empress Eugénie', *The Nineteenth Century and After,* vol. *LXXXVIII* (London).

Williams, S.T. (1935), *The Life of Washington Irving* (New York).

Zamoyski, A. (1987), *The Polish Way* (London).

Zeldin, T. (1958), *The Political System of Napoleon III* (London).

—— (1973), *France 1848–1945* (Oxford).

Index

314

Index